The Influence of French Symbolism
on Modern American Poetry

AMS STUDIES IN MODERN LITERATURE; NO. 9
ISSN 0270-2983

Other titles in this series:

No. 1. Richard E. Amacher and Margaret F. Rule, compilers.
*Edward Albee at Home and Abroad: A Bibliography,
1958 to June 1968.* 1973.

No. 2. Richard G. Morgan, editor. *Kenneth Patchen: A
Collection of Essays.* 1977.

No. 3. Philip Grover, editor. *Ezra Pound, the London Years,
1908–1920.* 1978.

No. 4. Daniel J. Casey and Robert E. Rhodes, editors.
Irish-American Fiction: Essays in Criticism. 1979.

No. 5. Iska Alter. *The Good Man's Dilemma: Social Criticism
in the Fiction of Bernard Malamud.* 1981.

No. 6. Charles L. Green, compiler. *Edward Albee: An
Annotated Bibliography, 1968–1977.* 1980.

No. 7. Richard H. Goldstone and Gary Anderson, compilers.
Thornton Wilder: A Bibliographical Checklist. 1982.

No. 8. Taylor Stoehr. *Words and Deeds: Essays on the
Realistic Imagination.* 1986.

No. 11 Clifford Davidson, et al., eds. *Drama in the Twentieth
Century.* 1984.

No. 12. Siegfried Mews, ed. *"The Fisherman and His Wife":
Günter Grass's "The Flounder" in Critical Perspective.*
1983.

No. 14. Arnold T. Schwab, ed. *Americans in the Arts,
1908–1920: Critiques by James Gibbons Huneker.*
1985.

No. 15. *Partisan Review Fifty-Year Cumulative Index: Volumes
1–50, 1934–1983.* 1984.

The Influence of French Symbolism
on Modern American Poetry

RENÉ TAUPIN

Translated by WILLIAM PRATT and ANNE RICH PRATT

Revised, Edited, and with an Introduction and Conclusion
by WILLIAM PRATT

AMS PRESS
NEW YORK

Library of Congress Cataloging-in-Publication Data

Taupin, René.
  The Influence of French Symbolism on Modern American
Poetry.

  (AMS Studies in Modern Literature: No. 9)
  Translation of: L'influence du symbolisme français sur la
poésie américaine (de 1910 à 1920).
  Includes index.
  1. American Poetry—20th century—History and
Criticism.   2. Symbolism in Literature.   3. American
Poetry—French Influences.   4. French Poetry—19th
Century—History and Criticism.   5. Imagist Poetry—
History and Criticism.   I. Pratt, William 1927–
II. Title.   III. Series.
PS310.S9T3813   1985   811'.52   83-45288
ISBN 0-404-61579-1

AMS PRESS, INC.
56 East 13th Street, New York, N.Y. 10003

MANUFACTURED IN THE UNITED STATES OF AMERICA

Contents

Acknowledgments

Grateful acknowledgment is made for the use of material from the following:

Hilda Doolittle, from the *Collected Poems of H. D.: 1912–1944*. Copyright © 1982 by the estate of Hilda Doolittle; reprinted by permission of New Directions Publishing Corporation.

T.S. Eliot, from *Collected Poems 1909–1962* and *Selected Essays* by T.S. Eliot; reprinted by permission of Faber and Faber Ltd. "The Hippopotamus" and excerpts from *Collected Poems 1909–1962*, are reprinted by permission of Harcourt Brace Jovanovich, Inc., copyright © 1963, 1964 by T.S. Eliot. From *Selected Essays*, copyright © 1932, 1936, 1950 by Harcourt Brace Jovanovich, Inc.; renewed 1960, 1964 by T.S. Eliot, 1978 by Esme Valerie Eliot. Reprinted by permission of the publisher.

T.E. Hulme, from *Speculations*; reprinted by permission of Harcourt Brace Jovanovich, Inc.

Ezra Pound, from *Personae*, copyright © 1926 by Ezra Pound; *A Lume Spento*, copyright © 1967 by Ezra Pound, all rights reserved; reprinted by permission of New Directions Publishing Corporation.

Wallace Stevens, from *The Collected Poems of Wallace Stevens*, copyright © 1923, 1931, 1935, 1936, 1937, 1942, 1943, 1944, 1945, 1946, 1947, 1948, 1949, 1950, 1951, 1952, 1954 by Wallace Stevens; reprinted by permission of Alfred A. Knopf, Inc.

William Carlos Williams, from *Kora in Hell*, copyright © 1957 by William Carlos Williams; reprinted by permission of New Directions Publishing Corporation.

INTRODUCTION

The French Origins of
Modern American Poetry

A STUDY IN LITERARY INTERNATIONALISM

by William Pratt

THE TIME is certainly long past when American literature might have been
understood in terms of a single national or linguistic origin. "Nothing," as
Wallace Stevens declared, "could be more inappropriate to American literature
than its English source since the Americans are not British in sensibility." Having
its people drawn from almost every country in the world, America had an
international destiny before it had a national destiny. Internationalism was clearly
asserted with independence at the time of the American Revolution (another time
when French influence was very strong), but a period of fervent nationalism and
sectionalism followed that lasted through most of the nineteenth century, and
really only ended with American entry into World War I. True literary independence, though often advocated by Emerson and others, proved even harder for
Americans to obtain than political independence, for the English language was in
many ways a stricter master than English sovereignty; yet eventually American
writers were bound to feel too much constrained by the English literary tradition,
and to seek a more broadly European, or international, tradition.

Such has been the case most notably with American poetry in the twentieth
century, which started a revolution in style that rejuvenated, and at the same time
effectively altered, the whole tradition of English poetry. Before 1900, America
had produced a number of able, but minor, English poets—Bryant, Longfellow,
Emerson, Lowell, Whittier, and Holmes, were the best-known names—and two
poets of genuine originality, Whitman and Poe. (Emily Dickinson, who was
virtually undiscovered before 1900, is best understood, along with Stephen Crane,
as a precursor of the Imagists, or in other words, as a "modern" poet.) After
1900, America produced any number of original poets of distinction, including
some major poets. What accounted for the difference? One factor was certainly
national destiny—America's rising power and responsibility in the world—but a

1

more important factor was the influence of France. "I look back to the dead year
1908," wrote T. S. Eliot in 1929, "and I observe with satisfaction that the current
of French poetry which sprang from Baudelaire is one which has affected all
English poetry that matters." That same year, the truth of his statement was fully
supported by a massive study of the French influences on modern American
poetry. René Taupin, then working for his doctorate at the Sorbonne, wrote a
treatise that linked two poetic movements in two languages. He produced his study
at a time when the modern movement was at its height, when many American
poets had either expatriated themselves, like Eliot, or were spending much of their
time abroad. The attraction of Paris was magnetic, for Paris was the capital of
the arts. "America is my country, and Paris is my home town," said Gertrude
Stein, and she could have been echoed by a chorus of American artists. As
Hemingway remembered it in a set of masterful period sketches, Paris in the
1920s was a "moveable feast" for all Americans, and all in some way partook
of it. Against that splendid backdrop, the French influence on American poetry
might almost seem a natural and inevitable thing.

But, in fact, what Eliot was speaking about, and what Taupin has so
thoroughly studied, was a movement which had much deeper roots. It had begun
even before World War I, the international event that brought so many Americans flooding to the gates of Paris. Eliot was speaking of a movement that had
started about 1910, in London rather than Paris, and that was in an advanced
stage of development by the time it reached Paris in the Twenties. Though it
developed at about the same time as the war, it had almost nothing to do with
the war, having its own battles to fight for the renewal of poetic language. In order
to understand the French influence on our modern poetry, therefore, we must look
behind the great attraction of Paris for Americans in the Twenties, behind even
the powerful force that drew Americans to Europe during World War I. We must
look at several decades of French influence on American writers, which reached
its culmination in the 1910s and 1920s, the period in which modern poetry in
our language was formed. For this purpose, there can be no better guide than
René Taupin's pioneer essay in comparative literature, which was published in
Paris more than fifty years ago. The intervening period has not substantially
changed the import of his book for American poetry, but in many ways has
confirmed its main conclusions and added further examples.

The full title of Taupin's work in French was *L'Influence du symbolisme
français sur la poésie américaine (de 1910 à 1920)*, but in reality his study
was much broader in scope than the closing parenthesis would seem to suggest.
It actually covers some fifty years of our poetry, beginning as far back as 1880,
and ending just short of 1930, when the book was published. With painstaking

thoroughness, it records every Symbolist influence of any consequence on American poetry between those dates, detailing the history of several short-lived and abortive movements before coming to the modern movement proper. Along the way, it gathers such rare specimens of poetic flora as the fin de siècle poets of the Nineties (transatlantic followers of Oscar Wilde and *The Yellow Book*), the American Decadents (who vied with Baudelaire, Verlaine, and Rimbaud in decadence, if not in poetry), and the so-called "American Symbolists," led by Richard Hovey (who thought they were following Mallarmé and Maeterlinck, but were really nearer to Whitman), before finally arriving at the group called the Imagists, who were able at last to make "American poetry speak French," as Taupin so aptly put it. For the period it covers and the work it sets out to do, Taupin's book is exhaustive, and it seems unlikely it could ever be replaced. It is the kind of work that could only have been done by a French scholar who had a thorough knowledge of the French tradition that produced the influence and an equally thorough knowledge of the English tradition that absorbed it and the American tradition that was shaped by it. He also had to be enough of a philosopher to understand the poetic theories of each literary tradition, and enough of a critic to recognize a literary influence at sight and judge how important it was. Taupin's central chapters on "Imagist Theories," on "The First Imagists," and on "The Second Stage of Imagism" seem as sound today as they were when they were written more than a half-century ago—proof enough of his critical acumen and his grasp of intellectual history. In short, his study itself demonstrates the sort of complete literary intelligence that helps explain why French thought has had such an enormous influence on writers in all modern languages.

1. THE QUESTION OF INFLUENCE

Literary influence is sometimes misunderstood as a lack of originality or dismissed as a question of academic interest pure and simple. The Welsh poet Dylan Thomas, for instance, liked to introduce his bardic recitals of poetry with "A Few Words of a Kind," in which he warned his audience that "This isn't a lecture about trends and impacts, and the influence of someone on somebody else; I am no dry and tepid don, smelling of water-biscuits." But he went on to add, a little ruefully, "Still I do wish I had learned some other languages, apart from English, BBC Third Programme and saloon, so that I could understand what some people mean when they say I have been influenced by Rimbaud." His embarrassment must have been shared by many modern poets in English, for so pervasive has been the French Symbolist influence on twentieth-century poetry that many poets who did not know a word of French have been affected by it, just as Thomas was—in spite of himself.

Among American poets, Hart Crane is probably the most instructive example of influence. With a natural gift for poetic composition, but with something
less than a high school education, he set out to acquire a knowledge of French
poetry on his own, being led to it by the examples of Pound and Eliot. Though
he read French only with difficulty, he absorbed enough of Rimbaud and Laforgue
to make a permanent difference in his style. Both the involved syntax and the
startling images of Crane's poetry are unmistakable signs that he had been reading
French, and reading it effectually:

> Bind us in time, O Seasons clear, and awe,
> O minstrel galleons of Carib fire,
> Bequeath us to no earthly shore until
> Is answered in the vortex of our grave
> The seal's wide spindrift gaze toward Paradise.

These haunting lines, which daringly mix metaphors of sky and sea, are among
the best Crane wrote, and neither the "minstrel galleons of Carib fire" nor the
"seal's wide spindrift gaze" are conceivable without French Symbolist influence;
thus the question of influence on his work cannot be taken lightly. Admittedly,
it makes for some distortion of language and even some unintentional obscurity—
faults which critics have often found in Crane's poetry—when a poet of Crane's
spontaneous talent takes in a sophisticated foreign influence, but it also makes
for phrases and lines of an unforgettable mystery and beauty, which invite the
reader to explore them and try to untangle their meanings. Crane's "fused
metaphors," as his friend and fellow-poet Allen Tate called them, are hallmarks
of his poetic style, and they are also clear proofs of his susceptibility to French
influence. Is it possible, then, that a poet can be most himself when he is most
influenced by other poets?

One might hesitate to say yes, but it is harder to say no, for Crane's case
is hardly unique among modern poets. It is unique only in its degree of self-
consciousness; other poets were more deliberate. "Be influenced by as many great
artists as you can," Ezra Pound advised his fellow-poets, "but have the decency
either to acknowledge the debt outright, or to try to conceal it."[1] The effect of
this advice in the modern period has been incalculable, and on no one more than
on Pound himself, whose poetry admitted more varieties of influence than would
have seemed possible in previous ages. The justification for such wholesale
borrowing can be found in one of the first poems Pound ever published. It was
called "Histrion" (another name for the *persona*, or mask, through which Greek
actors once spoke their parts), and it reads:

No man hath dared to write this thing as yet,
And yet I know, how that the souls of all men great
At times pass through us,
And we are melted into them, and are not
Save as reflexions of their souls.
Thus am I Dante for a space and am
One François Villon, ballad-lord and thief,
Or am such holy ones I may not write
Lest blasphemy be writ against my name;
This for an instant and the flame is gone.

'Tis as in midmost us there glows a sphere
Translucent, molten gold, that is the "I"
And into this some form projects itself:
Christus, or John, or eke the Florentine;
And as the clear space is not if a form's
Imposed thereon,
So cease we from all being for the time,
And these, the Masters of the Soul, live on.

This poem, which seems in so many ways archaic in diction and form, was published in 1908—the "dead year" Eliot looked back to twenty years later—and is actually one of the first expressions of the impulse toward a new poetry. Here, the question of influence is hardly literary at all: it is raised at once to the level of the metaphysical, and poetic imitation becomes a process which can only be described as *reincarnation*, in which the soul of the dead poet enters into the soul of the living poet, and expresses itself through his language. Startling as this doctrine may sound, Pound adhered to it with remarkable consistency. Later in his career, for example, he wrote this explanation of his experiments in poetic style:

> In the "search for oneself," in the search for "sincere self-expression," one gropes, one finds some seeming verity. One says "I am" this, that, or the other, and with the words scarcely uttered one ceases to be that thing.
> I began this search for the real in a book called *Personae*, casting off, as it were, complete masks of the self in each poem. I continued in a long series of translations, which were but more elaborate masks.[2]

The swift metamorphoses through which Pound passed in his poetry between 1910 and 1920 can only be accounted for by a new theory of literary influence, because it was his example which led the way toward the shaping of the modern poetic idiom. In founding Imagism, the first school of modern poetry, he depended heavily on French models, extracting the principle of "free verse" from the vers libre of Symbolists like Laforgue and de Régnier, and the principle of the "exact word" from the *mot juste* of Flaubert, but combining these with other, more remote models of poetic excellence, such as the Greek lyric and elegaic poets of the Classical period, which had long been an influence on English verse, and the more exotic Oriental form of the Japanese haiku. The result was the Imagist poem, a new vehicle of individual expression through which poets as diverse as Wallace Stevens and Carl Sandburg, William Carlos Williams and D. H. Lawrence, Amy Lowell and H. D., and many others, both English and American, were able to bring their talents to fruition. Never in the history of any poetry had such a diversity of traditions been brought together to produce such a variety of individual styles. In less than a decade, the Imagist school had proved that genuine freshness, originality, and individuality could come from the deliberate infusion of foreign influences into English poetry.

The experiments were enlivening, but the variety was bewildering. "That was a glorious confusion," John Crowe Ransom said when he looked back at the first period of modern poetry. What finally stabilized it was the appearance of a second major figure on the scene, in the person of T. S. Eliot. Eliot was responsible both for the introduction of further French influences into English poetry— Laforgue, in "Prufrock" and other early poems, and later Baudelaire, in *The Waste Land*—and for the deepening of this influence, by connecting it with the earlier English tradition of Metaphysical poetry. Eliot, in what Professor Taupin calls "the second stage of Imagism," was able to join the French and English traditions into a permanent alliance, following the example of Pound but with a profounder understanding of the connections and the consequences. Indeed, it was Eliot's essay on "Tradition and the Individual Talent" in 1917 which most fully expounded and clarified the doctrine of literary influence that Pound had intuitively practiced up to that time. The crucial importance of this early essay of Eliot's for the understanding of modern poetry can hardly be overestimated; and what the essay contains is, chiefly, a theory of influence.

Influence, or is it Tradition? The two words are redefined by Eliot in a new and illuminating way, a way that makes them essential to his grand conception that for the poet "the whole of the literature of Europe from Homer and within it the whole of the literature of his own country has a simultaneous existence and composes a simultaneous order." Influence, in his use of it, is a transmission of the creative force of earlier poetry to the living poet, and Tradition is the connection of all such influences in a continuous order. Eliot maintained that in reading a poet's work, critical attention should not be focused on the qualities that make him different from other poets, in the belief that these qualities constitute his individuality, his "peculiar essence." Instead, "if we approach a poet without this prejudice we shall often find that not only the best, but the most individual parts of his work may be those in which the dead poets, his ancestors, assert their immortality most vigorously." The burden of Eliot's essay is that a poet is successful, not when he aims at being most personal, but when he aims at being most *im*personal. "The progress of an artist is a continual self-sacrifice, a continual extinction of personality," he said. And if one asks, to what does the poet sacrifice himself?, Eliot might have answered "to the truth of his feelings," but he answered in a rather different and surprising way:

> The point of view which I am struggling to attack is perhaps related to the metaphysical theory of the substantial unity of the soul: for my meaning is, that the poet has, not a "personality" to express, but a particular medium, which is only a medium and not a personality, in which impressions and experiences combine in peculiar and unexpected ways.[3]

Though this essay of Eliot's halts, as he says, "at the frontier of metaphysics or mysticism," it has nevertheless speculated on the possibility that something so special and limited as an "influence" might be the key that unlocks the soul. Certainly no critic before Eliot's time would have dared to suggest such a thing, but in view of his own poetry and that of his most eminent contemporaries, it does not seem too serious a suggestion to make. The fact is, that in the modern period, and especially for American poets, "influence" has been raised to the level of "inspiration," and it has served to make this poetry both more international and more individual than the poetry of any previous age.

2. SYMBOLISM AND IMAGISM: THE CONTINUITY OF POETIC MOVEMENTS

If it is possible that through poetic influence, living poets may reincarnate dead poets, then it is surely conceivable that one poetic movement might give birth to another. In fact, in the history of art there is no such thing as a completely original movement; each new movement, each new period or epoch, is in some sense a rebirth of the previous one, though with its own distinguishing characteristics. What we call "Renaissance" is not confined to any one age in the history of Western culture, but is true of them all. If we think otherwise, it is because we have grown accustomed to restricting *the* Renaissance to that period from the fifteenth through the seventeenth centuries which seems richest in expression of all the ages of Western culture. We are also accustomed to thinking that each new poetic age is born from the age just prior to it, and in the same language, whereas it is probably true that the most striking cases of Renaissance have occurred when ages remote and languages foreign were involved in the change.

The Renaissance of the fifteenth through the seventeenth centuries in Europe was notable both for its renewal of Greek and Roman culture, and for the passage of influence from one modern language to another—from the Italian to the French to the English. In short, interlingual influences were primary, in the great age of European art and literature. It should not strike us as particularly strange, therefore, that modern American poetry sprang, not from nineteenth-century English poetry, but from nineteenth-century French poetry.

What may seem strange is the kind of poetry which resulted from the influence of French Symbolism. To some, it still seems unpoetic, lacking in both regular meter and rhyme, while to others, it seems written for a too exclusive and erudite audience. Modern poetry, like much modern art and music, continues to be thought of as unpopular, even though as the level of education has been raised, as a higher percentage of the population goes to college, there is a general increase in the audience for modern poetry. Perhaps the truth is that great poetry has always demanded an educated audience, and only the illusion of universal literacy makes us still wonder why poetry is not a more popular form of literature in the present century.

In a chapter on "Symbolist Poetry and the Ivory Tower," in Cleanth Brooks's landmark book, *Modern Poetry and the Tradition*, a plausible reason was given for the unpopularity of much modern poetry. "The symbolist poets," he wrote, "are akin to the metaphysicals in the subtlety of their descriptions of feelings, and in the subsequent limitation of their audience." Brooks did not blame either the Symbolist or the Metaphysical poets for their subtlety, which to him adds greatly to the pleasure of poetry. And he argued effectively against the position of Edmund Wilson, who in *Axel's Castle*, a book which owed much to Taupin's study, had accused the Symbolists of retiring to an ivory tower (though, in spite of the disparagement, Wilson's book remains a valuable study of the Symbolist tradition). Brooks accepted, as do committed readers of modern poetry, that when intellectual subtlety appears in poetry, it appears for a reason, and if a greater effort is required to understand it, that effort will be rewarded by a greater amount of meaning. It may even be that in certain periods of history only a poetry of great intellectual subtlety is capable of addressing itself to the human condition, and such would seem to be the case in our time.

> It is not a permanent necessity that poets should be interested in philosophy, or in any other subject. We can only say that it appears likely that poets in our civilization, as it exists at present, must be *difficult*. Our civilization comprehends great variety and complexity, and this variety and complexity, playing upon a refined sensibility, must produce various and complex results. The poet must become

more and more comprehensive, more allusive, more indirect, in order
to force, to dislocate if necessary, language into his meaning.[4]

So wrote T. S. Eliot in 1922, in an essay on "The Metaphysical Poets," and it
was an essay filled with quotations in French from the poetry of Laforgue,
Corbière, and Baudelaire (all Symbolists) to show that such a response to the
modern age already existed in another language—implying, as he did so, that no
comparable poetry had existed in English since the seventeenth century, when
John Donne, George Herbert, Henry Vaughan, and Andrew Marvell had written
their Metaphysical poems. Between then and the twentieth century, according to
Eliot's judgment, a "dissociation of sensibility" had taken place, in which thought
and feeling became separated in English poetry, not to be reunited until the
present century, except in the work of the Symbolist poets in another language.
If the modern poet was to be capable of expressing the complexity of his experience, so Eliot argued, he must either revert to an earlier poetic tradition in his
own language, or take the short cut into contemporary French poetry. It was the
latter course which most poets, including Eliot, chose to take.

To understand why it was French Symbolist poetry, rather than English
Victorian poetry, which provided the major influence on modern poets, we must
take note of two different factors involved in the change: one was certainly the
leadership of American poets, with their more international point of view toward
literary tradition; the other was the slow fading of the English Romantic dawn into
the dusk of Victorianism. In England, after the bright lights of Wordsworth,
Coleridge, Byron, Keats, and Shelley had gone out, only Tennyson, Arnold, and
Browning were left to bear the torch. But in France, after the Romanticism
of Hugo, there had followed an even more brilliant Counter-Romanticism,
led by such poets as Baudelaire, Verlaine, Rimbaud, Mallarmé, Laforgue,
Corbière—the whole body of French Symbolists. These poets were in a sense
inheritors of Romanticism, in that they continued to seek the bizarre and the
remote as subjects for their poetry, rather than the ordinary and commonplace,
but they did not seek it in China or Greece, the Lake Country or the Highlands—
rather they sought it within themselves, in the subjective reality of their own
experience. More importantly, they were Counter-Romantic in the sense that they
were not content to express the feelings alone, but put the conscious intellect to
work, replacing the cultivated innocence of earlier Romanticism with a cultivated
sophistication, and exchanging for the figure of the poet as peasant, happiest when
at home in nature, "dancing with the daffodils," the figure of the poet as dandy,
most at home amid the vices of the city, whose delight was in plucking the
"Flowers of Evil."

Les Fleurs de mal, published in Paris in 1857, was indeed the first book of modern poetry. It scandalized the reading public of that day quite as much as Eliot's *Waste Land* scandalized a later generation, and for much the same reasons. Both Baudelaire's book and Eliot's long poem contained descriptions of modern life which were repugnant to any reader's sense of decency. They reflected the general boredom of existence, the pursuit of novelty for its own sake, the sordidness of urban scenes and the perversity of human lives. But worst of all, to readers of refined sensibility, they implied that men and women were somehow responsible for the ugliness that existed around them, that they were involved inescapably in a common human guilt. Not just *some* men and women, not "Society" at large, but everyone alive:

> Tu le connais, lecteur, ce monstre délicat,
> —Hypocrite lecteur,—mon semblable,—mon frère!

These lines accosted the reader from the first poem in Baudelaire's book, and they accosted him again, in an altered context, at the end of the opening section of *The Waste Land:*

> "That corpse you planted last year in your garden,
> "Has it begun to sprout? Will it bloom this year?
> "Or has the sudden frost disturbed its bed?
> "O keep the Dog far hence, that's friend to men,
> "Or with his nails he'll dig it up again!
> "You! hypocrite lecteur!—mon semblable,—mon frère!"

In an essay on Baudelaire, a few years after he had written this poem, Eliot went so far as to say that "Baudelaire is indeed the greatest exemplar in *modern* poetry in any language, for his verse and his language is the nearest thing to a complete renovation that we have experienced."[5] It was not, he said, because the French poet delighted in shocking his reader, but because "actually Baudelaire is concerned, not with demons, black masses, and romantic blasphemy, but with the real problem of good and evil." However decadent Baudelaire's poetry may have appeared at first glance, its lasting effect was to convince its readers of the reality of evil in the human heart, and the certitude of human guilt. This effect, coming in an age when men were desperately seeking to convince themselves of the natural goodness of man, was salutary, and for it Baudelaire was publicly prosecuted by the indignant French bourgeoisie, and elevated almost to sainthood by the French poets who followed him—the *poètes maudits* ("accursed poets"), as Verlaine called them, who founded the Symbolist school.

But it was not for his moral perception alone that Baudelaire was admired; to the practicing poet, that was less important than his technical achievement.

To the poets of the Symbolist school of 1880, presided over by Mallarmé, Baudelaire had been the discoverer of new poetic laws. Their fascination was drawn toward the richness of his language, with its complex metaphors and its sudden ironies, its powerful sensuality that seemed to spring from a source deeper than any ordinary sensations. In particular, they centered their attention on his famous sonnet about the "Correspondences," where

> L'homme y passe à travers des forêts de symboles
> Qui l'observent avec des regards familiers.
>
> ("Man wanders through a forest of symbols
> Which observe him with insinuating eyes.")

The very word "Symbolist" may have originated in these lines, for they imply that symbolic meaning lies hidden within every common object. Moreover, as the poem develops its theme, with increasing sonority and eloquence, the symbolic power of words becomes an extension of the senses into a realm where

> Les parfums, les couleurs et les sons se répondent.
> ("Odors, colors, and sounds correspond.")

It is through the correspondence of different sense experiences that the symbolic effect of poetry is released, and ordinary language becomes resonant with the Divine Harmony of the universe:

> Comme l'ambre, le musc, le benjoin et l'encens,
> Qui chantent les transports de l'esprit et des sens.
>
> ("As amber, musk, benjamin, incense
> Sing the Transports of the soul and the sense.")

The doctrine of symbolism which is contained in this poem has been called *synaesthesis*, "the harmony or equilibrium of sensations."[6] Whatever name is given to it, it is a doctrine illustrated in all French Symbolist poetry. What made this poetry "symbolist" rather than simply "symbolic" was the deliberate juxtaposition of things, or sensations, or words which were not normally associated with each other, creating an initially jarring effect like certain metaphors of the English Metaphysical poets, but with no attempt to expound them by rational argument, as the Metaphysical poets often did. Rimbaud, for example, wrote a long poem about a "Drunken Boat," and a sonnet in which he described the colors of vowels; Mallarmé wrote an astonishing visionary poem about "A Throw of the Dice," and Laforgue wrote a series of tragicomic "Complaints," including "A complaint of the Pianos Heard in Better Neighborhoods." These were not spoofs, but serious, indeed brilliant poems, proving that poetic imagination was capable of synthesizing the most disparate materials of experience into significant relationships. Freedom of imagination was a Symbolist prerogative, and Rimbaud—who was the youngest, and boldest, of them all—even spoke of attempting "a rational disordering of the senses," with the aim of arriving at the beginning of all creation, and experiencing the radical spontaneity of God.

He did not succeed, needless to say, but the very audacity with which he used his imagintion was a Symbolist influence on all poets that followed. Baudelaire had once spoken of the mission of artists as being none other than to "discover the obscure laws in virtue of which they have created, and to extract from this study a set of precepts whose divine aim is infallibility in poetic creation."[7] Baudelaire cannot be said to have accomplished this aim, nor can the whole school of Symbolists together, but there is no doubt that they did penetrate further into the mysteries of the creative process than any poetic school had ever done before. They were originally impelled to this task, strangely enough, by Edgar Allan Poe (proving that there was first an American influence on French Symbolism!), who, in an essay which Baudelaire himself translated into French, had once tried to show how one of his poems— it was "The Raven"—"had proceeded, step by step, to its completion with the precision and rigid consequence of a mathematical problem." Saying of Poe that "he has subjected inspiration to method, to the most severe analysis," Baudelaire held that the artist is best when he both feels and analyzes his feelings, and this was the position of the Symbolists throughout. It was perhaps Mallarmé—and later, Valéry—who carried the critical intelligence farthest into poetry, seeking by indirect suggestion rather than by direct statement to produce a sense of ambiguity, like a faintly traced outline, to lead the mind of the reader to experience what Mallarmé called "the delicious joy of believing that it is creating." All the Symbolists sought in some way to make the creative process manifest in their poetry, so that the reader might share in it, and derive a new and more intimate satisfaction from poetry.

We may set down, then, as principal achievements of the French Symbolist movement: (1) a moral perception into the nature of evil, and the assumption by the poet of the role of "fallen man"; (2) a technical ability to bring beauty out of ugliness, by resolving the surface complexity of modern experience into new harmonies of poetic language; and (3) an aesthetic urge to lay bare the mysteries of poetic creation within the poem itself. The combined effect of this achievement was little short of monumental, for it brought poetry to a new stage of self-consciousness. As one French critic has summed it up:

> The moment arrives, in the course of the 19th Century, when
> poetry begins to take consciousness of itself as poetry . . . I believe
> that what has happened to French poetry since Baudelaire has a
> historical importance equal in the domain of art to that of the greatest
> epochs of revolution and renewal of physics and astronomy in the
> domain of science.[8]

The force of the Symbolist movement in France was so great that it gave
birth to similar movements in each of the major European languages, but on no
language was it more fertile in its effects than English, where the soil was barren,
and ready for new seed to be planted. It had been prepared, as Taupin shows,
by several decades of experiment by American poets, who were eager for a
change. But it was not until 1910, when the Symbolist movement in France had
largely spent itself, that a group of American poets appeared who were capable
of incorporating into their language the discoveries that the French poets had
made, and adding new discoveries of their own. The Imagist movement, as it was
called, was by no means a direct translation of French Symbolism into English.
It was a genuinely new poetic school, which developed its own theories and created
its own examples, and which in time produced poets of comparable greatness to
those of the French, yet in ways quite different from theirs. Taupin wisely observes
in the course of his study that "True influence consists in surpassing one's model,
not in reproducing it," and he rightly confines the major part of his study to the
examples of "true influence," dealing with the other kinds of influence only for
purposes of contrast.

In the history of the Imagist movement, as Taupin sees it, there were two
main stages of development, the first led by Pound and the second by Eliot, and
there were a number of divisions, or "schools," within each stage, dominated by
different poets. There were three such schools in the first stage of Imagism — the
"School of Images," led by T. E. Hulme in 1908–09; "Les Imagistes," led by
Pound, in 1912–14; and the group Pound nicknamed "The Amygists," which
Amy Lowell headed in the years 1915–17. These were separate and self-con-
tained groups, for the most part (only one poet, the Englishman F. S. Flint, was
a member of all three), but there was a definite line of development from one to
the other. Hulme was more philosopher than poet, and so his group contributed
more theory than practice to the first phase of Imagism; Pound was a prolific poet
as well as a theorist, and so the second phase contributed models, as well as
practical doctrines of poetic style; and Amy Lowell was a popularizer and propagandist more than a poet, and so the third phase extended outward in all directions
to include poets of the most widely divergent tendencies. What began in 1908
as an almost esoteric cult, known to a few, had by 1917 become the avant-garde

of a highly prolific movement, which dominated all the leading little magazines of England and America. The pattern of this development seems perfectly natural for a poetic movement to follow; what is surprising is that there should have been so much consistency in a movement aimed toward poetic freedom and individualism, as Imagism clearly was.

Of course, the word "individualism" was never mentioned by any of the three schools; it was simply implied in the variety of works produced. The key words that linked the three schools were the "image" as a vehicle of poetic expression, and "free verse" as a principle of form. Hulme was primarily responsible for the doctrine of the image, and Pound primarily responsible for the doctrine of free verse. The combination of these two doctrines, in the practice of a few skillful poets, made the Imagist poem what it was.

Though the name "Imagist" was Pound's invention, the theory of the image must be credited to Hulme, whose contribution to the philosophy of modern art has not yet been fully appreciated. That it has not, is partly owing to the forceful personality of the man and the belligerence with which he asserted his views, and partly to the shortness of his life. Hulme was a remarkable combination of things: part poet, part philosopher, and part prophet. In everything he wrote, he communicated the greatest sense of economy and urgency—as if he knew he had but a short while to live, and must get his work done quickly. The few essays, notes, and poems he left behind are all of the same character: brief, fragmentary, and full of meaning—like nothing so much as the *Pensées* of Pascal (which he greatly admired). Being opposed to most of the main tendencies of thought in his time— Romanticism, Humanism, Naturalism—he felt it necessary to be audacious in the pursuit of truth. It was as if his destiny was to be the first representative of a new intellectual type, rare at the time but increasingly frequent in the twentieth century: the revolutionary traditionalist. His doctrine of the image was at the same time a reflection of his own temperament, and a theory of the nature of thought and communication which had far-reaching consequences for the history of modern art, especially the art of poetry.

The root of Hulme's thought is perhaps to be found in his extended essay on "Humanism and the Religious Attitude,"[9] in which he attacks the former and defends the latter. Recognizing that "all English amateurs in philosophy are, as it were, *radically* empiric and nominalist," he proceeds to discredit the rational humanism of G. E. Moore and Bertrand Russell from a point of view outside the British tradition—a position which he had arrived at during brief periods of study at Marburg, under the influence of later German Idealism, and at the Sorbonne, under Bergson. In essence, Hulme maintained that the confusion of modern philosophy came from "the failure to recognize the *gap* between the regions of

vital and human things, and that of the absolute values of ethics and religion."
As a result of this failure, he went on: "We introduce into human things the
Perfection that properly belongs only to the divine, and thus confuse both human
and divine things by not clearly separating them." Romanticism, which he defined
as "spilt religion," resulted in his opinion from the mistaken effort to "place
Perfection where it should not be—on this human plane," and thus made a belief
in Progress "the modern substitute for religion." Against these views, Hulme
asserted what he called the "religious attitude," which recognizes that human
experience is relative, but that religious and ethical values are absolute:

> In the light of these absolute values, man himself is judged to be
> essentially limited and imperfect. He is endowed with Original Sin.
> While he can occasionally accomplish acts which partake of perfec-
> tion, he can never himself *be* perfect.

To take such an attitude, Hulme argued, was to give up believing in "man as the
measure of things," and to come to grips with "the *tragic* significance of life."
In doing so, he said, one experiences "a kind of conversion," which actually
changes his field of vision: "It radically alters our physical perception; so that the
world takes on an entirely different aspect."

Hulme's theory of the poetic image arises from this notion of a radically
altered perception of things; that is the revolutionary part of his philosophy. What
is interesting is that it developed out of a world view that was traditional and
conservative, which accepted Classicism in art and Christian orthodoxy in religion.
Hulme was perhaps the first to perceive that the pendulum of history was swinging
back from from the Renaissance view of a man-centered universe to the Medieval
and Greek view of a God-centered universe. He had a cyclical conception of
history, much like that which Yeats was later to express in *A Vision*. But instead
of seeing human experience as a sweeping set of gyres or wheels, in the manner
of Yeats, Hulme saw it as a series of disjunctive images rising out of a universal
flux. He was led to this vision by the influence of Bergson, the French philosopher
of "Creative Evolution," who was also a notable interpreter of art. In an essay
on "Bergson's Theory of Art,"[10] Hulme gave this summary of the Bergsonian
position:

> The process of artistic creation would be better described as a
> process of discovery and disentanglement. To use the metaphor which
> one is by now so familiar with—the stream of the inner life, and the
> definite crystallized shapes on the surface—the big artist, the creative
> artist, the innovator, leaves the level where things are crystallized out
> into these definite shapes, and, diving down into the inner flux, comes
> back with a new shape which he endeavors to fix. He cannot be said

to have created it, but to have discovered it, because when he has
definitely expressed it we recognize it as true.

The "shape" which the artist expresses, in whatever medium, is what Hulme
called the "image." Each image is individual, finite, and temporary, just as man
is, but it reveals for an instant a dimension of experience which is universal,
infinite, and eternal—in other words, the divine. When one sees a true image
embodied in words, or paint, or stone, Hulme says, "It means that a certain
individual artist was able to break through the conventional ways of looking at
things which veil reality from us at a certain point, was able to pick out one
element which is really in all of us, but which before he had disentangled it, we
were unable to perceive."

Though this may seem a complex explanation of a simple thing, it is
necessary for a full understanding of the importance of images in modern poetry.
When Pound, for example, defines the image in his 1913 Imagist Manifesto as
"that which presents an intellectual and emotional complex in an instant of time,"
he is putting into a single sentence what Hulme had taken years to formulate. And
when Pound, H. D., Aldington, and Flint began writing the first of their Imagist
poems, they were trying to put into effect the highly speculative ideas of Hulme,
though they were of course working inductively and intuitively from their own
experience as well, as artists in any medium must always work. What gave their
language its freshness and immediacy was the background of Hulme's new insight
into the nature of the creative process, together with the ever-present models of
French Symbolist poetry, which Hulme himself had often used as the best examples of "modern art."

If the 'image' as the Imagists understood it was really a new way of *seeing*
through the medium of words, free verse was a new way of *hearing* through
words. Just as poetic imagery becomes conventionalized through use and repetition, so does poetic meter, and there is a need in each age for a renewal of form
as well as of meaning. The iambic pentameter, or standard blank verse line, which
had been a fresh acqusition in Shakespeare's day, when it was a highly flexible
form that could be adapted to any poet's use, had by the late nineteenth century
lost most of its vitality, and was too often repeated by rote, rather than by ear.
Here, the French Symbolists were ready with a fresh technique, for they had
experimented with vers libre–sometimes, as in Laforgue's "Complaints," with
brilliant success. They had shown that an irregular and shifting rhythm was well
suited to the description of inner impressions and moods: their poems, like
Debussy's preludes (which were often based on them), changed as swiftly and
unpredictably as the mind itself. Their experiment became an Imagist principle:

> As regarding rhythm: to compose in the sequence of the musical
> phrase, not in sequence of a metronome.

In practice, this meant that the poet avoided fitting his image to a predetermined
pattern of rhythm and rhyme, but tried, instead, to fit the rhythm to the image,
following the natural cadence of speech. As Pound put it elsewhere, "I believe
in an 'absolute rhythm,' a rhythm, that is, in poetry which corresponds exactly
to the emotion or shade of emotion to be expressed."[11] His idea of free verse thus
was one of *organic form* in poetry—not, as was sometimes thought, of formlessness. Many poets since have testified that "free" verse is a greater challenge to
write than regular verse, for as Hulme had pointed out in the beginning: "It is
a delicate and difficult art, that of evoking an image, of fitting the rhythm to the
idea, and one is tempted to fall back into the comforting and easy arms of the
old, regular metre, which takes away all the trouble for us."[12]

Thus, the continuity between French Symbolism and Anglo-American Imagism can best be understood as a regeneration of poetic language, occurring first
in French then in English, together with a new understanding of the nature of
poetry. Both had their start in an intuition that, as Hulme expressed it, poetry
"no longer deals with heroic action, it has become definitely and finally introspec-
tive, and deals with expression and communication of momentary phases in the
poet's mind."[13] What the Symbolists meant by a "symbol" is very much like what
the Imagists meant by an "image," except that the latter was briefer in duration,
and "harder," or more concrete, in expression. Both schools acknowledged the
duality of human experience, and both tried to make contact, through visible,
sensible appearances with an invisible reality. The main difference between their
achievements was that while the Symbolists moved in the direction of the "pure
poem," and thus risked more and more subjective expressions, the Imagists
moved in the direction of realism and concreteness, toward a more objective
expression. The chief principle guiding the Imagists was that "images in verse are
not mere decoration, but the very essence of an intuitive language,"[14] and so they
relied—too heavily, at times—on the expressive power of things seen, rather than
on the suggestive power of things unseen, in the manner favored by the Symbolists.
But all in all, Taupin would seem to be justified in his major conclusion, that
"between the 'image' of the Imagists and the 'symbol' of the Symbolists there is
a difference only of precision."

To say that much of Imagism, of course, means to consider it as a movement
that did not end in 1917, when the third and last of Amy Lowell's Imagist
anthologies appeared, but carried on into a second stage under the leadership of
T. S. Eliot. This is Taupin's view, and it seems quite consistent with the facts.

For it was Eliot's poetry which deepened the Symbolist influence, at the same time as it widened the religious dimension of Imagism. It may be said that until Eliot began publishing his poems, the "religious attitude" Hulme had spoken of was only implicit in the Imagist movement, whereas after his work had made its impression, this attitude became more and more explicit—particularly after *The Waste Land* had exploded like a time bomb on postwar Europe. The effect of this one poem by Eliot on all the poetry that followed has been inestimable, and surely Pound was not exaggerating when he called it "the justification of the modern movement in poetry." *The Waste Land* may well be seen as the point at which the Symbolist and Imagist movements converged, for it is a poem constructed entirely out of images, connected not by plot but by an underlying myth which gives the whole poem its powerful symbolic force. No poem of the Symbolists, and certainly no poem of the Imagists before it, had carried such an overwhelming load of implied meaning. The multiple ambiguities and ironies of the poem place it squarely within the Symbolist tradition, while the economy and concreteness of the language show the full effect of Imagist concentration. Insofar as *The Waste Land* stands at the center of modern poetry in all languages—and there is much evidence that it does—it is the best witness we have to the salutary influence of French Symbolism on Anglo-American poetry.

PART ONE

FRENCH SYMBOLISTS AND DECADENTS AND THE AMERICAN POETIC TRADITION

IN THE LATE NINETEENTH CENTURY, French influence on American poetry was evident in the work of a few poets who were in revolt against the literary traditions of their country. But nothing of interest came out of this fin de siècle movement, whether it was inspired directly by French Symbolist and Decadent poets, or indirectly by them through the medium of English poets like Swinburne or Oscar Wilde. No poet had yet appeared who was powerful enough to overcome popular sentiment and organize a movement opposed to the strong English tradition of American literature. There were some poets who compromised, by studying and exploiting both Whitman and Verlaine, while others merely appropriated qualities (in this case faults) from the French that were already too evident in their own work. The example of Maeterlinck and Verlaine lured them in the direction of vagueness and indefiniteness, and so accelerated the mystical tendency already evident in their poetry.

It may be said that from 1890 to 1910, American poetry was feeling its way forward, subjecting itself to a great variety of foreign influences. Poets looked everywhere, but with little sense of purpose, and no constructive effort or serious work was accomplished during these two decades. The first effect of French influence on American poetry was not a reaction, but a weak imitation.

CHAPTER 1

The Eastern Tradition

IN 1912, when a new school of critics and poets surveyed American poetry, they agreed that the country had a poetic soul, that in many places an unmistakable artistic surge was to be felt, but that, nevertheless, "there is no man now living in America whose work is of the slightest interest to any serious artist."[1]

These writers felt that nothing dated before 1900 was worth reading, and that what the important reviews published were mainly echoes of the Victorian period. They were too observant, however, to doubt that there was a hidden poetic impulse, and they were right; today we know that a number of artists were privately seeking a style suited to their nationality and temperament. They could not hope for help from their predecessors, and, not knowing of each other, they could not form a group; thus their efforts were retarded, but their work in time bore fruit.

How is the conventionality of the poetry of this period to be explained? Why was it that the genius of the race could not find adequate means of expression? The question is complex, and the weaknesses of the period cannot be attributed to a single cause. Only if one traces the evolution of American poetry up to 1912 can it be seen that the state of literature from 1910 to 1912 was the product of different movements, attempts to find a new technique, a new inspiration—vain attempts that died in that period.

From 1880 to 1910, a series of tendencies were to be noticed. America was trying to fashion an artistic conscience; but whether because a literary tradition older than the Civil War continued, or because a national and democratic poetry was being sought, or because in the large cities artists were turning toward Europe and seeking to understand the new artistic movements of the Old World— no culture, no technique, no art was established.

Whistler, in a lecture given in London at that time, said that no country ever has such a thing as an "artistic period," yet no country ever had a period without art. This is a paradox, the truth of which is that in any period, men are capable of aesthetic emotions; as for achievements, however, they vary directly in proportion to places and times: they depend on circumstances as well as on chance. It is certain that one man can educate a people, or at least can give a people what they lack for producing art; but this same man, if he leaves the country, can only develop as circumstances favor him. In the same way, a foreign influence some-times suffices to complete the cultivation of a people; but in order for the transplanted seed to bear fruit, the climate must be favorable.

But, from 1880 to 1910, no seed bore fruit, no art prospered in America; and poetry had this disadvantage over the other arts, that one forgot it was *art*, and a number of versifiers made rhymes without the thought of being artists. Does this suggest there was no true poet to relieve the boredom of these thirty monotonous years? No, for Sidney Lanier, William Vaughn Moody, and Richard Hovey had true poetic temperaments. But their personalities, although vigorous, were not strong enough to provoke the sort of poetic awakening they so ardently desired. They were only half-successful in transcending their circumstances. To their vain but interesting efforts another chapter will be devoted. It will be best first of all to study the traditional American poetry of that time, the poetry published in magazines and read, not by a few exceptional people, but by the enlightened and respectable members of the American middle and upper classes.

The intellectual capital of the United States in this period was still Boston. But Boston and New England, though they were the center of civilization in the United States, were not its artistic center. Boston was a city as civilized as any other, if civilization is understood to mean philosophical and religious culture. But the city was closed to anything modern, artistic, scientific. Thoreau exiled himself from this New England by taking refuge in nature; Emily Dickinson, by shutting herself up in her own house. Theirs were the only means of escaping the constric-tion of an education framed by theologians, and a community life dedicated to prosperity and commerce. It is not surprising that when new ideas did penetrate these walls, when certain names, certain fashions achieved some modest success, they disappeared, to be almost immediately forgotten.

In *La Plume*, for July 1, 1892, "Marius," the French correspondent to the United States, described Boston as a city "with unlimited pretensions to every-thing in the nature of art, literature, and social advancement; a city excelling above all in everything pertaining to the advancement of women, having clubs, associations, and women's societies without number; a city where a variety of religions all have followers, where everyone is striving to be the first to advance a new idea, where Ibsen has been the rage of society women for a whole winter"—but where, as he went on to say, everything artistic was misunderstood.

This artistic poverty was by no means limited to New England. About the South, H. L. Mencken would write much later that "In that whole region, an area three times as large as France or Germany, there is not a single orchestra capable of playing Beethoven's C minor symphony, or a single painting worth looking at, or a single public building or monument of any genuine distinction, or a single factory devoted to the making of beautiful things, or a single poet, novelist, historian, musician, painter or sculptor whose reputation extends beyond his own country."[2]

Many corroborating opinions on the America of this period could be offered. For instance, there was the impression of Feodor Chaliapin, the Russian operatic star, who wrote from the United States to a friend in Russia on 12 April 1908:

> I am writing to you again to condemn this distant country, and to praise our Holy Mother Russia . . . Rarely have I seen such ignorance as that of the North and South Americans. Art for them is only an amusement, and if one tells them that art is a necessity, they open their eyes as wide as owls, slowly blink their eyelids, and say smilingly that money is the only necessity for men.[3]

In New England, which was the cultural capital of the country, the atmosphere was favorable enough for philosophy, but not for poetry. Philosophical poetry alone was read, and poets must first of all be moralists and rhetoricians. Minds shaped by the ideas and institutions of the intellectual capital of America were well equipped to achieve popular success, but not artistic success. These were the minds which had founded America, and they continued to direct it. In literature, the great names were those of men either born in New England or officially sanctioned by it. The only exceptions among poets were Poe and Whitman, who had been forced to find their inspiration in the realms of fantasy and "democratic vistas" of the future.

In short, the prevalent mind of the American upper class at the end of the nineteenth century was full of Puritanism and moral dignity, as it had been from the beginning of its history. It was suspicious of poetry and art in all forms, and was wholly confident of the rightness of its own traditions: it believed that the past had been full of success, and that the way was open for new success. Above all it feared any deviation from its course, such as the effects of beauty on the emotions. To the New England mind, it was fine to wander in the realms of thought, but fatal to get lost. It was a sin to make a mistake. It was guilty, as someone said of President Wilson, "of never having understood that an intellectual error is an innocent one." This prejudice killed in Americans the spirit of adventure and imagination. To escape error, they manufactured creeds. If one among them felt the strivings of a poet, his teacher soon taught him that poetry was not the aim of his life, and everywhere he would encounter such opposition that he soon returned to the straight and narrow path—that is to say, to respect for tradition and to intellectual apathy.

The means of expression which New Englanders were accustomed to was the sermon. In this medium it was not only possible, but easy, to lay bare one's soul. Those poets who by their temperament and art were also preachers were the best received: namely, Wordsworth and Browning. The poetry of Wordsworth was such as could express pious tenderness, deal with familiar subjects, interpret the dreams that Americans sometimes abandoned themselves to, and at the same time exalt their religious sentiments. Browning, more than any other, taught them to express their imaginary fears through dramatic monologues. For it was one of the most interesting characteristics of these Puritans, and one of the traits of their poetry, to turn the imaginations toward the pathetic, the mysterious, and even the macabre. Doubtless this was a deviation brought on by the strict nature of Puritan education. At any rate, minds and spirits of a troubled originality were not lacking in New England.

But Puritanism had become a system so vast, and—truly protean— had taken so many forms in order to shape all the activities of the country, that solitary souls absorbed in their individual lives and in the nostalgia of their small home towns became more and more rare. In adapting itself to modern conditions, Puritanism changed its methods; in order to capture the public mind, it propagated ideas which were intended to guide the people toward religion and social morality, but to thwart true culture and the critical spirit. Instead of remaining a religious ethic, intolerant, but applied only to the life of the mind, it became belligerent, aggressive, as organized as an army.

But while Puritanism was still a moral order and doctrine, rather than a social organization, it was capable of producing minds like that of Emily Dickinson. This woman, a stranger even to her family, whose reclusive existence was completely introverted, was one of the last followers of Puritanism: in her were embodied the indifference to the world, the melancholy reverie, the narrow culture, and the intense personality that are the most striking characteristics of early New England Puritanism.

The new Puritanism was exemplified by Thomas Bailey Aldrich. At home everywhere, writing poetry which was mediocre but always well received, Boston editor of *Every Saturday*, then of the *Atlantic Monthly*, Aldrich represented exactly the man of New England who adapted himself to everything, made his way everywhere, and never knew anything but success. He represented what was no longer exclusively the Boston spirit, but completely the spirit of the East. Puritanism had become a moral, religious, and political force which allowed little liberty in thought and art. Poetry was permitted as a pastime, an agreeable exercise, a recreation. If it carried a message, it would be best understood by the public. Thus there was an audience for humorous poets, and for poets with moralistic and social intentions.

The number of publications at this time was always increasing, and since poetry was enjoyed as a distraction, it was within anyone's reach: the monthlies, even the weekly magazines, published it, and anthologies began to multiply. The titles of some of these anthologies are enough to suggest what was in them: *Paradise of Dainty Devices, A Selection of Verse de Société from Modern Poets* (1884), *Flowers from Mother's Grave* (1884), *Love Poems* (1895), *Christmas Poems* (1897), *Nature Poems* (1900), and even *Poets' Dogs* (1895).

As for the large magazines, it would be difficult to believe that the best established ones of this period were created by adventurous men: *Putnam's, The Dial, The Atlantic Monthly,* which had once reacted against the banality and aimlessness of their time, had passed into the service of a respectable and unenlightened middle class. They did not change, and in 1912, Ezra Pound wrote that the only difference between the first number of a review that appeared in 1880, and the first number of the same review in 1910, was the date inscribed on the opening page.[4]

Poets sought inspiration in religious sentiments, domestic life, and memories of childhood. They were inspired by all the themes used by writers of the past, by mythology and history, by whatever made an agreeable pastime for a Saturday evening public which had little time for art the rest of the week. Thus an independent critic of the time reproached Boston for its love of the allegorical and the outdated:

> When Caius Scriblerius Bostoniensis prints a lyric about the light of Amatoria's eyes which disperses his melancholy moods, the average public, at least in Boston, cares nothing for it until somebody in lack of employment discovers that, as St. Patrick's snakes were heathen rites, and Beatrice Portinari was a system of philosophy, so Amatoria's eyes personify the sun myth! And Caius shoots into his eleventh edition.[5]

Poetry was a distraction for most of the poets, as well as for their readers. Almost all of them worked at jobs which had very little to do with it. Glenville Miller was known as "The singer of one song." Webster produced two or three poems; Bryant worked in an office; Lowell, Burton, Markham were schoolmasters; Bret Harte, a miner; Stedman, a New York financier. These examples could be multiplied; they explain why there was little care about perfecting technique.

It is hard to realize that these poets, in spite of the impression they give now, were not merely entertainers, occupied with easy ornamentation, or with effects of the most naive banality. But even in serious moments they had no desire for individualism, and their verse was weak both in feeling and in imagery; they lacked the technical virtuosity which allows the poet to become a performer. All true poets have been to some extent performers, and sometimes versifiers have acquired notoriety by technical virtuosity alone—but not in America at this time.

For a long time, Boston writers were not interested in form; for them, poetry was valuable above all because of the agreeable sentiments it expressed, but not because of any independent beauty. In this respect, Boston differed from New York. Later on, when a stultifying American literary organization stifled all individualism, it became necessary to stress form in order to hide the poverty of feeling and the absence of true technique. Then it was that the strictest forms quickly became the most popular; there was a vogue for the sonnet, and most of the celebrated poets of the time worked in it. Except for one book of Sidney Lanier,[6] the whole science of verse that was studied from 1880 to 1900 by reviewers—even those who wished to speak of the correspondence between the arts—consisted of a series of rules based on English poems from Shakespeare to Browning.

By inclination, poets imitated England. Because they spoke the same language, Americans felt bound to imitate the English. They did not realize that, separated from the English by an ocean and a civilization, they were no longer evolving in the same way. They were imitating Tennyson and all that was most artificial in Shelley in 1900, and in general behaving like Baudelaire's host, who, in a far-off French colony, still imitated La Harpe. Granted, this imitation was the result of a sincere love of the mother country; like Henry James, Louise Guiney had been sick with nostalgia for England: when she was finally able to go there, it was a passionate pilgrimage; she found her ideal at Oxford, and reverently touched the stones which covered her heroes and martyrs. For a long time, on the anniversary of the Restoration, she wore an oak leaf in her hat in memory of the Silurist (as the metaphysical poet Henry Vaughan was called).

Indeed, in all sincerity, American poets imitated Keats, Shelley, Tennyson, and Browning. The poetry of Tennyson had all the sentimentality, the ornate grace, which appealed to them, and they greatly loved his stories in verse. Only a musician by profession, like Lanier, dared to confide to a friend (the poet Bayard Taylor) that Tennyson was not a musician. He immediately added: "Let us not blaspheme against the gods." In September, 1892, the pastors of many churches were invited to pray for the health of Lord Tennyson; all students in the United States knew his most famous poems—and often, his least famous ones—by heart.

The influence of Browning, perhaps less general because of the obscurity of his works, was more durable. Men of talent, such as Lanier and Moody, agreed in admiring him and in imitating him, when Tennyson was beginning to be held in scorn. Louise Moulton visited the Italy that she admired through the poems of Browning; and in Boston, Miss Clarke and Miss Potter founded *Poet-Lore*, a magazine consecrated to Browning.

As early as 1880, Americans had begun to realize that they needed to regenerate their poetry. They said, and repeatedly, that the English influence was bad, because it encouraged mediocrity. But the imitations did not stop. In the West, poetry was written on the subject of pioneer life, but in a traditional style. The attempts at exotic poetry were as ridiculous as the little Chinese shops in New York; and Ridgely Torrence and Bayard Taylor wrote as though to children avid for color and novelty.

Strangely, what now began to be popular in New England was the adaptation of old French forms. In Boston, at the home of Louise Moulton, where there was a gathering of the literati enamored of Tennyson and Browning (and some who were more enlightened), the new English fashion was followed. From England, about 1885, had come the taste for adapting old French forms: rondeaus, ballades, triolets, and villanelles. Such experiments showed the interest in a reformation, above all of technique. But it was a demonstration too limited to have any effect.

Thus American poetry continued to follow imitative tendencies until 1912. Loyalty to the English was always the rule. Even after that date, Lizette W. Reese and Edna St. Vincent Millay continued the English tradition quite brilliantly. New England kept its vitality and, if it never sought novelty, it continued to produce men who distinguished themselves among their contemporaries by their cultivation. However, they were the last representatives of a long tradition.

Before the year 1912, all thought of poetry had disappeared from the normal activity of the country. Some people could be seen who recognized and approached the right ideals without attaining them. Poe and Whitman had only served to give scattered phrases to poets otherwise traditional and uninteresting. And when a new group of poets appeared on the scene to revolt against Puritanism, against American life, against tradition, their efforts found no support. When others, such as Edwin Arlington Robinson, made new use of the traditional Puritan spirit, it was not surprising that they had few followers.

In short, the faults of these thirty years may be summed up as a general disregard for art. It was against this fortress of prejudice and conventionality that independent spirits fought vainly. There was, from 1880 on, a breath of liberty coming from the West; and a tentative aesthetic individualism which sought its strength in Germany and in France. But the new tendencies struggled with difficulty against a literary organization whose strength was well entrenched.

CHAPTER 2

The Effort of the West

BOSTON, having given its culture to the whole country, ceased to be the intellectual capital of the nation. It faded little by little; it could not adapt itself to the new conditions of life, and remained the center of a province, instead of becoming the conscience of a great country. Among the most intelligent men of the East, there were a number who, without undertaking to produce it themselves, thought that the literature of the new land should reflect the national and democratic ideal of the whole country. They had read Whitman; and if they did not imitate him, it was only for lack of boldness and adventure. But they counted on the West to show what could be done.

Westerners had begun by imitating England and the Atlantic states. For a long time people in the new states were content to read the magazines they received from Boston and New York. If the West proved more original at the crucial moment in American literature, if Chicago showed more initiative than Boston, it was because, first of all, the people of the West, with their fresh and impressionable minds, were more eager to admit foreign influences; and because, more importantly, they felt less sympathy for England, which they regarded as a far-off and truly foreign country. They showed greater freedom in their expression, and gave indications that in time false ornament and decoration would disappear from their work.

But lacking any new technique, the poets of the West were content to tell new stories in old forms: Indian tales, the exploits of bandits and heroes were their subject matter, and their form was the ballad, chiefly. For a semiliterate public, such poetry was an agreeable novelty, but nothing more. Whitman unfortunately had no real successors. His individualism, and the free form of his verse, which had conveyed exactly the rhythm of his breathing and the vital energy of the man, could not start a movement in a country where literature was at the service of an indiscriminate public.

John Burroughs, Joaquin Miller, and Edwin Markham are representative enough of this literature of the West. These poets had all known and admired Whitman; Miller had crossed the Sierras in order to shake the hand of "The Good Grey Poet"; and Burroughs saw in him "the only mountain to be viewed up to now on our literary landscape." And here is how Miller translated the thoughts of Whitman: "And as there cannot be a great land on the page of history without first a great literature, so there cannot be a great literature without first a deep, broad, devout and loving religion, full of piety and love."[1] Thus he made Whitman into a Puritan prophet. Miller called poets "prophets" and "voices of the land"; he also spoke of American poetry much as Whitman had spoken of it. For the author of *Leaves of Grass*, this poet was to be "the soul of the nation; he should interest himself in man; in the national hero, and above all in 'the divine common man', in the divine average.' " Miller thought likewise: "Braver and better to celebrate the lowly and forgiving grasses under foot, than the stately cedars and sequoias overhead."[2] He reaffirmed Whitman's disdain for technique: "Will we ever have an American literature? Yes, when we leave sound and words to the wind."[3]

Whitman had exaggerated American democracy as a source of art: The "divine average" man much preferred Indian tales and love stories. Miller, Edwin Markham, Edward Rowland Sill, James Whitcomb Riley, Eugene Field, J. Russell, and G. Sterling, all of whom were in some way successors of Whitman, did not make a more national poetry for America, but a more popular poetry. It would be useless to make a detailed study of a style which merely delayed the development of American originality. But the East, until at least 1912, craved "red-blooded poetry" from Western poets.

John Hay, returning at this time from a long sojourn in Europe, saw that Western literature was in vogue, and began publishing "ballads" which he took less seriously than did his readers. Joaquin Miller succeeded by force of rhetoric in describing the canyons and mountains of California. But what stale epics, what trite language, what uncouth heroes! Yet Miller may be said to epitomize this period of Western poetry. Edward Rowland Sill, who had been educated at Yale, transported the Puritan culture of the East to the scenery of the West. He had read French writers—especially the realists, Daudet and Flaubert, and also Dumas père and George Sand. Besides his study and writing, he initiated social reforms, organized aid societies, and founded village libraries in the West. James Whitcomb Riley was the creator of a regional, domestic literature of the West. Eugene Field also had a large public. He wrote moralizing ballads for the newspapers—people seemed to love his poems in the morning after breakfast, before the day's work began. Edwin Markham's wish was to make the extraordinary familiar, and the familiar extraordinary. He sometimes displayed the style of Whitman, but also displayed his excesses.

Why such a vogue of Western literature? It is conceivable that all these ballads and narrative poems, written in trite images and familiar rhythms, couched in the dialect of the West, might have appeared amusing, sometimes even dramatic; but it is hard to believe that this vogue could have lasted half a century, or that many people once thought of these authors as inventors of an American poetry. It should be remembered that these works appeared at a time when Naturalism and Romanticism hung in the balance; people were reading Tennyson, Browning, Kipling, and Stevenson; and had begun to read Daudet, Maupassant, and Zola. The poets of the West effectively combined both styles, giving to a public which hesitated between them, stories that were realistic in dialect, but romantic in rhythm, images, and manner.

It seems strange that all these admirers of Whitman took so little influence from him, but it is clear that if he was not imitated he was read; people at least believed in him and in his ideas. Edwin Arlington Robinson has commemorated well the silent cult of Whitman at this period:

> We do not hear him very much today:
> His piercing and eternal cadence rings
> Too pure for us—too powerfully pure,
> Too lovingly triumphant, and too large;
> But there are some that hear him, and they know
> That he shall sing to-morrow for all men,
> And that all time shall listen.
>   "Walt Whitman," 1896

The number of imitators of Whitman increased, especially in the West. His true disciples, as we shall see, were those social poets who wrote around 1910. Certain of them studied his message then and took up his form. But in the period we are studying, a period encumbered by the past, his voice was too strident for their tender ears.

Nevertheless, it may be said at this point that the idea of a national poetry, as many of the critics of that time conceived of it, was condemned in advance. Whitman owed his success to his individualism, but this individualism contradicted itself, when the poet-patriot advised his successors to immerse themselves in the national spirit. Whitman, an excellent representative of the America of 1870, expressed all the faults of his countrymen: scorn for personality, exaltation of the mass mind, of quantity and mediocrity.

Alongside this poetry of the East and West, which accounted for most of the poetic production of the United States, we must now set still another, in order to understand fully the tendencies of American poetry in 1910, when something like an American Revolution began in poetry. This other kind of poetry reveals the first French influences, and the first signs of a movement toward aesthetic individualism.

CHAPTER 3

How French Symbolism Penetrated America

FROM 1880–1895—FIRST CRITICAL STUDIES

A ROUND 1880, in Paris, several young men met at a Naturalist salon, and the Symbolist school was born. In Boston, at this time, people were rereading Emerson, and removing from the hands of misguided adolescents the books of Tolstoi and Zola. Du Maurier was talked about; he was a charming novelist, but he had known the young models of the Latin Quarter rather too well. It was preferable to read Dickens and Stevenson; then Mrs. Phelps, William Dean Howells, and Louisa May Alcott. They were comforting, and showed that America had indeed remained pure, and had resisted European immorality. The public was resistant to Europe, without daring to admit that it was losing faith in its own national glory; Walt Whitman was no longer anything but an illustrious name, Thoreau a curiosity, and Lanier a nice poet.[1] Basically, people were weary, as yet scarcely recovered from the Civil War; they desired above everything else to escape the upheavals of Europe, to protect themselves also from its disturbing literature. This weariness, this desire for rest, accounts for the defensive attitude of America, and particularly of New England, toward Europe.

Lanier, certainly the most important poet of the period after Whitman, has described the spiritual isolation in which artists found themselves: "I will never be able to describe what a desert my life has been," he said, "when I think of the hosts of subjects one absorbs, I imagine, when he breathes an artistic atmosphere, in the commerce of men of letters, travelers, and people who have seen, written, or done great things."

It was then that a movement of expatriation began, which has not yet ended. America lost some of her great artists—Henry James, John Singer Sargent, and others.

In 1887, an expatriate returned to his native land: Stuart Merrill debarked in New York, with the idea of settling down there. At this time, he was already quite well known among the French Symbolists.[2] With Merrill as intermediary, it would seem that the influence of French poetry, and more particularly of

Symbolist poetry, should have made itself felt in America. Yet such was not the case. Stuart Merrill could not adapt himself to his country; in New York, he seemed to keep to himself, seeing very little of the young poets of the day, and among these, only the least talented ones.[3] Three years later, he took the boat back to France. In addition to translations, he had written during his stay several articles for the newspapers, one in particular on Gerard de Nerval, and three others on the music of Wagner, which attracted more notice in Paris than in New York.[4] Americans were to know the work of Merrill later on, as well as that of Vielé-Griffin, and to congratulate themselves on having given two poets to France. But this first visit of a French Symbolist failed to draw the least attention to the new French poetry. This failure was no doubt owing to the wide separation of American artists, and the apathy of a public that Merrill himself called "the crudest possible public in matters of art."[5]

It was, however, during the period of Stuart Merrill's sojourn in New York that the reaction toward Europe began. The provincialism of America had become so rigid that the freer minds revolted against it. University students were first, for they had known of Gautier and Baudelaire ever since Henry James had introduced them to the American public in 1878, in *French Poets and Novelists*.[6] They began to study these two poets, and to speak of "art for art's sake." Besides the young students, who were enthusiastic but poorly informed, there were well-known critics who wrote articles encouraging literary cosmopolitanism. Among the most cultivated and cosmopolitan of these, George Woodberry, Brander Matthews,[7] Harry Thurston Peck, and William Brownell must be mentioned. These last two interested themselves particularly in French literature and art.

The influence of W. C. Brownell was considerable. He published a large number of articles on France in *Scribner's*, and gathered them together in 1889 as *French Traits*. They were written with a good deal of critical sense and judgment, and constituted a first effort at giving America a saner idea of France. With his articles and his book *French Art*, he helped spread the knowledge of French art through the United States. He did more for the popularization of culture than for the awakening of a real critical sense; or perhaps this was a weakness of the period. It is regrettable at any rate that his books, like those of the more scholarly Woodberry, reached only a limited public.

It was around 1890 that people began to know contemporary French painting well. The names of the French masters became known to a wide public, thanks to the number of Americans who were studying in Paris. In addition to the articles of Brownell, popular magazines with a large circulation, like *Scribner's* and *McClure's*, regularly published illustrated studies of French artists, with interesting though mediocre reproductions. The favorite painters were decorative artists like Dagnan-Bouverer and Bouguereau. But soon there was a vogue for the masters of French poster art: Forain, Chéret, and Toulouse-Lautrec.[8] This imperfect knowledge of French art was extremely important, not only in itself, but because the interest in painting led to interest in French writing in America. From 1890 on, the results of the reaction toward Europe were to be seen everywhere.

By 1892, to judge by the articles in the magazines, the names of the greatest French poets and novelists were known in America. During his stay in the United States in 1893, Paul Bourget observed that Americans brought "enlightened interest to the reading of Verlaine and Mallarmé"[9] and he was surprised to hear in their conversation "constant reference to French authors of the most revolutionary kind." Bourget explained that this vogue reached even to society women, through the effect on them of painters who had gone to Paris to study.

Bourget discovered youthful literary clubs in Boston like the Tavern Club, which reminded him of the Club des Hydropathes of the Latin Quarter. The walls were covered with posters of Chéret, and the young Harvard boys discussed Baudelaire there. It was one of the numerous "Bohemian" clubs, where young artists made war on Victorianism and Puritanism, and looked to Europe for inspiration. Besides these, there was a minority who spoke of Americanism and national art. Here, for example, is what Mark Twain thought of the French influence, at the time of Paul Bourget's visit:

> What would the new teacher, representing France, teach us? Railroading? No. . Steamboating? No. . . . . Magazining? No. These are our own specialties. Government? No. Liberty, equality, fraternity, nobility, democracy, adultery? The system is too variegated for our climate. Religion? No, not variegated enough for our climate. Morals? No, we cannot rob the poor to enrich ourselves. Novel-writing? No, M. Bourget and others know only the one plan, and when that is expurgated there is nothing left of the book.[10]

This rather crude attack echoed the protest of the Puritan majority. If, however, students, young writers, and a few society people flattered themselves in 1893 that they knew French authors, it was because of the efforts of Brander Matthews and of Brownell; in addition to the knowledge gained through painters, there was the influence of the critics, whose articles in certain liberal papers and magazines drew attention to French writers.

But it was the English, really, who first introduced Symbolism to America, just as later they were the first to join the school of the French moderns. When the Symbolist school began to be known in France, about 1885, American criticism was closed to foreign influences, with some exceptions such as Woodberry and Brownell. It is not surprising, then, that the editors of *The Dial, The Critic,* and *The North American Review* were content to echo their more illustrious colleagues on the *Fortnightly Review* and the *Nineteenth Century Review.* The feeling that they were literary vassals of England was still very strong and deep. If some isolated men revolted against this respect for English opinion, and claimed independence of thought for America, the majority of the public was delighted to read articles from London in *The Living Age,* articles signed by Edmund Gosse, Saintsbury, or Arthur Symons. Beside these English reviews, American criticism was insignificant, consisting of a few recollections of an interview with a celebrity, or a few hasty and borrowed opinions. Americans learned about European literature by reading *Dial: A Year of Continental Literature,* which contained a few condensed articles that had first appeared in the *Atheneum.* When Londoners spoke of a French poet, people in New York were anxious to know him, but they would scarcely have thought of going to Paris to discover him. English articles on European authors almost invariably preceded American articles. Only later on did men of talent like Peck, Hovey, and Huneker begin to escape this slavery, and to insist that writers go directly to Paris to get their ideas. Until 1890, and perhaps until even later, the American public was interested only in England.

But England was at this time already much interested in French literature. George Moore returned to England more Parisian than Irish, and in his *Confessions of a Young Man*[11] and in *Impressions and Opinions,*[12] he described the studios, literary circles, and cafés that he had frequented during the previous ten years. He shocked the London public, which reproached him for his "foreignness of manner," the free tone of his criticism, his exasperating praise for almost everything that the English instinctively detested, and his scorn for those authors whom the English universally admired. However, the protests aroused by these articles attracted wide public notice. At the same time, Henry James, Andrew Lang, George Saintsbury, and Arthur Symons were speaking about the French and making themselves heard.

The English had known Baudelaire for a long time, as well as most of the Parnassians and Gerard de Nerval, about whom various studies had appeared from 1853 on.[13] The American public first knew these authors through James and Merrill, two expatriates.[14] In 1869, before James published *French Poets and Novelists.*[15] an unsigned article on Baudelaire had appeared in America.[16] Then an essay on him by J. A. Harrison appeared in the *Southern Review* in 1873,[17] and another by Henry James in the *Nation* in 1876.[18] These articles appeared at about the same time as the English critiques of Baudelaire.[19]

In *French Poets and Novelists,* Gautier and Baudelaire were described, but not altogether accurately. Henry James saw in Baudelaire only "the victim of a grotesque illusion. He tried to make fine verses on ignoble subjects, and in our opinion he signally failed." James admitted that "he had an extraordinary verbal instinct," but regarded him as "an altogether inferior genius to Gautier." James judged these two poets from a moral rather than an artistic standpoint, as the more provincial of his colleagues might have done. Great though James was as a novelist—indeed perhaps *because* he was such a great novelist, and his art consisted of delicately reproducing the opinions and feelings of a particular society—he had extreme difficulty in expressing an opinion different from that of his fellow-critics, except on matters concerning his own art of the novel.[20] Nevertheless, by means of his articles as well as by his expatriation, James served to direct the attention of his American contemporaries toward Europe.

At about the same time as *French Poets and Novelists* appeared, better balanced studies of Baudelaire also appeared. In February, 1890, some students at Harvard showed admiration for the poet's serious discipline, and even said: "It would be difficult to find a single false note in the whole of *Les Fleurs de mal.*"[21] However, certain American reviews were still announcing that the great poet of the future was François Coppée.

Verlaine seems to have been discovered fairly late by Americans, first through English critics, such as Edward Delille in the *Fortnightly Review* in 1891, and Arthur Symons in the *Academy*, in April of the same year.[22] The legend of Paul Verlaine, wandering from cafe to cafe, and the story of the squalid surroundings where George Moore found him, injured his artistic reputation in America. But students and artists knew him and were already under the spell of his influence, which was to be the most important of all in the period of the Nineties. Along with Verlaine, Rimbaud had been introduced to the English public in 1891, in an essay by George Moore called "Two Unknown Poets."[23] But Rimbaud, who was to have a great influence on the writers we are most concerned with, was not fully appreciated in America until many years later.

The first American article on Mallarmé was published by Harry Thurston Peck in April, 1896, in *The Bookman*, quite some time after the articles of Edmund Gosse and of Carrell in London.[24] The first serious study, which was by Peck, did not appear until 1898.[25] But soon the name of Mallarmé became a legend.

It was also through an English article that Emile Verhaeren was first introduced to Americans.[26] In New York, the names of Francis Jammes, Albert Samain, Henri de Régnier were known, but their works were hardly read before 1900. The same was true of Rémy de Gourmont.

The poet whose fame was most sudden and remained most lasting during this period was Maurice Maeterlinck. He was also introduced by the English. He was first talked of in Paris in 1889, following critiques by Albert Arnay and George Rodenbach. In 1890, an article by Octave Mirbeau in *Le Figaro* sang his praises. Mirbeau had just discovered "the Belgian Shakespeare." This expression was shocking to the English, but it attracted their attention. Paul Fredericq spoke of Maeterlinck in a survey of Belgian literature in July of 1891.[27] In September, a long article by William Archer consolidated the reputation of the Flemish poet in England.[28]

The American public, which read the column of Paul Fredericq in the *Dial*, soon knew the name of Maurice Maeterlinck. As early as 1891, *Les Aveugles* and *L'Intruse* were translated.[29] The author soon became a subject of discussion; certain people reproached him for having taught nothing about "men and women, God, and the mechanism of the universe";[30] others, on the other hand, admired him unreservedly. From this moment on, Americans, following the example of the English, wrote more about Maeterlinck than about any French poet.

As for the two American poets, Stuart Merrill and Vielé-Griffin, their work was scarcely known in their homeland. Their names were cited in articles on the Symbolists, with a certain pride that they were Americans, and that was all. Not a single serious study of these poets is to be found from 1889 to 1900. Stuart Merrill was the better known of the two, doubtless because of his visit to New York, a few articles written while there, and his acquaintance with a few men of letters in that city. In 1890, he published *Pastelles in Prose*,[31] which consisted of rhythmical prose translations of passages of verse and prose from Villiers, Huysmans, Baudelaire, Mallarmé, Ephraim Mikhael, and Henri de Régnier, as well as many less interesting poets. The book received scarcely any notice, at least from the critics. It must be admitted that the desultory selection and the hesitant English of Merrill prevented the work from having any great value.[32]

The English deserve the honor of having been the first to introduce Americans to modern French poetry. It was only after 1890 that American criticism slowly disengaged itself from English influence. In 1892, two original articles on the Symbolists appeared: "The Latest Literary Fashion in France," by T. S. Perry, in *Cosmopolitan* (July, 1892), and an article by the Paris correspondent of *Harper's*.[33] The latter tried very clumsily to define the theories of the "Symbolists," or "Decadents." He knew all the great poets of the group by name, and cited the names of Baudelaire, Verlaine, Laforgue, and Mallarmé, but admitted that he only vaguely understood their ideas. He excused himself readily, saying: "There are ill-balanced minds in the group . . . ," who have written "pages and even volumes that normal minds cannot comprehend at all . . . ." He added that "They are morbid and aristocratic," and show "a tendency to seek the rare, the precious, the exquisite, and even the perverse." It was a distorted portrait of Symbolism, but it was at least an attempt at analysis.

The article by T. S. Perry was much more serious. Like all Americans, Perry was inclined to exaggerate the obscurity of Symbolism, because of the poems of Mallarmé and the theories of René Ghil. He was bothered also by the term *Symbolism*, which he interpreted too literally, expressing surprise that the poetry of the school was not entirely "symbolic." He mistook ideas that were individual, such as René Ghil's theory of orchestration, for ideas held in common by the group. The reputation of the Symbolists in America for strangeness and abnormality may be attributed to errors of this kind. But Perry spoke of their search for perfection of form, and pointed to their importance in the evolution of poetry. All in all, this article described Symbolism to the American public fairly well.

In the following year, 1893, a number of studies of the French Symbolists appeared. First, a long article on the affinities of Poe and Baudelaire was printed in the *Nineteenth Century Review;*[34] then a review on Verlaine,[35] who was recognized as "the leader of the Decadents and Symbolists." This review had its importance: until 1910, Americans, more influenced by Verlaine than by any other French poet, considered him (though wrongly) the leader of the new poetic school. There was also a note about his lecture in London;[36] and another on the *Pélerin passionné* by Moréas. The latter was made to seem more comprehensible than the other Symbolist writings. In *The Nation* there was a rapid summary of the first reviews to be called "Decadent"; *La Revue fantaisiste* of Mendès; *La Plume; La Revue blanche;* and *La Revue indépendante* of F. Fénéon.

An article by Arthur Symons achieved considerable notice at this time.[37] Symons was the principal defender of Symbolism in England, and no study at that period was more important than his *The Symbolist Movement in Literature.*[38] But he was then mainly interested in Verlaine, and free verse seemed to him still "a whim of the noisy little school of Decadents, and the silly little school of Symbolists," and a natural consequence of Mallarmé's experiments with "the elasticity of rhythm and the rigidity of the caesura." He cited as examples of tolerable free verse the poems of Kahn and Dujardin; as intolerable, those of Moréas. The chief value of the article was in distinguishing between the terms Decadent, Symbolist, and Impressionist, which were being confused by Americans.

A little before Symons' article appeared, one of the best American studies of Symbolism appeared in *Scribner's.*[39] This study contained, along with a brief review of the works of Verlaine, Laforgue, and Rimbaud, a resumé of poets yet unknown in America—Gustave Kahn, Francis Poictevin—and the first intelligent statements about the work of Mallarmé. Miss Gorren's exactness helped to correct the false impression that less enlightened critics had given the American public.

This was the stage in the knowledge of French poetry that America had reached when Paul Bourget found, to his amazement, that he could discuss it with students, artists, and even society women in America.

Of course, the great event of the year 1893 for Americans was not the visit of Paul Bourget, but the Chicago Exposition—the World's Fair. Some people were expecting to see, in the rooms reserved for French art, paintings by the Impressionists whom they had read about in the magazines but whose work remained a mystery. But instead of the magnificent Renoirs and Seurats that Brownell had described in *Scribner's*, they saw only canvases of Bouguereau, Carrier-Belleuse, and innumerable unknown artists. The French government had sent 50,000 francs worth of valueless paintings as a gift to the United States, on condition that they be placed in American museums after the Exposition!

However, the interest in French poetry and in French art continued to spread, thanks to the critics. Maeterlinck emerged as the most fashionable author. In 1895, he accompanied L'Oeuvre's troupe to London, where they performed *L'Intruse* and *Pelléas et Mélisande*. The public was surprised and delighted with these performances. Important critics like William Archer and George Bernard Shaw praised the two plays. The American poet Richard Hovey, after talking with Maeterlinck and reading careful observations of the theatre and audience, left there persuaded that the renaissance of poetic drama was only a matter of time.[40] It was principally the inspiration of Maeterlinck that led Hovey himself, later on, to attempt a renaissance of poetic drama in America.

A new magazine was published in 1895, which did much for the cause of foreign, especially French, literature. It was Peck's *The Bookman*.[41] An English magazine of that name had existed since 1891. Peck, in his American *Bookman*, showed a profound understanding of what the public wanted, and his magazine was a success.[42] It was a thoroughly American magazine, in the worst sense of the word—a popular magazine for light reading. It would be a mistake, however, to call it only a commercial venture. Some good critical essays were published in *The Bookman;* the most remarkable were by Peck himself. He spoke freely, and without regard for English opinion, which was then law. His article on Mallarmé in November, 1898, was exceptional for the period.

In 1896, he founded the *Daily Tatler,* which lasted only two weeks. This paper was a successor to *Tattle,* which had lasted only one summer. It was in the *Daily Tatler* that Richard Hovey published articles devoted to French poets. There were also reviews of the foreign press, and *Cosmopolis* and *Magazine International* were often mentioned. When the *Daily Tatler* ceased publication, Peck took up his French propaganda in *The Bookman* again.

Peck's writings were those of a cultivated man, and his effort was courageous: he wanted to liberate America from its faults, by holding up to it the example of Europe. But like Brownell before him, he was only half-liberated himself, and his hesitations and concessions prevented him from accomplishing the work he set out to do. His importance lies in having made the names of Huysmans, Mallarmé, Rimbaud, Laforgue, and Rémy de Gourmont familiar to Americans.

It was also in 1895 that the book of Max Nordau, *Degeneration*, was translated into English.[43] In it, the author tried to show by weighty scientific arguments that the distinctive traits of decadent writers were pathological in origin: Baudelaire, Verlaine, and Mallarmé were all degenerates. These attacks were greeted with applause by the conservatives, and hisses by the partisans of the new literature. The battle raged for more than a year. Nordau had no more vehement adversary than James Huneker, who saw in him the most striking example of that bourgeois mind which had prejudiced America against France. At the same time that the French Symbolists were being defended in *La Plume* and *L'Ermitage*[44] Huneker attacked *Degeneration* in *M'lle New York* and in other respectable magazines. He redeemed Nietzsche, Baudelaire, Huysmans, and Barrès by his enthusiastic articles, praising their vibrant genius. Toward the end of his life, he could rejoice to see that the writers criticized by Nordau no longer needed defending: "Nordau's black geese have turned out white swans, which proves that a little prophecy is a dangerous thing."[45] Nordau's book was scarcely dangerous: even at the moment of its appearance, it did more good than harm for the cause of the French poets; if a few more philistines were convinced of their immorality by *Degeneration*, their reputation was greatly enhanced by the passionate arguments which the book aroused.

1895-1900—THE ACTIVITY OF THE LITTLE REVIEWS

In 1895, a peak of interest in French literature had been reached in America. Not until 1914 was such an interest in foreign literature to be seen again. It was in the year 1895 that the ideas of Nordau were so heatedly discussed, that Peck's *The Bookman* appeared, and that a host of revolutionary little magazines began to be published—magazines that imitated the French Symbolist journals, and devoted themselves for the most part to propaganda for the French school. The first and most important of these magazines was *The Chap-Book*. On May 15, 1894, two Harvard students, Stone and Kimball, brought out the first number. Several months later they left Harvard. They opened the publishing house of Stone and Kimball in Chicago, and *The Chap-Book* appeared again in October, 1894, edited this time by Herbert Stone and Bliss Carman. Among the contributors were most of the group of American "Symbolists": Richard Hovey, Bliss Carman, C. G. D. Roberts, Archibald Lampman, Duncan Campbell Scott, and Gilbert Parker. Included also were George Santayana and Eugene Field, together with a number of American poetesses: Louise Moulton, Louise Imogen Guiney, and Gertrude Hall, the translator of Verlaine. The common interest of these writers gave *The Chap-Book* a personal character that the larger periodicals lacked.

To emphasize the originality of his magazine, Bliss Carman made the first few issues look like almanacs or "chapbooks," once popular among countryfolk.[46] The first issues showed the revolutionary tendencies of the contributors and their enthusiasm for French literature. Verlaine was mentioned often. Gertrude Hall's translation of "Clair de lune" appeared there, along with Anatole France's article, "Paul Verlaine, à propos de 'Mes Hopitaux.' "[47]

Verlaine himself sent a collection of epigrams, which had not yet been published in France.[48] Translations of the poetry of Verlaine by Gertrude Hall and the dramas of Maeterlinck by Richard Hovey were announced in the magazine, as well as the founding of the Green Tree Library, which proposed to publish in English the best works of "Decadent" Europeans (that is to say, the Symbolists and other new writers).[49] *Les Loisirs de la poste* by Mallarmé was printed in French in the *Chap-Book* for December, 1894, and "Hérodiade," translated in blank verse by Hovey, appeared in the following number. One could even read (in French) Mallarmé's essay on Rimbaud.[50] The influence of Maeterlinck was also visible in *The Chap-Book:* in addition to articles on the poet, there were poems which reflected his manner.[51]

The magazine kept up with painting, and gave reviews of exhibitions as well as of French books; it reproduced sketches by French artists, portraits of Rimbaud and Mallarmé by Valloton (which were also to be found in *Le Livre des masques* by Rémy de Gourmont), and drawings which had appeared in the French reviews, especially in *La Plume*. Thus its readers could see illustrations of André des Gachons, Eugène Grasset, Chéret, and even Pissarro (whom they did not always understand). In September, 1895, the *Chap-Book* offered for sale, along with drawings by Aubrey Beardsley, a series of posters by Forain, Willette, Steinlen and Toulouse-Lautrec.

It was evident that *The Chap-Book* was in touch with the Symbolist journals which had inspired it. The editors sent copies of their magazine to *La Plume*, *Magazine international*, and *Ermitage*, the last of which did not think very well of their poems: "des vers, beaucoup de vers, c'est la partie faible, il faut l'avouer."[52]

The aim of *The Chap-Book* was to make itself the organ of American "Symbolist" poets, and young American writers with similar interests, and to acquaint the American public with the European literary movement. The success of the magazine was instantaneous, and from 1894 to 1896 it admirably filled the role it had chosen. But toward the middle of the year 1896, *The Chap-Book* began a swift decline. It seemed to lose interest in French writing, and began to speak of the novels of Huysmans and the illustrations of *Ymagier* as immoral. It no longer spoke well of Villon, Verlaine, or Baudelaire.[53] It spoke well of Kipling, Barrie, and the Americans Stedman and Thomas Bailey Aldrich. It was evident that *The Chap-Book* had enjoyed too much success. It was now an established magazine, aware of its own importance, and did not know how to be respectable without being reactionary. In January, 1897, it began to appear in quartos, after the custom of the *Atheneum* or the *Academy*. It continued, dull and respectable, until 1898, when it joined with *The Dial*. Its career was typical of the intellectual current of the period.

But already the extraordinary success of *The Chap-Book* had brought on scores of little magazines like it. Herbert Stone and Bliss Carman, the editors of *The Chap-Book*, collected 150 of them altogether. Every state in the union produced a few of the kind, especially the more remote Western States. Following the lead of Chicago, soon Milwaukee, Kansas City, and many smaller cities sought to produce their own little magazines and to become literary centers. Garishly printed, as a rule, these little magazines all looked like *The Chap-Book*, and all looked like each other. However, each one pretended to have its own artistic credo to defend, and its own personality to display. There were the university magazines, like the *Lotus* of Kansas City, which began in November, 1895, with the stated purpose of being "frank" but not "decadent," or the *Bachelor of Arts* of New York, which in May, 1895, dedicated itself to "university affairs and general literature." Actually, this last magazine contained little more than parodies of Maeterlinck and Nordau, and an article on Verlaine by the poet Trumbull Stickney. The *Optimist*, of Detroit, which appeared only once, and *Fin de Siècle* were decadent in the extreme. The latter, which was French in spirit as well as in title, had first appeared in 1890, four years prior to *The Chap-Book*, which later had shown scorn for "that unspeakable *Fin de Siècle*."[54] It was an interesting magazine nonetheless. Verlaine published his *Confessions* there, for instance, and besides the often sensational and shocking stories, there were to be seen poems in music by Marie Krysinska and a Parisian chronicle by Catulle Mendès.

When they were not copying the French journals, these little magazines took their inspiration from the English *Yellow Book*, which from April, 1894, to April, 1897, supplied all the little magazines with a model and all the larger magazines with a pretext for indignation. The *Yellow Aster* and the *Yellow Curtain* were as decadent as their color indicated. *Moods*, published in Philadelphia in 1895, was "a journal *intime*," and the *New Bohemian*, brought out the same year in Chicago, was "breezy." The *Clack-Book*[55] parodied *The Chap-Book*, and its only success was its title. The *Parisian*[56] sought "whatever is likely to interest and amuse American readers in current European literature." But it was conservative, and was more interested in the *Revue des deux mondes* and the *Revue de Paris* than in the Symbolist reviews. The *Echo*[57] was more lively; it reproduced modish sketches and caricatures. It contained illustrations from *La Caricature, Chic, Théâtreuse*, and even *La Vie parisienne*. Many other similarly unimaginative efforts could be cited, such as *The Pilgrim, The Lotos*, and *Truth in Boston*.

The *Criterion*, which had tried in 1889 to unite the widely scattered American writers, entered its second childhood in 1897.[58] It followed the lead of *The Chap-Book*, published poems in prose by Catulle Mendès, songs by Verlaine, but quickly degenerated into the dull magazine it had once been. The *Bibelot*[59] "will teach its readers to distinguish between real literature and the twaddle that has been circulated as literature in the respectable domestic magazines for the last two decades," and it did publish some poems by the English Decadents, and by Verlaine, as well as some articles by Arthur Symons on Symbolism. Although it was more intelligent than the rest, it had comparatively little success.

Most of these magazines lasted only a few months; fourteen appeared and disappeared in the first half of 1897. Some of them succeeded in sustaining themselves for a while, but were unable to escape eventual collapse. Such was the case with the *Flyleaf* ("A pamphlet periodical of the new, the new man, new woman, new ideas, whimsies and things."), and the *Philistine* ("A periodical of protest", East Aurora, N.Y.), which, without showing any more originality than the other magazines, pretended to be more serious. The *Philistine* was "a periodical of protest," and it protested vigorously and indiscriminately against everything. It seemed afraid of foreign influences, and recognized only American literature. The *Flyleaf* was also essentially American and "essentially modern," without being fin de siècle. It made fun of Symbolism and Impressionism, and attacked the Decadent Muse, that "Yellow Girl" whom English artists had had the audacity to import from Paris. These magazines were amusing for their variety and imagination, but they showed no real talent. Along with *The Chap-Book*, there were, however, two quite notable magazines: *The Lark*, edited by Gelett Burgess, and *M'lle New York*, whose editors were Vance Thompson and James Huneker.

The Lark ("a new note, some of the joy of the morning set here for the refreshment of our souls in the heat of midday") was born in a studio in San Francisco on May 1, 1895. The editors called themselves "Les Jeunes." They were Gelett Burgess, Bruce Porter, and Ernest Peixotto. Burgess could write and sketch with good humor, and his magazine was always gay. He addressed himself to his readers, not in Old English, but in French: "C'est une assez modeste creature que *The Lark* elle ne se mesle pas de personnalités; étant un oiseau matineux, elle s'occupe du ver."[60] It also "occupied" itself with painting, and conducted a "salon" in the manner of *La Plume.* The reader could find there, for his admiration, many caricatures of fashionable paintings. The sketches and verse satires in *The Lark* poked fun at the theories and affectations of the "Decadents" as well as at those of the intellectual conservatives of Boston. It also delighted in pure foolishness, of the sort that would be sure to mystify serious readers.[61] The engaging humor of this magazine guaranteed its success. But the sweetest pleasures are the shortest, and *The Lark* died quietly on April 1, 1897. To give its own funeral oration, the *Epilark* appeared for a single time the following month. *The Lark* had fought against outworn traditions and respectable fashions with the weapon of fancy, and had reacted against "decadence" with gaiety. Gelett Burgess announced further fanciful reviews which never appeared, such as *Phyllida or the Nutmaid* and the *Petit journal des refusés.* Perhaps the latter failed for lack of contributors; however, it did not reject any manuscripts: it accepted them all at a price of ten dollars per page. In the spring of 1898, Burgess announced the birth of *L'Enfant terrible,*[62] a magazine containing sketches, parodies, and improbable stories, in the manner of *The Lark.* But this "infant" that had strugged into birth lived for only one month.

Gelett Burgess obviously knew French, and liked to use it for humorous effects—and also as a way of mocking American "decadents" who were smitten with the French mode. But he cannot be said to have appreciated French influence or even to have judged it useful for American literature.

The French influence was so obvious in another magazine of the time that it looked exactly like a French journal. *M'lle New York,* which began publishing in August of 1895, took as its motto a line from Charles Wesley's hymn: "O Lord, the dark Americans convert!" To convert them, the editor, Vance Thompson, hoped to use the French example. He had just returned from Paris, where he had frequented theaters, studios, Symbolist salons, and editorial offices. His new magazine was the most risqué and "decadent" of them all, and it was also the one which showed the most talent.

Vance Thompson began by declaring that "*M'lle New York* would not cater to the public." The figure of "Mademoiselle New York" on the cover, wearing only a hatbox on her gloved arm and a feathered hat on her head, clearly showed an air of unconcern. The public thought the magazine "devilish, with the glare of red lights and the flavor of brimstone about her."[63] There were indeed more off-color stories and nude women to be found in its pages than in *La Plume*, but the French influence did not stop there. This was the magazine which published more French poems, translations, and articles on contemporary French literature than any other at that time. Thompson's *French Portraits* did not appear as a book until 1900, but was published chapter by chapter in his magazine, beginning in 1895. One of these chapters, "The Technique of the Symbolists,"[64] was remarkably good. Another, "Impressions of Verlaine,"[65] was much more superficial. Thompson admired French poets, but more for their poses than for their art, and his propaganda was thus of questionable value. James Huneker, on the other hand, who became co-editor of *M'lle New York* in October, 1895, was one of the best American critics. His knowledge of foreign literature was extensive, and the articles which he wrote on French poetry and music were more serious than those of Thompson. Unhappily, they were also less frequent.

Nearly all sides of the literary movement in Paris found an echo in *M'lle New York:* vers libre, "prose poems," mystical poetry (which the editors disliked), and "satanism" (which they loved). They vehemently defended the Symbolists against the attacks of Nordau. Among the poems which they published in French were those of Laforgue, Verlaine, "Le Violoneux" of Tristan Klingsor and "L'Archet" of Charles Cros. The translations were also interesting: they included the "Litanies" of Baudelaire, the "Prière" of Maeterlinck, "Il Était un roi de Thulé" of Laforgue, and some "Ballades" of Paul Fort. Also included were a story by Rémy de Gourmont, "Les Enfants assistes" by Jammes, the "Phénomène futur de Mallarmé," translated by George Moore, and "Hermès psychagôgos" by Marcel Schwob, translated by Vance Thompson.

Laforgue, Rémy de Gourmont, Jammes, Paul Fort, and Schwob were not known to the American public at that time. *M'lle New York* educated it in the importance and the diversity of the Symbolist movement. The magazine helped to correct the common error of connecting the word "Symbolism" only with the names of Baudelaire, Verlaine, and Mallarmé, and with the idea of obscure and tormented verses.

The activity of the little magazines had been a protest against the tyranny and the dullness of the larger magazines. Most of them were ephemeral, and of little literary value. Their editors often treated their work as an agreeable pastime; when they had ideas, they lacked talent for putting them to use. But all they wanted was to make themselves heard. The activity was important, because it claimed freedom, and expressed the search for individuality of all young writers of the period. *M'lle New York* played the leading role in this activity, because Burgess was too much a renegade, and the "Symbolists" of *The Chap-Book* were too sensitive to public opinion. *M'lle New York* preached the sort of extreme individualism, egotism, and intellectualism which was being sought by American artists ("Autolatry, it is the artist's religion," wrote the editors). And if it was interested almost exclusively in French Symbolism, the reason was that this movement seemed to offer the most striking example of artistic individualism, and could thus help American writers to discover their own personalities. If Huneker, Thompson, and their friends did not succeed in guiding the diverse artistic forces in the country to a definite achievement, they did work which needed to be done, and provided a useful preparation for later movements.

1895–1910—New Critical Studies

The first decade of the twentieth century was one of the emptiest periods in American literature. The little magazines of the time attracted almost no attention: examples were *The Stiletto* in New York, *Good Cheer* ("a magazine for cheerful thinkers") in Boston, *The Bachelor Book* in Chicago, *The Thistle*, a "magazine of protest," in New Rochelle, and *The Lotus*[66]—all of which disappeared about 1906. The larger magazines maintained their reputations, but did not attempt anything new. After 1898, interest in French poetry seemed gradually to disappear. Until 1910, Americans spoke of Symbolism as a school from which nothing more could be expected:

> We hear less and less nowadays of the Symbolists and Decadents—not that they have wholly vanished from the field of letters, but that many of them can no longer excite the enthusiasm they once awoke in tender hearts and not overstrong brains. Verlaine himself is not enjoying quite such a reputation as was manufactured for him, and it may well be that he in turn will pass out of sight like many another better and purer poet . . . And of the other less notorious writers who at one time attracted so much attention, what shall remain? Of Maeterlinck? Of Moréas? Of Mallarmé? They have striven after and occasionally attained new and quaint combinations of verse or words or letters, but they have not renovated poesy and they have not displaced the ancient idols.[67]

According to the *Atlantic Monthly*, in 1900 public opinion ranked French poetry fourth after that of England, Germany, and Italy.

However, several noted visitors came to this country to speak about the new French poetry. Early in 1900, the Harvard French Club invited Henri de Régnier for a visit; he accepted, and afterwards went as far as San Francisco, giving lectures on contemporary poets.[68] The following year, Gaston Deschamps came to the United States. Everywhere, people asked him what he thought of the "Decadents," and without understanding what Americans meant by the word, he answered: "I don't think anything of them—except that you seem to give great importance to a joke that once provoked laughter in the cafés of the Latin Quarter." Lastly, in 1904, the French government sent Paul Adam to speak at the St. Louis Exposition on the subject of contemporary aesthetic evolution.[69] If the number of articles devoted to French poetry was diminishing, there was still interest on the part of two men. In 1900, Vance Thompson's *French Portraits* appeared[70] and was coldly received by the critics. They were astonished that in this book "La Jeune France" was represented by authors such as Verlaine, Mallarmé, Barrès, about whom, in their opinion, there was nothing more to learn. However, Thompson also treated Samain, Signoret, Rodenbach, Jammes, and Rebell, who were almost unknown in America; but the tone of his remarks made serious critics, even Peck, doubt whether their names should be known outside the Latin Quarter. What Thompson offered were a few interviews and a few hasty comments. He gave the reader a few indignant remarks about the new writers: Barrès was "the drollest, saddest figure in modern French literature";[71] Jammes was "a shepherd whose flute is out of tune";[72] Heredia was "the last of the great French Negro writers."[73] The only great poet was Adolphe Rette. As for the two Americans, Vielé-Griffin and Stuart Merrill, their art was entirely explained by their origins. Finally, Thompson was firmly convinced that all modern French literature derived wholly from Poe and Whitman.[74]

However, Thompson proposed to admire these poets, and to offer them as examples to his countrymen. He even affected their style, and using a half-bantering tone to protect him from ridicule, he wrote in an eccentric manner meant to be taken as a translation of the worst French prose. He offered all the "impollués vocables" and "pléonasmes significatifs" prescribed by Moréas. Expressions like "a hyssop mood," "augural nights," "avid girls," "temptuous thighs," and "desultory suave serpents" rightly exasperated Americans. All things considered, the case of Vance Thompson is not unlike that of George Moore and his *Confessions of a Young Man*, which London condemned for its foreign thought and form. There was the same insolence, a little more affectation, and considerably less talent. Without meaning to, Thompson, who called himself a "Decadent," produced the same effect as the parodists of the Symbolist movement and the detractors such as Nordau, and he appeared to contradict the propaganda that he himself had made in *M'lle New York*.

His colleague Huneker was less clumsy, for if he was a disciple of the French, he was not a slave to imitation, but found his own personal style. In 1878, he had gone to study music in Paris, and had remained there several years. He recalled having seen Flaubert, and having listened to Villiers de l'Isle Adam one whole night in a café of the Batignolles. He tried journalism for a while, and sent articles to the Philadelphia *Bulletin*. He returned to the United States as a journalist, and was soon well known as a critic of art, music, and literature.[75] The extent of his acquaintances and connections was prodigious; his role as propagandist was also very important. It is not true, as some said, that Huneker was a critic "in the great French tradition"; he belongs to the tradition of French journalism, not French criticism. He was in touch with everything, and was always ready with his copy. He wrote a brilliant article on Huysmans the day Huysmans died, and another equally brilliant on the France-Brunetière quarrel, the day after Brunetière died. He deserves credit for having published in *M'lle New York* French poems by authors completely unknown in America, for having been the first to publicize post-Impressionist painters, and even the first to speak of Cézanne, Matisse, and Picasso. His articles on Barrès,[76] on Huysmans,[77] on Baudelaire,[78] and on Villiers de l'Isle Adam[79] provided the best explanation of the character of these writers to Americans. He made other discoveries, such as those of Francis Poictevin and Ernest Hello. Finally, it was he who introduced Rémy de Gourmont to Americans.

In 1897, the name of Rémy de Gourmont was mentioned as a completely neglected writer.[80] That same year, Huneker made de Gourmont's acquaintance, and their friendship began. Huneker wrote the only intelligent study of de Gourmont that appeared in America before 1910.[81] From that time on, he wrote scarcely an article without citing the opinion of his friend. In tribute to de Gourmont's book, *Promenades littéraires*, he entitled one of his collections of criticism *Promenades of an Impressionist*.[82]

For Rémy de Gourmont, as will be seen, Symbolism was principally the cult of individualism in literature. This was also what appealed to Huneker in the work of the Symbolists. Too intelligent to try to create a national literature, his aim was to save literature by encouraging the love of individualism. He had been the first in America to appreciate Nietzsche, his admiration dating from 1888. He also defended the most individualistic French writers: Stendhal, Flaubert, Baudelaire, Huysmans. The studies that he devoted to them were collected in a book called *Egoists; A Book of Supermen*.[83]

But Huneker was more of a moralist than a true literary critic: he loved arts and letters, but remained too involved in his emotions to concern himself with technique. Consequently, he could do nothing for poetry. He should be remembered for leading the individualist movement which originated in France and Germany, for speaking seriously to Americans about serious writers, whom he understood and judged from a consistent point of view, calling attention not to their decadence, but to their desire to express themselves affirmatively, and he thereby forced the American public to think of such writers no longer as a joke.

Following his example, several other critics, like Lucille Dubois and William Aspenwall Bradley (whose articles on Moréas and Barbey d'Aurevilly attracted notice, and who later wrote ably about Madame de Noailles and Valéry) continued to discuss contemporary French poetry with sympathy and accuracy. With these critics, as later with H. L. Mencken and Van Wyck Brooks, a need for criticism, for the appreciation of values, for the cultivation of ideas finally became felt: they provided the younger generation, which was ready to dedicate itself to literary pursuits, with a serious turn of mind for making its judgments.

CHAPTER 4

The American Symbolist School

1. RICHARD HOVEY

THANKS TO AMERICAN PAINTERS, travelers, and critics, knowledge of the Symbolist poets spread widely through the United States between the years 1888 and 1895, while at the same time, certain American poets were absorbing the influence of the new French school. The first to respond to this influence was undoubtedly Richard Hovey.

His first enthusiasms were in keeping with the taste of the time. He made his debut by writing imitations of Swinburne, Browning, Rossetti, and occasionally Shakespeare and the Elizabethans, in odes to his alma mater (Dartmouth) and other poems which hold little interest now. But he was talented in his imitations, and his verses were often musical. Following his journey to Europe, and his meeting with Mallarmé and Maeterlinck, his style became transformed. He began to understand, as Lanier once had, the value of studying verse technique, and he worked by turns at poetry in Greek and in French.

In 1896 and 1897, Hovey translated some poems of Verlaine, some songs of Maeterlinck, and some of the most difficult poems of Mallarmé. These translations were among the best of the period. It was a rare thing to find an American admirer of Mallarmé who was as much in earnest as the French disciples of the poet. For Hovey, the poetry of Mallarmé was a remote and musical realm, mysteriously calm, and he tried to render the sense of it in his own way:

> On battlemented Morningside
> The gold alembic days distil,
> The violet rocks remember yet,
> The winter winds that moaned and sighed.
> The grasses and the leaves are still.[1]

Hovey even went so far as to attempt a light version of Mallarmé's "L'Après-midi d'un faune." In this "faun," the poet, harassed by the city, flees to a maple forest populated only by chipmunks. There he catches a glimpse of the American "faun":

> There's a sense of a presence that lurks in
>   the branches. But where? . . .
> In vain—evasive ever through the glade
> Departing footsteps fail. . . .

The faun is finally tamed:

> Thou whom my soul desireth, even thou
> Sprawl'st at my side, who fled'st at my pursuit . . .
> I see the sharp ears through the tangled hair[2]

Hovey's translation was interesting, but where was the mystery of the Symbolist poem?

Hovey also admired Verlaine and Maeterlinck, whose dramatic form he studied, and knew Henri de Régnier, as these mediocre French verses prove:

> *Au Seuil*
> Le destin nous a pris de sa main forte,
> Il nous a pris en plein soleil, soudain,
> Il nous a pris avec son haut dédain
> Et il nous a montré la sombre porte . . .
>
> Peut-être—L'âme de l'homme est si folle!—
> On rencontrera le sourire d'un dieu
> Qui nous bénira de ses grands yeux bleus
> Et nous rassurera de ses mains molles.[3]

This must be taken as a parody. But imitations as conscious as this poem, or "The Faun," were very rare with Hovey. Desiring (like so many others) to create a national poetry, he resisted imitating foreigners. He wanted to play a role comparable to theirs, and to emulate them without being indebted to them. By experimenting with form, as he began to do in 1895, he was able to free himself to some extent from the poetic jargon of his early poems. His supple metrics often became a type of free verse—a free verse which owed nothing to Whitman, but which Hovey undoubtedly modeled on the French poets who interested him at this time. He began writing verses that were more modern in tone, and which have not become as dated as the rest of his work:

> I said in my heart, "I am sick of four walls and
>   ceiling.
> I have need of the sky.
> I have business with the grass."
> . . . .
> When I got to the woods, I found out

What the Spring was about,
With her gypsy ways
And her heart ablaze,
Coming up from the south
With the wander-lure of witch songs in her mouth.[4]

The sureness of these lines is worthy of the later Renaissance of American poetry. And the following lines, with their rhythm so well adapted to the subject described, give an indication of real mastery. Apollo is pursuing Daphne:

But she, with her maiden heart
Fluttered and frayed as a bird in snare,
Fled with fear-laden heart
Into the wood.
And Apollo up-leaping,
And rent with desire and despair
Sped after her, crying:
"Ah, leave me not, love . . ."[5]

Taliesin is generally cited as Hovey's tour dé force. It was praised for its more than thirty different meters, some of them original, and some adapted from Greek metrics. But unfortunately, neither the language nor the images were fresh, and the metaphysical subject of this "Masque" produced only an overwhelming boredom. A few fine verses alone survived.

If Richard Hovey's attempt at making the poetic medium alive and flexible had succeeded, his role would have been comparable to that of Verlaine in France and Henley in England. That at least was what he sought. But a lack of conviction always stopped him half-way, and his secret belief that the technique of a poem was less important than its philosophical meaning defeated him finally.

The plays of Hovey bore some resemblance to those of Yeats and Maeterlinck. The influence of the Belgian Symbolist, mixed with that of Shakespeare and Tennyson, could be seen in his *Launcelot and Guinevere*[6] and *The Birth of Galahad.*[7] The audience was immediately transported into a drama by the mysterious phrases which were repeated, and by the ominous setting: "Dreamy forests, skies lowering or resonant, parks and fountains, stretches of sea and dreary moats." This was clearly a Maeterlinck setting. The secondary characters were also Maeterlinck's: they consisted of valets, gardeners, and nurses. In *The Quest of Merlin*, the magician was reminiscent of the Merlin of Maeterlinck's *Joyzelle*, and the "Norms" were "The unknown forces" of Maeterlinck's drama: the "énormes puissances invisibles et fatales, dont nul ne sait les intentions."[8] But the form of these plays came from somewhere else; the technique of scenes in verse, alternating with scenes in prose, owes nothing to Maeterlinck.

These plays, which seem so outmoded today, apparently did not displease Mallarmé, who wrote to Hovey:

> J'achève avec délices, mon cher poète, la si musicale lecture de votre tragédie *The Marriage of Guinevere:* où l'exquisité de votre vers blanc neuf et jeune accompagne la beauté poignante, sauve et pure des lignes que donnent, dans leur attitude, vos personnages de rêve autant qu'humains.[9]

And Maeterlinck was equally complimentary of the American poet:

> Je viens de lire d'un trait *The Birth of Galahad*, je l'aime et je l'admire. Je l'aime surtout parce qu'il a le courage complet de l'amour, qu'l pose un beau probleme de morale humaine, et qu'il ose le résoudre par dessus l'étroite loyauté des âmes sans horizon et sans passion, dans une sorte de joie et de lumière.[10]

However, the translation that Hovey made of Maeterlinck's plays had unquestionably more influence on his contemporaries than his own plays.[11] The translation was interesting from another point of view. It was in the preface to it that Hovey announced the existence of a new poetic movement: American Symbolism.

In the hope of forming a new American Pléiades, Hovey had grouped several artists around him, who were a little more talented than most, but not enough to separate themselves from the mass or to rebel against it. They shared no poetic discipline, but only a desire to create a national poetry, and a taste for optimism and healthy morals which were considered typically American. Of the group, which included Bliss Carman, George Douglas Roberts, Archibald Lampman, and Gilbert Parker, all except Hovey were Canadians. These were the poets whom Hovey hopefully named "The American Symbolist School." He defined Symbolism as a universal movement, which was "not the imitation by the many of the eccentricities of one, but the spontaneous and independent development, in writers alien in race, residence, and experience, of similar traits and methods."[12] Of this so-called international movement, the principal figures were said to be Mallarmé in France, Maeterlinck in Belgium, Gilbert Parker in England, and— Hovey was modest—Bliss Carman in America.

The new "Symbolists" claimed absolute originality:

> William Sharp's *Vistas* and Oscar Wilde's *Salome* might perhaps not have been written had the authors been less familiar with the contemporary literature of the Continent. But Carman, Roberts, and Parker have evidently reached their results without any communication with France or Belgium. Their work is saner, fresher, less morbid.[13]

In an interview printed at this time in Boston,[14] Hovey issued something like a "manifesto" of American Symbolism. He said that the Symbolist movement sprang "from a root and branch democracy that will be satisfied with nothing less than the complete realization of the brotherhood of the race." The new American Symbolism, he said, would recognize that "the freedom of man must include the freedom of woman," and would speak freely of "those relations that her presence causes in the world." The keynote of Symbolism was "individuality," he said, and the new poetry would be characterized by "virility" and by "the Hellenic note of joy." Whether Hovey was more interested in morality or in poetry was not entirely clear, but it was clear that he was interested in technique, for he remarked: "The desire for spontaneity and sincerity has led to a greater freedom of technique, impelling the poets at once toward the simpler ballad measures, and toward the flexibility, complexity and naturalness of *vers libre.*" He mentioned Whitman as an earlier experimenter with free verse—"the first of American poets to probe its possibilities and to see how quickly and subtly it responds to every shifting shade of thought and emotion in the mind of the poet"—but added that the new Symbolists distinguished between "the principle of free verse and the personal style of the author of 'Leaves of Grass.' "

This "manifesto," such as it was, was not expressive of all Symbolist poetry, and though certain theories of the French Symbolists were contained in it, they were so adapted to American taste as to be scarcely recognizable. It was clear that the new poets had learned to experiment with free verse from the French, and that their philosophical idealism also came from the Symbolists—chiefly from Maeterlinck. The originality of American Symbolism was to be its expression of native qualities of virility and optimism, but these would be external to the poetry—and they were perhaps less American than Hovey liked to think, since he chose them in defiance of the prevalent taste in America for affected and sentimental poetry.

Unfortunately, the works of the heralded American Symbolists turned out to be a poor justification of their theories. Their leader, Bliss Carman, was called a "Symbolist" when he published *Behind the Arras; A Book of the Unseen.*[15] The title reminded many Americans of Maeterlinck. However, the book merely contained verse narratives such as people were reading everywhere. Really, Carman was never inspired by French poetry, which he knew very little about. Even his admiration for Verlaine was completely sentimental, and directed more to the Bohemian than to the writer. Carman had nothing Symbolist about him. His best poems may be found in *Songs from Vagabondia*, written in collaboration with Richard Hovey.[16] There are poems in that collection which smell of new-mown hay and morning air. In the rest of his work, this "Symbolist" was no more than a versifier, who sold out to the larger magazines as did his confreres. Nothing distinguished him from them except perhaps a little more elegance, a little more facility with rhvmes—and a facility with rhymes was one of the plagues of American poetry.

The poems of Archibald Lampman were inspired by the same "natural" emotions. They spoke of the joys of good health and walks in the country, in the most mediocre sort of verse.

Charles G. D. Roberts was more interesting. He began by singing of the Canadian wilderness in vigorous, manly, but conventional verses. In 1893, he came to New York, where he first learned about Rossetti, Swinburne, and Baudelaire. *In New York Nocturnes and Other Poems*,[17] he departed from the "robustious school" and began to write the "poetry of the city," wherein Symons thought the future of American poetry lay. In this volume, Roberts adopted the manner, the obsessions, the images, and the inversions of Baudelaire:

> Dawn like a lily lies upon the land
> Since I have known the whiteness of your hand.[18]

> Here is the street
> Made holy by the passing of her feet,
>   . . . And the place
> Is tremulous with memory of her face.[19]

Unfortunately, this influence of Baudelaire (which the critics deplored) was meaningless, since it was only a superficial imitation and did not enable Roberts to forge a new style. *In The Book of the Rose*[20] there are only further echoes of Baudelaire.

>   Such beauty seems
> To cry like violins . . .
> Your mouth, your throat, your eyes, your hands, your hair—
> To look at these is harps within my soul . . .[21]

> O take me into the still places of your heart,
> And hide me under the night of your deep hair,
> . . . .
> And touch me with the benediction of your hands![22]

Besides Hovey's group, there were a few isolated Symbolists, like Philip Henry Savage,[23] who died too young to produce anything definitive, and Josephine Preston Peabody, who was inspired by Yeats as well as Maeterlinck, and who wrote a Symbolist play that was nonetheless mediocre.[24] On these poets, the French influence was remote; they reflected common attitudes of the period. With the exception of Hovey and Roberts, these American poets knew Symbolism only through the ideas of English writers, through their verse, and through critics like William Sharp and Arthur Symons, in whose hands French Symbolism became a pale and weakened art. Thus they derived from this movement only a certain set of attitudes, weakening still further the already enervated art of the English poets of the Nineties.

Actually, the "American Symbolist School" existed only in the imagination of Richard Hovey. Roberts and Hovey occasionally produced an imitation of the manner of French poets, but it was without consequence, and Hovey showed an inclination toward modern technique inspired by the French, but it came to nothing. If Hovey did not succeed, it was because he was only half free of the prejudices he was fighting against in his contemporaries. He refused to make innovations that he admired in the French Symbolists, because of the illusion which possessed him and his whole generation that all foreign influence must be discouraged, in order to hasten the appearance of the virile literature that was supposed to flourish in American soil. National pride made them repeat this absurdity for years; it is printed still in certain American journals. It began to disappear on the day when people realized that art is autonomous as soon as it has found the technique that suits it, and that artists can only obtain this technique by studying poets who have mastered their own technique, in whatever country they exist. The patriotism of Richard Hovey did not give birth to a national poetry. At most, it flattered the vanity of the public for a time, and warped their taste by persuading them that poets as mediocre as the pretended "Symbolists" could be representative of America.

2. WILLIAM VAUGHAN MOODY

Richard Hovey died young, and those who hoped to see the birth of a modern American poetry explained its failure by his death. They transferred their hopes to another young poet, William Vaughan Moody, only to have them dashed again by his sudden death.

Moody had taken up the effort of Hovey some years later, and his work had a direct connection with the first American "Symbolist." While still in college, he had written some verses in the manner of Milton, Keats, and Browning, as well as of Rossetti, whose work he read avidly at Harvard in 1889. Moody spent his final year of study in Europe. He lived part of this time in France, but seems to have found there no more than passing amusement.[25] He returned there more than once, in 1895, and again in 1902. He knew French, but if he kept up to date on contemporary French literature, he did not look to it for models. He wrote in 1899:

> The Muses, I groundedly believe, reside at present on an obscure peak
> (not yet visited) of New Hampshire or Maine . . . At any rate that's
> where I purpose to seek them, and Europe be damned.[26]

Returning to America, he took for his poetic subject the problems of modern American life. "The Brute" glorified the frightening machine out of which the ideal city was to emerge; "The Quarry" was inspired by the foreign relations of the United States; "The Menagerie" was a poem about evolution. The form of these poems, however, was scarcely modern. Contemporary problems were treated allegorically; for this reason, Moody was called a "symbolist." But in his hands, the symbols stood for facts, rather than for ideas or feelings, and his symbols were mechanically imposed on things to the exclusion of all suggestiveness. This allegorical method was nearer to the French Parnassians than it was to the Symbolists.

The poems of Moody were often obscure, but the obscurity came less from hidden meanings than from a style encumbered by rhetoric and heavy with souvenirs of the classics. The vocabulary of Moody was elegant and artificial. It contained the familiar language of English poetry; "yonder," "twain," etc.; expressions borrowed from Shakespeare and Milton; and others like "bataillons," "Vesperine," "margent," "windelstise," which may have come from the French. While some of his poems showed vigor and even beauty, others showed an embarrassing sentimentality or religiosity ("Until the Troubling of the Waters," "Good Friday Night").

However, Moody sought the formula for a modern American drama. His letters spoke of this preoccupation:

> The thing I have most at heart just now is a poetic—I mean a *verse*
> —play.[27]
> I am heart and soul dedicated to the conviction that modern life can
> be presented on the stage in the poetic medium and adequately
> presented only in that way.[28]
> By all the Muses, we shall have an American drama.[29]

Moody by this time was working in the direction suggested by Hovey in *Launcelot and Guenevere* and in *Talliesin*. Moody also shared Hovey's interest in Greek tragedy, but not in Maeterlinck. He wrote a trilogy of poetic dramas: *The Fire Bringer, The Masque of Judgment,* and *The Death of Eve.* In a symbolic form, these philosophical dramas tried to represent the union of God with his creatures: *The Fire Bringer* was inspired by the *Prometheus* of Trumbull Stickney, a poet whose dominant influences were Browning and Verlaine. Certain lyrical passages of Moody's play were noticeably Symbolist in character, for example this one, in which voices are heard chanting in the dark:

Hush, hark, the pouring music! Never yet
The pools below the waterfalls, thy pools,
Thy dark pools, O my heart—![30]

Here, as rarely in Moody's work, the lines do not seek to express, but to suggest, and to suggest what is inexpressible. These lines are melodious and truly Symbolist, in a way that would not seem out of place in a Maeterlinck play.

The Death of Eve was only a fragment. Moody had discovered the idea for it in La Vision d'Eve of the Parnassian poet, Leon Dierx.[31] The American play was based on the central theme of the French poem:

Or les enfants jouaient. Soudain, le premier-né
Debout, l'ceil plein de fauve ardeur, la lèvre amère,
Frappa l'autre, éperdu, sous un poing forcené.

. . . .
Ève accourut tremblante et pâle de stupeur.

. . . .
Bientot tout s'apaisa, fureur, plaintes, baisers,

. . . .
            Et la femme
Immobile, ses doigts sous un genou croisés,
Sentit les jours futurs monter noirs dans son âme.

In The Death of Eve, it was Cain who brought on this scene in which for the first time he saw his mother's fear. The poem described the dark future which Eve foresaw:

Du fond de l'avenir, Azraël, menaçant
Te montrait-il ce fils, ayant fait l'oeuvre humaine,
Qui s'enfuyait, sinistre, et marqué par le sang . . .?

Azrael, the Angel of Death, reappeared also in the first act of Moody's play, which in retracing the terrible life of Cain in the city of Enoch, was an extension of this passage of Dierx's poem:

Le voyais-tu mourir longuement dans Enoch,
Rempart poussé d'un jet sous le puissant blasphème
Des maudits qui gravaient le défi sur le roc . . .?

But the poems came to completely opposite conclusions: Moody's Eve did not understand "que le mal était né, qu'il serait immortel; que l'amour périrait avec l'Aieule blond." On the contrary: this Eve continued to believe in the beauty of life, in spite of sin, and in the eternality of love; and she expected to justify herself and Cain before God.

This optimistic and Christian drama had all the traits which Hovey defined as those of "American Symbolism." Moody died before finishing it, but it is probable that if he had lived he would have continued to search persistently through all drama and all poetry for an American formula.

Thus, following in the footsteps of Hovey and the American Symbolists, another talented man had strained to bring a national poetry to birth. After him, American poetry fell into mediocrity, which lasted until the Renaissance of 1913.

CHAPTER 5

Fin de Siècle Poetry Inspired
by Verlaine and Baudelaire

THE POETS OF THE fin de siècle school—or rather, tendency—were more frankly in revolt against tradition than the American "Symbolist" group, and were not as concerned with artistic nationalism. They had begun to write before the "Symbolists," and continued to be heard from longer. Since they delighted in scandalizing the public (an easy enough thing to do), they imitated the most extravagant poses of the English and French fin de siècle poets: they proclaimed themselves the disciples of Baudelaire, Oscar Wilde, and Verlaine. Verlaine was their chief master.

Just as the American academic poets imitated the English academic poets, the American decadents imitated the English decadents. One of these English decadents, Arthur O'Shaughnessy, had died in Chicago in 1881. His poems, some of which were published by Louise Moulton in 1894, received little notice from the critics, who treated these morbid poems with "the same repulsion that they showed for so many of the paintings of the French Salon." But already O'Shaughnessy had disciples. He was one of the first imitators of Verlaine, and was responsible for one of the first translations of "Clair de lune" in America: he translated it under the title of "pastel" in his collection, *Songs of a Worker*, in 1881.

The most famous of the American decadents, Francis Saltus, began his schooling in France, and spent the greater part of his life in Paris. He was one of the protégés of Théophile Gautier, whose art served him constantly as a model. The work of Saltus offended all the American morals of the time: he was criticized for having imitated Baudelaire in his strangest fancies, for example, in dedicating a poem to every drink from beer to absinthe in his volume, *Flasks and Flagons;*[1] and more conclusively, for having "unchained the demon of carnal desire in his repugant book, *The Witch of Endor*,"[2] as one critic said, while another critic cried "Charles Baudelaire, what crimes are you not guilty of, in your own work and in that of your imitators!"

Here are some examples of this unrestrained imitation of Baudelaire, apparent in the mere titles of his book, *Honey and Gall*,[3] such as "Negra Venus," "Spleen," and "Landscape of Flesh."

> Mute pallid mass of withering flesh inert,
> Thou know'st the secret that I fain would learn.
>
> . . . .
>
> How must (I) loathe thy ugliness, and spurn
> Thy purple putrid swollen breast of dirt,
> Wherein each avid worm awaits its turn.[4]

The famous "Black Venus" of Baudelaire was encountered again in the "Zazza" of Francis Saltus:

> Zazza, fair pompous-breasted perfect queen
>   A marvelous glory of black flesh thou wert . . .
> Can I forget thy velvet-ebon skin,
>   Thy torse, grace flexile, and thine eyes
> Mirage of sultry prisms, flashing in —
>
> . . . .
>
> Can I forget thy coast, fair Zanzibar,
>   Deluged in gold, in verdure and in light?[5]

The Baudelairean echoes in Saltus's poems, however, were less frequent than the Verlainean echoes. Saltus and all his disciples practiced the art of *pastiche:*

> The night in June,
> The Silv'ry moon,
> The linnet's cry,
> The cobalt sky:
> The night when first we met,
> Can you forget?

And the patterns of sentimental *decor* were also Verlaine's:

> The serenade,
> The leafy glade,
> The pouring rain,
> The hurricane,
> The night my lips were wet,
> Can you forget?
>
> The lonely park
> The shadows dark . . .[6]

This same rhythm was continued for eight stanzas—and this was only one poem among many of a similar kind in Saltus's work. The facile charm of these lilting verses for a time obscured his unfortunate habits of negligence and sloppiness.

There was also a slight indication of the reworking of de Musset in some verses of about 1880:

In Vicenza the dark,
Not a light, save the spark
Of a torch.
With a red sullen flame,
O'er the duke's crested name
On his porch.[7]

Perhaps Saltus was better when he imitated Gautier: the precision of words and the solidity of phrasing gave him some idea of formal discipline; but unhappily he imitated Gautier as he imitated Verlaine, without seeking to understand the essential qualities. We will see later on what use the American poets of 1917 made of the study of Gautier's *Émaux et camées*, and how it helped to rescue American poetry from a new crisis brought on by excessive freedom and facility.

Here is the sort of imitation Saltus was addicted to:

Des losanges de plomb ceignent	Through fissured spire
Les vitraux coloriés	The sunbeam's gyre
Ou les feux du soleil teignent	Weaveth a magic web of rays
Les reflets errants qui baignent	Iris, gold gleaming as it plays
Les plafonds armoriés.	On marbled choir.
Cent colonnes découpées.	Long, dark, severe
Par de bizarres ciseaux,	The naves appear
Comme des faisceaux d'épées	In pious patriarchal gloom:
Au long de la nef groupées	Circled by columned walls, that loom
Portent les sveltes arceaux.[8]	Their shades austere.[9]

In his description of exotic countries, the choice of elegant words and proper names gave to Saltus's scenes an atmosphere like some of Gautier's poetry:

Seraskeer's turret, the Mosque,
Yena Djami, its kiosque,
And the dome of Selim—
Towered their portals and grees
Far above the yew-trees
Twilight dim,
Of bosk.[10]

Saltus even risked imitating Gautier in French:

Celle que j'ai le plus aimée
Avait la taille d'une almée,
De gros yeux bleus aux longs cils noirs,
Un teint de rose et de neige
Comme l'Albane et le Corrège
Seuls dans le rêve ont pu voir.[11]

The colors were there, but it was neither very French nor very pretty: Saltus should have done better things, rather than waste his time in juvenile imitations.

Besides Saltus, another expatriate whose name is worth mentioning was William Theodore Peters, who contributed to the *Quartier latin*, a review of the Decadent school, published in Paris. He brought out one collection of verses, *Poesies out of Rings*, and one play (*The Tournament of Love*, performed at the Theatre d'Application in 1894) which dealt with the Paris where he died in misery.

Francis Saltus had a brother, Edgar Saltus, who was one of the best known of the New York "decadents." About 1890, he frequented the "Fridays" of Edgar Fawcett, where he met Stuart Merrill, and Russell Sturgis, who had just translated Maupassant. He was to be seen in evening walks along Broadway, preceded or followed by three or four cats which he kept on a leash. Although he had written a collection of verses, *Poppies and Mandragoras*, he was more essayist than poet. He held a salon in the manner of Mallarmé for a few chosen disciples, who were invited to listen in silence while he read Chinese poetry and explained oriental art. The way of life of certain French poets made a greater impression on him than their work. The qualities of elegance in Saltus's writings later earned him a brief revival, but in his own time he was able to please only a few ardent devotees of Decadence; critics in general reproached him for admiring Villiers de l'Isle Adam too much, and for the French eroticism of his prose.

It was through the subjects of her poems that Isabella T. Aitkin also attained a certain notoriety; and it was by scandalizing the public that Vance Thompson achieved a greater notoriety; the style of his poems was as "purple" as his articles: his verse was full of phrases stolen from his American and French contemporaries. From time to time he imitated Laforgue, as in this fashion:

> I am the fool of Pampelune
> The consort of the vagrom moon;
> We fare together, she and I
> In vague and vast complicity.

For the readers of his *M'lle New York*, he translated some of the long poems of Laforgue, signing them without the least indication of their origin. Vance Thompson was something of a charlatan, and very little of a poet. When he was not turning out scattered light verses such as:

> I walked down Broadway to and fro
> Along the ghost of Edgar Poe,

he was scarcely worth reading at all.

About the same time, a friend of Vance Thompson's, an Australian adventurer named Lingwood Evans, published two volumes of free verse: *The Father of Livor* and *The Avenue of Farthingales*. In these collections, he imitated, according to the whim of the moment, the rhythms of Verlaine or of Verhaeren. And James Huneker, who wrote no poetry, often imitated Mallarmé and Huysmans in his poems in prose.

The nineteenth century ended without having launched the long-awaited renaissance of American poetry. Fin de siècle poetry lasted through the first decade of the new century. The interest, real or sensational, in French poetry was diminishing. The American "Decadent" artists, not troubling to find new masters, kept on repeating the same tired echoes of Verlaine and Baudelaire. About 1903, there appeared an anonymous collection of Baudelairean verses, entitled *The Book of Jade*.

In 1907, a book of decadent poetry by another exile, Wilbur Underwood, arrived from England. His *Book of Masks* contained a score of poems in a precious style embroidered on the themes of Verlaine's *Fêtes galantes*. And in the poems of Joseph Trumbull Stickney (a friend of William Vaughan Moody's, who died in his first year as instructor of Greek at Harvard), the memory of Verlaine was constant:

> It's growing evening in my soul,
> It darkens in
> At the gray window now and then
> I hear them toll
> The hour-and-day-long chimes of St. Etienne.
>
> Indeed I'd not have lived elsewhere
> Nor otherwise.
> Nor as the dreary saying is
> Been happier,
> To wear the love of life within my eyes.[12]

In his poems, Stickney did not model himself on Verlaine alone, but had the fervent hope of writing poetry in which the influence of Tennyson would temper that of Verlaine; the combination, however, threatened to be nullifying, for the unfinished work of Stickney is full of lackluster poems, half-Victorian, half-Symbolist.

This poet was the natural end of "Decadent" art, and of twenty years of systematic adaptation from the same foreign poets. It was not until 1912 that the critical study of French poets and the intellectual adaptation of certain of their techniques gave new life to an exhausted art.

A last Decadent, however, still believed in miracles. This was George Sylvester Viereck, who imagined that he could save American poetry by giving it "passion" — in other words, by imitating Baudelaire one more time. For Baudelaire had appeared to him:

> I heard a song, and I had no choice
> But to listen as into my heart it stole . . .
> Strange loves that speak with a siren voice,
> And lusts that rot both body and soul.[13]

Along with Baudelaire, he imitated Swinburne, that is to say, he repeated the experiments done twenty years before, (and with greater chance of success), by Francis Saltus, who nevertheless had failed. Viereck wrote with vigor at times, and sometimes captured the music of Baudelaire:

> I lay beside you. On your lips the while
> Hovered, most strange, the mirage of a smile.
> . . . .
> With all its beauty and its faultless grace,
> Your body, dearest, is a haunted place.[14]

Moreover, he never doubted his success: "I have given a new lyric impetus to my country. I have loosened the tongue of the young American poets . . . I may safely say that I am one of the leaders of the lyric insurgents."[15] The critics answered that Baudelaire, just like other *poètes maudits*, such as Byron and Swinburne, was no longer fashionable, that the theme of the sanctity of sin belonged to the past, that their ears had grown tired of loud cries of despair and passion long ago, and that the moment had come to find something new.

CONCLUSION

From 1889 to 1910, American poetry failed to evolve. In the course of these thirty years, attempts at liberation were made, but they came to nothing. The old traditions lacked vigor, and poets wrote without being satisfied with what they had done; hence France seemed to beckon as a possible model. Slowly the knowledge of French Symbolism invaded America, and soon no artist could be indifferent to it; some of them tried to adapt it to the public taste, but these attempts failed, without exception. French influence had to make itself felt against the resistance of the entire literate public. Of all the prejudices which warped public opinion, the prejudice against France was one of the most entrenched. Huneker attributed this prejudice to ignorance and middle-class morality, and these two faults showed no signs of disappearing. Moreover, the French influence—particularly that of

Symbolist poetry—was first felt by way of England, and along the way, Symbolism lost much of its force. Certain poets and critics took most of their ideas of Symbolism from Arthur Symons or Edmund Gosse; many had never made direct contact with the French poets, and had formed their idea of Symbolism through the works of Swinburne or William Sharp. They frequently confused the Symbolists with the Parnassians, and also with the Impressionists. Still, it was a curious fact that Symbolism had a mysterious attraction: the very word fascinated many people; and certain commanding names elicited an unaccountable respect: Baudelaire and Verlaine first, then Maeterlinck and Mallarmé, were thought to be the whole of Symbolism. Easier poets for foreign ears, such as Henri de Régnier, Samain, Merrill, or Jammes, might have given the movement a simpler and readier effect, but they were scarcely known before 1905.

But if no American poet knew how to draw essential resources from his knowledge of French Symbolism, it was because none had yet appeared who was daring enough. Ezra Pound wrote later that the trouble was that there were not yet enough adventurous spirits. Those who dared to fight against Puritanism were either literary jesters, or critics who were only half-liberated themselves, like Peck or Brownell. One person with vigor enough might have sufficed to rally the sparse forces, but no one appeared.

With the exception of a few "Decadents" who spent their lives writing light verses, the poets of this generation fell into the trap of nationalism. The public and the critics encouraged it: *The Forum* enumerated the virtues of an ideal literature thus: "A literature filled with national feelings proper to the race, and which would become, by the power of its interpretation, a true revelation of our life . . . The American people has not yet attained its complete national conscience . . . The body of the nation is so vast that its health depends on the perfect organization of its spiritual life . . . The services rendered by English literature are of a practical importance impossible to exaggerate. . . ." In conclusion, it proclaimed the necessity for a literature which would be at the service of the nation. But not one of the moralists, nor even one of the jesters, suspected the importance of technique: if certain of them rejected the influence of England, it was because of pure national pride; if certain others were interested in Symbolism, it was because of numerous sentiments which had nothing to do with a curiosity about technical innovations. And when one recalls that the major concern of Symbolism was with poetic technique, it does not seem surprising that the knowledge of this movement brought nothing vital to Americans at this time.

CHAPTER 6

The State of American Poetry
from 1910 to 1912

IT WOULD BE impossible to exaggerate the banality and indifference of poetic production in the United States about 1910. It is surprising, but true, that poets who were already well known had stopped publishing, as though waiting for the poetic revolution of 1912 to resume their artistic life. Edwin Markham published nothing between 1901, the date of *Lincoln and Other Poems*, and 1914, the date of *The Shoes of Happiness*. Lizette W. Reese remained silent from 1909 to 1920, the year she published *Spicewood*, a work which surpassed its predecessors in technique and in precision. Bliss Carman gave evidence of a certain discouragement between 1904 *(Songs of the Sea Children)* and 1913 *(Daughters of Dawn)*. Moody ended his career with prose dramas. Ridgely Torrence wrote his first book of poetry in 1900, *The House of a Hundred Lights*, and then waited a quarter of a century to publish his second, *Hesperides*. Edgar Lee Masters was no exception, for in this period of ferment and private enthusiasm, he was saving his strength for *Spoon River*, which did not appear until 1914, after the beginning of the poetic renaissance. The case of Sandburg appears to have been the same. The only exception worthy of note was Edwin Arlington Robinson, who chose exactly the date of 1910, when there seemed to be a discontinuity between present and past, to publish one of his most interesting books, *The Town Down the River*.

There was no doubt even then that this hesitancy on the part of the best poets of the time was a favorable sign. More than ever, people were waiting for a period of real poetry. With each new publication, the critics believed they saw the sign of a poetic awakening. While the poets of the past had been hesitant, awaiting a fruitful period, everyone now felt that poetry was in the air. If the authors hesitated, it was because they were tired of conventional verse. It had become too easy to write poetry and get it published. The renaissance occurred in opposition to the general tendencies of the time, which were as much those of 1880 as of 1905. Those who later achieved prominence—Pound, Fletcher, H. D., Gertrude Stein—were working in obscurity, and all of them had broken with the traditions of their country, some even with the life of their country.

Nineteen ten was a dormant year. The works that were published then (and

Louis Untermeyer's anthology[1] mentions only three) bore the same marks of traditionalism. This dormancy was doubtless the result of causes already described. To these causes—Puritanism, servility towards England, the partisanship of the reviews, and false orientation—must be added yet another: the lack of centrality. In 1912, Harriet Monroe complained that "In the United States today the poet is rarely able to devote his best energies to art . . . he suffers from the decentralization of literary taste and authority. His world is not a coterie in a capital, with an entrenched group of critics whose judgment, right or wrong, arouses comment; but a few inaccessible readers scattered over a wide area, and served by journalists who usually misconceive or ignore poetry altogether."[2]

There was no longer any literary center; no one would have dared to write, as Howells did in 1900, "the only criticism worth considering was that of Boston."[3] The East and the West had different tendencies, and in all the large cities there were independent schools which were hesitant about whether to take either of these two main directions, or to follow a new course of their own. In the East, the influence of New England was insurmountable; poets, and still more, painters, continued to submit to it. Percy MacKaye wrote a series of verse elegies to great men, dead and alive. F. E. Coates treated current ideas in traditional forms. In the West, descriptive poems about mountains and cities recalled Joaquin Miller and the period he symbolized.

If no event had occurred to change men's minds, the poetry of America would probably have continued in this direction. But even those whom we consider today to have brilliantly carried on the American tradition, such as Frost and Edgar Lee Masters, only fully emerged after the year of the revolution, 1913. Before this date, they were ready and waiting. Amy Lowell said, "America has produced only two great poets: Whitman and Poe. The other principal American poets were worthy and educated men, but they were poets of an English province, rather than of America, and obviously very inferior to their predecessors."[4] From Whitman's day to 1912, she found nothing of great value, and her evaluation was frank and true.

Even with these two facts in mind—that artists were working in the dark in search of a new way, and that the Renaissance must take place in opposition to the poetic tendencies current at the time—it was still difficult to predict what direction the long-awaited poetry would take. Certainly no new directions could be seen in the books of poetry listed in Lous Untermeyer's anthology for the years 1908-1911.[5] In these books were to be seen only the continuing imitation of the English, and a hedonism without the voluptuousness of the fin de siècle poets.

Nothing could be more instructive, for understanding the state of mind of American poets in 1912, than reading the first collection of poems by Amy Lowell, which appeared in Boston in that year under the title of *A Dome of Many-Coloured Glass.*

Amy Lowell spent her life in a compromise between the past and the present. Because of her name and her wealth, but also because she satisfied the average reader by combining new ideas with older habits of thinking, she achieved an undeniable success and influence in her lifetime. She invariably abandoned herself to the current fashion, and to the latest book she had read. For all these reasons, she was representative of the American poetic mind in 1912.

The title page of *A Dome of Many-Coloured Glass* carried two epigraphs, one drawn from Shelley and one from Samain. The poetry of Shelley, Keats, and Samain had exerted an influence on her early work, but this influence cannot be isolated. There is no great pleasure in reading her first book: some delicate verses in classical rhythm, legends, children's verses; a little more art than usual, a little more color, sometimes a poem which attempts to reproduce an impression; but no central idea: hers is still the classic collection of occasional verses, on the model of *Landmarks and Other Poems* or *The White Sail and Other Poems.* American poets had not yet taken possession of their individuality.

It was Keats who, more than any other poet, inspired Amy Lowell's first collection. But she had also read the French Parnassians, and the Symbolists who delighted in classical forms and brilliant colors, such as Samain and Henri de Régnier. She had read Francis Jammes, too, and it is surprising to find an imitation of him in this volume.

The titles of her poems alone showed a constant reading of the works of Keats. (There is even one called "To John Keats; suggested by a cover of a volume of Keats's poems.") Amy Lowell attempted a poetry as rich and sumptuous as that of Keats: using the same scenes, with finely traced details, the same intense and warm colors as the English poet, but not the same discernment and clarity in execution. The flowers with which she decorated her garden were the violets, hollyhocks, and poppies "with odor of honey" of Keats's poems. The second poem of the collection was a souvenir of "The Ode to a Nightingale"; "Azure and Gold" copied "Blue, 'Tis the Life of Heaven." In "Loon Point," on the other hand, are harmonized the end of "Callidore" and the "Soirs" of Samain. In other poems, Amy Lowell was inspired by Henri de Régnier. She often calls his images to mind, for example one of the swimmer coming out of the waves. Although all her images are obviously borrowed, it is impossible to isolate the elements common to the nineteenth century English poets from those of the French Parnassians. Thus, for instance, Amy Lowell wrote:

> To make a pavement for your feet I stripped
> My soul for you to walk upon . . .[6]

Yeats had already written:

> I have spread my dreams under your feet;
> Tread softly because you tread on my dreams.[7]

And Samain had also written:

> J'ai la fièvre . . .
> D'étendre sous tes pieds comme un manteau de roi
> Ma vie.[8]

One of her clearest and most successful imitations was the poem titled "Epitaph in a Churchyard, South Carolina," which borrowed agreeably from Francis Jammes. As for "Market Day," it was also a poem in the manner of Jammes, describing small objects humorously, but finishing on a sentimental note.

If Amy Lowell filled her imagination with images borrowed from all these authors, she did not seek to acquire their technique: there are "symbols" in her first collection, but there were no Symbolist poems. She might begin a poem with an image borrowed from Samain or Henri de Régnier, but she finished it in a more prosaic manner; her comparisons were only accidental associations, not real analogies; neither did she discover new musical patterns. If her first collection was more modern than the majority of volumes of poetry which stuffed the libraries at the time, the French influence in it was counterbalanced by the English, and went no farther than the borrowed images. It was to the more Parnassian of the Symbolists that Amy Lowell was indebted, and to those among them whose style was nearest to Keats. Of course, none of her poems were attempts at a new technique. The critic who wrote later that the effort of the new poetic school was "to write differently what others had already said"[9] was not familiar with the aims of this new school. But this first volume of Amy Lowell's was quite representative of what would have been written at the time by a young person endowed with poetic gifts. Very little in it gave any indication of Amy Lowell's second volume, where she professed to be inaugurating a new technique.

As a second example of the situation of American poetry in 1912, there was a publication called *The Lyric Year*,[10] which was greeted with transports of joy by Braithwaite in the *Boston Evening Transcript*, and by Charles Vale in the *Forum*. Did it give any inkling of the explosion of 1913? One has only to read this anthology to see that the Imagist movement could not have evolved logically from it. Scarcely any of the marks of a modern poetry are to be found in this collection.

But *The Lyric Year* was important as one of the first efforts to escape the exigencies of the mazagine, and to give poets the means of communicating directly with those who were more interested in poetry than in facts. In his preface, the editor remarked: "The poetry of our Twentieth Century is democratic, scientific, humane. Its independence shows the liberating touch of Walt Whitman, with admirable and robust optimism."

The mark of Walt Whitman was clearly to be seen in the collection. But Whitman, who for a time incarnated the spirit of his country, did not initiate a school. He had been admired by Western writers, who interpreted him wrongly. When, at the beginning of the twentieth century, Americans felt themselves forced by the critics — especially the English critics — to create a national poetry, and to spread the example of Whitman, some undistinguished imitators appeared on the scene, and their number increased. These poets thought they were freeing themselves from the conventionality of the time by taking up a forgotten idiom. The real successors of Whitman, those who adopted both his thought and his style, were the social poets, such as Ernest Crosby and Horace Traubel. The latter, in "Optimos" and in "Chant Communal," produced poems whose rhythm was that of prose rather than verse, and though he made too much use of repetition, in his poetry as in Whitman's there was an impression of great muscular vigor. His manner was full of a noble ease, but it was without originality.

In *The Lyric Year*, the disciples of Whitman were those who preached in verse against the evils of a materialistic civilization. In Pittsburgh, J. Oppenheim imitated him distantly; it was the Whitmanian style changed to a plaintive rhythm. The imitation succeeded less well in the hands of J. W. Lloyd, whose intentions were more didactic. "American," by H. Scheffauer, and "The Mob," by E. D. Schoonmaker, showed all the faults of Whitman's style without showing any of his forcefulness.

Reading this anthology, one could believe that the movement in favor of an industrial poetry, which had been encouraged several years before by Margaret Widlemer, Florence Wilkerson, Harriet Monroe, and others, was still going to emerge: the cultivated Western plains, the farms, the factories, the steel bridges, the elevated railways were among the subjects treated, but always in traditional meters. There was no further artistic effort than this. Except for these modern subjects, imbued with passion and revolt, all was translated into rhetoric, all tradition remained intact, all the common stock of poetic language and all the words approved by the academic mind, were accumulated in verses of the most disheartening banality. "To a Thrush," by T. A. Daly, is typical of the genre, and it won a prize. If, in the diversity of subjects treated, an attempt were made to discover tendencies, the poets could be grouped as follows:

1. The preachers, social reformers, descendants of the long Puritan line to which Hovey, Moody, and most of the poets of New England belonged.

2. Those called "cosmic poets," whom the English considered the most faithful representatives of American poetry: in July, 1914 Richard Aldington wrote in the *Egoist:* "We in England are rather apt to be scornful of American poetry—and rightly so, for there is nothing so appallingly boring as the average American cosmic poem. This sort of poetry, coming partly from Whitman and Swinburne, and partly from a profusion of capital letters, and vague and pompous expressions, tried to give a vision of the universe and everything under the sun in the same poem."

3. The writers of occasional verse, who were numerous, and all of whom used the same style.

4. The "moderns," who wrote sonnets about the Transcontinental Express.

If a predominant influence were looked for in this volume, it would be first Whitman, and then Browning. More modern influences might be seen in the poems of Eloise Briton, Ludwig Lewisohn, and Hermann Sheffauer. Among a hundred poems published in the same year by a hundred authors, at least ninety were mediocre. More importantly, none of them showed a real concern for technique. Yet a critic like W. S. Braithwaite could write of this volume:

> This book looks to the future with confidence, because it expresses the hopes and aspirations of national and individual life, whose soul and colors are based on solid moral principles, social obligations, humanitarian justice, moral responsibility, and spiritual vision, of a sort which, forming a unity that is artistic and essential, opens a new perspective on the future.[11]

And this was the state of poetry at the threshold of the modern era, when Pound, Aldington, and H. D. began publishing their first works in *Poetry* magazine in Chicago. The country still waited for a modern Whitman, a new American poet who could symbolize the spirit of the country according to an ideal more European than American. Those who entertained this illusion were able to see a certain richness of temperament in many poets, when they might easily have seen faults. One poem in the collection, "Renascence" by Edna St. Vincent Millay, was highly spoken of. It made an immediate appeal, even if the technique was not equal to the inspiration. The poetic force of such poems, together with the variety and modernity of the subjects treated, made readers forget the absence of art. But it was in the name of art, of artistic discipline and technique, that the poetic revolution was achieved, not in the name of modernity, whether scientific or industrial, or of tradition, whether English or American.

How then can the astonishing change of direction be accounted for? That is what we will try to explain later on in pointing out the results of French influence. What can already be determined, perhaps, is how an experiment which failed twenty years before could succeed in 1912. In the previous chapter, it was shown that the earlier French influence had not been profound, but it had been extensive. It was also shown that, after a passing period of influence which did not strike deep into the American literary consciousness, certain modern minds became interested in French art. These were not great artists, but were intelligent men who managed to gain the ear of the public. And it has also been seen that translations from European works were becoming more and more numerous: *Poet-Lore* was devoted almost entirely to translations (especially from Maeterlinck, Ibsen, and D'Annunzio). The field thus seems to have been slowly prepared for sowing new seed. In this same year, 1912, two new magazines appeared, one in Boston and one in Chicago. The one in Chicago, *Poetry*, was very receptive to foreign works. A group of poems by William Butler Yeats appeared in the December issue. Ezra Pound became foreign correspondent of the magazine, and supplied notes on European and even Asiatic art.

If the year 1912 did not bring forth any fruit, it was at least ripe with new seed.[12] Those who were indecisive that year were luminous the following year. But more than ever young writers were in revolt against the habitual way of writing, and against the ideas accepted by editors and publishers: they wanted to make something new. Masefield enjoyed a great American success, for new masters were being sought wherever they could be found. Then a revolt began to form against popular poetry, and soon reproaches were heard.

Finally, this rebellion against accepted ideas and customs, though based on no predetermined program, no new conception of literature, led to the establishment of some magazines, which were without philosophical principles, and had the sole end of giving anyone who showed talent the opportunity to see himself in print. The first issues of *Poetry* did not contain particularly interesting poems, but they did give the sense that something was in the air, and soon the magazine came to life, for though it had started with Whitmanian jargon and democratic propaganda still in evidence, it became a place where art was taken seriously. Its history was thus the reverse of those little reviews of the end of the nineteenth century, which began on solid ground and soon found themselves mired in custom.

But it should be noted at once that the first interesting verse in *Poetry* came from London—from Aldington, Pound, Yeats, and H. D.—that is to say, from English writers and Americans in exile; for it seems that in this period the only way of breaking out of the enveloping vacuum was by expatriation.

In 1914 in Chicago, at a dinner given by *Poetry* magazine to honor W. B. Yeats, the Irish poet spoke of the general sense then affecting writers:

Now, when I open the ordinary American magazine, I find that all that we rebelled against in those early days—the sentimentality, the rhetoric, the "moral uplift"—still exist here. Not because you are too far from England, but because you are too far from Paris.

It is from Paris that nearly all the great influences in art and literature have come, from the time of Chaucer until now. Today the metrical experiments of French poets are overwhelming in their variety and delicacy. The best English writing is dominated by French criticism; in France is the great critical mind.

The Victorians forgot this; also, they forgot the austerity of art and began to preach. When I saw Paul Verlaine in Paris, he told me that he could not translate Tennyson because he was "too *Anglais*, too noble"—"when he should be broken-hearted he has too many reminiscences."

We in England, our little group of rhymers, were weary of all this. We wanted to get rid not only of rhetoric but of poetic diction. We tried to strip away everything that was artificial, to get a style like speech, as simple as the simplest prose, like a cry of the heart . . .

Poetry that is naturally simple, that might exist as the simplest prose, should have instantaneousness of effect, provided it finds the right audience. You may have to wait years for that audience, but when it is found that instantaneousness of effect is produced.[13]

PART TWO

THE INFLUENCE OF
FRENCH POETRY IN THE
STRUGGLE AGAINST TRADITION

FROM 1910 ON, signs of revolt could be seen. Poets working privately, tired of decadent exhaustion, of Whitmanian and Kiplingesque rhetoric, made their escape to greener pastures. Thus Frost was seriously studying the ancient Greeks, Pound the troubadours. Sandburg, without going so far afield, found in American life and language an original and sound diction. When, in 1912, the first manifestations and first conquests of the new style were produced, partially liberated from eloquence and clichés, from overly familiar rhythms, poets young and old alike experienced a revelation: Masters, who had just started reading the Greek Anthology, was much struck with the first poems of Sandburg in *Poetry*, and Amy Lowell, who had imitated the most diverse poets in *A Dome of Many-Coloured Glass*, began to get interested in clarity of style and precise diction.

As for rhythm, it took longer to develop: neither the study of the Greeks nor that of the troubadours led to a complete remaking of English verse. Like Browning, Pound adapted the Provençal forms into English; Aldington read much of Southey, Landor, and Whitman, who had used some unusual rhythms. But it was only when they began to study modern French poets that "free verse" was discovered. It was the most important discovery, and in any case the one which caused the greatest sensation and was the most tangible innovation in the eyes of the public. It had the effect, among other things, of completing the development toward verbal precision and hardness; clichés and padding were no longer excused; poetry could be written with the freedom of prose, without losing its concentration. It was this development, attained by an intense reaction against the unpoetic poems of the generation of Shaw and Ibsen, and against the diluted Symbolism remaining from the last century, which was the clearest conquest of the years from 1910 to 1914.

The poets studied here show a common search for precision, for achieving realism by the briefest possible means; and all borrowed heavily from French poets, while correcting certain of their ideas and perfecting certain of their methods. It was from the second generation of Symbolist poets, and also from Laforgue, Corbière, and Gautier, that they took their point of departure. Some of the poets effected a compromise; approving of the desire for precision of the Imagists, they did not wish to ignore Henri de Régnier or Verhaeren, who inspired more sympathy in them than Corbière or Laforgue. These poets did little more than dispense the perfume already distilled by the French poets.

CHAPTER 1

The Imagist Attack

IN 1912, the break with tradition became definite; there were still some who believed in educating the public, and who made it their patriotic duty to explain artistic principles to America; but many escaped to exile in Europe, a freer place.

The new poets sent their work from London, but curiously enough, *Poetry* was prior to the London reviews in its date of origin.

In 1913, several American poets were in exile in London. Among them were Ezra Pound, H. D., John Gould Fletcher, and Robert Frost. The English air was easier for them to breathe. However, the literary situation there was essentially like that of the United States. The same conditions existed, but were called by different names: the evils from which they suffered were not Puritan or cosmic poetry, but a collection of maladies grouped under the name of Victorianism— that is to say , a manner of writing common to a number of mediocre poets, who clung to it because they saw there—or thought they saw there—the whole English tradition. The results of the fin de siècle movement in both countries were similar. The literary situation in England during these few years has been admirably described by Ford Madox Hueffer (Ford) in his book, *Thus to Revisit* (London, 1921). He said that since the fine days of *The Yellow Book*, "there had not been any movement in English letters—up until the appearance, just before the War, of the Futurists, the Vorticists, and the Imagists" (p.40).

Imitators of Swinburne still remained, misguided descendants of the fin de siècle and Symbolist movements that Arthur Symons had directed. But all in all, literary art had been neglected: a whole generation—that of Shaw and Wells— had something quite different in mind from the art of writing.

In 1915, Richard Aldington wrote: "The two poets whose literary influence has ruined what remained in England of poetic taste are Oscar Wilde and Francis Thompson." Aldington and his friends were at that time in revolt against this vaporous, decadent poetry. If the American "Decadent" mind was influenced indirectly by France, if all the echoes of Maeterlinck that were heard were only a discovery in French works of what were Anglo-Saxon qualities, if it was difficult to distinguish in 1912 between what came directly from and what had passed through England, the present period, in contrast, made a direct search for French qualities in French Symbolist literature.

77

It was the association in London of English and American poets united in a common cause that brought this decadent tendency to an end. Their alliance was based on a mutual scorn for current poetry, and their plan was a plan of war. The movement they launched, which was called "Imagism," provided the necessary catalyst for energies which were ready to be released in America. In studying the connections of Imagism with French poetry, it will help to have a brief history of the movement.

The following account is taken from F. S. Flint's "History of Imagism," published May 1, 1915, in *Egoist* magazine, London:

> Somewhere in the gloom of the year 1908, Mr. T. E. Hulme, now in the trenches of Ypres, but excited then by the propinquity, at a half-a-crown dance, of the other sex (if, as Rémy de Gourmont avers, the passage from the aesthetic to the sexual emotion, *n'est qu'un pas*, the reverse is surely also true), proposed to a companion that they should found a Poets' Club. The thing was done there and then. The Club began to dine; and its members to read their verses. At the end of the year they published a small plaquette of them, called "For Christmas 1908." In this plaquette was printed one of the first "Imagist" poems, by T. E. Hulme:

> *Autumn*
> A touch of cold in the autumn night
> I walked abroad,
> And saw the ruddy moon lean over a hedge,
> Like a red-faced farmer.
> I did not stop to talk, but nodded;
> And round about were the wistful stars
> With white faces like town children.

> In November of the same year, Edward Storer, author already of "Inclinations," much of which is in the "Imagist" manner, published his "Mirrors of Illusion," the first book of "Imagist" poems, with an essay at the end attacking poetic conventions. The first poem in the book was called "Image," here it is:

> Forsaken lovers,
> Burning to a chaste white moon,
> Upon strange pyres of loneliness and drought.

> Mr. Storer, who has recanted much since, was in favour then of a poetry which I described, in reference to his book, as "a form of expression, like the Japanese, in which an image is the resonant heart of an exquisite moment." A fair example of his practice is this from "Clarice-Henley":

Clarice! Clarice! The oasis of lunch,
We laid Arabian-Night-wise in the green
And pleasant desert of the field
For our most welcome selves,
And that rememberable canopy of white
And holy linen, that denied your face
Unto a hundred daisies' peeping glance,
We placed to bear the bread, the wine—the flowers
Of your dear hand.

I have always wished that Storer, in his after work, had brought more art to the exploitation of the temperament he displayed in the "Mirrors," which, for me, is a book of poetry. But he changed his manner completely.

At that time, I had been advocating in the course of a series of articles on recent books of verse a poetry in *vers libre*, akin in spirit to the Japanese. An attack on the Poets' Club brought me into correspondence and acquaintance with T. E. Hulme, and, later on, after Hulme had violently disagreed with the Poets' Club and had left it, he proposed that he should get together a few congenial spirits, and that we should have weekly meetings in a Soho restaurant. The first of these meetings, which were really the successors of certain Wednesday evening meetings, took place on Thursday, March 25, 1909. There were present, so far as I recall, T. E. Hulme, Edward Storer, F. W. Tancred, Joseph Campbell, Miss Florence Farr, one or two other men, mere vaguements in my memory, and myself. I think that what brought the real nucleus of this group together was a dissatisfaction with English poetry as it was then (and is still, alas!) being written. He proposed at various times to replace it by pure *vers libre*; by the Japanese *tanka* and *haikai*; we all wrote dozens of the latter as an amusement; by poems in a sacred Hebrew form, of which "This is the House that Jack Built" is a perfect model; Joseph Campbell produced two good specimens of this, one of which, "The Dark," is printed in "The Mountainy Singer"; by rhymeless poems like Hulme's "Autumn," and so on. In all this Hulme was ringleader. He insisted too on absolutely accurate presentation and no verbiage; and he and F. W. Tancred, a poet too little known, perhaps because his production is precious and small, used to spend hours each day in the search for the right phrase. Tancred does it still; while Hulme reads German philosophy in the trenches, waiting for the general advance. There was also a lot of talk and practice among us, Storer leading it chiefly, of what we called the Image. We were very much influenced by modern French symbolist poetry.

On April 22, 1909, Ezra Pound, whose book, "Personae," had been published on the previous Friday, joined the group, introduced,

I believe, by Miss Farr and my friend T. D. FitzGerald. Ezra Pound used to boast in those days that he was

Nil praeter "Villon" et doctus cantare Catullum,

and he could not be made to believe that there was any French poetry after Ronsard. He was very full of his *troubadours;* but I do not remember that he did more than attempt to illustrate (or refute) our theories occasionally with their example. The group died a lingering death at the end of its second winter. But its discussions had a sequel. In 1912 Mr. Pound published, at the end of his book "Ripostes," the complete poetical works of T. E. Hulme, five poems, thirty-three lines, with a preface in which these words occur: "As for the future, *Les Imagistes,* the descendants of the forgotten school of 1909 (previously referred to as the 'School of Images') have that in their keeping." In that year, Pound had become interested in modern French poetry, he had broken away from his old manner; and he invented the term "Imagisme" to designate the aesthetic of "Les Imagistes." In March 1913, an "interview," over my signature, of an "imagiste" appeared in the American review *Poetry,* followed by "A Few Don'ts by an Imagiste" by Ezra Pound. The four cardinal principles of "Imagisme" were set forth as:

1) Direct treatment of the "Thing," whether subjective or objective.

2) To use absolutely no word that did not contribute to the presentation.

3) As regarding rhythm: to compose in sequence of the musical phrase, not in sequence of a metronome.

4) The "doctrine of the Image"—not for publication.

Towards the end of the year Pound collected together a number of poems of different writers, Richard Aldington, H. D., F. S. Flint, Skipwith Cannell, Amy Lowell, William Carlos Williams, James Joyce, John Cournos, Ezra Pound, Ford Madox Heuffer and Allan Upward, and in February–March 1914 they were published in America and England as "Des Imagistes: An Anthology," which, though it did not set the Thames, seems to have set America, on fire. Since then Mr. Ezra Pound has become a "Vorticist," with a contradiction, for, when addressing the readers of *The New Age* he has made Imagism to mean pictures as Wyndham Lewis understands them; writing later for T. P.'s Weekly, he made it pictures as William Morris understood them. There is no difference, except that which springs from differences of temperament and talent, between an imagist poem of today and those written by Edward Storer and T. E. Hulme.

This description is precise and might be sufficient in itself. However, it seems indispensable, before considering the work of Pound, to review at least briefly that of the originator of Imagism, T. E. Hulme, in his relation with French Symbolism. T. E. Hulme gave many ideas to Pound and to Flint, who were his direct disciples. Hulme and Flint had been interested in French poetry well ahead of Pound; they converted him to it, and he converted Aldington and H. D.

Returning to the origins of Imagism, and rereading the unfinished work of T. E. Hulme,[1] one can soon see the extent of his debt to the French philosophers and theoreticians of style, such as Rémy de Gourmont and Jules de Gaultier. Hulme was a Bergsonian, and thus an enemy of the Cartesian rationalism traditional in France. He was a great believer in intuition and direct knowledge. Bergson had shown Hulme how and why the artist renders a service to man, by making him see reality unveiled, in all its violence. Emotion being at the root of all knowledge, art must search for a means to achieve direct communication between emotion and expression, between artist and public. Words, because they have been in use for too long, are an untrustworthy means, yet they are all the poet has to work with. Hulme thus posed the problem as Rémy de Gourmont and Jules de Gaultier had posed it: de Gourmont said that at the base of all knowledge there was emotion, and that almost always this emotion sprang from vision. T. E. Hulme wrote, "All emotion depends on real solid vision or sound. It is physical."[2] In other words, the style must convey the physical hardness of reality. "With perfect style, the solid leather for reading, each sentence should be a lump, a piece of clay, a vision seen . . . Never should one feel light vaporous bridges between one solid sense and another. No bridges—all solid: then never exasperated."[3] In order to avoid misusing words and phrases, one must use them with the value they possessed before overuse made them decadent: one must restore their value as images. "Aphra [a character invented by Hulme] sees each word with an image sticking on to it, never as a flat word passed over a board, like a counter."[4] As for thought, it must be for the artist an *analogy* not soiled by reason. "One thinks," said de Gourmont, "by means of images. An idea is only a stale sensation, an image that has been effaced; to reason with ideas is to assemble and combine, in a laborious mosaic, faded pieces that have become almost undistinguishable."[5] And T. E. Hulme said: "The demand for clear, logical expression is impossible, as it would confine us to the use of flat counter-images only."[6]

Poetry, which is thought in images, is the only powerful logic: "Poetry is no more nor less than a mosaic of words, so great exactness is required for each one."[7] His advice was, *"Always seek the hard, definite, personal word."*[8] This was the principal credo of the Imagist school for two or three years.

Old ideas about originality and the commonplace must be abandoned. Rèmy de Gourmont had already remarked that style was everything, the subject very little, for all the subjects that could be found have already been exploited. And Hulme wrote, with his own originality: "Literature a method of sudden arrangement of commonplaces. The *suddenness* makes one forget the commonplace."[9]

These ideas about words and images result in a poetry that is suggestive—the reader participates differently than in Descartes' *Discourse on Method*—but, and this is the Imagist doctrine in all its purity, the suggestiveness is not indefinite, as from handling words with gloves, but is direct comprehension through lively and strong expression, through new and striking images.

In the following passage, T. E. Hulme expressed ideas that had previously been formulated by Mallarmé: ". . . the very act of trying to find a form to fit the separate phrases into, itself leads to the creation of new images hitherto not felt by the poet. In a sense the poetry writes itself. This creation by happy chance is analogous to the accidental stroke of the brush which creates a new beauty not previously consciously thought of by the artist . . . The deed and the poem (are) always greater than the man."[10]

Hulme recognized his debt to French art. He knew also what he owed to philosophers like Bergson and like Ribot, whose theory of emotions he knew well. He was aware of using their theories as a point of departure. Hulme acknowledged also that he had a weakness for the study and analysis of modern art, "and in particular, Symbolism."

Pound eventually came strongly under the influence of these ideas. The other Imagists—those whose names are associated with Imagism: H. D., Aldington, Amy Lowell, Fletcher, D. H. Lawrence—forgot them too quickly; but it appears that around 1913 they all more or less held to these principles, and to the "Don'ts" published in *Poetry* by Pound, even if they neglected to apply them.

It was Pound who published the first anthology,[11] and who was the most consistent in his Imagism. He had already made the acquaintance of Amy Lowell, from whom he had accepted a poem at the last moment, entitled "In a Garden." Aldington did not think that this poem was worthy of the anthology; but Pound needed money for the anthology, and this was a way of procuring it. The first aim of the enterprise had been to make the poems of H. D. known, as much as, and perhaps more than, to found a school. Neither H. D. nor Aldington were part of Hulme's group, and in the year 1912 they knew very little about modern French literature; if the other names of the first anthology are examined, it might seem that modern French poetry was well known to the whole group, since Skipwith Cannell, James Joyce, Ford Madox Hueffer, and Allen Upward already knew much about it. But not one of those who participated in the Imagist experiment was much interested in French literature at the time: neither Pound, nor Aldington, nor Amy Lowell had yet begun their French study and propaganda. Flint was the only exception. The only other French influence at the beginning of Imagism was that which Pound drew indirectly through the agency of Hulme. Thus the work of Hulme was continued by Pound, who gathered Aldington and H. D. with him to form a group, from which he later separated, being replaced by Amy Lowell and John Gould Fletcher. In effect, Pound had found an idea in London to propagate, and he found Amy Lowell to finance the effort. In 1914, he pushed his Imagist idea to its extreme development in the "Vorticist" manifesto (which also was signed by Richard Aldington). He fell out with some of his friends, Amy Lowell among them. The English never took the movement very seriously. It was Amy Lowell who published the second anthology in 1915, and wrote the preface for it. She became the spokesman of the movement: it was thanks to her, to her name, her fortune, her crusading spirit that the school achieved its notoriety in America. She was also responsible for several historical errors: she was determined to have it forgotten that Ezra Pound was the organizer and instigator of the group much more than herself.

The second anthology was thus a transformation; Miss Lowell kept only Richard Aldington, H. D., J. G. Fletcher, F. S. Flint, herself, and D. H. Lawrence. This was certainly the collection which made Imagism popular. It contained the poem of H. D., "Oread," which became a classic; above all, it contained the preface, which unleashed a civil war in American poetry. In 1916, a third anthology appeared, followed by a fourth and last in 1917. The Imagist formula— it was a formula, not a broad doctrine like Symbolism— had fulfilled the role it chose to play: it had placed poetry once again among the arts, had "wrung the neck of eloquence," had put a ban on the use of the cliché by poets, and liberated poetic form. Such had been its great ambition.

For Imagism was a school, founded in the manner of the French literary schools, and destined to play the same role. In 1912, Pound affirmed truths that no longer needed demonstration in France. His role was like that played by Baudelaire against Romanticism, and like that of the first generation Symbolists against Romanticism and the Parnassians. Baudelaire tried to rid poetic art of all that was not essential to it. In England and in America, what people then called poetry was a series of regular verses, sustained by a general idea, and rhetorical in form. Flint and Pound demanded sincerity, and absolute honesty. The first necessity was to get rid of easy formulas, the enemies of expressive feeling. "The English Imagists," wrote Rémy de Gourmont, "obviously derive from the French Symbolists. That may be seen immediately from their abhorrence of cliché, of rhetoric and pomp, of the oratorical style, of the facile style, which imitators of Victor Hugo have made us disgusted with forever; they love precision of language, clarity of vision, and concentration of thought, synthesized into a dominant image."[12]

The theory of the Image was, along with the work of reconstruction, to create a true poetry, the indispensable credo of a firm discipline. Besides, it is implied in their very first principle, their definition of the poetic realm, their search for the nature of poetic art. "If we want form and color, we look at or paint a picture; if we want form in color, and in two dimensions, we look for sculpture; if we want an image or a succession of images, we look for poetry. If we want pure sound, we seek music."[13] It is evident that words are the medium of poets. However, this truism, which is the same as saying that cloth belongs to the tailor, and leather to the cobbler, needed to be brought home to the English, as well as to the Americans. Pound wrote it; Aldington repeated it: "A poet is an artist whose medium is words, who expresses in words thoughts, emotions, and sensations, as a painter expresses them in color, and a musician in sound."[14] But the Imagists had read Rémy de Gourmont, and were permeated with his *Problème du style;* they knew that words "can correspond only to a sensation, and primarily to vision."[15] and they knew also what de Gourmont thought of cliché. The words which one generation after another of poets have used become stale and flat; the word or expression which once conveyed great emotional richness, and presented a clear and striking image, becomes a dead weight. Rémy de Gourmont cited some examples; Amy Lowell cited others.[16] Thus, in searching for the word which makes an image, or the expression which presents an image, the Imagists were only filling in the gaps of the dictionary. To recover the word-sensation, the word-vision, the word-image that de Gourmont spoke of, was the very basis of the Imagist idea, a very sane idea, which would vivify the poet's means of expression, rejuvenate his language, and also importantly, his sensibility.

The image, the word-image, sprang out of the contact of young and alert senses with an ever present reality. The Imagists flattered themselves that they were returning to Nature, to the primitive; like the Symbolists, like Francis Jammes and Paul Fort, they had a sympathy for songs, for whatever was simple, vital in shape and emotion. Like the Symbolists, they soon discovered Oriental poetry.

But again, they were thinking in a direction parallel to that of the Symbolists: "Word-imagism denotes our way of presenting the subject, not the subject itself," obviously corresponds to what Tancrède de Visan said of the Symbolists: "The Symbolist epithet suited them marvelously, if one is alluding, not to their mode of inspiration, but only to their process of exposition."[17]

Considering only the principles which the Imagist group affirmed, the movement presented a series of essential analogies to French Symbolism that Rémy de Gourmont perceived immediately, and that the Imagists themselves were not ashamed to admit.

CHAPTER 2

The Imagists and France

By 1911, Arthur Symons, who at the end of the nineteenth century had done more than any other to make the modern French poetic movement known in England, was ill and no longer writing. His role had been filled by Ford Madox (Hueffer) Ford, whose aim was close to that of the Imagists; he appeared in their first anthology, and on many occasions joined forces with them. William Butler Yeats was strongly influenced by French Symbolism and had in turn influenced the new generation, but did not know French literature at first hand. T. E. Hulme, whose work was as yet incomplete, was interested exclusively in literature, not in propaganda. Thus, in 1911, Ford was the only serious artist interested in keeping up the influence of French literature in England.

During the autumn of 1911, H. D., Pound, and Aldington were meeting often for tea. Soon Flint joined them, and through his influence they began learning about French Symbolism; it was thus they discovered that their search for new form had already begun in France: the first authors they read were Henri de Régnier and Rémy de Gourmont.

It is worth repeating that neither Pound, Aldington, nor H. D. had used the French writers as models before this time, although all three had written definitive poems. They were feeling their way forward: H. D. in particular was discontented with her poems, and frequently destroyed them. When, one day, she came to Pound with a new group of verses, he saw the realization of what he and Hulme had been searching for; he christened this genre "Imagistes," and the group around Hulme, which had been greatly interested in French poetry, gave up its name to another group which owed nothing to the French; but still, the French influence on the whole group continued.

From the day when they realized that they actually had to simplify poetry in order to recover its true nature, and to place it once more among the arts, French poetry became an example for the Imagists to follow. Little by little, the need for this foreign import had been established. The success of F. S. Flint's fine study in 1912 in *Poetry Review* of London[1] shows how much was expected from France. Symbolism was at last regarded as a discovery in technique. In a panorama of poetry up to that time, Flint examined the principal French poets of the period, and presented them, not in isolation, but grouped into schools and movements. He described all the movements as deriving from the Symbolist movement, and he defined very accurately the various techniques of vers libre. What Flint gave his contemporaries was an insight into the rationale of French literature, the clear purpose established by their manifestos, and their concern for technique: finally, he showed how intensely these artists were trying to be a part of their century, to live the life of their contemporaries. He ended his presentation of "neo-Mallarmisme," "L'Unanimisme," "Paroxisme," "Impulsionnisme," and "Futurism," by this act of faith: "I salute in the poets of France an inextinguishable vitality!" Seeing this procession of French schools, Pound decided Imagism had as much right to a name as any of them.

Compared to Flint's study, which was the best informed and most important in England during the Imagist movement, the studies of Pound published the next year (1913) in *The New Age*[2] were those of a man who had just discovered a new land, and who was setting out to explore it. Far from being a model of composition or erudition, this series of articles was based only on the reading of a few volumes of verse, and several of the articles do not correspond to the plan announced in the first one. But their frankness is admirable, and also their critical assurance; they may have had little preparation, but they did have a definite aim: raising questions of art about each of the French poets, he went through their poetry with a practical intent, for he knew what he could learn from each of them. Thus he summed it up, as foreign correspondent of *Poetry:* "If our writers would keep their eye on Paris instead of on London—the London of today or of yesterday—there might be some chance of their doing work that would not be *démodé* before it gets to the press."[3] And he cited the authors studied in *The New Age:* "I think if our American bards would study Rémy de Gourmont for rhythm, Laurent Tailhade for delineation, Henri de Régnier for simplicity of syntactical construction, Francis Jammes for humanity, and the faculty of rendering one's own time; and if they would get some idea of intensity from Tristan Corbière (since they will not take their Villon in the original), there might be some hope for American poetry."

His intention, then, was clear: it was to find masters, and strict masters, experts in force and intensity of style. Of Tailhade he said: "It is a pleasing and erudite irony, such as should fill the creative artist with glee, and might well fill the imitators with a species of apostolic terror."[4]

Pound was the first to give Tailhade and Corbière credit for so much importance in the formation of a poet. But he had a sympathy for these older poets which was probably due to his own excellent discipline. Of Corbière he wrote, "The quintessence of style is precisely that it should be swift and mordant," and "He is more real than the 'realists,' because he still recognizes that force of romance which is a quite real, and, ineradicable part of our life. . . ."[5]

His sympathy for Rémy de Gourmont was primarily of the same kind. He was the first of his group to cite as an admirable example of the adaptation of rhythm to emotion de Gourmont's *Litanies de la rose*, which all the Imagists appear to have known by heart.

With regard to Francis Jammes, he again affirmed his aim to provide literary masters for "les jeunes" of England and America: "It is quite clear that there awaits a more definite place in our own literature for the man who will do for the English or American small city what Jammes has done for the French in *Existences*. And that is a silly sort of thing to say, for no one will."[6]

In 1913 and 1914, Flint gave a chronicle of French poetry in *Poetry and Drama*, thus completing his first study with a no less remarkable series of articles. There again, he tried to attach each piece of writing to a group, and to indicate the importance of literary movements, but still without making a choice, without any critical selection. He reviewed the latest books, placing among the most important those of the vers-librists: Paul Fort, Jammes, Claudel, and de Gourmont. He admired Verhaeren especially, and would soon refer to him as "the greatest European poet of our epoch."

But even better than the *Poetry Review*, better than *Poetry and Drama*, than *The New Age*, and than *Poetry*, was *The Egoist*, which showed the most enthusiasm for French poetry at this time.

The first number (January 1, 1914) contained the final installment of Pound's translation of de Gourmont's *Cheveux de Diomèdes*, which had begun in *The New Freewoman* [Predecessor of *The Egoist*]; a study of French philosophy, "France of Today: A Group of Thinkers," by Edgar A. Mowrer; and "Le Théatre du Vieux Colombier" by A. S. C. The issue of April 1 saw the inauguration of a column by Saint Fiacre, called "Passing Paris." In the same issue, there was another article by E. A. Mowrer on Leon Deubel. But it was the name of Rémy de Gourmont that was mentioned most frequently; for example, Aldington wrote of *Le Latin mystique:* "The work of M. Rémy de Gourmont has been probably more written about in *The Egoist* than in any other English periodical. That is because many of the younger people who are enthusiastic about literature feel that M. de Gourmont is the most fascinating literary artist now living in France."[7]

Alongside the column of Saint Fiacre (which was replaced in 1915 by that of Muriel Ciolkowska), and under the heading of "The French Word in Modern Prose," Aldington also did reviews of recent books: *Le Plateau de nacre, Le Latin mystique, Promenade littéraire,* and *Some Recent French Poems*. Sometimes he did studies of current French poets, whenever the occasion presented itself. Two of these were very good—one on Péguy, another on Tailhade.

Beginning in 1915, *The Egoist* published French poems in the original, such as Paul Fort's "Sur la mort de Hourcade," "Berçeuse," and "Le Chant des Anglais", as well as certain poems by de Gourmont, André Spire, and Stuart Merrill. Notable among the translated works were de Gourmont's "Tradition," done by Aldington; a page of de Gourmont's essay on Lautréamont; and a part of *Les Chants de Maldoror*, which appeared in the issue of October 1, 1914.

Finally, that same periodical, which became the organ of Imagism and of French influence in London, also publicized French painting and music. It was a magazine of philosophy and morals, as well as of art, and with its individualist program, literature did not seem out of place; *The Egoist* was reminiscent of those reviews of the Symbolist period in France, which did not shrink from omniscience.

It was in all respects the liveliest magazine in England at the time; it even attempted a direct exchange of artistic services between London and Paris. Jean de Bosschère published two articles on Ezra Pound in it, and Nicolas Beauduin published one on "La Nouvelle poésie française" (August 15, 1914).

This summary shows to what extent this Imagist review differed from those published ten years before. It exhibited a new and triumphant spirit, as well as a strong French influence: its readers had the pleasure of admiring poetry at first hand, not impeded by criticism or translation. Amy Lowell's book, *Six French Poets*,[8] shared something of both periods—that before 1913 and that after; it consisted of superficial studies of Verhaeren, Samain, Henri de Régnier, Rémy de Gourmont, Francis Jammes, and Paul Fort. The authoress gave ample illustrations from her point of view, but showed little originality and some degree of misinformation. Her book, which appeared in 1915, was of little importance for the understanding of Imagism, but of great importance for the understanding of Amy Lowell. It must be admitted, however, that it reached a much larger public than the other studies which have been mentioned.

In conclusion, if Flint was the most methodical and the best informed, Pound was also useful: with Flint defining free verse, and Pound speaking for the utmost literary discipline, they directed the efforts of themselves and their contemporaries. Pound always affirmed himself by opposition, and his opinions on French literature were stimulated by his dislike for the current English style. Aldington was perhaps the most French-minded, in his critical views, of all the Imagists: he judged one French work by another, and always with a balanced view. The criticism of Amy Lowell was of the finishing-school type, and contained biographical information which purported to explain the works. John Gould Fletcher wrote less about France than the others, but his study of André Fontainas was sympathetic and tasteful.[9]

If one were to make a list of the French writers for whom the Imagists showed the most sympathy, one would start with Rémy de Gourmont; then would come Henri de Régnier or Francis Jammes; Verhaeren would follow, on the vote of Flint and Fletcher, and last would come Tailhade and Corbière. But such a list would not get one very far in his search for influences.

One could judge the rise of these influences in England, and in America, by the state of literary opinion in 1918. The effect of Nordau's negative opinions had all but disappeared, and the French artistic influence was more alive than ever. The war of 1914 had served to heighten its prestige, while lowering that of "decadence." Many were affirming the superiority of French culture, as Aldington did in reply to a critic who was astonished at the increasing vogue of the French: "If I felt as Mr. Shanks does on the subject of French and German poetry I would not fight at all or I would fight for Germany. . . . French poetry is the foremost in our age for fertility, originality, and general poetic charm."[10]

To understand how far-reaching this influence was on Imagist thinking, one would have to see how eagerly they adopted the majority of de Gourmont's ideas on style, literary imitation, and tradition; one would have to hear how readily they judged their compatriots by comparisons with the French; one would have to know that Pound, in defending T. S. Eliot, told a critic to go and read the *Litanies de la rose*, Tristan Corbière, and Laurent Tailhade; one would have to see how Amy Lowell pushed the tendency to the absurd by explaining Robert Frost in terms of the French. F. S. Flint made a practice of reading one French book a day. Pound, Aldington, and T. S. Eliot wrote poems in French; indeed, at this time there was an artistic cosmopolitanism among Americans like that of the Symbolist period in France. Some were attracted by German literature, others by Italian literature. As for the Imagists, they admired qualities in the French Symbolists that they found also in the Greeks, in the Japanese, in Villon, in Cavalcanti, and in Heine: style, image, and sincerity. All in all, they felt they had the same cause to defend as the French Symbolists. Rémy de Gourmont, in *La France*, was not the only one who noticed this similarity. A. Mockel wrote to Ezra Pound:

> Trente ans ont passé sur la littérature et c'est de la folie d'hier qu'est faite la sagesse d'aujourd'hui . . . Alors le symbolisme naissait . . . Tout était remis en question. On aspirait à plus de liberté, à une forme plus intense et plus complète, plus musicale at plus souple, à une expression nouvelle de l'éternelle beauté . . . et surtout "no compromise with the public taste" . . . N'y a-t-il point la quelques traits de ressemblance avec l'oeuvre que vous tentez aujourd'hui en Amérique?[11]

Thus, as Pound saw most clearly, the only hope for American literature was to admit the influence of a foreign language. To those tired of the monotony of

English verse, a foreign influence, a new and different idiom was needed. The French Symbolists had once felt similar compulsions to read English poetry, to counteract the effect of too much Parnassian poetry. "Since the ideas and sentiments of French works differ so much from the ideas and sentiments of American works, I believe that Americans would have less chance of falling into servile imitation and would extract scarcely more than the virtues of the method."[12] Thus Pound expressed himself, in reproaching American writers for their subservience to England, and in the same article, he added that ever since Chaucer "all English poets have gone to school to the French." He soon proved his point.

CHAPTER 3

Imagist Theories

1. THE SYMBOL AND THE IMAGE

THE THREE IMPORTANT theoreticians of this first poetic Renaissance were Hulme, Ford, and Pound. Hulme and Ford attacked the problems of English style with French ideas in mind. Ford, for example, had studied the art of expression in the best French prose writers. It was from this study that he drew his conclusions about poetry and literary art in general. He was also the first, in point of time, of the English practitioners of free verse. His poetry was really fluid prose, in which the changing feelings were expressed by perfectly changing rhythms. He was an Impressionist: he sought to render every tremor of the forest leaves and every reflection of the sun on the water, by an expression as inevitable as possible. It may be said that Ford and Pound were somewhere between the two impulses which, in France, had split into the schools of Symbolists and Parnassians, but which had been reconciled in other French writers, Rimbaud in particular.

It was in the American poet's idea of the Image that the two impulses merged. The Imagists agreed with Rémy de Gourmont, that since emotion was at the root of everything, the poet must try to strike the senses. Through the Image, a fusion of two different things produced by an act of the mind, the poet can convey his emotion intact. With the Symbolists, the image had been partial, an element in the synthesis which the reader must make; it was only by a succession of images that the contours of the object could be described. For the Imagists, the procedure was different: the Image was itself the synthesis; the image, the fresh word, the completely new vision springing from the root emotion was to be directly communicated. For many Symbolists, the image was not an end, but a point of departure toward far-off mysteries. The image had a double sense for them: it expressed a sensation, then by extension, a whole vision behind it, for they delighted in evoking the mysterious. In their use, the image was inclined to disappear into the background, in the process of becoming symbolic. For the Imagists, the image had to be clear, pure, photographic—the center of the poet's thought. It was not to be allowed to remain hazy, but to be admired in all its clarity.

The symbol of the Symbolists was said to be "the affirmation of an essential analogy between a moment of duration of the self and a moment of duration of things."[1] This definition is similar to the one which Pound gave of the Image: "an emotional and intellectual complex in an instant of time."[2]

Thus, between the "image" of the Imagists and the "symbol" of the Symbolists, there is a difference only of precision. The symbolists tried to leave the image vague; they associated partial and multiple images in such a way as to render the emotion together with its overtones. The Imagists tried to make the image precise—sometimes to excess—and, through a total, unique image, to give the whole force of the emotion. But many Symbolists had also made use of total images.

Perhaps the difference was only a difference of sensibility. The Symbolist school had its disciples of Mallarmé, but it also had its "Imagists." It employed the word "Symbolism" to indicate the use of two types of metaphor, different not in their nature but in the rapidity of their association. It was said of the Imagists that "the passing event and its effect on the mind is everything to them."[3] Indeed, this was what Pound's definition seemed to imply: the image was a moment when the maximum of energy was released, giving a clear impression of the poetic aspect of the object. It was this moment which the poet had to seize upon, in order to fix it definitely on paper. Gustave Kahn had expressed a similar understanding of this moment, the name for which had once been "inspiration":

> Since we can only know what takes place in ourselves, we must be
> sure to seize it as rapidly and firmly as possible, in its essence, its form,
> and its impulse . . Hence the necessity for a poetry which is personal,
> immediate, observant.[4]

One feels certain that in 1915 any Imagist would willingly have subscribed to such a statement. However, this moment of pure clarity, when the emotion is transformed instantaneously into the image—this convergence of many lines into a single line—if it takes place in every reader, would not take place with the same frequency nor the same rapidity. Many factors enter in, including ultimately the different responsiveness of the senses. The Imagists, for example, never had their "demon of analogy": "a faculty at once poetic and childlike, of seeing everywhere, even in the most commonplace things, some fixed, eternal Idea 'which looks at one with familiar eyes.' "[5]

Albert Thibaudet has written of Mallarmé's "demon of analogy":

> These tenuous, capricious, tortuous analogies, which are imposed with
> one of the terms removed, so that it must be guessed—these are what
> the most extreme, most fantastically Mallarméan of his last poems,
> the "Tombeaux" of Baudelaire and Verlaine, contain.[6]

and in addition, he says:

> He embodies in his nature many authentic Christian traditions. The
> visible world furnished him, as it might have furnished a doctor of the
> Middle Ages, with the minutest signs of an invisible and real world,
> conceived by a mystical imagination and forced into new life by an
> artistic sensibility.[7]

Citing an Imagist critic on the poetry of Jean de Bosschère (a French poet
who may be considered a virtual Imagist) may serve to illustrate further the
difference between Imagist theory and Symbolist theory:

> Jean de Bosschère does not make use of symbols in the dilettante
> manner of the true *symboliste*. Or, rather, his is an inverted symbol-
> ism; a symbolism which is the opposite of Catholic, the opposite of
> Romantic, the opposite of the symbolism of Stéphane Mallarmé. It is
> much more akin to the symbolism of Greek religion with its adoration
> of the magic *sacra* than to the Christian religion with its unholy
> repudiation of the earth."[8]

Miss Sinclair could have writen the same thing about Imagist poetry, particularly
that of H. D.

The Imagist poets stripped their senses to the bone; their reactions to the
outer world were so alive as sometimes to seem painful; the slightest, most fleeting
event left its trace on them. But it is curious to see where this sensuous hyper-
aestheticism led them. They were attacked in a manner similar to that once used
against the Symbolists. People called the Symbolists "neurotic"; the American
critics called the Imagists "sick":

> They have the air of patients, of people under treatment; they *under-
> go* the things which other men observe or contemplate . . . The
> loneliness in which they dwell is almost polar; they are exiles who have
> actually accomplished the traditionally impossible feat of fleeing from
> themselves . . The man has vanished; what is left is a retina.[9]

It was also apparent to what extremes this stripping of the senses could lead,
if it became too subtle. The sensuous image could become as obscure as the image
produced by too great a subtlety of the mind. It is not difficult to understand this
image of Mallarmé:

> O Miroir!
> Eau froide par l'ennui dans ton cadre gelée.[10]

nor this image of a pool, by H. D.:

Are you alive?
I touch you,
you quiver like a sea-fish.[11]

But when this kind of transposition of one sense to another becomes too subtle, it may be difficult to find a sympathetic reader. These polished symbols of sensation, magnificently devoid of any artificial ornament, concentrated, bare, are sometimes also devoid of any association; they tend to be self-sufficient, to live a life of their own.

Thus H. D. and Mallarmé oppose each other, only to be joined by their relative obscurity. The obscurity of Mallarmé came from the fact that he tried to load his verses with too heavy a burden of sensation, that of H. D. from the fact that she gave only the flash of a poetic moment, only the dominant sensation, suppressing all harmonious associations, keeping only the two essential terms.

2. DIRECT AND INDIRECT PRESENTATION

The words "direct treatment" and "direct presentation" appeared often in Imagist manifestos. It was as though one were once again in France, during the period when poets were hesitating between the Parnassian and the new Symbolist school, arguing among themselves in the same terms. Art, for the Parnassians and Impressionists, consisted in being "direct"; for the Symbolists, it consisted in being "indirect." Mallarmé's purpose was "to evoke the object in a deliberate shade, by means of allusion, never by direct means." But later on, a group of Symbolists in La Phalange used these words again. Royère wrote about Mme de Noailles: "She is desperately direct; she has not the slightest trace of euphemism or symbolism in her writings," and about Claudel, who is of greater interest, "his hyperboles are systematic and his notations are direct." It would seem, therefore, although Claudel's case is somewhat reassuring, these words are fixed in two opposing and irreconcilable positions. The Imagists, along with the Parnassians and Impressionists, were opposed on this point to the Symbolists: they wished to be direct; that is to say, they rejected suggestion and replaced it by presentation.

Symbolism was based on the principle of suggestion. Suggestion was based on the psychology of the association of ideas. The Symbolists were most often content with rather vague connections, some of them ingenious, many of them fantastic, and they did not insist that the initial sensation must come from a unique image. On the contrary, in "L'Éventail de Mademoiselle Mallarmé, " the Symbolist poet, by a series of *associations of images*, suggests the object by slowly evoking its contours and shapes. The resultant pleasure of such poetry is in the atmosphere of dream brought on by the indefinite suggestivity of symbols. "For

Mallarmé, poetry must never paint, always name—and not name the object directly, for that would be, if not to paint, at least to sketch, but to name something nearby or even far away from the object, which will excite the emotion corresponding to the object."[12]

The Imagists never painted; they always named, and directly; and the pleasure of their poetry is not the satisfaction of discovering little by little, but of seizing at a single blow, in the fullest vitality, the image, a fusion of reality in words. The Imagist poem "is comparable to the irritated effort which one applies, say, ... to arrive at the clear vision which the blurred one hints at but fails to give."[13] What for the French was intellectual pleasure, was, for the Anglo-Saxons, physical pain.

Thus, it could be said that an Imagist analogy was an equation of the first degree, one immediately solvable; the Symbolist analogy was an equation of the second or third degree, depending on the subtlety of the poet. The Imagists did not suggest; they evoked immediately, by means of projection. The emotional value of the image depended upon rapidity; it was an instantaneous "click." While the Symbolist images, which were remote, surrounded the subject by envelopment or resonance, those of the Imagists, which were acute and vivid, took it by surprise. Notice, for instance, in the opening lines of a poem by H. D. the vision of the sea presented in a single image:

> Whirl up, sea—
> Whirl your pointed pines.[14]

or in these lines of Richard Aldington, the image of the snow:

> Are the halls of heaven broken up
> That you flake down upon me
> Feather-strips of marble?[15]

Beside these lines, those of Mallarmé seem to take, first a step forward, then a step back, in realizing the object:

> Ce lac dur oublié que hante sous le givre
> Le transparent glacier des vols qui n'ont pas fui![16]

"And in no case is the Image a symbol of reality (the object); it is reality (the object) itself. You cannot distinguish between the thing and its image."[17]

The Imagist analogy is an instantaneous process which captures the object alive, and transforms it in the same act. However, the Imagists defended themselves from the charge of being Impressionists. They never doubted that the artist was an extremely sensitive mechanism, one that operates with faultless precision.

But the artist's mechanism is unique: no man resembles his neighbor; if he uses the same language as his neighbor, he does not use the same images, and there is room for an infinite variety of analogies and groups of images. Because of this faith in the metaphorical power that is contained in the artistic principle of individualism, the Imagists were obviously opposed to the Parnassians and the Impressionists. Pound could be quoted in this connection: "By direct treatment we simply mean to say that once the image is obtained it must be kept from being hung with ornaments."[18] However, Pound and Flint only rarely used suggestion— they were direct and precise; but H. D., for example, used suggestion magnificently. Her images were clear, but she bathed them in a sort of atmosphere one can recall having breathed, but cannot recall where. Her art is extremely delicate; she was too careful about the rhythm, the form of the phrase, and the design of the poem, for her poetry to be read as one would read a satire of Boileau, or the poems of Kipling, or even many of those of D. H. Lawrence. The pure Imagists always avoided the word "suggestion,"[19] which would have seemed contrary to their public reputation. The group had arisen in order to attack the artificial poetry of the day with new weapons, and with principles radically opposed to the artificiality of the time. Thus, they opposed sentimentality by the pursuit of pure sensation; and they opposed Romantic metaphor by the direct, clear, complete image. The word "suggestion"—unless it is understood in the precise sense in which Mallarmé employed it—could be applied to that poetry of clichés the Imagists fought against, quite as much as to Romantic poetry, such as that of Swinburne and of Tennyson.

Even in France, Symbolism, after the work of the first disciples of Mallarmé, also turned toward a less fugitive poetry. Beginning as early as the last three years of the nineteenth century, the notion of poetry as Mallarmé understood it was under violent attack. In *La Plume* for March 1, 1897, this statement appeared:

> Be inspired directly by life. The more we let ourselves be possessed by it, and the stronger our expression of it is, the better will we suggest the idea of life. The more exactly we express ourselves, the more suggestive will we be: great writers have had no other secret. They felt intensely; they expressed themselves intensely; and thus we understood their emotions.[20]

The poets who followed profited from this kind of criticism. In so doing, they did not depart from the Symbolist ideal, but specialized it, forming a movement that tended to wander off into dreams, farther and farther away from the real. Passages from Claudel or even from Kahn could be cited to show that they had a similar understanding of the presentation of the subject. Indeed, it was in Claudel that F. S. Flint discovered, or rediscovered, his own ideas: "In the *Art poétique*, he has also said that his art is based on "la métaphore, le mot nouveau, l'opération qui résulte de la seule existence conjointe et simultanée de deux choses différentes . . ." and the whole of his work is upheld by the intensity of his visual imagination constantly creating new metaphors that have the power of primitive sensations."[21] It would appear, then, that it was following those Symbolist poets who (if one may unite two terms that are opposed only in appearance) made use of direct suggestion, that the Imagists sought to render the intensity of their emotions by a clear, lively, direct image; for so had Francis Jammes, Paul Claudel, Paul Fort, and Emile Verhaeren sought to do already.

3. IMAGISM AND THE REAL

Francis Jammes wrote, in the preface to his *Premier livre des quatrains:* "The poet arrives at an age when he says: the sky is blue, and finds this expression satisfactory." It was to such a simplicity that the Imagists directed themselves. The humblest objects could either draw their tears or charm their imagination, taking on an emotional or picturesque value that had been too long lacking in English poetry. People laughed at Aldington, when he wrote:

> That which sets me nighest to weeping
> Is the rose and white colour of the smooth flag-stones,
> And the pale yellow grasses
> Among them.[22]

One of the reproaches most often made of the Imagists was their lack of passion, to which they replied that for many centuries poets had filled their verses with violent and passionate sentiments, and that it was time for a change of style. "The natural object is always the *adequate* symbol," Pound wrote.[23] Pound, Flint, and Aldington sought to restore to ordinary objects their poetic value, and created, at least in America, a new habit of looking at things. It was this love of everything touching the senses, of everything alive, that they admired, for example, in Jean de Bosschère; and there was known to be a profound sympathy between this Belgian poet and the Imagist group. For him as for them, the natural object was always the adequate symbol. In Bosschère's poetry, objects—a house, its door, its roof, its dining room, its table, the bread placed beside the fruit on the sideboard—all have their symbolic sense. However, they symbolize nothing but their own existence. They lived, for Bosschère, as did the roadside, the olive trees, the flowers in the grass, even the household gods, in the poetry of H. D. and the early Greeks.

The Symbolists loved the image for its mysterious attraction. Imagist poetry, on the other hand, in its quest for the instantaneous flash of insight, for the precise word, was the enemy of all mystery. However, it is in the nature of the image to carry with it a train of echoes, to be so impregnated with emotions that, captured in all its freshness, it is still vibrant with the poet's sensibility. It is difficult for the poetic image *not* to be mysterious. The Symbolists searched consciously for mystery; the Imagists caught it by surprise, by the exteme bareness of their vision.

To return to H. D., and the dreamlike atmosphere of her poems,[24] it must be pointed out that she created it by means other than the image alone. She avoided defining the people in her dialogues; if she did not elaborate her images, she at least made a practice of showing their different aspects, and her dramas were set in distant countries, usually in a Greece far removed from the predictable pastoral setting, say, of Matthew Arnold. Her mysterious atmosphere seems born of the very precision of details; it is a "mystère précis," an "accurate mystery." The minutiae, the precision of her images attracted the interest of the reader, making him sense aspects of things he had never suspected. Common things are thus made to appear strangely new.

This was a logical development of the new Symbolism, being more and more directed to the real, the living, finding there the same artistic pleasures that had once been found in the dreams of an imagination closed to reality.

4. INDIVIDUALISM

The individualist sensibility was accompanied by a need for independence, freedom of expression, and sincerity; by a need for refinement and delicacy as well. The Imagists had, in common with the Symbolists, a highly developed sense of individualism. Clearly, it was in that sense, which took them beyond Naturalism and Impressionism, that the two schools were united. Ford Madox Ford in his book, *Thus to Revisit*, explains this point exactly. He speaks of three related groups, which he calls the Imagists, the Symbolists, and the Vorticists.

> Actually, I fancy that the main point of their sympathy and contact was their desire to impress on the world their own images. Or, let us put it that the first point of their doctrine would be that the artist should express by his work his own personality.[25]

And he continues by reporting a conversation that he once had with Pound and another "young genius," in the course of which the "genius" said to him: "What the public wants is Me . . . Because I am not an imbecile, like the component members of the public."[26]

Pound had from his very first poems affirmed his faith in the vitality, the love of life, the turbulent energy, which enter into his work of art. His whole work is written with force and vigor, with frequent eruptions of astonishing and penetrating remarks. He succeeds best in his short poems, those which contain a concentration of forces in an instant of time.

Pound's confidence in his own powers, which prompted him to reject Whitman at first, later prompted him to acknowledge Whitman as an equal.[27] Pound's individualism is affirmed in other poems, as in the line:

I beseech you learn to say 'I'.[28]

But on this point, as on many others, the Imagists avowed themselves to be the descendants of the French Symbolists. In the preface to *Some Imagist Poets* (1916), one reads:

> The great French critic, Rémy de Gourmont, wrote last summer in *La France* that the Imagists were the descendants of the French Symbolists. In the preface to his *Livre des Masques*, M. de Gourmont has thus described Symbolism: "Individualism in literature, liberty of art, abandonment of existing forms . . . The sole excuse which a man can have for writing of a world which mirrors itself in his individual glass. He should create his own aesthetics—and we should admit as many aesthetics as there are original minds, and judge them for what they are, and not for what they are not." In this sense, the Imagists are descendants of the *Symbolists;* they are Individualists.[29]

However, their individualism appears to take on fresh form, like that of primitives who have just discovered their strength; in this respect, they would not seem to differ from the French Symbolists, who had recognized Whitman as a sympathetic soul. Did not Mallarmé write, in definition of the artist, that he was "l'homme primitif suprême"?

But, like the Symbolists, the Imagists had read the German philosophers, and, spontaneous as their individualism seemed, it was in part the artistic culmination of those Nietzschean ideas which America absorbed in the first decade of this century. It is not without significance that the Imagists grouped themselves in London around a magazine which was devoted to the cult of individualism, *The Egoist*, advertised as "An Individualist Review." It was also in the years 1913, 1914, and 1915 that *The Little Review*, which was soon to become Pound's vehicle of expression, devoted several articles each month to Nietzsche. It was at this time *The Phoenix* was founded,[30] also dedicated to individualism. The Imagists were part of a general movement in the direction of individualism, and they espoused it enthusiastically.

But while the Symbolists of 1880, in their scorn for what they called the world of appearances (which the Imagists called "the real world"), had a tendency to abandon life and seek for intellectual perception, far from sensation, the Imagists thought, with the Symbolists of 1910, that the domain of the senses was the proper one for the poet. Their egoism was a mark of their belief in life, in all its manifestations, and in the reactions of the five senses to contact with the real.

5. STYLE—THE EXACT WORD

Le style est une spécialisation de la sensibilité.
—RÉMY DE GOURMONT

When the Imagists began to write, a style of writing was current in England which was loaded with familiar words and turns of phrase long consecrated by the example of the greatest English poets. This habit, if it can be called a "style," was considered indispensable to anyone who wrote iambic pentameter. Ford Madox Ford, who was, along with Joseph Conrad, the most original prose stylist in England at the time, wrote in his book, *Thus to Revisit:*

> I have discovered this for myself from my own practice in verse. I found that as soon as I came to write a "poem", I automatically reduced my intelligence to the level of one purely childish. And looking one day through the Collected Edition of my own poems that some misguided publisher issued some years ago and that no soul appears to purchase to read—looking them through again then, I was appalled to observe that in the whole affair there were not twenty lines that, had I been writing prose, I should not have suppressed. Everything: every single group of words was what in French is called *chargé* . . . It was not so much that the stuff was rhetorical; it had not the marmoreal quality of true rhetoric—the kind that one finds on tombstones. It was just silly—with the silliness of a child. . . . [31]

In other words, poetry at that time was a poetry of words only; the poet was permitted to pad out his lines with useless phrases, provided that the words were agreeable to an ear accustomed to the Victorian poets.

It was against these habits of laziness that the Imagist group directed its main efforts. These poets thought that the problem to be resolved was that of style. Aldington, for example, wrote: ". . . let me now say from memory what I, as an Imagist consider the fundamental doctrines of the group. You will see that they are all practically stylistic."[32] The Imagists prided themselves on having rediscovered the true criterion of poetry: style, the test of the poet's sincerity.

Their first rule was that it was necessary "to employ always the *exact* word, not the nearly exact, nor the merely decorative word,"[33] and they also insisted on employing the common word. It was, then, neither the Parnassian word, nor the Symbolist word that such poets as Moréas or Stuart Merrill would have sought, the word that was cultivated for its "resonances." But it was the word that Corbière, Tailhade, and Jammes used, and above all the word as used by the great French prose writers, Flaubert and Maupassant, for it was in reading these poets and prose writers that the Imagists formed their taste. But their truest guide was de Gourmont, in his book, *Le Problème du style.*

It was from this book that they imbibed most of their ideas on style. Ford repeated de Gourmont's judgment that the masters of French style were Chateaubriand, Flaubert, and Maupassant.[34] When Aldington, Pound, Amy Lowell, and later, T. S. Eliot, set forth their ideas on metaphor and cliché, or chided their contemporaries, it was often in a way that was reminiscent of de Gourmont. *Le Problème du style,* however, did not prohibit the use of adjectives, and on this point the Imagists may have let themselves be influenced by the Futurist doctrines of Marinetti, although they did not agree with him on other matters. What they prohibited was the overuse of adjectives, as opposed to condensation and direct expression.

The Imagists were pleased by what Rémy de Gourmont said about them in *La France,* May 4, 1915. He acknowledged their descent from Symbolism, saying it was apparent in their horror of clichés and high-flown metaphors, of the sort which "the imitators of Victor Hugo have made us disgusted with forever."[35] Aldington, discussing this opinion, said that the English equivalent for "imitators of Victor Hugo" would be Swinburne, Tennyson, and Francis Thompson.[36] It is easy to see the agreement between de Gourmont and the Imagists on matters of style. They declared war on the cliché, on all that was called "poetic language," on all that was not fresh; the Imagists carried out an intensive search for the new word, the exact word—the word which, springing from the sensibility of the artist, gave his vision precise expression. Aldington cited J. K. Huysmans in further support; "The Imagists," wrote Aldington, wished to use "the word which makes the image, the unexpected and exact adjective which describes from top to toe and gives the sense of the thing it is trying to capture, the color which glistens and vibrates."[37]

Like Rémy de Gourmont, the Imagists thought that "Style is to feel, to see, to think—and nothing more";[38] also like him, they thought that the concrete was preferable to the abstract; and like him, they thought that an idea is "an image, but one that has been effaced and deprived of force." Since sensation was for de Gourmont "at the root of everything, of the intellectual life as well as of the physical life," it was the word-image—a direct transformation of sensations—that the artist needs, and not word-ideas, which are transformations of word-images, or word-sentiments, which are transformations of word-ideas.[39]

They thought it necessary, for the same reason, to avoid joining the concrete to the abstract: "Don't use such an expression as 'dim lands *of peace.*' It dulls the image. It mixes an abstraction with the concrete. It comes from the writer's not realizing that the natural object is always the *adequate* symbol."[40] This is another way of saying that there is no special style for poetry; that in the final analysis the language of poetry and the language of prose are the same, except that the poetic word must be chosen with more care.

Such statements did much to demolish current ideas about style, and caused critics to say that one could find in the work of the Imagists all sorts of foreign traditions, but nothing English.

Thus, there was really only one art, that of prose—or rather, that of poetry, since the poet is the one who must show the greatest care in his choice of words, and must strive for concentration, the fullest sense, the richest meaning. Mallarmé thought there was poetry as soon as there was style. Flint thought that "There is only one art of writing, and that is the art of poetry,"[41] and in that way the Imagists were very close to the Symbolists, who wanted poetry to capture emotion in a definitive, perfect fashion: poetry was to express what no other form of writing could express as perfectly.

No one insisted on this point more than Pound; for him, the difference between prose and poetry was that poetry was ten times more condensed than prose, and for that reason poetry was able to render pure emotion. Prose explained; poetry presented, without commentary. Hence prose admitted a great number of equally good styles; poetry admitted only one, which is definitive in rhythm and in words—the very emotion itself. This idea was not new; it had passed from Gautier down to the latest Symbolists; it was at the bottom of what was called "la poésie pure." All serious poets devoted themselves to discovering this perfect form: H. D. and Pound often seemed to find it; Amy Lowell and Fletcher, through carelessness or neglect of principle, were less successful in their attempts.

For clear vision, and acuteness of sense, they sought a style with definite colorations, which could be engraved in the marble of their verse forever. Such was at least the impression their poetry gave: it contained sensations so alive and so vivid that they permeated the words. It could be said that "their words don't merely convey color to you; they *are* the color."[42]

When, after this sound discipline, they began to develop more complex symbols, the Imagists continued to use words in a way that produced the shock of an electric wire. It was after their technique had been perfected that T. S. Eliot was able to make his successful combination of the nonchalance of Laforgue and the profundity of the Elizabethans.

Thanks to the study of French stylists, the Imagists were able to teach writers of English the importance of style, the principle that "The style is the man." They now knew that whenever there was sincere emotion, there was style: "And, when you find sincerity, style and personality in writing, you have found poetry," said Flint.[43] In 1918, T. S. Eliot, one of the last to arrive, wrote that style could be reduced to "a few simple physical movements,"[44] and he referred his readers to Rémy de Gourmont's *Le Problème du style* for a more thorough treatment of the matter. "The style is the man," one reads there, "is the proposal of the naturalist who knows that the song of the bird is determined by the shape of its beak, the position of its tongue, the diameter of its throat, and the capacity of its lungs."[45]

6. THE IMAGISTS AND MUSIC

Imagist verse, compared with that of Swinburne, Verlaine, or Samain, does not seem musical. Its charm is perhaps in its absence of music: its poems seem to live in an atmosphere where things do not sing, but have a mute harmony, truer for not being sustained by music.

Pound once criticized Swinburne for neglecting the value of words as words, and for concentrating on their value as sounds. The Imagists always avoided direct imitation of music (with the exception of Amy Lowell and Fletcher, who were not pure Imagists), but they often declared the importance of studying music, and Pound thought those poets incomplete who had refused to learn anything about the musical art. Among other things, he held Swinburne guilty of "a remarkable ignorance of music." It was not that the Imagists deprecated music, for they shared the French Symbolists' discovery, through the teaching of Schopenhauer, that music was the perfect art; in essence, the Symbolists believed it supreme because it seemed to owe nothing to the exterior world, remaining always in the domain of the sensibility.

This idea persisted, for some of the Imagists maintained that, since emotions translate themselves first into rhythms and colors, music is the most direct art; but they also felt that poetry could become as direct, whenever the rhythms produced by the emotion were exactly reproduced in the image and the poetic phrase. Pound wrote in this regard: "I believe in an 'absolute rhythm,' a rhythm, that is, in poetry which corresponds exactly to the emotion or shade of emotion to be expressed."[46]

What resulted from this thought was a search, not for poetic composition as understood by Mallarmé, but for a harder individual discipline. The Imagists believed that "A new cadence means a new idea."[47] Each poet had to find this cadence within himself. From this principle, the necessity of free verse follows logically: "To compose in the sequence of the musical phrase, not in the sequence of the metronome."[48]

7. THE IMAGIST POEM—FREE VERSE

The Imagist poem was successful if it presented a single image, not a juxtaposition of images, and achieved the sort of concentration which is the very essence of poetry. It was composed of two elements: the indication of the subject (often in the title), and a name-image.

Successful poems, based on these principles, are to be found in the Imagists' work, or at least poems which come near the ideal. "Papyrus," by Pound, is a good example:

> Spring . . .
> Too long . . .
> Gongula . . .[49]

In the effort to synthesize into a single image a moment rich with emotion, the Imagists discovered Japanese forms, just as the French Symbolists had discovered them earlier, in their search for the clear sensation. The aim of poetic concentration, pushed to the extreme, provided a necessary corrective to the poetry of the day; the Imagists "corrected" poems by reducing them to a fifth of their size.

Having made their point, they allowed poems in the later anthologies to grow longer — at first rather awkwardly, then with more and more skill. But it was on this first principle of concentration that they developed their art of composition. By composition, they did not mean the tyranny of the classical hexameter, or of fixed forms generally. Their form was not determined numerically, by external laws. Just as a single word could be a poem for them, and as twelve syllables were not required for every idea, so the Imagist poem developed according to an interior rhythm, not by being poured into antique molds.

The poem, as they conceived of it, was to be the thought itself, and any modification of the form would be a modification of the thought: the poem was in no case to be a compound of separable elements, each one having an independent value. The poem in their theory is a state of mind, and this state of mind gives the poem its length and its form, drawing it in straight, curved, or broken lines. "The idea engenders the form, as the tortoise or oyster engenders the scales or pearl of its shell," as Rémy de Gourmont had once expressed it.

The Imagist poem could be a revery, prolonged or broken sometimes by clear visions and precise images. It could be a succession of images, evoked by the same object, and sustained by a central image. It could be a thought of the poet, haunted by an image which returns many times and is always the same. The Imagists used the stanza, or strophe, to mark the succession of images. With Henri de Régnier, they thought that the poetic stanza was only a word, only a "prolonged verse, the multiplied echo of an image, of an idea, of a sentiment which reverberates, varying through changing lines to recompense itself at the end."[50]

Like the image which is elemental to it, the poem must spring from the emotion with a definitive movement, clear in its pattern. The Imagists represented the poem as a pattern, not as an arabesque, like the poem of Mallarmé; all its curves were to respond in a symmetry which is not predetermined, but which is realized when the emotion is sincerely felt: "Emotion is an organizer of forms," as Pound once said.

Efforts to prove that Imagism derived either from Poe, or from Oriental poetry (in which the Imagists were greatly interested, but not from the very beginning) have failed. In the same way, efforts to prove that the new free verse derived from the free verse of Whitman have also failed. If Amy Lowell, toward the end of her life, allowed herself to say that the Imagist movement derived indirectly from Poe, because it came from the French Symbolist movement, which in a sense came from Poe, the reason was that some American source had to be given, if only to satisfy ardent nationalists among the American critics. But neither she nor her group founded their ideas of poetic composition on Poe, nor did they ever read him very much. As for what is called the "free verse" of Whitman, only those ignorant of poetic form could maintain that Imagist free verse derived from it. To say that Richard Aldington had read much of Whitman in his youth, and that he saw the possibility of justifying freedom of rhythm by Whitman's example; to say that Whitman influenced French poets—the *Unanimistes* in particular—and that these poets in turn influenced the Imagists, is to say almost everything about the alleged influence of Whitman.

Free verse, then, belongs by right to Imagism, as it had belonged by right to Symbolism. It was the most fertile discovery of the Imagists: the need for breaking fixed forms was such that once the first example was given, this form was not long in conquering all the young poets of America. Whitman had been able to do nothing for them, and this fact is proved by the technique of free verse employed by the Imagists, which owed nothing to him. In 1910, free verse was a curiosity as rare in England as it was in America. Free verse had been transplanted to London by Symons, Henley, and Ford Madox Ford, but without much success. Aldington said that before the first experiments of H. D., in 1912: "vers libre was practically unheard of outside of France,"[51] and T. S. Eliot wrote, in 1917, that until shortly before that time it had been impossible to get free verse published anywhere but in the magazines where Pound had influence. However, from 1915 on, *The North American Review* and the *Atlantic Monthly* began to accept it. Its success had been almost instantaneous.

The Imagists did not hide the fact that they had borrowed their technique from the French. In 1912, F. S. Flint wrote a series of essays on contemporary French poetry, in which he made a study of free verse as it was used by current French poets. He had not himself begun to write in free verse at that time; he had started out with traditional verse, and acquired great dexterity in it. In 1909, in "Palinode,"[52] he had said: "I have grown tired of the old measures wherein I beat my song," but in that whole volume, and even in his following one, he had used only traditional verse forms.

In this respect, as in many others, the Imagists profited by the latest experiments of French poets. Just as they had renewed Symbolism by keeping the essential part of it and suppressing the artificial, they made use of the latest rhythmic discoveries of French poets while avoiding the mistakes of the first groping attempts.

For in France, the art of vers libre had made much progress since its beginnings. It is true that from 1904 to 1909 the subject had not been much discussed. There was even some talk that vers libre had failed. But then, in 1909, Robert de Souza wrote a series of articles which had the effect of manifestos, and revived enthusiasm for vers libre.[53] In 1912, the articles were collected into a book,[54] which was hailed by many reviewers as authoritative. What Gustave Kahn had accomplished through intuition and reason, de Souza accomplished scientifically, aided by observations made with laboratory apparatus at the Collège de France by Abbé Rousselot. Like Gustave Kahn, de Souza had arrived at the conclusion that a vers libre was possible which would keep all the essential characteristics of *vers classique*, but would free it from the encumbrances which usage had made to appear indispensable. But Kahn had not demonstrated the possibility; de Souza did. He showed that what is essential in French verse is rhythm, and that rhythm is impossible without accent. This accent is not, as in English, an accent of intensity, but rather an accent of duration. This accent cannot be fixed (as Kahn had also said); it varies according to the thought and the emotion. It falls on the last syllable of important words, and as the emotion varies in strength, so does the accent vary in strength. Rhyme, assonance, and alliteration make no difference to the accent; when there is a powerful emotion, the rhythm is powerful; this process is a physical law as inevitable as the beating of the heart.

Thus, the poetic line is a basic unit of emotion. Rhythm is present in all human speech, in prose as in verse, but with this difference, that in progressing from prose to verse the rhythm increases in intensity: the accents are compressed; words brought in through pure logic tend to disappear; all that is indirect tends to vanish. The importance of this book, *Du Rhythme en français*, had been to give definite proof to what had long been taken for granted.

It was in this book that Flint found his grounds for poetic discipline. He began with de Souza's principles, and never lost sight of them. He wrote in 1920 in *The Chap-Book:*

> In cadence, free verse or prose, the strong and weak beats of speech fall into a natural order, and the stronger the impulse of the writer, the more marked will the rhythm be. This may also be said in less degree of metrical writing; but in the latter the meter is always there to be juggled with as well.[55]

If Flint was the first expert, Amy Lowell was the most active proponent of free verse, and she pursued her research extensively. She agreed that rhythm was to be marked, not by the number of syllables, but by the accent. She even made some experiments—like those made by de Souza in the laboratory of the Collège de France—in W. M. Patterson's laboratory at Columbia University, and these convinced her that in free verse there was rhythm, because *the time that elapsed between two accents was approximately the same*, in spite of the differences in the number of syllables.[56]

In short, the principle of the new free verse, as practiced by the Imagists and by the later generation of French Symbolists, was that it must be read aloud, that it must address itself to the ear and not to the eye since the ear can hear rhythm even when the rhythmical groups do not have the same number of syllables. It was this principle which de Souza had observed in his book, and which Amy Lowell was intent on demonstrating in her long article:

> ... *vers libre* is ... assuredly poetry. That it may dispense with rhyme, and must dispense with meter, does not affect its substance in the least. For no matter with what it dispenses, it retains that essential to all poetry: Rhythm.
>
> Where stanzas are printed in an even pattern of metrical lines, some sense of rhythm can be gained by the eye. Where they are not, as in *vers libre*, the reading aloud becomes an absolute condition of comprehension. If the modern movement in poetry could be defined in a sentence, the truest thing which could be said of it, and which

would include all its variations, would be that it is a movement to restore the audible quality to poetry, to insist upon it as a spoken art.[57]

The number of syllables remains a very important matter, but the Symbolists tended to neglect it, and so did the Imagists. They knew that suppressing one syllable can destroy the whole design of a poem; but as they no longer counted syllables on their fingers, trusting to instinct instead, they were inclined to speak less about it. In English, the question of syllable count is less important than in French, for English words are not so easily measured as are French words, every syllable of which is pronounced with a nearly equal value. That is why free verse is perhaps more logical in English than in French, since syllabication is less strict; it would seem curious, in view of that fact, that Amy Lowell treated a final unaccented syllable as a "feminine ending," equivalent to the French "silent 'e.' "[58] English, however, just because it is more diverse and more strongly accented, needs a more severe discipline, in order to mold its accents to the rhythm of the poem.

In spite of these differences in the languages, Amy Lowell and Professor Patterson arrived at the same conclusions as de Souza had, showing the progressive gradations of rhythm from prose to verse; and with de Souza, establishing that rhythm was the unit of direct emotion. Also like de Souza, they felt that the link between modern poetry and classical poetry was stronger than ever; as Patterson said, "It is certainly significant to hear in our most recent verse the harp of our ancestors."

If Amy Lowell deserves credit for pursuing scientific studies of rhythm the furthest, she was not responsible for originating the theory of unrhymed cadence, or "free verse." The whole Imagist group, and especially Flint, were responsible for its origin. In the preface to their anthology of 1915, the Imagists were quick to refer those interested in the question of free verse to Gustave Kahn, de Souza, Rémy de Gourmont, Vildrec, Duhamel, Henri Ghéon, and André Spire.[59]

De Souza's book did not provide a ready-made technique, immediately applicable to the writing of poetry. But there were at the time two very practical ideas: the "analytical strophe" of Ghéon, and the theory of the "rhythmic constant" of Vildrac and Duhamel. Of the two, Flint preferred the latter; and he criticized the former in this way:

> . . . his expression, *analytical strophe*, is as bad as that of *vers libre*, and in no way can it be opposed to the *verse;* for many ideas, sentiments, and emotions do not lend themselves easily to this passionate shortening of our breathing — since small rhythmic elements set apart by themselves demand stoppages and renewed respirations; besides, there is a natural physiological tendency to pronounce in one

breath successive groups of rhythmic feet, and the rhythmic content in this average length of a breathing can be called a verse.[60]

Then with greater sympathy, Flint explained the theory of Vildrac and Duhamel:

> A *poetique*, they say, is based on metrical and phonetic relationships. The cadence of a strophe or poetical paragraph is due to the repetition in each verse of a fixed numerical quantity or *rhythmic constant*, which beats the time of the continuous melody. The traditional alexandrine had a rhythmic constant of six syllables, and a line was composed of two of these. But the modern verse is composed of a constant of any number of syllables, plus an element numerically variable, which gives it an individuality closely adapted to the sense. The rhythmic constant has no fixed place in the verse; it may begin it, support it in the centre, or terminate it. A strophe may be governed by one or two rhythmic constants, and although the constant has been given a numerical value, this may be modified by the quantity of the syllables, the only law here and always being the instinct of the poet.[61]

It was to Vildrac and Duhamel's *Notes sur la technique poétique* that the Imagists returned most often.[62] Pound, in speaking of the *Odelettes* of Henri de Régnier, wrote: "There one sees him moving in a direction which anticipates Vildrac." And if one were to ask which French poets the Imagists most admired for rhythm, they would be Henri de Régnier of the *Odelettes*, Rémy de Gourmont of *Les Litanies de la rose*, and finally, the poems of Vildrac and Verhaeren. It was from these theoreticians and artists that the Imagists drew their theory and practice of "unrhymed cadence," or free verse.

The preference for these authors is proof that the Imagists sought strongly marked rhythms, obtained by the repetition, at varying intervals, of the same quantity of syllables: the *Odelettes*, for example, were formed from regular lines recurring at intervals among shorter lines, serving as links that give cohesion to the whole, and perfectly joining together movements which would otherwise be separated. The poems of Verhaeren were obviously in freer verse, but a whole series of repetitions, balances, and equilibriums were always evident in them, assuring a force and harmony in their total execution. The example of these poets proved to Flint and the other Imagists that rhythm was the very essence of verse. The techniques proposed by Vildrac and Duhamel for mastering the art of rhythm were those employed by Verhaeren, and Pound and Amy Lowell thought that they were also employed by Henri de Régnier, in *L'Accueil* and the *Odelettes*.

There was no great originality in the views of the London group about free verse: the *Notes* of Vildrac seems to have been the source of them all. Thus the Imagists declared: "The definition of *vers libre* is—a verse form based upon cadence. Now cadence in music is one thing, cadence in poetry quite another, since we are not dealing with tone but with rhythm."[63] De Gourmont meant the same when he said, "the sense of cadence in prose has nothing in common with the sense of cadence in music: it is a completely physiological sense; one feels the beat of its rhythm. . . ." And Vildrac said likewise: "The music of verse is to actual music what color in a watercolor is to color in an oil painting."[64]

On the question of rhythm and cadence, Vildrac and Duhamel had said: "It is frequently noted, in modern form, that the cadence of a strophe or poetic paragraph is due to the repeated presence in each verse of a metrical unit that may be called the rhythmic constant, which beats time in a continuous melody."[65] De Gourmont had already written that "The common measure being the real number, a full verse must appear at nearly regular intervals to reassure the ear and guide the rhythm. There is no poetry without rhythm, and no rhythm without number."[66]

This idea of the "rhythmic constant" and of repetition (the two ideas are different, but obey the same laws) was appropriated by the Imagists. Richard Aldington wrote: "Free verse is not prose. The cadence is more rapid and more marked, its *rhythmic constant* shorter, and more regular."[67] Much the same thing was said by Amy Lowell, when she asked: "But, in fact what is prose and what is poetry? Is it merely a matter of typographical arrangement?" and answered by defining the "unit of *vers libre* as the 'strophe'—which may be the whole poem, or may be only a part. Each strophe is a complete circle: in fact, the meaning of the Greek word 'strophe' is simply that part of the poem which was recited while the chorus were making a turn round the altar . . . ."[68]

The Imagist preface of 1916, in fact, said metaphorically what Vildrac and Duhamel had stated flatly: "L'équilibre rythmique" became "the perfect balance of flow and rhythm." The Imagists did not give all the methods of combining rhythmic constants that were given in *Notes sur la technique poetique*, but it was true, nevertheless, that for the pure Imagists, this book was the guide. They condemned rhyme for the same reasons the French writers had: "Rhyme," wrote Flint, "is to poetry what earrings are to a beautiful woman—a ridiculous orna-ment, or rather, no ornament at all, a toy trinket added to poetry."[69] They were more sparing than the Unanimistes in the use of rhyming devices. They wanted their verse to depend only on what was essential, that is to say, on the repetition of rhythmic elements and combinations of them, while leaving out devices which were useful only for maintaining rhythm or filling in the meter. Thus they did not make a practice of repeating a whole phrase, in the manner of the Unanimistes:

Tout cela remplit sa songerie
Tout cela remplit de bruit sa chambre.

Vildrac had admired this childlike device in Whitman; the Imagists, who took nothing directly from Whitman, nevertheless borrowed indirectly from him through the agency of Vildrac; however, they did not give themselves over to repetitions as freely as the Unanimistes had done. A quick examination will show the extent of their debt:

1. Harmony between verses:

Et maintenant, devant ce papier,
Et maintenant dans ma maison,
Je suis encore en moi et j'y étouffe.
          VILDRAC, Le Livre d'amour

long, long before we came to earth
long, long before we rent our hearts
with this worship, this fear
and this dread.   H.D.

Il s'agissait de justifier nos pas;
Et puis nos pas.
Il s'agissait de repérer ma route
Sur mon plan confus.
          VILDRAC, Le Livre d'amour

Fruit can not drop
through this thick air:
fruit can not fall into heat
that presses up and blunts
the points of pears
and rounds the grapes.   H.D.

a. Succession of phrases phonetically different but numerically the same:

Et l'on entendait
Le long des boutiques,
Derrière les stores,
Toutes les pendules
Qui sonnaient midi.
          VILDRAC, Le Livre d'amour

You are proud; I praise you;
Your mouth is set; you see beyond us;
and you see nothing.
          F.S. FLINT

b. Succession of lines beginning with the same words:

You stand about in the streets,
You loiter at the corners and bus-stops,
You do next to nothing at all.

You do not even express our inner nobilities;
You will come to a very bad end.
          EZRA POUND

2. Harmony between strophes:
Here, both the French poets and the Imagists obtained their effects by the same techniques: whether by exterior likeness, an identical *silhouette;* or by echoes and repetitions of the same movements in different stanzas, or strophes. Flint liked to give several stanzas the same silhouette, as in "Swan" or "Trees"; H. D. made much use of repetitions and echoes, for example:

If I could break you
I could break a tree.

If I could stir
I could break a tree,
I could break you.

H. D.

Finally, the use of assonance and alliteration was frequent with the Imagists as with the French poets.

All in all, the Imagists added nothing new to the French discoveries in regard to vers libre. Actually, there was very little that could be added to the principles which these poets set forth: only the poetic practice could vary. The pure Imagists did not pursue their research into French techniques much beyond this point; only Amy Lowell and Fletcher tried out all the experiments which the French poets had made. What is important is that the free verse which they developed, out of the theories of de Souza and Vildrac, was well suited to a poetry which aimed at rhythmic expression of emotion, and at concentration of meaning. De Souza had showed that a strong rhythm corresponded to a strong emotion, in a physiological chain. "We beat time to our feelings obscurely, as in cries of joy or of sorrow," de Gourmont had said, and Pound thought that the logic of sensation and of emotion should be allowed to speak for itself. Free verse, Aldington added, "is or ought to be about five times more concentrated than the best prose and about six times more emotional."[70] For all of the Imagists, poetic rhythm was the beat of the heart.

The Imagists tried to restore to English poetry its human value, its spontaneity. They tried to speak in human terms, with no false emotion, so that no artificiality would interpose itself between the emotion and its expression. Gustave Kahn had said before them: "We follow popular instinct; we scan in a conversational tone." And the Imagists agreed with the idea: "Mr. Hueffer says that the unit of our rhythm is the unit of conversation. I daresay he is right."[71]

7. CONCLUSION

The Symbolist school proclaimed that the symbol was the very essence of poetry. About 1885, that was a remarkable intuition: later, modern psychology helped to make it precise. The Symbolists saw in the symbol the expression of the unconscious; the psychologists, Ribot in particular, saw in the image the expression of emotion. The Imagists obviously profited by the findings of psychology. They had the happy idea of making use of it to construct their poetic style.

At this period in France, the same attacks were made against the French Symbolists that Aldington for example made against the fin de siècle poets in England, that they had lost themselves in all sorts of extravagance and intoxications. Fin de siècle poetry was a café poetry, a poetry of the idle inebriate; if the poets were not condemned for their debauches, they were condemned for abandoning themselves to dreams. A reformation had to take place. In bringing it about, the new poets used expressions once common to the Symbolists—such as "deep wellsprings," "soul," "real," "direct and indirect expression"—while correcting certain misconceptions attaching to them from previous use. Paul Claudel and André Spire were the most active reformers. These poets wished to return to the real, above all, to direct expression. From 1890 on, the words "direct" and "indirect" appeared to divide the artists into opposite camps. These terms had been current for some time, and by 1890, painters were divided into the school of the "direct" and the school of the "indirect." Gauguin and Van Gogh were of the "indirect" school; the Impressionists were of the "direct" school. As for the poets, naturally the Parnassians favored "direct" expression, and the Symbolists "indirect."

The Imagists advocated "direct" expression, but their use of words allowed for additional meanings. Thanks to modern psychology, they had learned that the symbol, if it was total, was the most direct expression possible. When the mind expresses itself freely, it does so in images, as is evident in dreams, and often even when awake. Before the Imagists appeared, Claudel and Spire in France had corrected and reaffirmed Symbolism with this idea in mind. Edouard Dujardin followed, making use of the same discoveries. Dujardin succeeded in giving to poetic expression qualities both of precision and of evocation. He invented the formula of "symbolic realism," which the Imagists recognized as parallel to their own doctrines.[72] He brought attention to the symbolic value of movements, gestures, and faces, when they are chosen and detached from the rest of experience by the spontaneous activity of the mind, and thus presented in their maximum reality.

Of course, excessive precision of treatment sometimes impoverishes the symbol: too clear a presentation in words reduces the overtones, the effective qualities of expression. Both the second generation of Symbolists and the Imagists were guilty of this excess at times. But it should be noted that while "direct" expression meant abstract expression to the Parnassians, to the Symbolists it meant concrete expression—the image—and they held fast to this idea. Pound said, with good cause: "go in fear of abstractions."

John Gould Fletcher was correct in saying that "Imagism is not Symbolism, but it proceeds from it."[73] The two movements were opposed at a number of points, but particularly in regard to the meaning of "evoke." The Symbolists sought a diction descriptive of the state of dreams, translating somnolence into words, evoking feelings in a musical revery. But neither Rimbaud nor Corbière, nor especially, Rémy de Gourmont, nor Francis Jammes proceeded in exactly this fashion. The originality and essence of the Symbolists must be seen in their desire to show man more exactly and profoundly than he had ever been revealed before. They pursued an art devoid of artificiality, of learned expressions and false traditions. They sought to strike the senses by word-sensations and word-images; they avoided clichés and trite expressions, even trite rhythms, creating in the process a new rhythmic art. Free verse belonged to them by right; in the same way, it belonged to the Imagists.

In its surprise at contact with the external world, the mind loses consciousness of itself, forgets its familiar notions, and gives itself freely to a magical act by which vision is transfigured. Thus this creation of the free imagination, an act purely human, directly expressive and vibrant with emotion, has the effect of a shock to which the poet submits himself. It is from this experience that Pound drew his formula for the "Image," and it was the faculty for it which artists sought to cultivate.

The facts show that Imagism, at least in its beginnngs, did not owe as much to Symbolism as might be supposed. But it is certain that there was a seed planted by Symbolism which Hulme transplanted and caused to grow in England, and that very soon after it sprouted, the whole Imagist group began the avid reading of French works, where they found that most of their experiments had already been tried successfully.

The French influence was only one among many on the Imagists. Curiously, one may even say that the French qualities found in their poetry had been obtained through the study of other literatures, mainly that of classical poets, who long ago had known all there was to know about rhythm, concentration, and images. It was by the example of Greek poets that H. D. had brought her art to the level of the French Symbolists. It may even be said that those who were least contented with modern literature were the greatest innovators, as is especially true of Pound and Eliot, the former seeking the essence of poetry in the classical and medieval periods, and the latter in the peaks of classicism in all languages, especially in the Elizabethans. On the other hand, poets who, like Amy Lowell, were satisfied with contemporary poetry, whether American or English, and were most eager to combine it with French poetry, succeeded only in weakening the force of the discoveries by their enthusiasm for novel effects.

CHAPTER 4

The First Imagists

F. S. FLINT, RICHARD ALDINGTON, EZRA POUND, H. D.

IT IS MORE accurate to consider Imagism not as a doctrine, nor even as a poetic school, but as the association of a few poets who were for a certain time—a matter of weeks rather than of months—in agreement on a small number of important principles, and who advanced their ideas in the hope of saving poetry from the disease of decadence which had infected it for a long time.

But in associating themselves, they did not sign any manifesto; they did not abandon their individual liberty. From their first anthology on, they were separately identified and even opposed to each other; that is why the Imagist doctrine can only be described by showing its evolution, from T. E. Hulme's ideas to Pound's declarations, up to the time of his Vorticist manifestos. By that time, the most interesting ideas of the movement had been expressed, and Imagism ceased to exist as a doctrinaire school, releasing those individual poets who had been loosely associated in it, and who then evolved independently of one another—sometimes, however, helping one another by uniting their efforts.

Judging them by how well they obeyed the rules agreed upon in 1913, and in particular, the second rule: "Use no superfluous word," one would single out as the truest Imagists: Aldington, Pound. H. D., and to a certain extent, Flint. Amy Lowell and John Gould Fletcher would be put into a neighboring group, for only occasionally did they take the trouble to abide by the rules and be direct; but we would also be obliged to include T. S. Eliot among the Imagists, because, coming later, he benefited by the intelligent directions set forth in 1913, and enriched the manner created by Pound.

It may be seen that the influence of French literature on these poets, even if it came after other foreign influences, had a vital effect: to the poets of the first group, it brought freedom of verse form.

1. F. S. FLINT

Neither F. S. Flint or Richard Aldington properly belong to this study, since they are English, but as they both did much to introduce modern French poetry to the

116

Imagists, it will be well to indicate what their relations were with the American group. Flint was always the disciple of someone, and his role consisted perhaps more in understanding the works of others than in judging them, and in drawing out the essentials for his own work. He began by espousing the ideas of Hulme, from whom he benefited greatly; being at the heart of the group, he was able to make certain of the ideas more precise, and to formulate them; it was he who said, echoing Rémy de Gourmont: "The test of poetry is sincerity; the test of sincerity is style," (de Gourmont had said that style is proof of the sincerity of the poet) "and the test of style is personality." And it was Flint who said, as many French poets before him had said: "There is only one art of writing, and that is the art of poetry. . . ."[1]

Flint played a dual role among the Imagists. First, at the crucial period around 1912, he was probably the Englishman who knew most about the French poetry being written at that time, and it was he who introduced it to his Imagist friends. Second, in studying the schools and theories of the vers-librists that were appearing or developing then in France, he contributed to the founding of a free verse theory appropriate to the Imagists.

Although his authority in poetry declined, his authority in matters of French literature continued. It has already been noted that his studies of French poets were the best informed and broadest of the time. It was his unselectiveness and indecisiveness, however, which limited his influence, for it is certain that the poets who exercised the greatest influence on their generation knew how to accept certain tendencies in French poetry and reject others. But a well-informed man was useful at the time, and his observations were beneficial up to the moment when other Imagists were in a position to choose from the mass of words to which he had introduced them.

Finally, Flint found directly in France the novelty of verse forms that the others had been seeking either in earlier English poets or in classical literature; and from his study of the French vers-librists he drew his theory of free verse as "unrhymed cadence" which the other Imagists, especially Amy Lowell, were quick to accept. This theory, as we have seen, derived from several French works on prosody; it consisted not in grouping words so that each group had a constant number of syllables, but so that each group had a similar impulse, or cadence, which was not obtained by counting syllables but by observing the duration of syllables, and of accents given to certain words. Amy Lowell did say that the free verse of the Imagists derived from the vers libre of the Symbolists, but she did not see that Flint had been the principal agent.

Flint's influence ceased rather early, however, and his role as temporary schoolmaster ended. It was certainly not his poetry that won him admiration. In

1908, this poetry had been clearly inspired by the English and French Decadents, his greatest admiration being for Oscar Wilde and Francis Thompson.

The influence of Ford Madox Ford, that of Hulme, and of the Imagist poets generally led him to abandon this inferior Symbolism, in order to search for a more severe discipline, for a stricter style, and for a freer verse form. In his case, theory preceded practice, while his friends had been developing in inverse fashion. For several years, he practiced the Imagist technique. While Pound, Aldington, and H. D. sought beauty outside the modern world, Flint tried to express in his verse "the soul of London," a thing which Ford had already done successfully in prose. He occupied a place of his own in the ranks of the Imagists, some of whom would eventually render the poetry of modern civilization better than Flint, who succeeded only half-way, his subjects often escaping into marginal themes.

He made excellent translations of Verhaeren and Jean de Bosschère,[2] and his own poetry shows the effects. The volume of memorable verse by him is quite small, and his influence of short duration. However, he is important for having brought the influence of France into the midst of the group which centered around pound, H. D., and Aldington, and he was at one time a serious Imagist, who made lively surveys of French poetry for leading London magazines, and who, more than any other, gave a reasonable justification for free verse.

2. RICHARD ALDINGTON

Like Pound and H. D., Richard Aldington had started writing, and had even found his style, before hearing either of Imagism or of modern French poetry. Before he was twenty, he had formed his style by studying the choruses of Euripides, the *London Voluntaries* of Henley, certain poems of Southey (a poet whom he did not admire as a poet, but as a metrical experimenter), the *Hellenics* of Landor, and the poetry of Whitman. His taste had always been for the purest classicism, though he did not try to codify his taste into theories. In college, the Greeks had been his chief study, because they were the source of that classic beauty so well represented in both French and English poetry. His Greek models showed him the necessity of being concise, of poetic imagery which was concrete and direct, and of a supple poetic form free of the tyranny of rhyme and meter. The choruses of *Hippolytus* provided him with the most perfect example of what he would like his poetry to be. He found similar qualities in the English poetry of Landor, hence his attraction for it.

In 1913, one of Aldington's first poems, "Choricos," appeared in *Poetry* magazine. It was one of his best, containing the sort of intense, harmonious feeling that one finds in Greek lyrics, and with a broad, flowing, and uninterrupted rhythm:

The ancient songs
Pass deathward mournfully,
. . . .
            the songs pass
From the green land
Which lies upon the waves as a leaf
On the flower of hyacinth,
And they pass from the waters
The manifold winds and the dim moon
And they come . . .[3]

There did not seem to be any modern influence in this classic poem, not even
any discernible English influence. It was Euripides that Aldington had studied, but
if he had borrowed techniques from him, they were so well assimilated that there
is no evidence of imitation. He also imitated Sappho, but if an image like
"swallow-dark halls of Persephone" was borrowed directly from her, the Greek
is remote enough, and the emotion of the poem strong enough so that it is not
noticed. This poem, which was afterward cited as an Imagist poem, had been
written before Aldington met Pound, and before he had read any modern French
poets—even Henri de Régnier, the French poet for whom he came to feel the
greatest sympathy.

As has been pointed out, Flint was the last to join the group of "Imagistes,"
which included Pound, H. D., and Aldington, and it was with his coming that
French poetry was introduced into the circle. Pound knew a little about it already,
having associated earlier with Flint and Hulme, but he had not yet begun to speak
openly about French poetry of the modern sort.

That was in 1911 and 1912; soon Aldington became avidly interested in
modern French poetry, where he discovered men who had made the same
experiments as himself. In the beginning, Flint found Aldington and the others
a little resistant to French influence, because of their devotion to Greek poetry.
It was Henri de Régnier who first appealed to them. Aldington read much of this
poet's work, but it does not appear that he drew anything more from it than the
assurance and strength to continue on the road he had chosen for himself, the
confidence that the way was possible, and some new rhythms and harmonies to
try out.

It was when the Imagists, following the example of the young continental
poets, organized themselves into a school, that they found French writers most
useful, both for arguments to support their cause, and for the prestige of associating with them. Remy de Gourmont had already expressed admirably many of the
things which they wanted to say. Like the other Imagists, Aldington made de
Gourmont his master. It was not the poet he admired in de Gourmont—although

the *Litanies de la rose*, which had a peculiar influence on all the Imagists, enriched his imagination with its rhythms—it was the thinker, the critic, the "free spirit." Pound made greater use of de Gourmont for propaganda purposes, but Aldington probably had more sympathy for him and was more greatly in his debt than Pound. He continued his study of him, eventually publishing an essay on his work, and an anthology of his writings with a complimentary introduction.[4]

In the first of these works, he noted carefully the stages of de Gourmont's evolution: "De Gourmont's maturity really dates from the time when he finally learned the necessity for limiting himself, when he abandoned that foolish ambition of knowing and feeling everything. When he made this decision, he gave his tacit acceptance to the tradition of his own race."[5] In his introduction to the anthology of de Gourmont's writings, Aldington indicated exactly how important he thought de Gourmont's work had been for his contemporaries; he showed how it fostered the search for freedom in all forms and aspects. He pointed out how much aid and comfort de Gourmont's individualist philosophy could give to those who were engulfed in the mass mind of their time; he also showed why the critic was so important to the artist, because he prepared the way for creative work. Rémy de Gourmont turned the attention of Aldington toward a particular French literary tradition which included the most liberal works of the French mind: toward the works of the eighteenth century and of the Renaissance. Alldington studied and translated a great many of these.

Aldington was probably the first of the Imagist poets to receive official recognition, or, what passes for it in England, the support of some time-honored institutions, a not inconsiderable honor for a writer who never abridged his freedom of speech. Aldington, along with Pound and H. D., remained faithful to the essential principles of Imagism: he was more classical than H. D., in a sense, for his poetry was more humane, less severe; on the other hand, he never achieved the condensation of the finest poems of Pound, but often attained a notable mastery of poetic form.

3. Ezra Pound

"His true Penelope
Was Flaubert,"
And his tool
The engraver's.

Firmness,
Not the full smile,

His art, but an art
In profile . . .

"Mauberley," 1920, I

Ezra Pound represents, in the Imagist movement, the passion for fashioning a poetry "hard as marble." It was toward an ever purer "hardness" that he patiently advanced, dissociating himself from Imagism as soon as that movement admitted, along with Amy Lowell and John Gould Fletcher, "suggestion" and "spirituality," the vague and the indecisive. But his work had many links with the Imagist school, even after he left it, although Amy Lowell excluded him from a prominent place in her *Tendencies in American Poetry*, because in her personal resentment she wished to lessen his importance. But because he had been the leader and organizer of the movement, his moral influence continued to be strongly felt by the Imagists even after he resigned from official membership. The severity of his principles, his resolute tone, the timeliness of his propaganda had made and continued to make him one of the leading lights in American poetry.

He did not seek originality alone; he had faith in the good sense and hard work which directs a poet toward perfection of form; no one insisted on these essential points more than he. That is why he looked to older poets for discoveries in technique: a certain poem of Rimbaud, for example, might show him the means of attaining the crystalline hardness he sought; another poem by de Régnier might give him a good but incomplete idea which he could try to perfect.

> There are two ways of being influenced by a notable work of art: the work may be drawn into oneself, its mastery may beget a peculiar hunger for new sorts of mastery and perfection; or the sight of the work may beget simply a counterfeiting of its superficial qualities. This last influence is without value, a dodge of the arriviste and of the mere searcher for novelty.[6]

It would not displease Pound to say of him that he was a sort of Gautier: like Gautier, he was an excellent instigator; like him, he insisted on telling newcomers to the art of poetry what they needed to know before they could begin to master it. It was he who drew up the list of "Don'ts" published in 1913 in *Poetry*, a set of recommendations which Gautier would no doubt have found agreeable: at an interval of more than half a century, the same commonplaces, the same simple rules appeared to need reviving, as if at regular periods the errors of the Romantic school had to be corrected by a stricter discipline.

The French helped Pound to make this discipline more precise: his aims were fixed before he became acquainted with the French moderns, but he found in France experimenters who had similar aims, and who had made discoveries from which he could profit.

In the same way that Aldington had sought his liberation in the reading of classical, especially Greek, poets, Pound sought his in the poetry of Browning, and in Provençal literature, into which he had been initiated, while still in America, by his studies in Romance philology. That much is evident in his first collections of verse: *A Lume Spento*, which was published on his arrival in Venice, in 1908, and *Personae*, which was published on his arrival in London, the following year. These were not his first writings; before his departure for Europe, he had written a great many sonnets which he later destroyed. The fact that he had chosen this form, the strictest and tightest traditional instrument, proves that he had always pursued condensed expression and immutable rhythm. But his orientation was not definitely established, until the day when he chose Browning for a master, and he has acknowledged a great debt to that poet.

Readers of Pound's first two volumes admired him for his originality, enthusiasm, and energy. He was already using a language filled with unexpected meanings and strange resonances. Browning and the Provençal poets had taught him the art of intensification, by concentrating the meanings of words, and they had given him the idea of new poetic forms. Browning's influence is evident in such poems as "Mesmerism," "Cino," and "Famam Librosque Cano."[7] Jean de Bosschère remarked in the *Egoist* that Pound was the first to use five Provençal lyric forms in English: the ballade, the sestina, the canzon, the pastourelle, the aube.[8]

He had begun by translating Bertran de Born's "Song of Battle," Pierre Vidal's "Song of Breath," an anonymous "Alba Innominata"; and *The Sonnets and Ballate of Guido Cavalcanti* (published in Boston by Small, Maynard & Co., 1912). Translation, and the translation of these works in particular, was the best discipline that a writer could choose. The poetry of the troubadours was so far from anything that was being written at the time, that there was little likelihood a conscientious translator would use familiar phrases, expressions, and rhythms in putting them into English. Browning and Yeats had made similar experiments, and these two poets were prime influences on Pound's work.

At the same time, Pound introduced a new music into English. He examined classical and medieval poetry with the aim of restoring to English poetry its musical or quantitative measure: free verse itself, to him, was only "the sense of quantity reasserting itself in poetry." He wrote, "when men began to write on tablets, and ceased singing with the *barbitos*, a loss of some sort was unavoidable. Propertius may be cited as an exception, but Propertius writes only one meter." And he also praised the troubadours for their return to a song-poetry. But in none of the attempts which Pound made to adapt the qualities of Provençal poetry did he depart from the natural evolution of English poetry.

It was Pound's study of poetry in the Romance languages, *The Spirit of Romance*, published in London in 1910, which best showed what he was thinking at the moment when he decided to join the Imagist group. He wrote, in the preface to it:

> I am interested in poetry. I have attempted to examine certain forces,
> elements or qualities which were potent in the medieval literature of
> the Latin tongues, and are, I believe, still potent in our own.

In this literature, Pound found the first principles of his own poetry, for the Tuscan poets had cultivated an art that he defined as objective, brilliant, and striking in its truthfulness. "Dante's precision both in the *Vita Nuova* and in the *Commedia* comes from the attempt to reproduce exactly the thing which has been clearly seen."[9] Pound took from Provençal poetry examples of diction which were frank, direct, and intimate, qualities that he saw as continuing in Villon. At the same time, he discovered in these poets certain laws of prosody: the importance of quantity, the art of the *strophe*, or stanza, and the disposition of rhymes.

By means of this study, along with that of certain Latin poets, such as Catullus, "qui avait une conception fort nette à plusieurs mille ans,"[10] Pound formed his poetic consciousness. He even believed, remaining basically a philologist, that he was carrying on the current of European literature: "La France a appris de l'Italie et de l'Espagne, l'Angleterre de la France, et la France ne peut rien apprendre de l'anglais . . . . tel a été le courant linguistique, et tel le courant littéraire."

It was after these discoveries, after his translation of such poets as Cavalcanti and Heine, that, under the influence of the Imagist group, he began to read the French moderns. However, he never cultivated them as he did earlier poetry. In his youth, he had, like any young American, read his share of Baudelaire, Verlaine, and Gautier; but none of these authors, except Gautier, left evident marks on his work. It was not that his first poems were lacking in traces of Symbolism, but that no definite French influence can be found there. On the other hand, influences from the Nineties of Swinburne, William Morris, of the "Aesthetic School" of the late nineteenth century, had evidently been assimilated by him. In some poems, the direct influence of Yeats was to be seen, and perhaps, in the final analysis, the indirect influence of France, but there is little of it in these early poems. More interesting is Pound's own affirmation that, after Browning, the next date in his literary education was the reading of Flaubert: Browning had taught him to eliminate superfluous words, to increase the density of his style; Flaubert taught him the art of the *mot juste*, of presentation, of direct statement.

Then he spent some time in Paris, but his short stay there did not encourage him to learn much about modern French poetry; it was the year of Catulle Mendès's triumph, and neither the poetry of Mendès nor of the academic poets who acclaimed him aroused Pound's curiosity.

Flint wrote of Pound at this period, as we have already seen: "he could not be made to believe that there was any French poetry after Ronsard. He was very full of his *troubadours;* but I do not remember that he did more than attempt to illustrate (or refute) our theories occasionally with their example."[11] Pound has been accused of embracing one idea after another, of submitting himself to every influence, but actually, in passing from the study of the troubadours to that of the modern French poets, he did not change his opinions, and scarcely his influences—he merely changed his examples. The ideas that Arnaut Daniel, Guido Cavalcanti, Dante, and Villon had exemplified could as well be exemplified by Rémy de Gourmont, Corbière, and Tailhade, while each contributed something more—some new technique, perhaps, which could well be added to the assets of medieval literature he had already acquired.

It was around 1912 that Pound became interested in modern French poetry; in the same year, he became foreign correspondent to *Poetry* magazine. In September, 1913, he began a series of articles in *The New Age,* entitled "The Approach to Paris." Pound had suddenly discovered that some French poets had followed the same course he was following, that they had searched for answers to the same questions, and had resolved them in a fashion similar to his own. It was clear that Rémy de Gourmont, who had investigated primitive art, and the Latin works of the Middle Ages, and had made a general study of poetic rhythm, particularly attracted Pound's curiosity, as he attracted that of nearly all the first Imagists. It would be a mistake to make too much of this early series of articles; they were written in haste, and were not entirely disinterested in their purpose. Some of them were based on the opinions of long-time friends of French literature; moreover, Pound himself did not appear to take them too seriously. However, they are well worth rereading, for the just and intelligent remarks they often contain, and because they reveal what Pound and the Imagist group were seeking at this moment. They all believed that Rémy de Gourmont was the cleverest poet in France in the handling of vers libre. Pound wrote, for instance:

> I suppose M. de Gourmont knows more about verse-rhythm than any
> man now living; at least he has made a most valuable contribution to
> the development of the strophe. It seems to me the most valuable since
> those made by Arnaut Daniel, but perhaps I exaggerate.[12]

For Pound, as for many of his friends, the *Livre des litanies* of de Gourmont was a masterpiece; like many others, he studied these poems and imitated them. Like

T. E. Hulme, who had drawn his theory of language directly from de Gourmont, Pound was greatly influenced by the author of the *Problème du style*. But he also read Henri de Régnier, and it may be said that at this time, the Imagist group admired de Gourmont most as a philosopher, but preferred de Régnier as a poet. Pound's opinions of de Régnier's poetry appear to have been borrowed from Flint, and though he was not enthusiastic about de Régnier's free verse, he could appreciate the natural and clear syntax, the elegance, the sort of harmony in de Régnier's verse which he had found before in the medieval Tuscan poets. His admiration for Corbière and Tailhade seems to have been more personal. He praised Corbière for his clear-cut images, his absence of rhetoric, his brusque rhythm, his "hard-bitten" words, his puns, and his intense irony. It was through the example of Corbière that he defined his own principle of style: "The quintessence of style is precisely that it should be swift and mordant." What he admired in Corbière was the density of his thoughts and feelings; his irony was animated by a very rich and humane nature. Pound said with justice: "He is more real than the 'Realists,' because he still recognizes that force of romance which is a quite real and apparently ineradicable part of our life."[13] In Tailhade, Pound admired what he later called "the prose quality of poetry." His views of Jammes, for whom he had only a passing sympathy, were still more pointed; there again, he appears to have been giving the opinions of others, though the force of his originality can be felt. "When the form is new," wrote de Gourmont, "the thought is also."

Among contemporary French poets, in other words, Pound discovered the same qualities he had already admired in the Provençal and Latin poets. In so doing, he had gone a step farther than either Ford, who was aware of the *mot juste* in Flaubert, or Flint, who was well acquainted with the art of vers libre in French poetry, had gone.

Though at first a little reluctant to accept modern French poetry, Pound soon became a fervent admirer of Corbière, Tailhade, Rémy de Gourmont, and, a little later, Rimbaud and Laforgue. At one time, Pound considered writing in French, in order to get his free verse published, but he found the French language less rich for poetry than the English. He soon replaced Flint, who up to that time had been the best advocate of French poetry in London. Flint, as has already been noted, lacked severity in his judgments: though he published a well-informed study of French poetry in 1912 in the *Poetry Review*, he refused to leave anything out—quite the contrary, he unrolled a whole panorama of French poetry, which was admirable as a panorama, but was lacking in critical discrimination. Pound, however, even in his very first articles, upset established opinions and went straight to the mark, approaching each poet with the undisguised intention of extracting whatever was worthwhile to himself and others.

It is difficult to say how much his poetic work at this time reflected his new studies: Pound had evolved toward a style which seems more French than his previous style, but it cannot be shown that one French writer affected him more than another in this process of development. It may well have been the influence of T. E. Hulme and other early Imagists which affected him more directly, giving to the poems of *Ripostes* (1912) an imagery and tone more like the French. The same could be said of the poetic theories Pound was advancing at this time. He owed to Hulme his basic concept of the Image, and Hulme had studied de Gourmont and the Symbolists. Pound had not read the weightier Symbolist writings, which had been directed toward the philosophical nature of the Symbol and the Image, and his own definition of the Image, striking though it was, was no more than a precise formulation of Hulme's thought.

It was in the rhythmic experiments of *Ripostes* that the influence of the French Symbolists could be most clearly seen. Pound advised the young poet at this time to "fill his mind with the finest cadences he can discover, preferably in a foreign language, so that the meaning of the words may be less likely to divert his attention from the movement."[14] It is entirely likely that this advice was dictated by his own experience, and though the power of a foreign idiom has been felt by other poets, none thought of advocating it as actively as Pound.

The exactness that Pound sought in his choice of words and syntax, he also sought in his choice of rhythms: "I believe in an 'absolute rhythm,' a rhythm, that is, in poetry which corresponds exactly to the emotion or shade of emotion to be expressed."[15] *Ripostes*[16] represented a movement toward this exactness of rhythm, this perfect accord between the cadence and the poetic vision, which was achieved in such poems as "The Return."

Besides the Imagist cadences which appear in *Ripostes*, and which seem to have been the common property of the group at this time, for example:

> My City, my beloved, my white![17]

and:

> Tree you are,
> Moss you are,
> You are violets with wind above them.[18]

there are, in this volume, many cadences which are reminiscent of French poetry. It seems that at this period Pound was becoming interested in the free verse of Henri de Régnier. The influence of de Régnier is to be seen in those poems of Pound which move with a rhythm between free verse and regular verse, a characteristic of many of de Régnier's poems, particularly his *Odelettes*. It is also to be seen in the use of regular or equal patterns of lines set above short lines, which serve as hinges:

> The tree has entered my hands,
> The sap has ascended my arms,
> The tree has grown in my breast—
> Downward,
> The branches grow out of me, like arms.[19]

De Régnier's influence may also be seen in poems where the rhythm is set by a group of lines which are repeated at intervals: proof of this influence may be had by comparing de Régnier's "Ode. III," where the rhythm is set by the phrases: "Je t'ai connue, Chère ombre nue," with Pound's "N. Y.," where it is set by the phrases: "Listen to me—attend me—I will breathe into thee a soul." In this poem, the placement of "rhythmic constants" is very close to that of de Régnier, who puts them at the beginning and the end of a poem to achieve a harmonious balance. Pound gave a great deal of attention to de Régnier's method of grouping lines into strophes, as can be seen in "Apparuit," the beauty of which is like a painting, with its colors, its subtly yet clearly perceived images:

> Green the ways, the breath of the fields is thine there,
> open lies the land, yet the steely going
> darkly hast thou dared and the dreaded aether
>   parted before thee.[20]

and the movement of these images is affirmed by a perfectly balanced stanza. The whole rhythm of the poem is in the composition of stanzas, the regularity of which corresponds to the sustained emotion and clear vision of the poem. It seems certain that, before reading modern French poets, Pound knew the value of stanzaic form: Browning, Arnaut Daniel, and the Tuscan poets had given him many examples of the kinds of stanzas possible in poetry. But it is equally certain that the poetic work of Rémy de Gourmont, and the *Litanies* in particular, confirmed his earlier studies. In "Apparuit," for example, though it does not show the influence of any particular poem of de Gourmont, there is evident a literary experience which has created a new rhythmic power. The repetitions of the Litanies are echoed by Pound in repeated syntactical forms, as by the use of the same grammatical construction in the first and last line of each stanza. In *The New Age* series, Pound had observed of the *Litanies:*

> The artist may find these poems provocative, by which I mean that
> they may stimulate his old habits of perception, or they may even
> bring into being new modes of perception. He may begin to think about
> rhythm in a slightly different manner; or to feel sounds, or to gather

up sounds in his mind with a slightly different sort of grouping. He may, it is true, imitate M. de Gourmont but such imitation is scarcely more than a closer study of the original. . . . For those who seek refreshment in the arts, a new principle of grouping is far from negligible.[21]

The only poems in *Ripostes* which can be called "imitations" of French poems— conscious imitations, that is—are "The Return" and "The Alchemist"; one is derived from Henri de Régnier, the other from Rémy de Gourmont.[22]

In "The Return," Pound had sought to surpass the excellent title-poem of de Régnier's collection, *Médailles d'argile*. Pound's admiration for the poem made him wish to produce an equivalent in English, if possible one that would be better than the original. The rhythmical strength of his poem echoes that of de Régnier, and is obtained in the same manner: by frequent pauses and broken lines:

> See, they return: ah, see the tentative
> Movements, and the slow feet,
> The trouble in the pace and the uncertain
> Wavering!

Thus the poem continues, repeating pronouns and conjunctions as in de Régnier's poems:

> Une à une, vous les comptiez en souriant,
> Et vous disiez: Il est habile:
> Et vous passiez en souriant.
> > DE RÉGNIER, "Les Médailles d'argile"

> See, they return, one, and by one,
> With fear, as half-awakened;
> As if the snow should hesitate
> And murmur in the wind,
> > and half turn back . . .

And it ends with further repetitions of the sort de Régnier used, though they are more skilfully handled by Pound:

> Celui-la ruisselant d'algues et d'eau,
> Cet autre lourd de grappes et de bleu,
> Cet autre aile
> ·
> Et celui-ci toujours voile,
> Cet autre encore
> > "Les Médailles d'argile"

These were the "Wing'd-with-Awe,"
        Inviolable.

Gods of the wingèd shoe!
With them the silver hounds,
            sniffing the trace of air!

Haie! Haie!
        These were the swift to harry;
These the keen-scented;
These were the souls of blood.

Slow on the leash,
        pallid the leash-men!

But only certain movements of de Régnier's poem were used by Pound; out of several rhythmic patterns in the French poem, Pound fashioned a single movement, thus increasing the unity of his poem. In view of what each poet accomplished, it would not be fair to judge between them. The two poems remain as excellent examples of free verse in each language, with Pound's poem being perhaps the better executed.

"The Alchemist" is also a successful poem, though it smacks a little too much of the *pastiche*; whereas in "The Return," Pound has profited from the discoveries of others, in "The Alchemist" he imitated almost to the point of parody. He made use of names which appear in de Gourmont's *Litanies* and composed them into what he called a "Chant for the Transmutation of Metals"; this repetition of chains of proper names, accumulating as the poem progresses, and becoming more and more metallic, gives a strange charm to the language.

Ripostes, therefore, contained techniques of prosody which were not to be found in Pound's earlier books; the French poets did not make Pound over, but helped him perfect his technique, making certain of his ideas more precise and strengthening him in his principles as he saw that the French poets had made experiments similar to his own.

Toward 1914, a new crystallization was taking place in his poetry. There was still to be seen in *Ripostes* a "softness" which was not to be seen in *Lustra*, published in New York in 1917. The first years of the war had brought forth new energies in London, breaking out in unexpected shows of violence. Pound renounced the Imagists, and formed the "Vorticist" magazine, *Blast*, which published only two issues: in June 1914 and July 1915. Quite straightforwardly, he made it the culmination of Imagism:

Every concept, every emotion presents itself to the vivid consciousness in some primary form. It belongs to the art of this form. If sound, to music; if formed words, to literature; the image, to poetry; form, to design; colour in position, to painting; form or design in three planes, to sculpture; movement to the dance or to the rhythm of music or verse.

Elaboration, expression of second intensities, of dispersedness belong to the secondary sort of artist.

Vorticism is art before it has spread itself into a state of flaccidity, of elaboration, of secondary application.[23]

And Pound gave as his ideal poetic model the Imagist poem "Oread" by H. D.

Whatever the Vorticist venture represents in the career of Pound, at this moment it was an affirmation of his continuing force. The Imagist movement was being feminized, and the Vorticist movement was a sudden masculine explosion, brief but symptomatic of the time. Pound declared himself against all weakness of rhythm or expression; he linked himself with Ford and Joyce (who were long-time disciples of Flaubert) and Wyndham Lewis, and began broadening his activity in all directions, propagandizing for the new movement and developing verse satire as a medium of expression. He now took a lively interest in Tailhade's poetry, which further whetted his appetite for precision.

He directed his new impulses toward both intensity and precision. There was no better way to express these qualities than by satires of contemporary manners, and this was the vein which Pound began to work. Also at this time, he extended his campaign for French poetry, using it as an example to American poets of the sort of verse they should write. In spite of this vigorous assertion, Pound's poems in *Blast* show very little French influence.

Corbière and Tailhade gave him models of intensity, and a modern style for depicting manners. Corbière was the model for his rugged, consonantal style; Tailhade was the model for simple scenes, or tableaux, ending with a brusque and lashing final line. In "Salutation the Third," the violence of the invective, the vividness of visceral metaphors, the movement that breaks off into a point-blank question—all these give the effect of a poem by Corbière or Tailhade: the brusqueness and violence are typical of Corbière; the images are typical of Tailhade.

In fact, Tailhade may have influenced Pound even more than Corbière. Pound admired in him the same qualities he had found earlier in Propertius, Catullus, and Villon: the number and kind of images, the general freshness of style. With Tailhade, he agreed that the poet brings to language not only new emotions and an original sensibility, but the clear articulation of contemporary manners. One of his poems, in fact, is dedicated to Tailhade: "Our Respectful Homage to M. Laurent Tailhade," (*Blast*, July 1915).

Such was his new manner, from April 1913 (with the poems published in *Poetry*, under the title of "Contemporanea") until 1916, with the poems grouped together in *Lustra*, his collection of that year. "The Garden," in this collection, is especially reminiscent of Tailhade; and so is "Les Millwin": some gestures and movements of Tailhade's "Vendredi Saint" and "Place des Victoires" are repeated here, and even some of the subjects: old women, unhappy married couples, literary vices of the time. His brand of insults would have pleased Tailhade:

> You slut-bellied obstructionist,
> You sworn foe to free speech and good letters,
> You fungus, you continuous gangrene.[24]

Compare these lines by Tailhade:

> Coeur de lapin, ventre de porc, nez de gorille,
> Incarnation des plus saumatres Wisnous,
> Debut de la forêt qu'une gale essorille,
> Étant un pur gala, rayonne parmi nous.
>
> "Gens de lettres"

But most of the poems of this kind that appeared in *Lustra* and in *Blast* are quite inferior to Pound's other poems. If Pound has the gift of irony, he does not have the genius of insult; his talent is for perfecting expression, and he cultivates it best through patience; anger does not suit him. He only surpassed Tailhade in a few perfect sketches, where he fixed some contemporary foible precisely.

The poem which appeared at the end of *Lustra*, "To a Friend Writing on Cabaret Dancers,"[25] was replete with the influence of French poets—Gautier, Rimbaud, Corbière, Tailhade—its movement is rapid, but controlled. Again, the vocabulary of Tailhade is recognizable: "Until the last slut's hanged and the last pig disemboweled," and even one of Tailhade's images: "Vous dont la gorge flotte en amont du corset" is reproduced by Pound in the lines:

> on the up-pushed-bosom—
> It juts like a shelf between the jowl and corset.

Some of the lines have a cadence like that of Tailhade's "Vieilles actrices," but one passage is nearer the satiric style of "Pays du mufle":

> Old Popkoff
> Will dine next week with Mrs. Basil,
> Will meet a duchess and an ex-diplomat's widow
> From Weehawken—who has never known

Any but "Majesties" and Italian nobles.
Euhenia will have a *fonda* in Orbajosa.
The amorous nerves will give way to digestive;
"Delight thy soul in fatness," saith the preacher.
We can't preserve the elusive *"mica salis,"*
It may last well in these dark northern climates,
Nell Gwyn's still here, despite the reformation . . . . [26]

In the beginning, Pound seemed to be trying for a classic satirical poetry, and his interest in Tailhide and Corbière was in keeping with this effort, since the French poets gave him the example of a style cutting in its abrupt images. It is not surprising, then, that Tailhade's style left the greatest mark on his poetry of this period—especially on the poem quoted above, which is full of influences of Tailhade. The influence of Corbière is no less certain, but it is mixed with other voices that are as clear and as human as his—Villon in particular. The influence of these two vagabond poets on Pound has been translated into permanent discipline, providing a constant direction for his style, and is not the accidental appropriation of a moment's convenience. Basically, the influence of Tailhade is superficial, beside the more pervasive ones of Corbière and Villon, but for that very reason it is more easily detected.

Another influence, too accidental to dwell on, is that of Francis Jammes, which is visible in certain sections of *Moeurs contemporaines.* Pound praised in Jammes qualities that are not to be found in his more characteristic poems; for instance, he judged *Existences* as Jammes's best work, "perhaps the best work by a living French author." What he admired in Jammes is more often found in Tailhade: tableaux of manners, scenes of family life.

The poem entitled "Soirée," in *Moeurs contemporaines"* [27] is very close to the scene in "Le Poète," a poem in Jammes's *Existences:*

C'est drôle . . . Cette petite sera bête
Comme ces gens-là, comme son père et sa mère . . .

And the influence of Jammes's style is to be seen in "Clara," another poem of the same sequence, in which each line is a separate sentence, and the poem consists of a series of direct statements. Also, the poetry of reminiscence, reflecting old-fashioned costumes and manners, is notable in "I Vecchii," and can only have been inspired by Jammes:

And he talked about "the Great Mary,"
And said: "Mr. Pound is shocked at my levity."
When it turned out he meant Mrs. Ward.[28]

The same poetry of reminiscence is evident in another poem of this sequence, "Ritratto":

> "You remember Mr. Lowell,
> "He was your ambassador here?"

which ends:

> She was a very old lady,
> I never saw her again.[29]

This brings us to 1917, which is an important date in the evolution of Pound's work. From this time on, it becomes possible to disentangle from the skein of influences evident in his work the more accidental and the more essential ones. But first, a resumé of his career will be helpful.

Pound left for Europe with the sort of literary knowledge which any well-educated young American might have had; he knew certain French poets, including some Symbolists (Gautier, Baudelaire, Verlaine); he was already interested in certain contemporary English poets—in Yeats, to whom all the poets of Pound's generation were in debt, and in Browning, who became his chief master, and whose example helped him to remove the inessential from his poetry. Thanks to the study of Browning, and of the Provençal poets of medieval France, he was able to reform his own meter, perhaps as early as 1905. The study of Flaubert, who was held in esteem by certain English writers at the same time, taught him the value of the exact word, or *mot juste*, and the beauty of the unadorned style, or direct statement. With these influences, he had found his orientation by the time he arrived in London and fell in with the group which had formed around T. E. Hulme. In this group, there was much talk of France, and of Symbolist poetry in particular, as well as of the "Image." Pound prided himself on having had a definite idea of the Image and its role in poetry before reading the theories of the French Symbolists, but he admitted owing much to Hulme, who in turn owed much to Rémy de Gourmont. He began to read modern French poets around 1911, and wrote his first articles about them in 1913, benefiting by some of their rhythmic inventions, and letting himself be influenced superficially by Laforgue and Tailhade, as well as by others such as Gautier, Rimbaud, and Jammes. These poets did not change either his principles or his direction, but they enriched his poetic style and helped him to perfect his verse technique, impelling him to make experiments which were not always successful but were always valuable.

It was not until 1917 that one could see what literary tradition Pound's work belonged to: his tradition was European, with a very evident French flavor. If his poetry were stripped of superficialities, there would still remain a current of Latin influence to which Browning and Yeats were linked, and which has always flowed through French literature. The French moderns rode this same current, and channeled it into many fruitful streams, from which Pound and his generation of American poets took their water of life.

From this time on, Pound agreed with Stendhal that "on n'émeut que par la clarté"—"One 'moves' the reader only by clarity." And he added: "In depicting the motions of the 'human heart' the durability of the writing depends on the exactitude. It is the thing that is true and stays true that keeps fresh for the new reader."[30] From this time on, he accepted the rationale by which Stendhal had condemned poetry, and he regarded Flaubert as the man in the 19th Century whose work was most interesting and the best guide to literary taste. In 1929, he wrote of later French literature:

> Departing from *Albertus*, Gautier developed the medium we find in the *Émaux et camées*. England in the 'nineties had got no further than the method of *Albertus*. If Corbière invented no process he at any rate restored French verse to the vigour of Villon and to an intensity that no Frenchman had touched during the intervening four centuries. . . . Gautier, Corbière, Laforgue, Rimbaud, redeem poetry from Stendhal's condemnation. There is in Corbière something one finds nowhere before him, unless in Villon.[31]

He had by this time decided that the distinction between prose and poetry (as Ford and Flint had already said) was that "The language of prose is much less highly charged, that is perhaps the only availing distinction between prose and poetry. Prose permits greater factual presentation, explicitness, but a much greater amount of language is needed."[32]

The same branch of Latin literature which produced Gautier, Corbière, Rimbaud, and Laforgue also produced the work of Pound. For Gautier, he had held a long admiration. He believed him the greatest of the Parnassians, and believed that Heredia and Leconte de Lisle had only diluted the essence distilled by Gautier.[33] It is true that no one has gone farther with the lyric of direct statement than Gautier; and the phrase "Carmen est maigre" fascinated both Pound and T. S. Eliot in turn, who held the pure diction of the *Émaux et camées* in the same high esteem.[34] As for Rimbaud, Pound was persuaded that he had brought poetry to its fullest contemporary expression: "The actual writing of poetry has advanced little, or not at all since Rimbaud," he wrote in 1918.[35] And in 1929, he had not changed his opinion: "In Rimbaud the image stands clean, unencumbered by non-functioning words; to get anything like this directness of presentation one must go back to Catullus, perhaps to the poem which contains *dentes habet.*"[36] At about the same time, in a personal letter, he added:

"Ce que Rimbaud avait atteint par intuition, par pur génie, je l'ai érigé en une esthétique consciente ... j'en ai fait une esthétique plus ou moins systématique."[37] The poems of Rimbaud which he particularly admired were "Au Cabaret vert," "Vénus anadyomène," "Les Chercheuses de poux," "Roman," and "Comédie en trois baisers."

These poems show, no doubt, how Rimbaud had developed to perfection the poetry of simple statement, which had been initiated by Gautier. Pound's opinion shows how well he himself understood this kind of poetry, and saw its essential value: "Cézanne was the first to paint as Rimbaud had written—in, for example, Les Assis. . . ." Then, speaking of "Vénus Anadyomène," he said: "Tailhade has painted his 'Vielles actrices' at greater length, but smiling. Rimbaud does not endanger his intensity by a chuckle. He is serious as Cézanne is serious."[38] Realism is expressed with such intensity by these two artists, in other words, that it attains a lyric quality, which is lacking in the work of Tailhade, even at its best.

It would be wrong to suppose, however, that the influence of Rimbaud is conspicuous in the work of Pound. These two poets had no common traits of character, and Pound owes to the French poet only a certain manner of expression. He took him as a model, because only in Rimbaud among contemporary poets could he find "such a firmness of coloring, such certainty." He most resembles Rimbaud when his intensity and force of vision are strongest, as in an image like: "their smile full of teeth." This is an image which has the spontaneity of Rimbaud's most characteristic images. At other times, Pound slipped into Tailhade's class.

Laforgue's influence on Pound was of the same nature, though more superficial, perhaps, and more evident. He does not seem to have discovered Laforgue before 1915, when he first read Eliot's poetry. In any case, in his series of articles in The New Age, where he mentioned the French poets most important to him in 1913, he did not discuss Laforgue. But in 1918, in his later series on French poetry for The Little Review, he included him among the three fundamental poets of Modern France.

Pound may have felt ill at ease with Laforgue's kind of subtle irony, for he preferred a more violent satire. He was no sentimentalist, and was not happy singing, as Laforgue did, cosmically desperate songs, to the accompaniment of "pianos in the better neighborhoods." He wrote with justice of Laforgue: "He is, nine-tenths of him, critic—dealing for the most part with literary poses and clichés, taking them as his subject matter—and this is the important thing when we think of him as a poet—he makes them a vehicle for the expression of his own very personal emotions, of his own unperturbed sincerity."[39] But he added, less justly: "He writes not the popular language of any country but an international tongue common to the excessively cultivated . . . ." This may be true of a large number of Laforgue's expressions, but not of others, which were very popular and very Parisian in Laforgue's day.

Laforgue's influence, through the media of Eliot's poems and Pound's propoganda, did not reach America until after the vogue of Imagism; it had the attraction of a more complex poetic style than poets disciplined in the pure Imagist manner were able to achieve. Laforgue would have been a bad master for American poets five years earlier, but in 1917, his influence signaled a new tendency in American poetry—not, however, in that of Pound. For, from this time on, Pound was inclined to divide poetry into three distinct branches, corresponding to its three elements: Images, words, music. There were possible, then, three kinds of poetry: Imagist poetry, Verbalist poetry, and Musical poetry. He understood the second of these types chiefly through the example of Laforgue, saying: "There is good verbalism, distinct from lyricism or imagism, and in this Laforgue is a master."[40]

Of Laforgue's verbalism, consisting of the intertwining of words, expressions, and ideas harmonized by rhythms and refrains, little is to be found in Pound's writing. A few good imitations and translations serve as witnesses to his admiration, however. A prose poem entitled "Our Tetrarchal Précieuse, a Divagation after Jules Laforgue,"[41] is a successful jest, which shows how well Pound understood Laforgue. He thought of Laforgue as a poet whose irony had corrected the cumbrous historical detail of Flaubert's realistic school, and who had fashioned a style common to the highly cultivated of all countries.

Pound's "Divagation" was an attempted reproduction of Laforgue's "Salomé." Pound imitated, in the best verbalist manner, what was briefest and surest in Laforgue, and added a hardness of his own. When Laforgue's style was at its most condensed, Pound translated it accurately, but as soon as Laforgue began to play with words, or digress, Pound corrected him by shortening the passage, and altering the humor of it.[42]

His translations, exact as they are, confirm the earlier criticism of Pound: he did not grasp the poignant melancholy of Laforgue's songs: his greater vigor deprives them of their characteristic tone.

One may find in Pound's own poetry, however, a number of parallels to that of Laforgue. For example, this succession of learned words in *Mauberley:*

> Incapable of the least utterance or composition,
> Emendation, conservation of the "better tradition,"
> Refinement of medium, elimination of superfluities,
> August attraction or concentration.[43]

Or, again, in the same poem, the pleasure in cosmic metaphors:

> He had moved amid her phantasmagoria,
> Amid her galaxies,
> NUKTIS 'AGALMA[44]

Also, one finds Pound using clichés in a manner that makes them "a vehicle for the expression . . . of his own unperturbed sincerity," as he said in praising Laforgue. For example, again from *Mauberley:*

> Unaffected by "the march of events,"
> He passed from men's memory in *l'an trentiesme*
> *De son eage;* the case presents
> No adjunct to the Muses' diadem.[45]

> Conduct, on the other hand, the soul
> "Which the highest cultures have nourished"
> To Fleet St. where
> Dr. Johnson flourished;[46]

> —Given that is his "fundamental passion,"
> This urge to convey the relation
> Of eye-lid and cheek-bone
> By verbal manifestations;[47]

or this remark:

> Knowing my coat has never been
> Of precisely the fashion
> To stimulate, in her
> A durable passion;[48]

Nevertheless, it is possible to say that the poetry of Laforgue has not left important traces in the work of Pound. It is necessary to distinguish "ideas" from "influences" here: Pound's work owed little to Laforgue and even less to de Gourmont; however, his admiration for these two authors was great, and he often referred American poets to their examples. In doing so, he was working for them, not for himself, in order to civilize American prejudices. There is no question that he succeeded remarkably well.

It was Pound who introduced Americans to Laforgue by his translations and essays, just as it was Eliot who introduced him by direct poetic influence. And the qualities which Pound had found most outstanding in Laforgue were the ones most sought after by young American poets.

Thus Pound had studied Rimbaud, Corbière, and Laforgue, and had discovered in their poems the essential qualities of modern poetry. He had acquired these qualities in his own writing without resorting to direct imitation.

If, in the work which he wrote after 1918, the influence of Rimbaud is fundamental, but not at all apparent, and if that of Laforgue is apparent but largely superficial, the influence of Gautier is both apparent and important. From 1913 on, Pound had recommended Gautier to young poets, for language purged of all eloquence, and for hardness of style.[49] His admiration never ceased, and his study of the master of the Parnassian school exerted an influence of great significance on his work.

Between the American and the French poet, there was a resemblance that was more than literary. There was a certain common temperament, a similar taste for the real, a similar passion for life, a similar energy, even a similar propaganda. Their roles appear more and more parallel, their literary influence and their prestige correspond, given the different languages and times.

Pound wrote in his *Mauberley* sequence:

> "His true Penelope
> Was Flaubert,"
> And his tool
> The engraver's.
>
> Firmness,
> Not the full smile,
> His art, but an art
> In profile.[50]

This is precisely the manner of Gautier, and the kind of style which it defined. The comparison with the engraver and sculptor is clearly recognizable as Gautier's, and the second stanza quoted seems an acknowledgement of Pound's debt to the French poet, especially in its resemblance to Gautier's lines:

> D'une main delicate
> Poursuis dans un filon
> D'agate
> Le profil d'Apollon.[51]

The same search, for profile carved from marble, for eternal profiles, was the search of Ezra Pound. His work bears more resemblance in this respect to Gautier than it does to any of his lineal descendants—Rimbaud, Corbière, or Tailhade.

If Rimbaud's poetry may be said to resemble the painting of Cézanne, and Corbière's that of Goya, neither Gautier nor Pound seem to represent any single style of painting; their scenes are almost without "atmosphere": they are precise, in their sharp economy of detail, but they do not attain the eloquent synthesis of Rimbaud's best poems. Both Pound and Gautier see the world as a design of artistic forms and colors, as an arrangement of objects, and both are able to present their symbolic vision in very brief expressions, even seeking a deliberate abridgement of language in order to make the expression clear. Gautier would have appreciated such a scene as this one, from Pound's *Moeurs contemporaines:*

> And by her left foot, in a basket,
> Is an infant, aged about 14 months,
> The infant beams at the parent,
> The parent re-beams at its offspring.
> The basket is lined with satin,
> There is a satin-like bow on the harp.[52]

It was in *Hugh Selwyn Mauberley* (1920) that the influence of Gautier was most evident, and it was an influence which Pound had deliberately cultivated. He and T. S. Eliot, wishing to put a stop to the flood of free verse which flowed from every pen into the pages of the American little magazines, had decided to write, with Gautier as a model, poems in metered verse and regular stanzas.

It was then that Pound wrote *Mauberley*, combining the influence of Gautier successfully with that of Byron—Gautier for poetic form, Byron for vehement tone and descriptive power. Some of the verses of this poem parallel those of Gautier directly; others are Gautier transmitted through Eliot. Some poems in the sequence begin, as Gautier began so many of his poems, with a simple declaration:

> Gladstone was still respected,
> When John Ruskin produced
> "King's Treasuries"; Swinburne
> And Rossetti still abused.[53]

Each stanza in this poem continues in the same fashion. Other poems in the sequence begin by presenting a scene, and letting it determine the tone of the passage:

> In the cream gilded cabin of his steam yacht[54]

Or, to take another example close by:

> Beneath the sagging roof
> The stylist has taken shelter . . . [55]

Finally, Pound resembles Gautier in constructing complex stanza patterns, to accord with the complexity of his feelings. It was by employing well-sculptured stanzas in the fashion of Gautier that Eliot and Pound hoped to check the carelessness that had replaced personal discipline in the composition of free verse. Their success was evident in an increased control of rhythm and diction by American poets after this time.

But if the influence of Gautier is most visible in *Mauberley*, it is present in all his work; it simply does not betray itself by obvious imitation. It is one of those directing influences in Pound's poetic career, and it may be said that the study of the three volumes of Gautier's poetry had as much to do with the formation of Pound's poetics as did the study of the Symbolists, or of Villon, or of the Tuscan poets, or of Catullus.[56]

Pound was certainly the most important poet of the Imagists. He was responsible for bringing the poets together in a group, with the strong intention of submitting them and himself to a harder discipline, in order to purify their style and condense their expression. The Imagist anthologies of 1915, 1916, and 1917 were not edited by him: they were responsible for whatever popularity the Imagist movement had, being better suited to an undiscriminating public than Pound's first anthology, *Des Imagistes*; but Pound never ceased to act as preceptor, and the Imagist movement, though it continued without him, was never able to renounce the principles which he had first imposed, in spite of its majority vote.

It was in French poetry, where the classical virtues had been best preserved, that Pound sought the sort of technical perfection necessary for American poetry. He was criticized for changing his models too often, but it is not difficult to prove that he always remained himself, in spite of changes. When he found a new model, he accepted it only if it suited his tradition, which was that of Villon, Gautier, and Corbière. He did not imitate these authors, as has been shown, but studied them and compared them with the great poets of the Renaissance and Middle Ages, and absorbed qualities of their style. Because he always knew how to see, in every example, what the literature of his country needed, and because he also knew the tone that was needed, he had immense influence on his generation, and, both by his own work and by the introduction of French poets who were his masters, he contributed more than anyone else to giving American poetry the French qualities of style which it now possesses.

4. H. D.

The poet who, properly speaking, might be called the purist Imagist was H. D. Her poetry is as clean as new marble; tradition left no impurity in it. She is completely devoid of old habits of writing. If Fletcher and Amy Lowell were able to expiate their sins, H. D. seems to have been born in a state of grace. Throughout, her work is pure, and like only to itself.

It is evident that in the beginning she carefully destroyed all her poems until she had discovered her own formula, and that perfection was as natural to her as declamatory lyricism was to Whitman. With the freshness of youth, with senses wide open, she saw and touched nature in its most minute detail: flowers, blades of grass, footprints. Her clear visions hold the truth that can only come through eyes not blurred by points of view or by education. Only to see—and "all the rest is literature." There is little music in her poetry, and little verbalism. No example could better fulfill Rémy de Gourmont's ideal of style than hers.

But this poet, extremely sensitive and even a little wild, lacks some of the charms which are the fruit of civilization. The flowers which abound in her work, for all their color and clear outline, have no perfume. The sentiments are all physical joys and sorrows; the pains are what one might feel in touching a thorn; the pleasure is that of breathing the pure air. Her poetry is extremely feminine, but is lacking in sensuousness.

Her temperament required a highly personal poetry, an art without preparation or adornment. The grace and harmony of her poetry is not embellished: it is a naked art.

Still, her poetry breathes the atmosphere of a far-off country: ancient Greece. After all, it had to be born somewhere, and to acquire a certain degree of education in order to survive. The poetry of Henri de Régnier is French, and is content to be found in the Gardens of Versailles; that of H. D. belongs only to Greece, to a world where sensibility was most acute and freest from artificiality.

It was of H. D. and Richard Aldington that the editor of *Poetry* was thinking, when she first wrote that the Imagists were: " . . . a group of ardent Hellenists who are pursuing interesting experiments in *vers libre;* trying to attain in English certain subtleties of cadence of the kind which Mallarmé and his followers have studied in French."[57] It was in the Greek Classical poets that H. D. sought the elements of her art. Among the French moderns, she had read Rémy de Gourmont and Henri de Régnier, who were the only French Symbolist poets with a taste for the same sharp outlines, clear colors, and pure atmosphere. But in her case, one cannot speak of imitation: scarcely any reading or conversation brought new qualities to her work. If one happened to find an image or rhythm of H. D.'s which reproduced an image or rhythm of de Gourmont or de Régnier, one would not be a step closer to proving that her art derived from French Symbolism. It would only show that it was impossible, around 1913, for a poet as natural and independent as H. D. to escape the enveloping influence.

That H. D. and Henri de Régnier had traits in common, may be seen from the following lines, where the images and expressions are very much alike, and produce a similar harmony:

> The night has cut
> each from each
> and curled the petals
> back from the stalk
> and under it in crisp rows . . . [58]

or, again, in these lines:

> I made image upon image for my use,
> I made image upon image, for the grace
> of Pallas was my flint
> and my help was Hephaestos.
>
> I made god upon god
> step from the cold rock . . . [59]

or this harvest of flowers, fruits, and souls:

> each of us like you
> has died once,
> each of us like you
> stands apart, like you
> fit to be worshipped.[60]
>
> They have melted
> . . . .
> each from his plinth,
> each one departs.[61]
>
> Fringe upon fringe
> of blue crocuses . . . [62]

It is curious that the most striking resemblances are found in her later poems, rather than her earlier ones; thus, in "Lethe," and in "The Islands," the rhythms of de Gourmont's *Litanies* are recollected—too sharply in the second of these poems, but very agreeably in the first:

> Nor skin nor hide nor fleece
>   Shall cover you,
> Nor curtain of crimson nor fine
> Shelter of cedar-wood be over you,
>   Nor the fir-tree
>   Nor the pine.[63]

Generally speaking, H. D.'s poetic technique is like that of de Régnier's *Odelettes*, which are among the masterpieces of vers libre, and are excellent examples of the theories formulated in Duhamel and Vildrac's *Notes sur la technique poétique*. These theories stated that rhythm in poetry results from the grouping of certain words into phrases, directed by a natural impulse toward short lines, and from repetitions of phrase, achieving a fixed balance based on the shortest lines in the poem, those which appear most often at the beginning and the end.

H. D.'s "Sea God," for example, is noticeably similar in stanza pattern to de Régnier's "Odelette I":

> For you will come,
> You will yet haunt men in ships.
> You will trail across the fringe of strait
> and circle the jagged rocks.
>
> You will trail across the rocks.
> and wash them with your salt.
> . . . .
> You will draw back,
> and the ripple on the sand-shelf
> will be witness of your track.
> . . . .
> For you will come,
> you will come,
> You will answer our taut hearts,
> You will break the lie of men's thoughts
> and cherish and shelter us.[64]

The internal composition of the stanza is also the same as de Régnier's, with its pauses and its lengthenings. As with de Régnier, a long stanza may consist of only one phrase which has been broken in two, and which tends to unify itself by the force and weight of successive associations, reinforced by rhyme and assonance.

Ceux qui passent l'ont entendu
Au fond du soir en leurs pensées,
Dans le silence et dans le vent,
Clair ou perdu,
Proche ou lointain . . .
Ceux qui passent en leurs pensées
En écoutant au fond d'eux-mêmes,
L'entendront encore et l'entendent
Toujours qui chante.

Each of us like you
has died once,
each of us like you
has passed through drift of wood-leaves
cracked and bent
and tortured and unbent
in the winter frost
then burnt into gold points
lighted afresh,
crisp amber, scales of gold-leaf,
gold turned and re-welded
in the sun-heat.[65]

A prolonged comparison would show other analogies between H. D. and de Régnier in the art of repetition and balance of phrases:

> Think, O my soul,
> of the red sand of Crete.
> Think of the earth; the heat,
> burnt fissures like the great
> backs of the temple serpents;
> think of the world you know;
> as the tide crept, the land
> burned with a lizard-blue
> where the dark sea met the sand.[66]

These resemblances are enough to show that the free verse of H. D., while not issuing directly from the French poets in question, had at least attained the same degree of development, from personal experiences and conversations shared with poets who knew the technique of French vers libre thoroughly. There is also the fact that more resemblances to French poets are to be seen in the verse she published after 1918, which would tend to prove a certain degree of French influence through the Imagists.

As for the rest of her style, even if all her originality is shown in her images and the use she makes of them, nevertheless she might well have been accepted in one of the Symbolist groups. Her art sometimes seemed to be in direct opposition to the Symbolists, whose verse was too often characterized by sugges-tion, vagueness, and reverie, and whose style often appeared very difficult, complicated as it was by nuances of all sorts and by the full use of evocative language to excite the senses. The art of H. D., on the other hand, seems a spontaneous expression, with its simple rhythms and its concrete words. The Symbolists employed their symbols with multiple ambiguities; H. D. employed her images with the greatest simplicity. But the differences are not essential: her poems can be as difficult as Symbolist poems, and if she seeks effects other than theirs, she needed just as much skill to obtain them.

The image—a projection of feeling by means of concrete objects—is the expressive element which both H. D. and the Symbolists used. But, and this was quite evident in her most typical poem "Oread," H. D. transcribes brutally, making her images as sharp as possible, reducing her analogies to two terms only, and muffling all overtones. But in the end, the process was the same, and she used it to the same artistic ends.

The Imagists had been developing, little by little, toward more complex symbols, with increasing overtones of meaning. The same was true of H. D., whose later poems tended to become more evocative. While preserving her precision, she began to express more than physical pain; now, both pain and pleasure produced passion—an unusual combination, but agonizing. The passion of H. D. compares with that of Mallarmé, but is of another order: he was tormented by an ideal of elegance, by the desire to create harmonies of the most subtle and delicate kind; she had a passion for the beauty of nature, for broad landscapes, and for violent actions within these landscapes. Mallarmé's was an intellectual or sensual passion; H. D.'s was a physical passion—hence their difference.

H. D. expressed herself in straight lines; Mallarmé in curves. H. D. used emotive symbols, solitary and always lucidly defined, which could remain symbols and still be appreciated for themselves. While Mallarmé sought connections by means of drifting, transient images, enveloped in dreams, H. D., by her directness, her clarity, her sharpness of details, worked for a sudden vision of truth, or, failing that, a simple pleasure for the eyes. Consequently, there is little in her of the suggestiveness of dreams: for example, in her fine poem, "Lethe," the succession of negatives convince the reader that death does not exist, by an effect like that of a litany.

> Nor sight of whin nor gorse
> Nor river-yew
> Nor fragrance of flowering bush,
> Nor wailing of reed-bird to waken you,
> Nor of linnet,
> Nor of thrush.[67]

What H. D. realized poetically was the intensity of an emotion, not its variety, its resonances, its overtones.

Readers have sometimes found H. D.'s poems obscure. Mallarmé's obscurity came from the subtlety of his associations, the tenuous links between his images, and the multiple meanings with which he charged his words. H. D.'s obscurity came, if at all, from the lack of connections between images, and from the excessive intensity of emotion with which her images often vibrate: being too simple, too concrete, her straight lines sometimes do not meet, whereas Mallarmé's curved lines sometimes cannot be disentangled. Their poems must be read as poems, not as prose, in order to arrive at a full understanding of their meaning. That is proof, at least, that they escaped the perils of Parnassianism, the rules for which made it difficult to express concrete objects at all, because of the restricting principles of "stability" and "immortality."

Mallarmé escaped by means of word-images of motion, which are vehicles of prolonged emotion. H. D. escaped by means of word-images, also, but by images which were palpable, the equivalent of her emotion, and by strong and varied rhythms. Their mutual efforts to avoid a frigid concreteness resulted in a comparative obscurity, but in a fullness and perfection of form.

The poetry of H. D. had a similar importance for the Imagists that Mallarmé's poetry had for the Symbolists. They both fought against the worst qualities of Romanticism: the unrestricted freedom, the rhetorical excesses, the lyric intoxication; and at the same time against the worst qualities of Parnassianism: expression without emotion, facile elegance, false local color, and exoticism. H. D. had an admirable sensitivity, a vibrant contact with nature, without a trace of sentimentality, and she inspired other poets by her spontaneity—especially Pound and Aldington.

Her influence on lesser poets was also great: her fresh style had numerous imitators, who lacked her gifts and her deceptively simple rhythms, and who produced volumes of short verses full of repetitions and minute descriptions. But in contrast to Pound, who corrected taste, made many friends and many enemies, and stirred up passions on every side, H. D. rarely wrote anything but poems, and contented herself with being an imperturbable model.

CHAPTER 5

Two American Symbolists

AMY LOWELL AND JOHN GOULD FLETCHER

A MY LOWELL and John Gould Fletcher followed the French poets, but did not surpass them, for they never were able to detach themselves from the conventions and shortcomings of earlier American poetry. Their concern had been to express the same themes as the preceding generation of American poets, but with the help of techniques popularized by French disciples of the Symbolist masters. Moreover, they were never able to divest their poetry of moral and sentimental overtones, and their admiration for Albert Samain, Paul Fort, and Emile Verhaeren was dictated more by the sentiments and the subjects which these poets dealt with than by their art. They were, in fact, so little free from earlier habits of writing that once their youthful period of experiment had passed, they fell back to easy rhetoric and moralizing, even to imitating once again the poetry of Whitman, whose purely poetic influence was always unfortunate on other poets.

1. AMY LOWELL

Amy Lowell is still considered by some as the leader of the Imagist movement. There is no doubt that, around 1915, a great number of American readers looked on her as the champion of innovation. She had come late to poetry: her first collection of verse, *A Dome of Many-Coloured Glass* (Boston: Houghton, Mifflin, Co., 1912), appeared when she was almost forty, but within a few years she was one of the most celebrated of the new poets. To aid her in achieving public reputation, she had a famous name and a large fortune, and a constitution which exuded energy. This energy was real: she was capable of working for eight years without publishing anything, in order to astonish the public with her first volume. But this first collection of her verse passed almost unnoticed, and it was then that she sought her fortune by joining the avant-garde poets. She met the Imagists in London, and in particular Pound, who accepted one of her poems ("In a Garden") for his first anthology, *Des Imagistes*. When Pound separated himself from the group, she then took charge of publishing the Imagist anthologies in three successive years, 1915, 1916, and 1917, and wrote the prefaces for each of them.

When her second volume, *Sword Blades and Poppy Seeds* (New York: Macmillan Co., 1914) appeared, she became recognized as the leader of the Imagists. That was when the battle was joined between the vers-librists and the classicists. To defend the experimentalists, Amy Lowell wrote articles for the most respected and conservative periodicals in America. She delighted in making public appearances, and she defended her ideas zealously by means of lectures in large cities and well-known universities. Since she loved a good fight, her lectures were lively, and she played an important role in attacking the intellectual apathy of the time. Being diplomatic as well as aggressive, she knew how to take criticism. As a result, the anthologies of the period contained more of her poems than those of any of her contemporaries, but it was principally her propaganda that gave Amy Lowell a place in the poetic renaissance of America.

It was she, more than anyone else, who made the French Symbolists known to a wide public in America. She seems to have become familiar with French poetry rather early in her life, and she could recite it very effectively in public. But she became actively interested in French poetry in London, when she joined the Imagist group. During the winter of 1914–1915, she gave a series of lectures in Boston, prepared in London during the summer of 1914. In 1915, she published these lectures under the title of *Six French Poets*. No study of this magnitude had appeared in the United States since the impressionist criticism of Vance Thompson's book, *French Portraits* (1900). The book performed a useful service, for the authors that she treated (de Régnier, Samain, Verhaeran, Jammes, de Gourmont, Fort) had published almost all their important works after 1900. She spoke neither of Rimbaud, nor of Laforgue, nor of Corbière, nor of Vielé-Griffin, whom she considered as belonging to an earlier period and as not being "modern." She had the right to do so, of course, but some critics wondered why she had included Samain: Flint raised the question at once, but Miss Lowell did not deign to answer it.

The book was not a unified study, either of the Symbolist movement or of the development of free verse. The author chatted agreeably about the lives and works of the poets, but without showing their relative importance in the period or in the movement to which they contributed. Amy Lowell's poetry may have owed something to French technique, but her criticism unfortunately did not; the absence of style, critical judgment, and coherent purpose left little residue of value in her studies. A few sentences from the text will suffice to show her faults: for example, she said of Paul Fort: "Not even Byron has so fine an irony as he,"[1] and of Francis Jammes, she said that he had "never been moved by reason," and that he was "a charming child on one side, and a most lovable genius on the other. But a man of mature and balanced intellect he certainly is not."[2] Her criticism made strange bedfellows: "Zola and Jammes are the only men who have known enough about life to mingle poetry with their 'realism.' "3

The book had little critical value, for everything that Miss Lowell said had already been said elsewhere; but it presented the French authors in a fashion which was assimilable by even the most casual readers. Her frequent quotations, most of which were borrowed from the anthology of Van Bever and Léautaud (from which she recited, with excellent effect, at her lectures) made a great impression on the reading public.

The articles that she published in the newspapers at the time displayed the same virtues, and the same faults, as her book. She had a figurative way of defining ideas which was disturbing to the more demanding critics, but was easily remembered by the less discriminating, for instance, phrases such as "unrhymed cadence," and "unrelated method." She knew well how to make slogans of new ideas. But she deserved credit for having insisted on the necessity of poetic technique, and for having recognized how much the new poetry owed to France: "Before the works of Parnassians like Leconte de Lisle, and José-Maria de Heredia, or those of Henri de Régnier, Albert Samain, Francis Jammes, Rémy de Gourmont, and Paul Fort, of the more modern school, we stand rebuked," she wrote, and added: "It is because in France, to-day, poetry is so living and vigorous a thing, that so many metrical experiments come from there."4 Lest there be any misunderstanding of the origins of the new American verse, she made the point very clear: "Often and often I read in the daily, weekly, and monthly press, that the modern *vers libre* writers derive their form from Walt Whitman. As a matter of fact, most of them got it from the French Symbolist poets, they were nearest to our time . . . ."5

Certainly Amy Lowell's role in the dissemination of French ideas of poetic technique was considerable: she attracted much attention and stirred a great many people up—poets as well as readers. Her own poetic work is interesting for the fact that, from beginning to end, it is a series of experiments. She first gave all her attention to free verse, seeking its essential principle, and showing scientifically that the rhythm of free verse was as sure as that of regular verse. She tried to make her own verse echo the rhythm of music and the movements of things. If her experiments were repetitions, for the most part, of experiments which had already been tried in France, and if John Gould Fletcher was the only important poet who followed her example, it is nevertheless true that she brought important issues into focus.

In *Sword Blades and Poppy Seed*, her second volume, there were thirty-two examples of free verse poems, and three examples of "polyphonic prose." She was already drifting far from Imagism, forcing herself to apply these two free forms to narrative and dramatic poems, and when the Imagist formula reappears in her poetry, it is already corrupted by the search for "suggestion." The suggestive value of words, proper names, and selected details made many of the poems in the collection true Symbolist expressions. She had not yet rid herself of artificial poetic vocabulary, imitating Keats and adopting his archaic expressions often. She rhymed "life" and "strife," "breeze" and "trees," "kiss" and "bliss," and "love" and "dove." Her third volume, *Men, Women and Ghosts* (New York: Macmillan Co., 1916), only continues the experiments already made in *Sword Blades and Poppy Seed;* however, the contact with Imagism had purged her style of clichés and conventional rhymes. She continued to seek a formula for the long narrative poem, and "polyphonic prose" seemed to her the most suitable vehicle for historical subject matter. She treated the historical subject in a new and lively manner, carrying the reader back into the ordinary life of a vanished period. And, as Fletcher did in his "Symphonies," she attempted to adapt musical technique to poetic technique:

> I think it was the piano pieces of Debussy, with their strange likeness
> to short *vers libre* poems, which first showed me the close kinship of
> music and poetry, and there flashed into my mind the idea of using
> the movement of poetry in somewhat the same way that the musician
> uses the movement of music.[6]

In "The Cremona Violin," the free verse translates the sound of the violin; in "Three pieces for String Quartet," the verse transcribes the movement of a Stravinsky symphony. Generally speaking, *Men, Women and Ghosts* exhibits considerable progress in the technique of rendering subtle colors by means of words.

In the period when she wrote *Can Grande's Castle* (Boston and New York: Houghton Mifflin, 1918), she had become interested in Oriental poetry. "Sea Blue and Blood Red," the first selection, uses poems of Japanese inspiration to break the monotony of recitals in "polyphonic prose." In 1919, two years after the *Japanese Prints* of Fletcher appeared, she brought out *Pictures of the Floating World*. In this volume, she produced short poems in imitation of the Japanese haiku, but without rigorously sticking to their form. In 1921, in *Fir-Flower Tablets*, she set into verse some translations from the Chinese by her friend Florence Ayscough, and in the same year, *Legends* appeared, which repeated the manner of *Can Grande's Castle*, but abandoned the histories of people in favor of legends. In this book, she returned to American subjects, making use of Indian legends and legends of New England. Her last three volumes[7] marked a definite return to American subjects and more regular forms; and they were clearly inferior to her previous volumes, lacking the freshness which gave charm to her first volumes.

Imagism According to Amy Lowell

Amy Lowell appears to have had very few emotional experiences; she came from New England, and though she left her region and traveled widely, though her activities carried her far into the interior of the United States, she still remained emotionally in the confines of her library. Her development can be explained entirely in terms of the reading which she did, and the poets whom she met. These influences mingled, but without creating artificial divisions in her work, it is possible to separate them into definite periods.

The Imagist influence was the first and most important on her work. Without it, Amy Lowell would have continued to write for some time as she had in her first book. She publicized Imagism, but she was never an Imagist in Pound's, H. D.'s, Flint's, and Aldington's sense. She did not stick to the principles set forth in *Poetry* magazine in 1913 by Flint and Pound. Her fancy, her love of color and of shining ornaments, makes up the whole of her poetry. She monopolized Imagism, and denatured it, changing the sense given by Ford, Hulme, and Pound to the expression "le mot juste": For the critic, she said, "the 'exact' word means the word which exactly describes it as it is. To the poet . . . the 'exact' word is the one which best renders this suggestion."[8] Pound and his followers thus become "critics," while Amy Lowell places herself among the poets. She carried this emphasis on "suggestion" even further, saying that "Modern poetry is using a different idiom from that of its predecessors . . . If I were obliged to define the dominant characteristic of the idiom in a word, I should say that it was 'suggestion': the invoking a place or a character rather than describing it."[9] Thus she made off with Imagism, and turned it into Symbolism again. This emphasis on "suggestion" helps to explain the importance she gave to poets like Paul Fort and Emile Verhaeren, as well as her choice of Albert Samain to represent the earlier Symbolist school. Her impulse was toward diffusion, while the Imagist impulse had been toward concentration. She employed the convenient symbol, while the Imagist had sought the clear, new, and total image. In some of her poems, she even went so far as to develop a symbol and then rob it of its force:

> My cup is empty to-night.
> Cold and dry are its sides,
>
> . . . .
> But the cup of my heart is still
> And cold, and empty.[10]

In all her search for ornament, for decoration, for the art of suggestion, and in her development of free verse, she followed the example of the French Symbolists.

Amy Lowell and the Parnassians

Amy Lowell began her study of French poetry with the Parnassian school. As she wrote in her Preface to *Sword Blades and Poppy Seed;* "For the purely technical side I must state my immense debt to the French, and perhaps above all to the, so-called Parnassian School. . . ."[11] Many poems in that collection, such as "Irony," "The Pike," and "Convalescence," are simple descriptions in the pure Parnassian manner. Thus the description of the fish in "The Pike" is like that at the end of the Parnassian poem, "Récif de Corail," by Heredia:

> Un grand poisson navigue à travers les rameaux;
> Dans l'ombre transparente indolemment il rôde.
> Et brusquement, d'un coup de sa nageoire en feu,
> Il fait, par le cristal morne, immobile et bleu
> Courir un frisson d'or, de nacre et d'émeraude.[12]

Amy Lowell repeats these images in a somewhat different order:

> Thick and silver-sheened in the sunshine,
> Liquid and cool in the shade of reeds,
> A pike dozed.
> . . . .
> Suddenly he flicked his tail,
> And a green-and-copper brightness
> Ran under the water.[13]

The form of such a poem as "Convalescence" is also like that of Heredia; and it shows what she had learned from the Parnassians about describing human gestures:

> He toils toward the sounding beach, and stands
> One moment, white and dripping, silently,
> Cut like a cameo in lazuli.[14]

However, the imagery of this poem also resembles that of Henri de Régnier:

> Nageur victorieux de l'onde qui l'assaille,
> De l'élan de ses bras et de son corps roidi,
> Surgira-t-il, prestigieux de nacre pâle,
> Nu héros, hors du flot, tout debout et bondi.[15]

What she took from the Parnassians was not only certain techniques and subjects but also the colors and aspects of things. She loved nakedness: a poem such as "Clear, with Light, Variable Winds"[16] is a study in nudity, reminiscent of Heredia's "Bain des nymphes."; "Thompson's Lunch Room—Grand Central Station (Study in Whites)"[17] is another such poem, but it is far from having the value of Gautier's "Symphonie en Blanc Majeur" or Pound's "Albatre."

This Parnassian influence in her poetry disappeared in late volumes. It was, however, from certain nominally Parnassian poets like Henri de Régnier and Albert Samain that Amy Lowell was to borrow a new technique and manner.

Amy Lowell and Henri de Régnier

It was natural enough that at the time when she was experimenting with free verse most seriously, Amy Lowell would have given considerable attention to the French poet whom the Imagists regarded as the master of free verse, Henri de Régnier. Indeed, the last two stanzas of the title poem of de Régnier's *Médailles d'argile* appear on the opening page of *Sword Blades and Poppy Seed*. This was the same poem which Pound, as we have already seen, used as a model for "The Return." It is apparent that Miss Lowell had studied this poem very attentively, for she reproduced its irregular stanza in "The Captured Goddess."[18] The rhythm of the verses, sometimes short, sometimes long, pauses near the middle of each strophe on a short line of two or three feet, then springs onward to the end:

> Over the housetops,
> Above the rotating chimney-pots,
> I have seen a shiver of amethyst,
> And blue and cinnamon have flickered
> A moment,
> At the far end of a dusty street.

Some of the echoes and repetitions are characteristic of de Régnier:

> In the city I found her,
> The narrow-streeted city.
> In the market-place I came upon her,
> Bound and trembling.

She used the same verse pattern in a simplified form in "Apology," where the enjambement at the end of each stanza is exactly like that of certain of de Régnier's poems:

> The stuff of happiness,
> No less,
> Which wraps me in its glad-hued folds
> Of peacock golds.[19]

Compare this with de Régnier's lines:

> Les deux serpents en caducée
> D'autres encore . . . .
>
> Et j'ai fait les plus belles de belle argile
> Sèche et fragile.[20]

In certain of her poems, such as "The Precinct. Rochester,"[21] Amy Lowell's use of free verse resembles that of de Régnier's longer strophes, where the rhythm is nonchalant and full of echoes. For in Henri de Régnier's practice, free verse was "only a prolonged line, the multiplied echo of an image, of an idea, of a sentiment which reverberates, varying itself through many modifications and then recomposing itself."[22]

In Amy Lowell's poem, "The Precinct. Rochester," the impression of calm is a motif which is echoed throughout the poem, as in the practice of both de Régnier and of John Gould Fletcher. It is a characteristic Symbolist technique:

> The tall yellow hollyhocks stand,
> Still and straight,
> With their round blossoms spread open,
> In the quiet sunshine.
> And still is the old Roman wall,
> Rough with jagged bits of flint,
> And jutting stones,
> Old and cragged,
> Quite still in its antiquity.

In her famous poem, "Patterns," she displayed a sureness of technique in handling free verse which was acquired through the study of de Régnier. But one can also see that, whereas H. D. and Pound borrowed prosodic elements from de Régnier and perfected them, Amy Lowell imitated him strictly; her verse is long and sinuous, suggestive, but neither in meter nor in cadence. This strict imitation of the model makes her poem seem dated now.

More even than for his technique, Amy Lowell was attracted to de Régnier for his depiction of the elegant manners of an earlier epoch. Very much taken with the eighteenth century, she had recreated its atmosphere about her by means of objets d'art and bric-a-brac. The same taste is to be found in her poem:

> The clock on the mantel-piece
> Was a gay conceit of porcelain flowers springing from
> fantastic sprigs of ormolu . . .

The smell of clipped box floated in from the garden outside,
   and the sound of a rake
On gravel stirred the silence with an impression of placid
   order
Peacefully repeated through a season and seasons perhaps,
   but the odour of the box was an ache
After the same perfection which existed inevitably in every
   parterre and border.[23]

De Régnier had described a similar scene inside a garden:

Le pendule hâtive et l'horloge au pas lent
Où l'heure, tour à tour, se contrarie et boîte;
Le miroir las qui semble une eau luisante et morte,
Une fenêtre sur l'odeur du buis amer
Ouverte, et sur des roses d'où le vent balance
Le lustre de cristal au parquet de bois clair.[24]

Amy Lowell preferred *La Cité des eaux* to all the rest of de Régnier's volumes. She used it directly in her poem about Venice, "The City of Falling Leaves," in which the same lights, the same colors, and the same feelings are expressed as in de Régnier's book. She also imitated certain of his *Vignettes;* for example her lines in "The City of Falling Leaves":

The little black slave with the yellow satin turban
Gazes at his mistress with strained eyes . . . [25]

are very much like de Régnier's "Le Singe" in *Passants du passé.*

But it is De Régnier's influence on the free verse technique of Amy Lowell which is most worth remembering. It makes little difference whether she imitated a certain image or subject which de Régnier had used; these minor influences, satisfying as they may be to the recognition of one author's presence in another author's work, do not lead very far, and most often they occur without producing any profound influence on the technique.

Amy Lowell and Albert Samain

The influence of Albert Samain on Amy Lowell was to give her a certain sense of atmosphere, but only rarely did it give her the technique by which he attained it. Amy Lowell had a liking for indefinite effects in poetry, such as Samain so often created, and she said of the atmosphere of his poems: "It is chamber-music, as tenuous and plaintive as that played by old eighteenth-century orches-tras, with their *viole de gamba* and *haut-bois d'amour.'"[26] This judgment is vague, but it does describe the impression one generally feels in reading Samain's work. In a poem such as "A Lady," there is the poetry of fading things, so familiar to readers of Samain:

> You are beautiful and faded
> Like an old opera tune
> Played upon a harpsichord;
> Or like the sun-flooded silks
> Of an eighteenth-century boudoir.[27]

In "Music" (*Sword Blades and Poppy Seed*), "The Painter on Silk" (*Men, Women and Ghosts*), and "Nuit blanche" (*What's O'Clock*), the same note of melancholy is to be found. In fact, if "Nuit Blanche" is compared with the poem of the same name by Samain (in his *Au Jardin de l'infante*), many of the same images will be found. Perhaps Amy Lowell also owed to Samain some of the Symbolist comparisons which she so freely used:

> My heart is like a cleft pomegranate,
> Bleeding crimson seeds
> And dripping them on the ground.
> My heart gapes because it is ripe and over-full,
> And its seeds are bursting from it.[28]

Generally speaking, it was the style of elegance which she excelled in, and reading Samain helped her to cultivate this talent.

Amy Lowell and Francis Jammes

Upon seeing South Carolina for the first time, Amy Lowell exclaimed:

> What would Francis Jammes, lover of dear, dead
>   elegancies,
> Say to this place?[29]

The love of bygone graces was what attracted her to the poetry of Jammes, as it had to that of Samain. She understood instinctively his nostalgia for the period of the early eighteenth century. The charm of such a poem as her "Roxbury Garden" is in the evocation of old gardens, old interiors, and little girls playing with hoops:

> The tall clock is striking twelve;
> And the little girls stop to watch it,
> And the big ships rocking in a half-circle
> Above the dial.
> Twelve o'clock!
> Down the side steps

Go the little girls,
Under their big round straw hats . . .
Twelve o'clock!
An hour yet before dinner.
Mother is busy in the still-room,
And Hannah is making gingerbread.[30]

Such lines are very reminiscent of Jammes' "J'écris dans un vieux kiosque."

The influence of Jammes is also clear in certain small phrases and minute descriptions of "The Precinct. Rochester":

The Dean is in the Chapter House;
He is reading the architect's bill
For the completed restoration of the Cathedral.
He will have ripe gooseberries for supper,
And then he will walk up and down the path
By the wall,
And admire the snapdragons and dahlias,
Thinking how quiet and peaceful
The garden is.[31]

Since Amy Lowell was seeking the formula for a narrative poem, she was naturally attracted to the work of Jammes. She remarked how, in Jammes's *Jean de Noarrieu*, the beauty of descriptive passages broke the monotony of the narration: "But what is really interesting in the poem is the long succession of pictures of landscapes, and places, and labours. The book smells of hay, and freshly dug earth, and the sweet breath of cows."[32] A little of this flavor is to be seen in her "Pickthorn Manor" and "Cremona Violin" (both in *Men, Women and Ghosts*). The first of these paints scenes like those of *Jean de Noarrieu*, and the interiors of the second recall those of other Jammes poems.

Jammes's influence did not result in a single remarkable poem of Amy Lowell's work; it is evident in certain techniques which she can scarcely be said to have improved upon, and which are irritating in the way that some of Jammes's less successful poems are irritating—for their triviality.

Amy Lowell and Rémy de Gourmont

The influence of de Gourmont on Amy Lowell was slight, though she had great admiration for him, and even gave him financial support (without revealing her name) during a period in his life when he was in need of help.[33] She made much of de Gourmont in her *Six French Poets*, although she admitted that for his poetic work alone he did not deserve a place among the most important writers of his time. But she echoed the rhythms of his *Litanies*, which the whole Imagist school had found so appealing:

Venice anadyomene! City of reflections! A cloud of rose and
violet poised upon a changing sea. City of soft waters washing marble
stairways, of feet moving over stones with the continuous sound of
slipping water. Floating, wavering city . . . [34]

She even borrowed from de Gourmont, on one occasion, the expression "vert
lunaire," translating it into English as "moongreen." Regrettably, she was not
often inspired by such delicate coloring as de Gourmont practiced, which might
have softened her violent use of colors.

One of her most famous poems, "Lilacs," is also in the style of de Gourmont's *Litanies*, although its vigorous rhythm is quite different from the delicate
movement of the French poem. However, the means of establishing rhythm at
the beginning and end of each strophe is exactly like that of Rémy de Gourmont
in the *Litanies*.

Lilacs,
False, blue,
White,
Purple,
Color of lilac!

Amy Lowell and Paul Fort

The influence of Rémy de Gourmont is very complex, and cannot easily be
isolated: it made its impression on a whole generation. His *Litanies*, in particular,
gave a number of American poets the sort of rhythmical technique they seemed
to need. What he said about vers libre was read and repeated everywhere:
American free verse owes him a surprising debt, in view of the small number of
his poems.

But to speak of the influence of Paul Fort on Amy Lowell is to speak of two
minds that are very sympathetic, and the influence of Fort's *Ballades
françaises* on her work was of the greatest importance. Around 1914, Paul Fort
was hardly known in America. When he was chosen "Prince of Poets" in 1912,
some periodicals mentioned the event with astonishment, wondering why the title
had not been given to Rostand. The *Literary Digest*, for example, wrote of the
election: "Paul Fort, a poet whom few in this country are likely to have ever heard
of, has been elected to the station of 'Prince of Poets' . . . The constituency, which
finds its local habitation in the cafés on the left bank of the Seine, consists of five
hundred men and women of letters."[35] In 1914, Fort was so little known in
America that Amy Lowell remarked on the fact that not a single one of his books
could be found on the shelves of the Boston Public Library. However, in 1919

his new books were noticed and criticized by all the important reviews, and *Poetry* spoke of him as "one of the best known among the French poets . . . a man of whom everyone has read something." During these years, Fort had done nothing to extend his fame, except to be discovered by Amy Lowell. She always tried to persuade her countrymen that Fort was the most French of French poets, and also the most readable. From the time of her first book of modern poems, *Sword Blades and Poppy Seed*, she had avowed her debt to him:

> Three of these poems are written in a form which, so far as I know, has never before been attempted in English. M. Paul Fort is its inventor, and the results it has yielded to him are most beautiful and satisfactory. Perhaps it is more suited to the French language than to the English. But I found it the only medium in which these particular poems could be written. It is a fluid and changing form, now prose, now verse, and permitting a great variety of treatment.[36]

Her explanation followed that which Fort himself had made of his style: "J'ai cherché un style pouvant passer, au gré de l'émotion, de la prose au vers et du vers à la prose . . . la prose, la prose rythmée, le vers ne sont qu'un seul instrument gradué."[37]

Paul Fort wrote what was nearly regular verse, printed in an irregular manner; but certain of his poems followed the irregular and changing design which Amy Lowell admired—for example, his "Henry III," "Monthléry la Bataille," "Coxcomb," and "Le Roman de Louis XI." She owed her own flexible technique to this rather accidental method of Fort. She always admitted her debt to Fort, though there were some critics who attributed her "polyphonic prose" to Whitman, particularly to the "Song of Myself." Of course, poetic prose was one of the solutions long proposed by writers who sought a free expressive form with all the virtues of verse. Baudelaire was perhaps the first to try out this technique, and in the preface to his *Petits poèmes en prose*, he wrote:

> Quel est celui de nous qui n'a pas dans ses jours d'ambition, rêvé le miracle d'une prose poétique, musicale, sans rythme et sans rime, assez souple et assez heurtée pour s'adapter aux mouvements lyriques de l'âme, aux ondulations de la rêverie, aux soubresauts de la conscience?

And Baudelaire had American disciples in this form: in 1915, a collection of poems appeared in Philadelphia which imitated his method, while even earlier, James Huneker had experimented with Baudelaire's "prose poem."

But whereas the "prose poem" makes little use of either rhyme or meter, the poems of Fort employed these two poetic devices as much as classical poems had. The "prose poem," as Baudelaire developed it, was not completely satisfactory, since it lacked a prevailing rhythm. But soon the Symbolists sought a theory of vers libre, and found a variety of rhythmic variations possible, some of which were very near to the form which Paul Fort later used, and which Amy Lowell adapted in 1914. She was aware of the earlier experiments, and wrote that, in addition to free verse, "The second characteristic modern form, and the only one really deserving the epithet 'new,' is 'polyphonic prose.' " She went on to define this form as "the freest, the most elastic of forms, for it follows at will any, and all of the rules which guide other forms." And, after explaining that the form had been developed in the Eighties and Nineties by Saint-Pol-Roux and Paul Fort, she maintained that "in taking over the form invented by Saint-Pol-Roux and Paul Fort, I have had so to adapt and alter it as to make it practically a new form."[38]

What made the difference between the "polyphonic prose" of Amy Lowell and the idiom of Paul Fort was the fact that he based his rhythm on the French alexandrine, and she based hers on oratorical prose. Amy Lowell, however, borrowed from the French poet all the tricks which he used to ornament his style: repetitions, refrains, the contrast of passages of verse with passages of prose. She even went so far as to say that "repetition is the most characteristic trait of poetry," and added, that "the characteristic is so clear that the distinction between prose and poetry may be said to consist more of the repetition of certain groups of words than in the length of rhythm."[39]

It may be said of three poems in *Sword Blades and Poppy Seed*—"In a Castle," "The Forsaken," and "The Basket"—that repetition serves as the basis of the composition. A line may be repeated once or twice in each strophe to establish the unity of rhythm, then, in the following stanza, it may appear again in an identical or slightly altered form, tending to bring together the separate strophes, much as a melody in a symphonic composition might do. The process is more evident in "The Forsaken" than in the other poems, but it must be remarked that Paul Fort seldom used the technique of repetition in so primitive a manner as Amy Lowell. In general, he took two or three lines as a rhythmical unit, and these two or three lines were then echoed in each strophe. Amy Lowell used a similar method in many of her poems, as may be seen by comparing her "The Basket" with Fort's "La Pêche miraculeuse," citing the principal motifs of each:

> The air is silver and pearl, for the night is liquid with moonlight.
> See how the roof glitters, like ice!
> . . . beside it stand two geraniums, purple because the light is
> silver-blue, to-night.
> The bellying clouds swing over the housetops.

These elements reappear in the following way:

> The silver-blue moonlight makes the geraniums purple, and
> the roof shines like ice.
> ...... The bellying clouds are red as they swing over the
> housetops.
> ...... The air is of silver and pearl, for the night is liquid
> with moonlight.
> ... He sees the silver-blue moonlight, and set in it, over
> his head, staring and flickering, eyes of geranium red.

Fort's more rhythmical use of repetition may be seen:

> Maître Olivier, puceau, faisait le guet sur la berge,
> à grandes enjambées froissant l'herbe ...
> Maître Olivier, puceau, avait l'esprit ailleurs ...
> Les asticots filaient, filaient ...
> Et les goujons spirituels, battant
> des ouïes, applaudissaient.
> Maître Olivier, puceau, faisait le guet sur l'herbe.
>
> "Roman de Louis XI," *Ballades françaises*, I

The repeated elements reappear at the beginning, middle, or end of the strophes, customarily, though with both poets they may appear isolated between strophes—a practice which Paul Fort uses more often than Amy Lowell, as may be seen by comparing the same poem, "The Basket," with Fort's "Henri III."

Certainly Miss Lowell understood well what this essentially fluid and versatile form could accomplish, especially in the expression of changing moods. She recognized that it was best suited to narrative and dramatic poems, where each person and each action could be given the treatment most appropriate to it. For this purpose, she studied, translated and imitated Fort's "Henri III" in detail, using it as a model for the "polyphonic prose" narrative of "In a Castle," where she told a different story, but used the same descriptive details and the same stylistic method.

She had admired the way Fort introduced his poem: "notice how the tone is given by the first lines: 'Les rideaux des croisées sont clos. Les meubles dorment'; and a little farther on, 'Trois petites flammes bleues dansent sur le foyer ... Plus rien. L'obscurité chasse les quatre murs.' "[40] She used a similar opening in her own poem, and a similar setting:

> Over the yawning chimney hangs the fog. Drip—hiss—drip—hiss fall
> the raindrops on the oaken log which turns, and steams, and smokes
> the ceiling beams. Drip—hiss—the rain never stops.[41]

In "Henri III," Fort recounted the visit of the king to Catherine after having a hallucination that the Valois had been riding on the wall of his room. The bed figures in the center of the scene, and from this bed Henri envisions the terrifying cavalcade. In Amy Lowell's poem, the bed is also central to the story: the Chevalier has made love to his mistress there, and now sees her in the arms of another. The thematic phrases, as they appear in Amy Lowell's poem, and in her translation of Fort's poem, are comparable:

Henri III	In a Castle
The bed, all shivering, gives a human wail . . .	The wide state bed shivers beneath its velvet coverlet . . .
Sometimes the royal bed gives a long moan . . .	The state bed shivers in the watery dawn . . .
The room, where everything wavers, is a prey to phantoms.	The room is filled with lisps and whispers . . .
. . . the iron of a halyard, caught in the fluttering stuff, lifts up an easy curtain.	The arras blows out from the wall . . . .
The dark fireplace comes to life and shines, Three little blue flames dance on the hearth . . . [42]	Above, in the firelight, winks the coronet of tarnished gold . . .

Here, the comparison is too direct to need illustration; and at other times, Amy Lowell borrowed wholesale from Paul Fort, even to his childish tricks of onomatopoeia:

> Le main de justice vole de serrure an serrure (circ crac).
> Trente pirouettes . . . Deux, trois, cinq. Deux trois cinq
> rrrrrrran.
> > "Henri III" and "Les Deux clowns"

> And tap! She cracks a nut! and tap! another. Tap! Tap!
> Drip—hiss—the rain never stops.
> > "The Basket" and "In a Castle"

More importantly, she used certain effects of sound repetition and alliteration in the manner of Fort:

> Heigh-ho! See my little pecking dove? I'm in
> love with my own temple. Only that halo's wrong. The
> colour's too strong, or not strong enough. I don't
> know. My eyes are tired. Oh, Peter, don't be so rough;
> it is valuable. I won't do any more. I promise. You
> tyrannise, Dear, that's enough.[43]

It is easy to see that Amy Lowell had read and admired Paul Fort, in such passages as this one, for example:

> Non, me faut aimer, me faut traîner ma peine, pleurer
> contre la pierre ici, que voici, où j'inscrivis son nom
> entre un héliantème et cet oeillet couleur de coeur. Suis
> transi. Je vais herborisant au clair de la lune, cherchant
> sous la mousse l'herbe qui rajeunit.[44]

Such are the first poems of Amy Lowell in "polyphonic prose." They are not especially remarkable; and their only value seems to have been in attracting some sharp criticism. But she was not discouraged, and continued to work at her method, trying to avoid a too facile imitation. With "Red Slippers" and "Lead Soliders" in *Men, Women and Ghosts*, she achieved a degree of originality. John Gould Fletcher wrote an article[45] in praise of this new form, trying to prove that Miss Lowell had invented it. He admitted that Miss Lowell herself had said it could be found in the works of Paul Fort, but contended that it was only modesty which prompted her to do so.

Certainly, the prose poems of *Men, Women and Ghosts* were superior to those in her earlier volume in technique, and were also more original; but the influence of Paul Fort is still evident—though only obviously so in one poem, "Bombardment," which is too much like Fort's "La Cathédrale de Reims," a mediocre poem that Amy Lowell greatly admired.

By this time, she was in full possession of the method of the prose poem, and had gotten rid of excesses of onomatopoeia, alliteration, and assonance. She maintained a surer rhythm, and made a surer use of repeated phrases and light rhymes. She made as much use of description as Fort had, but with greater originality. "The Crossroads," for example, is an instance of her improved style, showing how she was able to bring together lyric and dramatic techniques.[46]

Fletcher's article had been a little premature, but in *Can Grande's Castle* Amy Lowell justified some of the claims which he had made for her, and proclaimed in her preface that she had indeed invented "polyphonic prose":

> In the preface to "Sword Blades and Poppy Seed", I stated that I had found the idea of the form in the works of the French poet, M. Paul Fort. But in adapting it for use in English I was obliged to make so many changes that it may now be considered as practically a new form. The greatest of those changes was in the matter of rhythm. M. Fort's practice consists, almost entirely, of regular verse passages interspersed with regular prose passages. But a hint in one of his poems led me to believe that a closer blending of the two types was desirable, and here at the very outset I met with a difficulty. Every

form of art must have a base; to depart satisfactorily from a rhythm it is first necessary to have it. M. Fort found this basic rhythm in the alexandrine. But the rhythm of the alexandrine is not one of the basic rhythms to an English ear . . . Putting aside one rhythm of English prosody after another, I finally decided to base my form upon the long, flowing cadence of oratorical prose. The variations permitted to this cadence enable the poet to change the more readily into those of *vers libre*, or even to take the regular beat of metre, should such a marked time seem advisable.[47]

This was her explanation for the use which she made of repeated motifs, or thematic phrases, for assonance and alliteration, for the use of "echoing" images and sounds. It is difficult, however, to see how the technique of "polyphonic prose" differs from the French prose poem, or from poetic prose in general. Take such a typical passage as this one:

> Ah, the beautiful palaces, with their gateways of gilded iron frilled into arms and coronets, quilled into shooting leaves and tendrils, filled with rosettes, fretted by heraldic emblems! Ah, the beautiful taste, which wastes no time on heavy stone, but cuts flowers and foliage, and flourishes, and ribbons out of—stucco![48]

Neither the faint assonances nor the modest alliterations suffice to transform the prosaic rhythm of this passage into poetry. If, applying Amy Lowell's own rule, what differentiates prose from poetry is that prose rhythm is longer and does not repeat itself, while verse rhythm is short and balanced, then the "poems" of *Can Grande's Castle* are clearly prose.

In these poems, Amy Lowell availed herself of popular subjects just as Paul Fort had, but dealt as well with subjects of her own choosing. She made use of French history, of modern life, of American legend, of Japanese scenes, seeking her fortune wherever she could find it. It is curious, though, that just as she seemed to be breaking free of the close imitation of Fort, she returned to him in an obvious way in one of her historical descriptions: in "The Bronze Horses," she described the taking of Constantinople by the Crusaders in a way that echoed Fort's description of the siege of Beauvais in his "Louis XI":

> Now, now, you crossbowmen and archers, you go first . . . Such a pounding, pummeling, pitching, pointing, piercing, pushing, pelting, poking, painting, punching, parrying, pulling, prodding, puking, piling, passing, you never did see. Stones pour out of the mangonels; arrows fly thick as mist. Swords twist against swords, bill-hooks batter bill-hooks, staves rattle upon staves. One, two, five men up a scaling ladder. Chop down on the first, and he rolls off the ladder with his skull in two halves; rip up the bowels of the second, he drips off the ladder

like an overturned pail. But the third catches his adversary between the legs with a pike and pitches him over as one would toss a truss of hay.[49]

"What else did they throw at them—and no lie?"
"Ah! many objects very bruising, cutting, sharpened, whetted, ball-shaped, socket-shaped, ganulated, horned, toothed, beaked, of earth, of sheet-iron, of freestone, of iron, of steel, curved, bristled, twisted, confused, everything that was badly used up, moss-grown, rusted, frayed, in thongs, in wedges, hollow, sieved, cross- shaped, screw-shaped, hooked, ringing, grating, whistling and snoring, going humph, ouf, louf, pouf, bring, sring, tringle, balaam, bottom, betting, batar, arara, raraboum, bul, bul, breloc, relic, relaps, mil, bamb, marl, broug, batacl, mirobol, pic, poc, quett, strict, pac, diex, mec, pett, sec, sic, soif, flic, faim, bric, broc, brrrr ... which battered in skulls, enlarged noses, banged ears, widened mouths, made fly teeth, fingers, elbows, arms, chins, cheekbones, and married eyes disdaining an omelette of one, bonded shoulders, brutalized chests, discouraged hearts, thrust into bellies, pried first into one buttock then another, pulled out false bowels, made wool of thighs, billiard-balls of knee-pans, and enlarged feet, or cut a man into five, six, seven—really."[50]

Amy Lowell also made use of Japanese forms and subjects in the second poem of her book, "Guns as Keys: And the Great Gate Swings." These subjects were familiar to readers of her work, for in *A Dome of Many-Coloured Glass*, her first volume, the poems "A Coloured Print by Shokei" and "Blades" showed the influence of Japanese material. From 1915 on, a wave of Japanese influence passed over American poetry; the Imagists were the first to feel it: its main features were the search for the image and the stylization of sense impressions. This Japanese influence followed the French influence on American poetry, and did not have the same degree of importance. Most of the Imagists did not pursue Japanese technique, but treated subjects in a superficially Japanese manner. Amy Lowell did not seem greatly interested in earlier attempts at adapting Japanese poetry, though many had been made by French poets, including Paul Fort. W. L. Schwartz, in *The Imaginative Interpretation of the East in Modern French Literature*[51] gave a full account of these influences, and showed that Amy Lowell had sought in the French adaptations only knick-knacks, trimmings, and orna-ments, not the essential Japanese effect; therefore, this influence is outside the range of the present study.

Amy Lowell seems to have grown tired of "polyphonic prose," for the volume which followed *Can Grande's Castle* was *Pictures of the Floating World*, and it contained only two quite mediocre poems in this form. But she returned to it again in *Legends*, in 1921, which included some of her best poems in free verse as well as in polyphonic prose. The tendency of Amy Lowell was now to move toward a certain degree of regularity, even if not of the classic sort. In *Legends*, there are a number of pieces in which passages of pure prose are used to frame passages of regular verse.

It was between 1914 and 1921 that she was most influenced by the example of Paul Fort, and it was also during those years that she wrote almost entirely in free verse and polyphonic prose. Paul Fort had not been her only model, but he was her chief master. He had not given her rhythmic technique alone, but had also taught her a new method of telling a story. Fort wrote a rather small number of purely lyric poems; the majority of his work consisted of narrative and descriptive poems of varying lengths. It is interesting to note that one of Amy Lowell's first attempts at narrative poetry, "The Foreigner," appeared in *Poetry* (April, 1914) along with "The Forsaken," which was her first experiment in the manner of Paul Fort. And *Sword Blades and Poppy Seed*, which marked the beginning of Fort's influence on her, contained fifteen narrative poems. In 1916, in the preface to *Men, Women and Ghosts*, she wrote: "This is a book of stories." *Can Grande's Castle* and *Legends* contained only narratives and polyphonic prose. In 1921, the decline of Paul Fort's influence was marked by the publication of greater numbers of lyric poems and fewer narratives, and she returned to polyphonic prose only rarely after that time.

She had remarked in 1915 that Paul Fort was a popular poet, who drew his inspiration from French legends that were close to the heart of the people. And she had quoted from a French critic about Fort: "He has listened to the instinctive songs in which the soul of the race shivers; which are born, so to speak, of themselves, each like the others, clumsy and sincere . . . It's there, the raw, inexhaustible treasure, which germinates through the length of the centuries in epics and odes, in epigrams, in romances, in legends . . . . "[52]

When *Legends* appeared, in 1921, she warned her readers in the preface that it was a book of legends—"stories as such, they emphatically are not, since all have that curious substrata of reality, speculative or apprehended." It might be thought that she was putting American legends into verse as Fort had done with French legends, but she did not possess the spirit of her race as Fort had: the accent of sincerity was not to be heard in her legends, and consequently they lacked vitality. As a critic justly remarked, she did not have the breadth of vision to express her race's origins. Notably, two legends about New England, "Before the Storm" and "Four Sides to a House," were the most believable in the book.

Amy Lowell said that the World War made history come alive to her, and that in her poems she hoped to bring about the same transformation in her readers, to present the past to them as it actually was. In her book on the French poets, she had made mention of Fort's success in the vein of historical reconstruction. She called her reader's attention to the familiar manner in which Fort had treated French history, and as an example of his method she cited "Le Siège de Beauvais," and all of "Henri III," both of which she later imitated; she said of the latter poem that it was "eight pages in which is contained the whole Middle Ages."[53] She attempted her own poetic versions of history, choosing for settings Rome, Byzantium, and Venice, and for style, that of Paul Fort.

One receives the same impression, almost, from reading Fort's "Louis XI" as from reading Amy Lowell's "Malmaison" and "The Fruit-Shop," in *Men, Women and Ghosts* or "Sea-Blue and Blood-Red" in *Can Grande's Castle*. These poems plunge the reader into the common life of earlier periods of history, and a sense of the comic adds to their charm. However, in her versions, Miss Lowell was careless of certain elements, or failed to carry them through. She represented history as it was lived by the common people, and, in spite of the easy tone, as it was in its most serious moments, while Fort had employed all his erudition to achieve comic effects. Her poems were sometimes agreeable, but often superficial; they had several imitators, of whom John Gould Fletcher was the best.

The narrative and dramatic poems which compose the greater part of Amy Lowell's work owed much to the work of Paul Fort, but it was her shorter lyric poems which were mainly responsible for her success, and if the influence of Fort was important to her technical innovations, she drew the greatest artistic benefit from her studies of Jammes and, above all, de Régnier.

The posthumous work of Amy Lowell was much less interesting than her earlier work. It showed her in reaction against her time, proving that she had never left New England except as a traveler, and that she had never entirely separated herself from Boston. In her last writings, her heredity reasserted itself, and not only her subjects but her style showed a return to the traditional. All the experiments that she had made during the vital period of her life seemed to have been lost. But of her total work, these earlier poems must be considered as the most essential, for they were the ones which caused a sensation and produced an influence. It seems true that she exploited the most diverse authors, one after the other, without ever achieving a personal art form of her own: she imitated Keats, de Régnier, Paul Fort, Poe, Keats again, even Rossetti, Oriental poets, and longer American poems of an earlier period; but her most important poetic experiments were made with the example of the French in mind. The influence of Poe and Whitman on her work my even be attributed, in part, to the esteem in which these poets were held by the French, and it may be said of her much more than of Pound that her popularity depended on the fact that the American public did not know the French poets she was imitating and adapting at will.

Much the same was true of John Gould Fletcher, and his evolution as a poet was similar to hers. Both Amy Lowell and Fletcher were Symbolists: by virtue of their technical experiments, they were contemporary with the second Symbolist generation of Verhaeren and Paul Fort; like these poets, they sought to create musical poems, in which the sound and rhythm of the world would be accurately expressed by means of onomatopoeia and evocative language. They cultivated subjective lyricism and idealism, and they experimented with the ornate style and the long poem—all those things which the Imagists had instinctively reacted against. They remained somewhere half-way between Imagism and the older Symbolism. To be sure, their Symbolism was not that of Arthur Symons or Francis Saltus, who had been imitators of Baudelaire and Verlaine, the first generation of Symbolists, but it was also true that they did in English what some French poets had already done in French, but what no one had yet done in England or America: studying prosody, making experiments with rhythm, advancing ideas about imagery and suggestion—all of which they took from the second generation of French Symbolists. Their work seemed an innovation in the America of 1913, but it was a stage which H. D. and Pound, for example, had already passed beyond.

In their country, both Amy Lowell and Fletcher enriched the native tradition, and so earned themselves a name, but the modern American poets who count most are those who have influenced the history of poetry in European countries. To remake something is inevitably to dilute it; she gave the momentary illusion that she was making something new, but it was soon seen that the essence was lacking, which commonly comes from original invention and personal discovery.

Amy Lowell, however, by obediently following the French poets contemporary with her, studying them carefully, speaking for them, helped to establish the current French influence which affected the whole of American poetry in her generation, and her name must be placed with that of Pound at the head of those who in one way or another helped to make an American poetry out of a combination of French influences.

2. JOHN GOULD FLETCHER

Coincidence alone made an Imagist of John Gould Fletcher. Only a very small part of his work can be linked to this movement, and it is no exaggeration to say that most of his work was a continuation of French Symbolism, but not an addition to or a completion of it. Long before he knew of the Imagist group, he had studied contemporary French poetry. When he was eighteen, he had read Gautier and Baudelaire in translation, like most of the young people of his time. In 1911, he read Verhaeren's poetry for the first time, and found it a revelation, a fact noted by Amy Lowell in her *Tendencies in Modern American Poetry*. After that, he had read all the poets quoted in Van Bever's and Léautaud's well-known anthology. The poetry of Rimbaud was another great discovery of his youth, just at the period when he was beginning to write. In 1913, five slight collections of poems, which had been composed between 1910 and 1913, appeared in London. These were *The Book of Nature, The Dominant City, Visions of the Evening, Fool's Gold,* and *Fire and Wine.* These represented attempts of Fletcher to orient himself, and it was in French poetry that he found his orientation. Memories of Tennyson, Keats, and Shelley, whom he had read at the age of twenty and earlier, faded away before other and more vital memories, those of Baudelaire, Rimbaud, and Verhaeren. But these were still only echoes; there was no new style, no synthesis, only the elements of other styles.

In the first book, there was a prevailing atmosphere reminiscent of Samain and Stuart Merrill:

> To my soul which is as drunken
> With Summer's anguish of silent leaves
> Dead infantas go trailing by.[54]

And, besides the translations of Baudelaire's poems, such as "Couvercle," there were many obvious borrowings from *Les Fleurs du mal:*

> Last night, I lay disgusted, sick at heart,
> Beside a sodden woman of the street
> Who drowsed, oblivious of the dreadful mart,
> Her outraged body and her blistered feet.[55]

There were similar examples in *Visions of the Evening,* a book which was dedicated to Baudelaire, such as these lines from "Invocation to Solitude" which recall Baudelaire's "Réversibilité":

> O solitude, evil angel, come to me . . .
> . . . .
> O solitude, evil angel, let me kiss . . .
> . . . .
> O solitude, evil angel, let me sleep . . .

Judging from these early poems, it would appear that images of Baudelaire and of Verhaeren were engraved in Fletcher's memory. For example; the lines

> The pleasure, like a vast cat, stirred herself,
> And yawning stretched forth her velvet paw
> To clasp the city in her long curved claw.[56]

recall the more powerful lines of Verhaeren:

> Les chats d'ébène et d'or ont traversé le soir
> Avec des bruits stridents de vrille et de heurtoir,
> Et des griffes en l'air vers les étoiles.[57]

The titles of these two poems would not have seemed surprising among those of the early Symbolists. The city evoked in *The Dominant City* was a nervous, nightmarish place, like the cities Verhaeren envisioned.

Another of his five early books, *Fool's Gold*, was dedicated to "Mes Poètes Maudits: Tristan Corbière, Comte de Lautréamont, Arthur Rimbaud, Jules Laforgue, C. Albert Aurier, John M. Synge." But in the book, aside from an agreement of tastes and an attraction for the same subjects, there was no clear influence from any of these poets.

In *Fire and Wine*, some critics discerned the influence of Verlaine, but what they were seeing was a vague and general Symbolist influence. The vocabulary was of the sort dear to the fin de siècle:

> The clarions of the autumn, sombre and sonorous, wind me
> Forth, go forth to the sunset's sumptuous pain.[58]

In this book, the poems inspired by Rimbaud are more than mere imitations. Fletcher loved music and painting as much as he loved poetry, and from the time of his youth, he sought to introduce into his poetic manner techniques which belonged to the other arts. Rimbaud's famous sonnet about the vowels immediately attracted him, and he wrote a poem which projected similar correspondences of his own invention. It took all of Amy Lowell's enthusiasm to say that this poem was more perfect than Rimbaud's:

> A, light and shade, E green, I Blue, U purple and yellow, O Red
> E, parakeets of emerald shrieking perverse in the trees,
> Iridescent and restless chameleons tremulous in the breeze,
> Peace on the leaves, peace on the sea-green sea.[59]

Rimbaud, once he had made his discovery, had the good sense to leave it behind and not attempt to apply it. But Fletcher tried to use logic as a means of justifying style. He meant to construct in his poem a theory of language: he sought to use words which designated green objects, and which were composed of the letter "E," for example, hoping to demonstrate that the words had been formed with the aid of sounds which determined their color, but probably only demonstrating that, by the force of words, we are accustomed to see green in our mind's eye when we hear the English sound "E," because "green," "trees," and "leaves" have forever associated in our minds this sound and these green things. But

Fletcher happily did not continue this line of argument, although he never abandoned the search for "correspondences" between sounds, colors, and emotions.

What Fletcher admired in Rimbaud was his youthful vigor of expression, the keenness of his sight, which could see colors in all their vibrancy. He sought to obtain the impassioned speech, the burning images, the sparkling colors of the French poet. The result of this ambition may be seen in the following lines:

> I am the anvil of moods and slave of the fulminate world
> That, like a prismatic Kaleidoscope, leaps instantly through
> My soul: flamboyant flamingoes 'Gainst torpid tortoises hurled
> Chrome corollas confused with corollas chrysoprase blue.[60]

One can see here how much Fletcher favored alliteration and repetition of sounds, and other devices common to the Symbolists.[61]

Thus, as early as 1913, Fletcher showed—not that he had found his style (it is doubtful whether he ever found it)—but that he was searching for it among the French masters, where he continued to search for it the rest of his life. His life was spent in a constant search, which began at this period, and if he never found a solution to the problem of style, it was because he proposed a solution which had already been made. Thus he was dogged by a certain anxiety and indecision: to redo what has already been done, if one has talent and serious ambitions, is to lose oneself in badly constructed imitations and gropings for style. True influence consists in surpassing one's model, not in reproducing it.

Fletcher, who had profoundly studied the technique of the French Symbolists, seemed to take a variety of manners from them, but never to arrive at a synthesis. He wrote of himself on one occasion:

> I have always considered the French poets as showing me what I wanted to do: finding a way of painting nature and life in a non-realistic manner, a method opposed to that of Robinson, Masters, Frost, and Sandburg, and making use of what is most lyric in my temperament. Have I imitated their method? That is a question which I cannot answer. I have always felt an emotional parenthood in Rimbaud and the Symbolist school in general. The vision of nature can be the same, without there being any definite desire to imitate the style exactly. The difference that exists between the two languages explains that.[62]

In these early years, the French painters were confirming his vision of the world. In 1912, in particular, Fletcher saw in London an exhibition of French Impressionist paintings. Amy Lowell said that this exhibition had succeeded in destroying what was left in Fletcher of conservatism. He believed from then on that poetry, like painting, needed a new idiom, and it was then that he began to write in free verse. He also began writing art critiques, among them a study of Gauguin which was published in 1918. Around 1914, he met the members of the Imagist group. He did not appear in the first anthology, *Des Imagistes*, but appeared in the following ones, edited by Amy Lowell. His first contribution, "Excursion to London," showed that Imagism was largely a verbal discipline on his work: the image was not clarified, as it was with Pound, H. D., and Aldington. It was only a flight of fancy, though often a very pleasant one:

> It is evening and the earth
> Wraps itself in a blue shawl.[63]

This is a passage which compares with Hulme's "Autumn":

> I walked abroad
> And saw the ruddy moon lean over a hedge
> Like a red-faced farmer.

And Fletcher's image, also in the Imagist anthology:

> The trees, like great jade elephants
> Chained, stand and shake 'neath the gadflies of the breeze.[64]

compares favorably with H. D.'s "Oread," another of the original Imagist poems. In the image of H. D.'s poem, there is an inevitability and a swiftness which brings one as close to the sensation as language can; in Fletcher, the mind and the imagination are trying to suggest, by a roundabout route. It is worth noting that poets who had little sympathy for Imagism, and criticized it for excessive precision, were admirers of Fletcher. Thus Conrad Aiken praised the musical quality in his poetry, and deplored the lack of it in other Imagists.[65] Moreover, Fletcher himself criticized the Imagists in a similar way:

> A critical examination of the work of these young poets, Aldington,
> H. D., Flint, Pound, proves that their efforts have not been completely
> successful. The art of poetry demands as great a mastery of sound
> qualities as of poetic substance. An expression that is condensed and
> full of subject matter is not enough. The ear instinctively demands that
> the nude skeleton be decently covered—with beautiful and subtle
> orchestrations of assonance, alliteration, rhyme, and rhythm.[66]

Such were the qualities which he admired in the Symbolists. He owed very little to Imagist techniques, other than the facility of writing in free verse, since he had not studied Rémy de Gourmont and Henri de Régnier with the same interest as he held for the earlier Symbolists. Rimbaud and Verhaeren were the poets for him, and they had been little enough imitated by others. But in these years he was interested in everything that came from France, being in the habit of reading a French book every day.

Irradiations, which was his best collection of poems, was published in 1915, and marked the end of his apprenticeship, though it still contained some of the initial flaws of style that were present in his earlier collections. He wrote *Irradiations* in 1913; the *Symphonies* in 1914, and the first part of *The Tree of Life* in 1915 and 1916. These are the works which show the strongest French influence, for it is less in evidence in the works he published later.

Irradiations, Sand and Spray

Irradiations, (Boston: Houghton Mifflin, 1915), was dedicated to Amy Lowell, whose development had been closely parallel to his. The preface he wrote for the volume was in the vein of her preface to *Sword Blades and Poppy Seed,* which had appeared in the preceding year. In it, he made no mention of Imagist technique; he said simply that "The good poem is that in which all the effects are properly used to convey the underlying emotions of its author, and that which welds all these emotions into a work of art by the use of dominant motif, subordinate themes, proportionate treatment, repetition, variation . . . ." This is the same basis for poetry as that understood by such Symbolists as de Régnier and Verhaeren.

The first poem of the book was an excellent application of the principles stated in the preface. An indecisive state of mind—the melancholy of afternoon—was rendered by appropriate sounds, colors, and perfumes. Variations performed on a central theme were the essential method of the poem:

> The spattering of the rain upon pale terraces
> Of afternoon is like the passing of a dream
> Amid the roses shuddering 'gainst the wet green stalks
> Of the streaming trees—the passing of the wind
> Upon the pale lower terraces of my dream
> Is like the crinkling of the wet gray robes
> Of the hours that come to turn over the urn
> Of the day and spill its rainy dream.
> Vague movement over the puddled terraces:
> Heavy gold pennons—a pomp of solemn gardens
> Half hidden under the liquid veil of spring:
> Far trumpets like a vague rout of faded roses
> Burst 'gainst the wet green silence of distant forests:
> A clash of cymbals—then the swift swaying footsteps
> Of the wind that undulates along the languid terraces.

Pools of rain—the vacant terraces
Wet, chill and glistening
Towards the sunset beyond the broken doors of to-day.[67]

The volume abounded in similar harmonies. There were very few examples of the Imagist type in it. Fletcher's verse was different from that of the other members of the group: it was not based on "rhythmic cadence," but on older metrical verse: whereas the Imagists generally chose rhythms that were short and quick, he preferred those which were long and slow. Following the example of Verhaeren, he used echoes, assonance and alliteration, and a vocabulary with frequent strange and sonorous words. Perhaps his contribution to the American poetry of his time consisted in this fact, that he knew how to write poems that were well orchestrated, with a command of the verse instrument that gave him the power to express musical effects in reverie or fantastic dreams. The art was not original with Fletcher, but in English no one had yet attempted the same combinations of effects.

Apparently Verhaeren was his chief inspiration in this poem, for the shock of consonants imitated the noise of ship engines, as Verhaeren had once imitated the sound of bells and revolving wheels:

Like black plunging dolphins with red bellies,
The steamers in herds,
Dive and roll through the tumult
Of green hissing water[68]

Et ce Londres de fonte et de bronze, mon âme,
Où des plaques de fer claquent sous des hangars.[69]

Fletcher also used internal rhymes in the manner of Verhaeren, and sometimes placed a long adverb at the end of the line, also after his fashion; e.g.: We consecrate and acclaim them tumultuously."[70] And Fletcher undoubtedly took from Verhaeren's free verse strophe the final explosive energy and breathless rhythm:

With green-grey eyes,
With whirling arms,
With clashing feet,
With bellowing lungs,
Pale green-white in a gallop across the sky,
The wind comes.

The great gale of the winter flings himself flat upon earth.[71]

But it was not only the musical quality of Verhaeren that Fletcher assimilated; his vision and the landscape of his poems is also like that of the Flemish
poet. The towns and the countryside have the same symbolic sense in both poets'
use, and the same anxiety was expressed by them over the sight of a deserted
street, a mysterious woman (as in *Irradiation*, II), or the misery of the poorer
quarters.

In these lines:

> A monotonous procession of black carts
> Full crowded with blood-red blossom:
> Scarlet geraniums
> Unfolding their fiery globes upon the night.
> These are the memories of day moulded in jagged flame:
> Lust, joy, blood, and death.[72]

the symbolic combination of red and black has a value similar to that of gold and
black in the poetry of Verhaeren, where it was used to represent exaltation and
depression. But Fletcher was less the artist than Verhaeren, in that he explained
his symbolic colors in the poem too explicitly, and thus missed the concise beauty
of Verhaeren's lines:

> La mort a mis sur le comptoir
> un écu noir.[73]

or these:

> Vers les lunes de mes deux yeux
> Vers les lunes de mes deux yeux en noir.[74]

In the same fashion, Fletcher obtained what Amy Lowell called "the strange
magic reality of Verhaeren," by passing from the plane of fact to that of
hallucination: taking a gesture or a line and carrying it beyond the realistic:

> "From long white high roads whipping in ribbons up summits."[75]

> The lifeless chilly slatey sky with no blue hope is lit,
> A rusty waddling steamer plants a smudge of smoke on it.

> Stupidly stand the factory chimneys staring over all . . . [76]

Verhaeren achieved a similar detachment from reality in the gesture of the
rope-maker who "attire à lui les horizons."[77]

The title of *Irradiations* suggests a close analogy to Rimbaud's *Illuminations*, and the influence of this other French Symbolist was to be seen in Fletcher's
book. For example, the lines:

> Whirlpools of purple and gold,
> Winds from the mountains of cinnabar,
> Lacquered mandarin moments, palaquins swaying and balancing . . . [78]

show a talent for grouping images that are colorful and harmonious, in the manner of Rimbaud.

Finally, one can see in *Irradiations* the influence of the French Impressionist painters. It is to be seen especially in certain poems where the minute and vibrant images give the effect of heat and light on a summer afternoon. One passage alone will demonstrate this effect, though it is not the only one to be found in Fletcher's poems:

> The iridescent vibrations of midsummer light,
> Dancing, dancing, suddenly flickering and quivering
> Like little feet or the movement of quick hands clapping,
> Or the rustle of furbelows or the clash of polished gems.
> The palpitant mosaic of the midday light
> Colliding, sliding, leaping and lingering:
> O, I could lie on my back all day,
> And mark the mad ballet of the midsummer sky.[79]

Goblins and Pagodas

In 1916, Fletcher published *Goblins and Pagodas* (Boston: Houghton Mifflin). In the first section of it, entitled "Ghosts of an Old House," he evoked the presence of an ancestral mansion with its stored-up memories. This kind of poetry also had its origin in the French Symbolists, with Rimbaud's "Le Buffet" as the first example, and Francis Jammes's "La Salle à manger" as a further development. Fletcher used twenty-five poems to describe his subject. As Rimbaud had written in "Le Buffet":

> O buffet du vieux temps, tu sais bien des histoires,
> Et tu voudrais conter tes contes, et tu bruis
> Quand s'ouvrent lentement tes grandes portes noires.

So Fletcher wrote in "In the Attic":

> Legless chairs and shattered tables
> Seem to be crying
> Softly in the stillness
> Because no one has brushed them.[80]

Sometimes his poetry resembles that of Jammes in its reminiscences, its simple and precise presentations:

In this room my father died:
His bed is in the corner,
No one has slept in it
Since the morning when he wakened,
To meet death's hands at his heart.[81]

Certain of the poems in this first section were pretty, but there were too many of them.

The second section of the book was far more important than the first; it contained the "symphonies," which were the most personal of Fletcher's poems. These poems attempted to express the harmony of a symphonic composition by means of a scene with a dominant tone. The sounds, colors, and emotions are intended to form a perfect correspondence—thus Fletcher continued the idea of his "Vowels" sonnet, or perhaps the ideas of René Ghil or of Scriabin, both of which were then in vogue. But the poet of the "Symphonies" was principally interested in the connection between feelings and colors. He had grown up trying to apply the theory of "Vowels," following the good example of Rimbaud. For, in "Blue Symphony," the dominant sound is "o," which, according to Fletcher's poem, should evoke the color red. But the blue tone is given instead by the color of the descriptive images.

Basically, Fletcher's idea was related to Scriabin's only in point of origin. Fletcher decided, very intelligently, that poetry need not give colors by means of sound, since it could give them directly by means of words and images. It was rather feelings that were conveyed by sounds and by color-images. So for a time Fletcher experimented with the relation between poetry and painting, recalling the search he had made in his earlier poems to paint reality in an unreal manner, following the Post-Impressionist painters. They had sought to represent life and nature, not by photographic copies, but by emotions and dreams, in a symphonic arrangement of colors and forms. Thus Gauguin had said, for instance: "Nous sommes allés à la mer peindre la campagne et à la campagne peindre la mer." What they tried to paint was not the scene, but the plastic elements corresponding to the feelings it produced. The grouping of these elements, the gradation and agreement of colors, was meant to provide a harmony as much musical as plastic.

The images of Fletcher's "Symphonies" were equivalent to the plastic elements in the paintings of Gauguin and Van Gogh: they suggested emotions which were not directly described. The French Symbolists had done the same thing, but had felt that it was an effect more of music than of painting, and they did not venture as far as Fletcher did in the direction of painting. These "Symphonies" achieve a synthesis at their best which is like that of a canvas of Gauguin. The decorative harmony is due to the agreement of neighboring colors, and is much in evidence in "Blue Symphony," the first of them, where the black mass of clouds and the green mass of the prairies are put into balance with each other. A single tone dominated the scenes, as in the paintings of Gauguin, who once advised "chercher l'harmonie et non le contraste, l'accord et non le heurt des couleurs."

Fletcher admired the violent character and the primitive temperament of Gauguin, and discovered the same qualities in Rimbaud. In certain of his "Symphonies," one finds the same violent landscapes, evoked by clusters of exploding images of color:

> In the evening I listen to the winds' lisping,
> While the conflagrations of the sunset flicker and clash
>   behind me,
> Flamboyant crenellations of glory amid the charred ebony
>   boles.[82]

The same exaltation and the same mystical sense of nature as Rimbaud expressed is to be seen in these lines of Fletcher:

> I sway to the movement of hooded summits,
> I swim leisurely in the deep blue seas of air.
>
> I hug the smooth bark of stately red pillars . . . .
>
> I will abide in this forest of pines:
> For I have unveiled naked beauty,
> And the things that she whispered to me in the darkness,
> Are buried deep in my heart.[83]

The influence of Verhaeren is also apparent in the "Symphonies." The two familiar symbolic colors of the Belgian poet are the basis for the "Symphony in Black and Gold." Sometimes, in fact, Fletcher seems obsessed with the rhythm, tone, and imagery of Verhaeren, but surely the Flemish poet would have been pleased by this image:

> Elsewhere the crane's gaunt muscles
> Tug the city up to the stars.[84]

And he would also have liked this animated description:

> The chimneys rank
> Their motionless forces
> Against the swift movement
> Of tugs in the stream;

Against the flame-chariots
Of the Embankment;
Against the bowing trees,
Against the blowing smoke,
Against the busy rain.[85]

The most notable qualities in "Symphonies" are just these strong and violent movements, sustained by an appropriate and effective free-verse form. The idea underlying the poems is less convincing, perhaps: one wonders whether it is possible for poetry to create "symphonies," still less symphonies of color, and for that reason, the originality of Fletcher's conception seems questionable, though that does not keep one from admiring the movement of his verse, its variety and its vigor.

Japanese Prints

But this essentially Symbolist technique of Fletcher lacked concentration, and was capable only of rendering indecisive emotions. The next collection which he published, called *Japanese Prints* (1918), was nearer the Imagist method. It was part of the general vogue for Japanese subjects at that time in America, which was best expressed by Pound's book, *Cathay* (1915). Fletcher's book has less of the Oriental flavor than Pound's, probably because it was inspired by the Japanese effects of some French Impressionist painting, rather than by Oriental poems, although Fletcher certainly must have seen the Oriental influence in French poetry, as well.

Here is the sort of vague Japanese effect he created:

> Spring rain falls through the cherry blossoms,
> In long blue shafts
> On grasses strewn with delicate stars.
>
> The summer rain sifts through the drooping willow,
> Shatters the courtyard
> Leaving grey pools.[86]

The Tree of Life

In his next collection, *The Tree of Life* (1918), Fletcher returned to Symbolism, but not completely: he was somewhat more direct, less suggestive and indefinite, but on the other hand some of his pleasure in words had disappeared, along with his power of making images. The influence of Verhaeren was still to be seen, as in these lines:

Along the street,
Dismally perched on a crazy cart
That creaks and wobbles dolefully,
With a starved white horse
Between the shafts,
Goes the giver of empty days.[87]

And, in general, the influence of French Symbolism seems to have become more pervasive, and at the same time better controlled, in Fletcher's poetry.

Breakers and Granite

Fletcher was always interested in the experiments of Amy Lowell, and for a period these two poets worked together. When Amy Lowell discovered "polyphonic prose," Fletcher wrote an enthusiastic article on the new form. She seemed to him to have hit on a formula for the orchestrated poem, which he had long sought. In 1915, he published some experiments in "polyphonic prose" in *Poetry*, and later included them in his collection, *Breakers and Granite* (New York: Macmillan, 1921).

Amy Lowell's influence dominated the whole book, even to the subjects chosen: they were largely historical narratives and American legends, of the sort that she was writing at the time. Like her, he imitated old folksongs and even Indian chants, and since she had taken her idea for "polyphonic prose" from the study of Paul Fort, Fletcher indirectly absorbed this influence in his experiments, as can be seen in such passages as "The Song of the Wind":

O my soul of purple and gold, the earth is green, the sun is gold! The wind that whoops, ho! ho! in the noonday . . . The wind that stops awhile and then comes on in multitudes, flickering, licking dry wavelets, screaming, fighting, tingling, tossing, clanging, prowling, growling, howling, rasping, soaring, crashing and ebbing away.[88]

This might seem like a parody of Amy Lowell, but Fletcher always made his imitations seriously and sincerely. At other times, he put into the new form the sort of visions which Verhaeren had given him:

Restless hammers are carving new cities from the stagnant skies.
Beneath, the earth is propped and caverned; monstrous halls drop with vaulted echoing roofs dripping and sorrowful far below; the bells toll and the trains start slowly, clanging, shaking the earth and the sad towers above them as they go banging their cargo of lost ones towards the secret gates of the sea, falling, falling with thunder and flame, roaring and crawling, shooting and dying away.[89]

Other poems in the book showed Symbolist elements in their composition and rhythmic movement, and many were reminiscent of Verhaeren. For instance, "The Windmills" recalled his French poem of the same name, "Le Moulin," in its subject and descriptive imagery. The windmill is the central figure in Verhaeren's poem; around it are grouped houses and gardens which are obedient to it, which look to it and admire its majesty. Fletcher's scene uses different colors, and his windmill does not tower over small huts, but over trees and plants that are rich with color; however, the houses have the same place as in Verhaeren's poem. In both poems, the first verse describes the majestic movement of the windmill:

> The windmills, like great sunflowers of steel,
> Lift themselves proudly over the straggling houses.[90]

Then the two poems show how the windmill exerts its influence over all the landscape, and even penetrates to the very smallest and most hidden part of the houses. Finally, Fletcher's poem ends with the vision, calm and sad, of the windmill again solitary, and:

> Turning, turning, forever turning
> In the chill night-wind that sweeps over the valley . . . [91]

A final influence is that of de Gourmont's *Litanies*, which until this book had not affected Fletcher as it had the other Imagists.

> City of night,
> Wrap me in your folds of shadow.
>
> City of twilight,
> City that projects into the west,
> City whose columns rest upon the sunset, city of square,
> threatening masses blocking out the light:
> City of twilight,
> Wrap me in your folds of shadow.[92]

The Symbolist technique is discernible here, as in the other poems of this collection, but is more superficial than in the others. Amy Lowell and Fletcher both returned to American subjects, but he was less successful at them than she. The return is easily explained in Fletcher's case: the tumultuous life that attracted him in Verhaeren's poetry, the youthful exuberance that he admired in Rimbaud, also drew him toward Whitman and American civilization. However, Fletcher lost many of his finer stylistic qualities in his return to America: his impetuosity was of a more aristocratic nature than Whitman's, and his talent more European.

Fletcher did not carry Symbolism forward; he simply repeated it. Consequently, he only succeeded in emulating some of the second generation of Symbolists, the disciples of Verlaine and Mallarmé. He went no further than Lowell had gone. For real success, as their example proves, the American poet had to be inspired by French Symbolism, but to react against certain of its qualities while cultivating others. Those who did so not only attained personal originality, but also created a new poetry, more genuine and more durable than the old.

Fletcher's criticism is worth mentioning, for it was a notable part of his writing. He had the knowledge necessary to speak of Gauguin or of Fontainas, of the painter or the poet. He had a powerful sympathy for his subjects, and knew how to understand their lives as well as their work. For example, he depicted very movingly the tragic force which animated Gauguin: he spoke of the art and character of the Post-Impressionist painter without apparent artifice, and his book was a serious and moving study of Gauguin's life and work.

In 1919, he published a short study of the poetry of André Fontainas. The book showed a real knowledge of Symbolism; in fact, it was almost a homage to the movement. The technique of Symbolism and that of Fontainas were thoroughly examined, with a solid simplicity, making the reader feel strongly that the sympathy of Fletcher was for the art and sensibility of a poet like Fontainas: a delicately descriptive symbolism, a musical and perfectly appropriate vers libre.

CHAPTER 6

The Second Stage of Imagism

T. S. ELIOT

T S. ELIOT appeared on the scene when American poetry, thanks to the Imagists, had once again become an art, and when some of the rules that had once been necessary could be abandoned without risk. If Imagism, up to a certain point, appeared to be behind the evolution of continental European literature, American poetry, after the advent of Eliot, entered into the front ranks of that evolution, and even into the avant-garde.

It was to Pound that Eliot clearly affirmed himself in his first works, particularly because Pound still maintained many of the Imagist ideas. Pound provided the example of a clear style, of direct expression, of the art of satire, and probably of a common admiration for French poetry. But these two poets complement one another, for Eliot showed Pound new directions to take, and his influence is evidenced in *Hugh Selwyn Mauberley*, where Pound's unilinear energy was developed into a more complex energy. It was also after meeting Eliot that Pound modified some of his judgments about French poets, placing Laforgue among the three "permanent" French poets. It would be best to say that these two poets mutually benefited each other, that they had a similar artistic under-standing, a similar artistic education, and that Pound formed a solid link between Imagism and the more modern poetry which Eliot produced.

Having appeared after the Imagist experiment began, Eliot succeeded in making certain of its principles more precise: the importance of presenting the real emotion without any artifice; the necessity for criticism—he maintained that the poetic mind and the critical mind are inseparable; and the importance for the poet of knowing his own time, his own country, and the inheritance of the past, implying an extensive knowledge of European literature.

T. S. Eliot profited by all the work which had been done during the few years that preceded his entry into the poetic movement: not only the work of Hulme, of Rémy de Gourmont, and of the Imagists, but also that of the Surrealists, and even of Paul Valéry. He had the advantage of arriving at the time when numerous experiments had been made, and a determination of values had been accom-plished, that is to say, when a Classicism could be solidly established in England as it had been already in France. He had been drawn into the Imagist movement, thanks to Pound, Aldington, and H. D., but these poets, who had come to the fore after a period of artistic poverty and debility, had not yet dreamed of creating a systematic poetic criticism.

To speak of the Symbolism of T. S. Eliot is to realize that he consciously continued this movement, with the clear intention of profiting as much as possible from the discoveries of the French. The Imagists had already performed a critical act, by extracting the most precious elements from French Symbolism. Eliot took additional elements from it, particularly those which could form the strongest connection with the English poetic tradition. These elements were essential to him in the same way as those he took from the English Metaphysical poets. The search for tradition had always been one of the principal quests of the Imagists.

It is possible to account for the French influence on Eliot in two particular ways: by seeing how the criticism of Rémy de Gourmont helped him to form a classic conception of poetic art, and by seeing how the Symbolism of Baudelaire and Laforgue helped to determine the literary tradition to which Eliot attached himself, and which he in turn enriched.

1. T. S. ELIOT AND RÉMY DE GOURMONT

Eliot had the same admiration for Rémy de Gourmont that the Imagists had shown. He wrote that "Of all modern critics, perhaps Rémy de Gourmont had most of the general intelligence of Aristotle. An amateur, though an excessively able amateur, in physiology, he combined to a remarkable degree sensitiveness, erudition, sense of fact and sense of history, and generalizing power."[1]

Eliot owed much to de Gourmont, but he surpassed his master: he also had read the *Problème du style,* and although he had the same understanding of literary style as de Gourmont, he carried his ideas considerably further. He agreed that "style" means to think and to feel—that is everything. He once wrote to Pound: "I have tried to write about certain things which have really moved me."[2] He also agreed with de Gourmont in maintaining that style is a specialization of sensibility. The artist has both an artistic sensibility and a human sensibility, but the latter is interesting only as it is absorbed into the other, as the personality of the artist is effaced in the work. Eliot cited approvingly de Gourmont's statement:

> L'écrivain de style abstrait est presque toujours un sentimental, du
> moins un sensitif. L'écrivain artiste n'est presque jamais un sentimen-
> tal, très rarement un sensitif.[3]

It was in pursuing this idea of de Gourmont's that Eliot arrived at his well-known conclusion regarding the art of poetry:

> Poetry is not a turning loose of emotion, but an escape from emotion; it is not the expression of personality, but an escape from personality. But, of course, only those who have personality and emotions know what it means to want to escape from these things.[4]

These passages from Eliot's early essays are so clearly influenced by the reading of the *Problème du style*, that Eliot even takes from de Gourmont his examples of the "sentimental style": politicians and scholars.

In statements such as this one, de Gourmont gave Eliot a basis for his ideas: "Tout mot, tout grand style correspond d'abord à une vision." Eliot carried this idea forward when he wrote: "The end of the enjoyment of poetry is a pure contemplation from which all the accidents of personal emotion are removed; thus we aim to see the object as it really is . . . And without a labour which is largely a labour of the intelligence, we are unable to attain that stage of vision *amor intellectualis Dei.*"[5]

The criticism of Eliot was undoubtedly sharpened by contact with that of de Gourmont, who furnished him with problems to solve, and the example of lively and at the same time sound intelligence. When he praised Henry James for example, Eliot praised him as de Gourmont might have praised him, for having "a viewpoint untouched by the parasite idea."[6] But Eliot surpassed de Gourmont in the breadth of his criticism. The author of *Le Problème du style* did not arrive at the stage of pure vision which Eliot spoke of; he always remained enclosed in the domain of the senses and of sensuality; and he always thought that there were no books worth reading except those in which an author expressed the sense of his own age. Eliot, on the other hand, recognized the author's task as that of forming structures of emotions and experiences; he understood poetry as a living organization of feelings experienced in various ages, a part of the living whole of all the poetry that has ever been written.

One of the problems that de Gourmont had posed for him was that of literary tradition. De Gourmont had resolved it for himself in an article that was translated by Richard Aldington and published in *Poetry* in 1914: "Ma tradition n'est pas seulement française, elle est européene."[7] And Eliot recommended that the writer must know the European mind as well as the mind of his own country, in the living stages of its evolution, the phases of its active development: "He must be aware that the mind of Europe—the mind of his own country . . . is a mind which changes. . . ."[8] Eliot also maintained, as de Gourmont had, that the real artist, in joining a tradition, modifies that tradition.

But Eliot and de Gourmont were opposed in the freedom they sought for the writer: de Gourmont, profoundly classical and profoundly French, needed to have the sense of freeing himself from his tradition, of becoming a tradition to himself, by bringing together the most diverse moments in literature; it was a necessary illusion, by means of which he freed himself from many fetters without losing any of his classical clarity of mind. Eliot, on the contrary, entering the English tradition after a period of vague sentimentalism, and not having enjoyed the strict discipline that French culture imposes on its adherents, early felt the need for placing himself inside a literary tradition. He recognized the justice of de Gourmont's ideas, but had to see tradition from his own point of view.

2. THE CLASSICISM OF T. S. ELIOT

Starting with these ideas of literary tradition, Eliot developed them in the direction of a poetry detached from sentimental subjectivity, and an objective criticism of poetry. These two aims are the basis of Eliot's classicism, which is no less his own in being connected with parallel movements in France, inspired by ideas best expressed by de Gourmont, and corresponding to contemporary theories of other French critics, or even in developing certain of the salient ideas of Pound. With Eliot, these ideas took on such depth and precision that they can be considered original.

Eliot's classicism, which aimed at an avoidance of pure emotion, and imposed as a consequence the formal and almost architectural study of literary works, and as a further consequence the determination of an artistic tradition, had begun with Pound and the Imagists. But they had stopped short of the mark, perhaps at the point where Rémy de Gourmont had stopped. Eliot completed the development. Pound had studied poetic diction; Eliot studied style. Pound had defined the image; Eliot defined the synthesis of images, their "structure." Thus Eliot carried each idea a step forward.

Pound had defined the image as the projection, on the objective plane, of sensation and emotion. Eliot went further:

> The only way of expressing emotion in the form of art is by finding an "objective correlative"; in other words, a set of objects, a situation, a chain of events which shall be the formula of that *particular* emotion; such that when the external facts, which must terminate in a sensory experience, are given, the emotion is immediately evoked.[9]

Pound defined poetry in much the same way, making certain ideas of de Gourmont more precise:

Poetry is a sort of inspired mathematics, which gives us equations, not for abstract figures, triangles, spheres, and the like, but equations for the human emotions. If one have a mind which inclines to magic rather than to science, one will prefer to speak of these equations as spells or incantations; it sounds more arcane, mysterious, recondite.[10]

But Eliot called for a more complete detachment of the artist, and a more complex architecture in the work, than Pound.

Like Pound, but with slightly different intentions, Eliot sought the definition of his classicism in the Greeks and in the Middle Ages. *The Divine Comedy* seemed to him to contain the sort of pure vision at which he himself aimed. Pound had already written of Dante's poem, but less systematically than Eliot; both considered it a masterpiece of architectural construction, in which the emotions were perfectly projected into the objects, which stood out in clear relief.[11]

It was after making this study that Pound began to be interested in modern French poetry: it completed, for him, the literary tradition that had, as its summits, Catullus, Dante, Villon, Browning, Gautier, and Corbière. Eliot's tradition was different, but bore some resemblance to Pound's, containing more of the French Symbolists and of the Classical poets. While most of the young poets after Pound had been content to repeat his ideas in different form, Eliot found the means of establishing links between the poetry of Laforgue and that of the English Metaphysicals.

The poetry of Eliot proves that John Donne and Jules Laforgue are compatible poets. The possibility of such a combination was critically examined by Eliot in his essay on "The Metaphysical Poets,"[12] where he showed a similarity of intention in the modern French and the earlier English poets, the latter trying to modify the eloquence of the Elizabethans, the former the eloquence of the Parnassians, the latter transposing emotional experience into philosophical terms, the former transposing emotional experience into terms of science and superstition, and both thus augmenting the power and richness of poetry.

In his essay on "The Metaphysical Poets," Eliot called attention to the qualities in certain Elizabethan poets which, according to him, are present in all great poetry, and which he professed to find, to an equal degree, in certain French poets, particularly Baudelaire. Thus, in the work of John Donne, he remarked on the contrasting images in such a line as: "A bracelet of bright hair about the bone," where, as he said, "The most powerful effect is produced by the sudden contrast of associations of 'bright hair' and of 'bone.' "

Eliot also noted in his essay on "Andrew Marvell," the juxtaposition of lightness and seriousness in Elizabethan poetry, and said that the same effect was to be found in French poets such as Gautier, whose lines he quoted:

Le squelette était invisible
Au temps heureux de l'art Païen.

And again, in the essay on "The Metaphysical Poets," he used the French example to define another important quality of the style he admired; objecting to Samuel Johnson's criticism that "the most heterogeneous ideas are yoked by violence together," he said:

> But a degree of heterogeneity of material compelled into unity by the operation of the poet's mind is omnipresent in poetry. We need not select for illustration such a line as:
>
> Notre âme est un trois-mâts cherchant son Icarie;
>
> we may find it in some of the best lines of Johnson himself ("The Vanity of Human Wishes").[13]

On the poetic image itself, the example of the Elizabethans led him to the same conclusion, for in the best poets the idea and the simile are one: as he said of Donne, "A thought to Donne was an experience; it modified his sensibility." And as he went on to say of modern French poets:

> Jules Laforgue, and Tristan Corbière in many of his poems, are nearer to the "school of Donne" than any modern English poet. But poets more classical than they have the same essential quality of transmuting ideas into sensations, of transforming an observation into a state of mind.[14]

Eliot noted how Racine, Baudelaire, and Donne, who were great masters of poetic diction, were also great explorers of the human soul, which meant not only the "heart," but "the cerebral cortex, the nervous system, and the digestive tracts." And he concluded that the modern poet could well learn by their example:

> We can only say that it appears likely that poets in our civilization, as it exists at present, must be difficult. Our civilization comprehends great variety and complexity, and this variety and complexity, playing upon a refined sensibility, must produce various and complex results. The poet must become more and more comprehensive, more allusive, more indirect, in order to force, to dislocate if necessary, language into his meaning. . . . Hence we get something which looks very much like the conceit—we get, in fact, a method curiously similar to that of the "metaphysical poets," similar also in its use of obscure words and of simple phrasing.

> O géraniums, diaphanes, guerroyeurs sortilèges,
> Sacrilèges monomanes!

Emballages, dévergondages, douches! O pressoirs
Des vendanges des grands soirs!
Layettes aux abois,
Thyrses au fond des bois!
Transfusions, représailles,
Relevailles, compresses et l'éternal potion,
Angélus! n'en pouvoir plus
De débâcles nuptiales! de débâcles nuptiales![15]

It might be possible to maintain, assuming that certain Symbolist poets like Mallarmé and Laforgue had been influenced by English poetry, which they knew, that Eliot only reclaimed from France properties which once were common to English poetry; then the French qualities which are found in his poetry would only be English qualities that had been given a new value by French artistic endeavor. But it is enough to observe that there seems to be a general law, which directs that for two elements to be successfully united, they must have certain affinities and certain oppositions, and that the Symbolist influence in England was probably ruled by this law, so that English poetry was able to recover from French Symbolism a lost tradition and vanished qualities of style, by seeing them in a richer and more propitious light.

3. THE SYMBOLISM OF T. S. ELIOT

Since Eliot associated the English Metaphysical poets with Corbière, Laforgue, and the French Symbolist poets, it must be understood that to speak of the "Symbolism" of Eliot is to speak of the qualities he has in common with French Symbolist poets, and also with Donne, Webster, and other Elizabethan poets. But he took from both these groups something more than ideas of poetic style. His poetry is as complex as the civilization about which he spoke, and if he drew on a great variety of experiences, he also drew on a great variety of authors, whose lines he put in a new context, giving them new life as Ronsard had given new life to the Greek verses he used.

It would be difficult to separate all the influences which Eliot so successfully combined in his poetry, for sometimes in the same verses he has imitated the rhythms of Gautier while borrowing phrases from Donne:

> . . . Who clipped the lion's wings
> And flea'd his rump and pared his claws?
> Thought Burbank, meditating on
> Time's ruins, and the seven laws.[16]

As for the more modern French poets, Eliot sought them as models of concrete style, where emotion is transcribed by an object or an association of objects, without any mixture of abstraction. Like the Imagists, he profited from the example of Jean de Bosschère, particularly from his poem, "Homère Mare Habite Sa Maison de Planchese."

> Pendant quatre saisons Homère voyage
> Et dans chaque ville il est un autre personnage;
> Bleu sous le ciel bleu, gris à Londres
> Recueilli à Paris; perverti à Rome
> Parmi l'ordre de la tombe des tombes
> Byron dans les îles et Shakespeare encore
> Dans la poussière d'hommes de Rome
> Mais jamais il n'est Mare.[17]

While he was in Paris, Eliot knew both Guillaume Apollinaire and André Salmon, and their influence is audible in certain of his poems. Salmon's "La Maison du Veuf" and other of his works bear a resemblance to Eliot's "Sweeney" poems. Eliot also borrowed some techniques from Apollinaire, for example, that of changing the time and place abruptly at the end of a poem. Thus Apollinaire, at the end of "Marizibill," wrote:

> Je connais gens de toutes sortes
> Ils n'égalent pas leurs destins
> Indécis comme feuilles mortes
> Leurs yeux sont des feux mal éteints
> Leurs coeurs bougent comme leurs portes.[18]

It is enough to compare the "Sweeney" poems with certain of Apollinaire's poems in *Tirésias*, in order to see that these two poets have a similar way of grouping the most diverse objects, in a unique rhythm and for a unique effect, and of introducing into the most serious discourse a personal aside:

> La duègne a secoué ses jupons
> (Chargez le ciel!—La herse flambe.)
> Le rat de Hamlet, ce bouffon,
> Vient de passer entre ses jambes.
>
> Chassez les rats, chassez les veufs,
> La vieille fermera la porte,
> Rose enfile le maillot neuf
> D'une soeur rivale enfin morte.[19]

In 1907, in his collection *Féeries*, André Salmon had stated the purpose of expressing "impersonal emotions," and of "creating things by verbal description." And, in his "Prikaz," he attempted the crystallization, as on a strip of film, of "a feeling, stronger than any information, of the most poetic element of the time, the Bolshevik Revolution." It was with a feeling of a similar order that Eliot wrote *The Waste Land*, and there is good reason to think that French Symbolism had the same importance for Eliot as it had for the French poets who grouped themselves around Apollinaire just before World War I.

Apollinaire belonged to a generation which was aware of its Symbolist heritage, and which took it as an asset on which to build a new fortune: his was a generation which knew what it owed to the Symbolists. With a similar kind of gratitude toward the Symbolist poets, Eliot wrote:

> A poet, like a scientist, is contributing toward the organic develop-
> ment of culture: it is just as absurd for him not to know the work of
> his predecessors or of men writing in other languages as it would be
> for a biologist to be ignorant of Mendel or De Vries. It is exactly as
> wasteful for a poet to do what has been done already, as for a biologist
> to rediscover Mendel's discoveries. The French poets in question have
> made "discoveries" in verse of which we cannot afford to be ignorant
> . . . .[20]

Apollinaire is better understood in relation to the Symbolists than apart from them. Yet, as one critic pointed out, in introducing his work, he cannot be entirely understood as a Symbolist, either: "Ne cherchons pas à le faire deriver tout entier de Mallarmé. Pourquoi apparier deux choses que l'incompréhension où elles sont ne suffit pas à faire jumelles?"[21] Jean Royère was also in accord on this point, writing of Apollinaire: "Son art est souvent une sorte de Mallarmisme renversé."[22] In view of these opinions, one can think of Apollinaire as a Mallarmé *libre*, a sort of mirror image of the Symbolist poet, but as sharing a common poetic tradition with him.

The poetry of Eliot belongs to the same tradition: it is a skillful grouping of highly imaginative sense impressions. The art is one which Eliot learned partly from the school of Apollinaire, partly from the Elizabethans, and partly from Laforgue, just as he learned from Baudelaire and from Corbière certain practices of diction and the choice of images. To some extent, his position was the same as that of Apollinaire: he continued the Symbolist tradition following a short anti-Symbolist reaction, led in England by certain novelists and dramatists, and accompanied by a degeneration in poetry.

In attempting to distinguish the elements in Eliot's poetic style which derived from the French Symbolists, it is natural to begin with Baudelaire. Eliot wrote of him once, "He had something to do with the nineties and he has a great deal to do with us."[23] Eliot received from Baudelaire a very personal sense of religious values (although he was not the only poet of his generation to respond in this way to Baudelaire). One cannot make of Baudelaire a religious poet, and the sense of religious values does not necessarily imply a belief in God or a desire to believe in a Christian sense of the consequence of all appearances. A sense of this kind, Christian and Baudelairean at once, infuses Eliot's poetry and gives it an intensity of emotion without ever betraying itself by accidental exposure.

Baudelaire was obsessed by the inevitable attraction of vice and sin. Eliot did not have the same obsession, but some of his lines are Baudelairean in their import:

> Think
> Neither fear nor courage saves us. Unnatural vices
> Are fathered by our heroism. Virtues
> Are forced upon us by our impudent crimes.
> These tears are shaken from the wrath-bearing tree.[24]

Human folly, error, sin, wickedness appear as frequently in Eliot's poetry as they did in Baudelaire's.

Moreover, Eliot attained his dramatic effects by the same essential means as Baudelaire—by the choice of very concrete images, as in the famous opening lines of "The Love Song of J. Alfred Prufrock":

> Let us go then, you and I,
> When the evening is spread out against the sky
> Like a patient etherized upon a table.

or as in the lines of "Rhapsody on a Windy Night":

> A twisted branch upon the beach
> Eaten smooth, and polished
> As if the world gave up
> The secret of its skeleton,
> Stiff and white.

Another means common to the two poets was the contrast of the agreeable and the hideous, creating a strange fusion which destroys neither the agreeable nor the hideous. The contemplation of the hideous and the sordid was for both poets a necessary negative aspect of the search for beauty. And the artistic value is great: the shock which passes between two contrary poles of sense is powerful, and gives an objectivity that makes the author seem to disappear. A notable example of Eliot's Baudelairean style is to be found in the early "Preludes."

The influence of Baudelaire is present in many of Eliot's lines.[25] Wherever the dramatic force of images is strong, and the sardonic and pathetic are blended together, one senses in Eliot the same personality and intention as in Baudelaire; but nowhere is the influence more evident than in these lines from *The Waste Land:*

> Unreal City,
> Under the brown fog of a winter dawn,
> A crowd flowed over London Bridge, so many,
> I had not thought death had undone so many.
> Sighs, short and infrequent, were exhaled,
> And each man fixed his eyes before his feet.
> Flowed up the hill and down King William Street,
> To where Saint Mary Woolnoth kept the hours
> With a dead sound on the final stroke of nine.
> There I saw one I knew, and stopped him, crying:
>   "Stetson!
> "You who were with me in the ships at Mylae!
> "That corpse you planted last year in your garden,
> "Has it begun to sprout? Will it bloom this year?
> "Or has the sudden frost disturbed its bed?
> "Oh keep the Dog far hence, that's friend to men,
> "Or with his nails he'll dig it up again!
> "You! hypocrite lecteur!—mon semblable,—mon frere!"

The art of T. S. Eliot is strongly Symbolist, but without the extreme reticence of Mallarmé, or the subjective lyricism of Laforgue, and enriched by techniques which neither of them had. "Prufrock" and "Portrait of a Lady" are symphonies, as are "Preludes" and "Rhapsody on a Windy Night," and if the word "symphony" could ever be applied to poetry, it would be proper to these poems, which are composed of a music of images. Each one of the movements of his symphonies is clearly defined; the rhythms are skillfully varied, from fragments of conversation to rhetorical questions; and the emotion is sustained by all these means, but is never given over to subjective lyricism.

Mallarmé made use of a similar technique, but his language was less rich than Eliot's, if perhaps more perfect, since such rationalization of the emotions as Mallarmé practiced often may result in pure technique. But it was by the same process of moving from the emotional into the speculative realm that both succeeded in forming their poem-symbols, consciously creating them out of accumulations of images. Both Eliot and Mallarmé are highly self-conscious artists, in whom all thought of abandonment to the unconscious is suppressed, and also all thought of error or imperfection, which might result from such abandonment. And it is true of Eliot perhaps even more than of Mallarmé, for if the poems of Mallarmé seem sometimes to float in a dreamworld, those of Eliot continually break out of the dreamworld by the intensity of a word or the incision of an image.

Neither the technique of Eliot nor of Mallarmé can be described in a few sentences: it would take a detailed comparison to show the means by which they are able to translate the abstract into the concrete, the emotional into the visionary, and to arrive at a full understanding of what Mallarmé called "synthesis" and Eliot called "structure." Short of such a comparison, Eliot himself provides the best understanding of his relation to Mallarmé, in an article he once wrote for a French journal:

> Donne, Poe et Mallarmé ont la passion de la spéculation métaphysique, mais il est évident qu'ils ne croient pas aux théories auxquelles ils s'intéressent ou qu'ils imitent à la façon dont Ovide et Lucréce affirmaient les leurs. Ils se servent de leurs théories pour atteindre un but plus limité et plus exclusif: pour raffiner et pour développer leur puissance de sensibilité et d'émotion. Leur oeuvre était une expansion de leur sensibilité au dèlà des limites du monde normal, la découverte d'une nouvelle combinaison propre à susciter de nouvelles émotions—transmutation de l'accidentel en réel.[26]

It was in the relation between speculative thought and feeling that Eliot profited from the example of Donne and Marvell, but in the search for release from personality that Laforgue gave him the most valuable model.

4. THE INFLUENCE OF LAFORGUE

Laforgue gave Eliot the technique of self-effacement by means of a special kind of irony. It must be remembered that Laforgue's influence was quite general, both in France and England, in the second decade of the century, but it was in 1908 that Eliot discovered him, before he became a vogue. What Laforgue's poetry, especially his *Moralités* and *Complaintes*, presented to the world was a new point of view, in which personal feelings were elevated to the plane of epochal events, and a critical poetry was created in which the age was allowed to satirize itself in terms of its own romantic literature and popular songs. Eliot made use of the same point of view for treating his own later generation. Particularly in his *Moralités*, Laforgue made an effort to unify the whole of his experience, to make the echoes of the past and the portents of the future audible, and thus the passage of time felt, throughout his poems.

In view of Eliot's obvious debt to Laforgue, Richard Aldington's attempt to absolve Eliot of the "sin" of imitation seems misguided. He wrote:

The reader will amost certainly have noticed that when the syllables "T. S. Eliot" are pronounced, the reply "Laforgue" is elicited as invariably as an automatic machine produces a very small piece of chocolate when pressed with a penny. Now it is certainly true that Mr. Eliot's poetry has some affinity with Laforgue's poetry; but is it not a perfect example of muddled thinking to deduce imitation from affinity of mind, just as the same muddled thought deduces affinity of mind from imitation? . . . To say that Mr. Eliot imitates Laforgue because they have a common faculty for unexpected juxtapositions of ideas expressed with ironic wit is as foolish as it would be to say that Mr. Eliot imitates Ausonius because both frequently quote other poets in their verse.[27]

Aldington's warning is useful, but it fails to apply to the case of Eliot and Laforgue. That Eliot and Laforgue had similar intelligences is certainly evident, but it was exactly for that reason that the younger writer imitated the older one, if the word "imitation" has any favorable sense at all.

"Moreover," Aldington added, "Mr. Eliot has quite as much affinity with Rimbaud and Corbière"—but this statement is simply not true: Eliot profited from Corbière, but there is less sympathy in his work for Corbière than for Laforgue; as for Rimbaud, not even the profoundest reading of the poetry of Eliot could discover any secret affinities.

For Eliot as for Laforgue, the problem was one of being able to speak, in a precise and modern language, of history and everyday life, as a man of his time using the style of his time (Paris for Laforgue, Europe for Eliot). To that end, both had the ambition of being painters, but painter-philosophers. They projected in their poems, as setting for the modern man, such sketches, landscapes, and circumstances as were necessary to give the sense of modern life, together with such moments of the past as continued to act effectively upon the present. Eliot and Laforgue constructed groups of images and reflections, and fixed them in a language in which moments of direct observation and affirmation exist side by side with moments of verbal wit. Eliot's work maintains a perfect equilibrium between verbal virtuosity and groups of violent images. The study of the Elizabethans, of Laforgue, of Pound, and of Gautier, among others, gave Eliot the skill necessary for balancing these opposing modes of expression.

Laforgue's artistic aim was to create a perfect grouping of emotions, of accumulated images of life, around a poetic theme, and so to make a sort of musical composition of images, the harmony and order of which was the sole determinant of poetic value. Laforgue wrote, in his *Mélanges posthumes:*

Je ne serai jamais un compositeur, mes eaux-fortes ne sont que cochonnées et mes vers demeurent plats, et je n'ai pas le temps surtout

... Et pourtant si je savais le métier—et la patience—je ferais de
la sculpture polychrome qui révolutionnerait, de la musique qui serait
le dernier mot du ravissement dans l'Imprévu Infini, des vers philoso-
phiques à Bible définitive.

But too often in Laforgue, one finds an intoxication with words, which produces
phrases around which images whirl; in Eliot, the images are not so much the slaves
of sheer word power: the progress Eliot made was to realize a proportion, a distinct
equilibrium between words, ideas, and images. Eliot took up Laforgue's art where
he had left off, and brought his flooding images under control—images, as
Laforgue also wrote in his *Mélanges posthumes*, "d'un Gaspard Hauser qui n'a
pas fait ses classes, mais est allé au fond de la mort, a fait de la botanique naturelle,
est familier avec les ciels et les astres, et les animaux, et les couleurs et les rues
et les choses bonnes comme les gâteaux, le tabac, les baisers et l'amour."

Laforgue died, still in his adolescence. The poetry of Eliot is not that of an
adolescent, but in it, the images of adolescence are crystallized into the solidity
of art. Laforgue and Eliot saw the same sights. They heard the same voices. They
listened to the same complaints—of rainy days:

> The showers beat
> On broken blinds and chimney-pots,
> And at the corner of the street
> A lonely cab-horse steams and stamps.
> And then the lighting of the lamps.
>
>   "Preludes. I"

—of wasted hours:

> For I have known them all already, known them all:—
> Have known the evenings, mornings, afternoons,
> I have measured out my life with coffee spoons . . .
>
>   "Prufrock"

—of the change of seasons:

> She turned away, but with the autumn weather
> Compelled my imagination many days,
> Many days and many hours:
> Her hair over her arms and her arms full of flowers.
>
>   "La Figlia Che Piange"

—of barrel-organ tunes:

> I remain self-possessed
> Except when a street piano, mechnical and tired
> Reiterates some worn-out common song . . .
>
> "Portrait of a Lady"

Eliot's subjects have much in common with those of Laforgue: the manners and surroundings of the people of his time, the banalities of their conversation, the neighborhoods in which they live—and central to them all, the concealed but passionate observer. His "Portrait of a Lady" offers a complete tableau of contemporary manners among the respectable, which is more complete, more visual, and more artificial than those of Laforgue. It contains one line: "Well! and what if she should die some afternoon," which is very near to one of Laforgue's:

> Enfin, si, par un soir, elle meurt dans mes livres
>
> "Autre Complainte de Lord Pierrot"

Similarly, Eliot's "Prufrock" is a blood-brother to Laforgue, and like him aspires to "bleed the silence":

> On voudrait saigner le Silence,
> Secouer l'exil des causeries;
> Et non! ces dames sont aigries
> Par des questions de préséance.

But Laforgue's poem, "Complainte de certains ennuis," does not have the power of "The Love Song of J. Alfred Prufrock." The feeling of melancholy which pervades Laforgue's poem is replaced in Eliot's by a sense of vision and of drama; Eliot surpasses his model:

> No! I am not Prince Hamlet, nor was meant to be;
> Am an attendant lord, one that will do
> To swell a progress, start a scene or two,
> Advise the prince; no doubt, an easy tool,
> Deferential, glad to be of use,
> Politic, cautious, and meticulous;
> Full of high sentence, but a bit obtuse;
> At times, indeed, almost ridiculous—
> Almost, at times, the Fool.

Eliot's "Conversation galante," is too obviously Laforguean, even to its title, to need comparison; the tone and situation are exactly that of Laforgue's "Autre Complainte de Lord Pierrot":

> I observe: "Our sentimental friend the moon!
> Or possibly (fantastic, I confess)
> It may be Prester John's balloon
> Or an old battered lantern hung aloft
> To light poor travellers to their distress."
>   She then: "How you digress!"

"La Figlia Che Piange" is also Laforguean; its nearest parallel is "Sur une défunte." But in this case the imitation has borne new fruit: the emotion is more intense, the irony more refined; all the mannerisms of Laforgue are there, but masterfully used to evoke the precise emotion. There is the same polite, considerate gesture of the man to the woman:

> I should find
> Some way incomparably light and deft,
> Some way we both should understand,
> Simple and faithless as a smile and shake of the hand.

There is the same detached sympathy:

> And I wonder how they should have been together!

And there is the same ironic goodbye:

> Sometimes these cogitations still amaze
> The troubled midnight and the noon's repose.

As for Eliot's imagery, it bears some striking resemblances to that of Laforgue, but to compare the two is not to suggest that a serious writer really "steals" images from another (in spite of what Eliot has had to say on this subject): if one finds similar images in two poets, it is because they have observed the same figures crossing the same landscapes, or perhaps because Eliot's profound sympathy for Laforgue has produced in him an identical feeling, so that he actually sees things from the same point of view, or else because certain images have struck him with their realism, and so, after a period in which they are stored in his memory, they reappear at the summons of an artistic purpose. Thus it is with the geraniums of Laforgue, which left a definite impression on the poetry of Eliot. Laforgue wrote, for example, in his brief "Rigeurs à nulle autre pareilles":

> Dans un album
> Mourait fossile
> Un géranium
> Cueilli aux Îles.

> Un fin Jongleur
> En vieil ivoire
> Raillait la fleur
> Et ses histoires . . .

Eliot repeats this image in two different and striking ways in his "Rhapsody on a Windy Night":

> And through the spaces of the dark
> Midnight shakes the memory
> As a madman shakes a dead geranium.
> . . . .
> The reminiscence comes
> Of sunless dry geraniums . . .

One is on surer ground in speaking of the verbal irony of Eliot and Laforgue. When Pound translated or imitated Laforgue, it will be remembered, he added qualities which the French poet did not possess, among them precision of words. It may be that to foreigners, even when they know French as well as Eliot and Pound, certain imperfections of form are not apparent; but even so, it is a little surprising to hear the American poets say that Laforgue had language always under his control, that his irony was as carefully wrought as if it had been sculptured, for in France he has the reputation of being satisfied with the nearly perfect effect, of being a master at poetic sleight-of-hand. In any case, it is certainly true that Pound and Eliot both corrected Laforgue's imperfections in transcribing him into English—which proves that the important thing, when an artist is looking for masters, is to make them his pupils.

The verbalism of T. S. Eliot was never the result of a moment's inspiration, or of an intoxication with words. All plays on words are something of a sport or game, but sports and games have rules which cannot be ignored if one wants to master them. Laforgue himself recognized his faults, and in his last poems worked to correct them.

Still, Eliot is capable of using words much as Laforgue used them, as in the deliberate repetition of polysyllables:

> Et que jamais soit tout, bien intrinsèquement,
> Très hermétiquement, primordialement.

Thus Laforgue; and Eliot:

> And all its clear relations,
> Its divisions and precisions . . .
>   "Rhapsody on a Windy Night"

Again, Eliot echoes Laforgue in using proper nouns for emphasis:

> . . .The eternal Footman . . .
> Almost, at times, the Fool.
>> "Prufrock"

and in certain turns of phrase:

>> "So intimate, this Chopin . . ."
>> "Portrait of a Lady"

and on one occasion he even repeats Laforgue, in slightly altered form:

> Là, voyons, mam'zell' la Lune
> Ne gardons pas ainsi rancune . . .
>> "Complainte de cette bonne lune"

> "Regard the moon,
> La lune ne garde aucune rancune . . . "
>> "Rhapsody on a Windy Night"

With these examples in mind, one might say that Eliot's kind of irony and verbal wit is less a matter of playing with words than of playing with actions and situations: his manner is less joking than Laforgue's, but more gripping. He has refined Laforgue's irony, and corrected his nonchalance. Laforgue, for all his sophistication, is sometimes too obviously clowning; Eliot's buffoonery is never crude.

As for the device of using clichés, which both poets enjoyed making fun of, Eliot is the more careful handler of the trite phrase: he leaves Laforgue to his popular ditties, and elects only phrases that are in good taste. The result is a loss of some comic effect, but a gain in elegance. He takes Laforgue only at his best; for example, in "Portrait of a Lady":

> This music is successful with a "dying fall"
> Now that we talk of dying—
> And should I have the right to smile?

At other times, he uses quotations to good effect, in the way that composers often use borrowed melodies in a sonata or a symphony—not as clichés, but as added enrichments of style.

All in all, there is really no essential difference between the art of Laforgue and that of Eliot: if one can call Laforgue a Symbolist, one can certainly apply the same term to Eliot. Eliot preserved the best of Laforgue, correcting and ordering his digressions, avoiding his sentimentality (even when the sentimentality is hiding under a cloak of irony), and making his diction more precise, to correspond exactly with the emotion. With all these improvements, some of Eliot's poems appear quite different from Laforgue's, in their length, their clarity of vision, their controlled proportions; but it is nonetheless true that all the techniques of Laforgue are in them, from the organization of images to the verbal irony they display. Eliot plays all the instruments so well that the symphony sounds new, just as Picasso uses all the techniques of Cézanne so skillfully that his paintings seem wholly original—but in both cases, there is direct influence, and there is organic evolution.

5. THE INFLUENCE OF CORBIÈRE

Richard Aldington was the first to call attention to the considerable influence of Corbière on Eliot, particularly in regard to the poems which Eliot wrote in French. Aldington said:

> The poem of Mr. Eliot, *Mélange Adultère de Tout*, demands for its effect that the reader understand the reference to Corbière's poem, *Epave Mort-né*. But Mr. Eliot has completely purged Corbière of his unpleasant romanticism and his self-pity. He has his own hardness:
>
> > En Amérique, professeur;
> > En Angleterre, journaliste;
> > C'est à grands pas et en sueur
> > Que vous suivrez à peine ma piste.
> > En Yorkshire, conférencier;
> > A Londres, un peu banquier,
> > Vous me paierez bien la tête.
> > C'est à Paris que je me coiffe
> > Casque noir de jemenfoutiste.
> > En Allemagne, philosophe
> > Surexcité par Emporheben
> > Au grand air de Bergsteigleben;
> > J'erre toujours de-ci de-là
> > A divers coups de trà là là
> > De Damas jusqu'à Omaha.
> > Je célébrai mon jour de fête
> > Dans une oasis d'Afrique
> > Vêtu d'une peau de girafe.
> >
> > On montrera mon cénotaphe
> > Aux côtes brûlantes de Mozambique.

The desire to parody, the allusion to Verlaine, the condensation, the jesting way in which it passes over the events of a varied life are all characteristic of modern poetry. All the French poems of Eliot correspond perfectly to the development of the French poets of the younger generation. The disillusioned tone of *Lune de Miel* and *Dans le Restaurant* would find quick approval among our "dear colleagues." At least one can be sure that the author of the following lines, whose inferiority to those of Mr. Eliot is very evident, would have saluted him as a poet:

> Voyez le vieux Goethe; il sautille
> Comme une chèvre sur le Vesuve;
> Il porte un livre grec, un hervier,
> Un filet à papillons;
> Il casse des gros morceaux de Vésuve
> Et en remplit ses poches,
> Car la fin des Vacances d'Eckerman
> Approche . . . etc.

Here is no question of imitation nor of similarity of manner, but of the same stage of intelligence attained by both.

There is no need for extending this comparison. The French poems of Eliot are excellent *pastiches*, excellent exercises, which show how much discipline Imagist poets submitted themselves to in order to obtain a sureness of technique that might otherwise have escaped them. A French reader would not necessarily agree that Aldington chose the best of Eliot's French poems—a greater virtuosity, in fact, is shown in "Le Directeur":

> Malheur à la malheureuse Tamise
> Qui coule si près du Spectateur.
> Le directeur
> Conservateur
> Du Spectateur
> Empeste la brise.
> Les actionnaires
> Réactionnaires
> Du Spectateur
> Conservateur
> Bras dessus bras dessous
> Font des tours
> A pas de loup.
> Dans un égoût
> Une petite fille
> En guenilles

Camarde
Regarde
Le directeur
Du Spectateur
Conservateur
Et crève d'amour.

Other of his poems might be more pleasing to foreign readers, for they contain more color and more varied images. *Dans le restaurant* is the most important of them, ending as it does with the lines which later become the "Death by Water" section of *The Waste Land:*

Phlébas, le Phénicien, pendant quinze jours noyé,
Oubliait les cris des mouettes et la houle de Cornouaille,
Et les profits et les pertes, et la cargaison d'étain:
Un courant de sous-mer l'emporta très loin,
Le repassant aux étapes de sa vie antérieure.
Figurez-vous donc, c'était un sort pénible;
Cependant, ce fut jadis un bel homme, de haute taille.

It is in this realism of extraordinary intensity and density that Eliot was a true follower of Bosschère, Pound, and Corbière. In such poems as "Mr. Apollinax" and "Gerontion," each word is a direct presentation of a real object, stripped of all emotionalism and sentimentality. The poetry of Corbière is sometimes tainted with sentiment, but modern French poetry has no poet more massive than he, no voice that is more rugged and lashing:

—Seul—mais toujours debout avec un rare aplomb,
crenélé comme la mâchoire d'une vieille,
Son toit à coup de poing sur le coin de l'oreille,
Aux corneilles bayant, se tenait le donjon,
Fier toujours d'avoir eu dans le temps sa légende . . .

With his last traces of Romanticism removed, Corbière attained pure aesthetic states through masses of images, in "Un Riche en Bretagne," or "Frère et soeur jumeaux." His method, systematized by Eliot, produces poems of the force of "Rhapsody on a Windy Night" and "Gerontion," some lines of which are very close to Corbière:

My house is a decayed house,
And the jew squats on the window sill, the owner,
Spawned in some estaminet of Antwerp,
Blistered in Brussels, patched and peeled in London.
The goat coughs at night in the field overhead;

Rocks, moss, stonecrop, iron, merds.
The woman keeps the kitchen, makes tea,
Sneezes at evening, poking the peevish gutter.

Obviously, Rimbaud had attained a similar detachment, in certain of his poems which Pound admired, and a harmony of realistic images, pure enough to evoke a state of intense emotion. But these were scenes, not dramas, which Pound justly compared to the paintings of Cézanne. Eliot achieved in his best poems both the harmonic proportions of Rimbaud and the freedom of expression, the movement, the prolific imagery of Corbière.

6. THE INFLUENCE OF GAUTIER

From Corbière and Rimbaud, Eliot moved on to rejoin the tradition of Gautier. Both Pound and Eliot, as we have seen, profited from his example in putting a check on the excessive freedom of free-verse writing in America. And they were successful, for their use of the controlled quatrains of Gautier soon produced new disciples.

At the time when Eliot was imitating Gautier, he became a master of his method, with all its tricks of variation and turns of phrase; as a poet who had developed out of Imagism, he already knew the value of detachment and clear statement; he also knew how many lines and stanzas there were in the first poems of Gautier and in his most famous collection, *Émaux et camées*. He knew that in Gautier's poems were unrealized possibilities of expression, as well as models of perfect form. Certain of Gautier's stanza-patterns were exactly reproduced by Eliot—notably, this one:

> Carmen est maigre—un trait de bistre
> Cerne son oeil de gitana.
> Ses cheveux sont d'un noir sinistre,
> Sa peau, le diable la tanna.
>
> "Carmen"

which becomes:

> Grishkin is nice: her Russian eye
> Is underlined for emphasis;
> Uncorseted, her friendly bust
> Gives promise of pneumatic bliss.
>
> "Whispers of Immortality"

Eliot's imitation of Gautier turns into parody, when he employs bizarre and intriguing proper names, in the manner of the French poet; or when he arranges scenes with "local color":

> Gloomy Orion and the Dog
> Are veiled; and hushed the shrunken seas;
> The person in the Spanish cape
> Tries to sit on Sweeney's knees
>
> "Sweeney among the Nightingales"

Finally, even the composition of individual poems of the "Sweeney" period follows that of Gautier's *Émaux et camées*, for Gautier worked from a surface impression at the beginning to an exploration of the depth of each personage and subject, with a description complete in each line, up to the point where he felt the effect was obtained, and then he stopped short, or at most permitted himself, on rare occasions, a rapid comparison which would not dull the total impression. By progressive descriptive images, Eliot like Gautier makes use of repetitions and echoes phrases:

> The couched Brazilian jaguar
> Compels the scampering marmoset
> With subtle effluence of cat;
> Grishkin has a maisonette;
>
> The sleek Brazilian jaguar
> Does not in its arboreal gloom
> Distil so rank a feline smell
> As Grishkin in a drawing-room.
>
> And even the abstract Entities
> Circumambulate her charm;
> But our lot crawls between dry ribs
> To keep our metaphysics warm.
>
> "Whispers of Immortality"

Pound, in *Hugh Selwyn Mauberley*, and Eliot, in his "Sweeney" poems, and in "Burbank with a Baedeker, Bleistein with a Cigar," "Whispers of Immortality," "Mr. Eliot's Sunday Morning Service," and above all, "The Hippopotamus," have succeeded in using the style of Gautier with a dexterity equal to his, and especially in the case of Eliot, of making caricatures which surpass the Romantic sketches of *Émaux et camées*.

The best example of this type of imitation—not exactly a parody, because it does not hold its model up to ridicule, but employs all the other techniques of parody—is "The Hippopotamus," which has its source in Gautier's poem of the same name, "L'Hippopotame," in his *Poésies diverses*. The two poems begin alike, then diverge:

L'hippopotame au large ventre
Habite aux jungles de Java,
Ou grondent, au fond de chaque antre,
Plus de monstres qu'on n'en rêva.

Le boa se déroule et siffle,
Le tigre fait son hurlement,
Le buffle en colère renifle,
Lui dort ou paît tranquillement.

Il ne craint ni kriss ni zagaies,
Il regarde l'homme sans fuir,
Et rit des balles des cipayes
Qui rebondissent sur son cuir.

Je suis comme l'hippopotame:
De ma conviction couvert,
Forte armure que rien n'entame,
Je vais sans peur par le desert.

The broad-backed hippopotamus
Rests on his belly in the mud;
Although he seems so firm to us
He is merely flesh and blood.

Flesh and blood is weak and frail.
Susceptible to nervous shock;
While the True Church can never fail
For it is based upon a rock.

The hippo's feeble steps may err
In compassing material ends,
While the True Church need never stir
To gather in its dividends.

The 'potamus can never reach
The mango on the mango-tree;
But fruits of pomegranate and peach
Refresh the Church from over sea.

At mating time the hippo's voice
Betrays inflexions hoarse and odd,
But every week we hear rejoice
The Church, at being one with God.

The hippopotamus's day
Is passed in sleep; at night he hunts;
God works in a mysterious way—
The Church can sleep and feed at once.

I saw the 'potamus take wing
Ascending from the damp savannas,
And quiring angels round him sing
The praise of God, in loud hosannas.

Blood of the Lamb shall wash him clean
And him shall heavenly arms enfold,
Among the saints he shall be seen
Performing on a harp of gold.

He shall be washed as white as snow,

By all the martyr'd virgins kist,
While the True Church remains below
Wrapt in the old miasmal mist.

Considering Eliot's poem as a parody—and although the author has not insisted on its being taken as such, he has not taken any precaution to prevent its being admired in this way—it is an admirable success. Considered as an original poem, it is perfectly successful; and in fact, if one knows that it was composed after a careful study of the qualities and form of Gautier, he can only admire the techniques which the American poet was able to draw from the French poet, and the means by which he gave them a greater value than had been perceived up to that time.

Everything that is in Eliot's poem is to be found somewhere in the work of Gautier—repetitions, contrasts, characterizing words and images, are carried even further by Eliot. Gautier's poem ends in a fashion less brilliant than Eliot's: its force of caricature suddenly gives way, for the resemblance between the two things compared (the hippopotamus and the poet) only appears at the end, and is not carried all the way through the poem, as in Eliot's comparison of the hippopotamus and the Church. The imitation is evident in the first line of Eliot's poem, which is simply a translation of Gautier's, in the idea which informs the poem, in the vision, in the rhythm, in such a way as to be self-evident; the differences, in this case, are more important than the resemblances.

The aim which Pound and Eliot pursued had been attained: the strict forms of Gautier's poems passed by means of their work into the English poems of Herbert Read, and into the American poems of Elinor Wylie, Hart Crane, and Archibald MacLeish, among many others.

But this was not the only influence of Eliot in America, for he has continued to have a dominant influence on poets until this day. Wherever irony, or anguish, or tragedy appears in American poetry of the modern period, it usually owes something to Eliot's example.

Eliot enriched the Imagist movement, and made its technique capable of expressing a greater variety of subjects. The Imagists had been criticized for their narrowness of vision; Eliot, without sacrificing any of the Imagists' precision or the realism of their images, strengthened their poetic vehicle so that it was capable of sustaining more varied objects and more diverse observations. In doing so, he tended to bring American and English poetry nearer to French Symbolism—not the vague Symbolism of Samain, nor the Symbolism of forms and colors of De Régnier, but the Symbolism of Baudelaire when it expressed human torment by means of concrete images, that of Corbière when it made one see the hard edges of an object, that of Laforgue when it clothed with irony an emotion twisted and tortured by the conventional politeness of the world.

CHAPTER 7

Conclusion

THE SUCCESS OF IMAGISM

IN 1916, Ezra Pound declared that America at last had a group of young poets worthy of comparison with their French contemporaries. He added that such a group had not existed before 1912, and it is clear that he had tried to create such a group when he made up the first of the Imagist anthologies. This book, *Des Imagistes*, included some poets who did not appear in Amy Lowell's subsequent anthologies, but who went their own way—for example, William Carlos Williams, Skipwith Cannell, James Joyce, John Cournos, and Allen Upward. Pound's anthology, as F. S. Flint said, "set fire, if not to the Thames, at least to America." By 1916, it can be said that Pound and Amy Lowell, in different ways but with equal energy, had become the directors of the American poetic destiny.

The Imagist movement had flooded the little magazines in America with free verse, until editors began complaining that every morning's mail was filled with Imagist and Vorticist imitations. Taking the issues of *Poetry* alone, between 1914 and 1918, one could cite a whole host of more or less successful imitators of Imagism: Max Michelson, Clara Shanafelt, Rosalind Mason, Robert A. Sanborn, Alice Corbin, Helen Hoyt, William Saphier, Dorothy Dudley, Muna Lee, Jeanne d'Orge, Mary Carolyn Davies, David O'Neil, Agnes Lee, Louis Gilmore. For the most part, they added nothing new to the Imagist experiment, contenting themselves with the rules as Pound had laid them down, but nearly all their poems were interesting, and they bore witness to the vitality of the Imagist doctrines.

Imagism even led to parody, the most successful being that of Witter Bynner (under the pen name of "Emmanuel Morgan") and Arthur Davidson Ficke (under the pen name of "Anne Knish"), who published an anthology called *Spectra* in 1916. The effort was well timed, for the moment was ripe for mystification: many critics had attacked Imagist poems when they were new, and then had seen the poems quickly become classics. They had grown more prudent, and as a result a number of respected periodicals, including *The Forum*, took the "Spectra" hoax seriously, although it was as obvious as the notable parody of French Symbolist poetry, the *Deliquescences* of "Adoré Floupette."

The "manifesto" of the "Spectrist" group was more instructive:

> Emmanuel Morgan, father of the poetic school of *Spectra*, was for
> many years interested in painting, and now begins to publish his works
> in verse. He returned recently to Pittsburgh, his native town, after
> having lived for twenty years in Paris. Some years ago, he made the
> acquaintance of Rémy de Gourmont, and this acquaintance ripened
> into an intimate friendship. It was Gourmont, he attests, who sug-
> gested that Mr. Morgan write in the new form which he had invented.
> Mr. Morgan does not pretend that M. de Gourmont has accepted the
> poetic theories formulated and expressed in *Spectra*.[1]

in particular, mocking their expatriation and their cult of French authors. Its
literary "theories" were reminiscent of the Imagist prefaces: "It is the intention
of the Spectric group to advance poetic expression to new heights, to attain a
brilliant and fresh style, by a method not greatly different from that of the Futurist
painters." In metaphors worthy of Amy Lowell, the parodists announced their
intentions:

> If the Spectrist wishes to describe a landscape, he will not attempt a
> map, but will put down those winged emotions, those fantastic analo-
> gies which the real scene awakens in his own mind. In practice this
> will be found to be the vividest of all modes of communication, as the
> touch of hands quickens a mere exchange of hands.

Announcing that "The Spectric method is as yet in its infancy," they made
allusions to Oriental art, as the Imagists had done, and licensed the use of either
free or regular verse. The hoax was soon exposed, and if the ruse cast some
ridicule on the Imagists, it also gave them further publicity.

The years 1912 and 1913 had been years of doubt, when poets shifted from
one position to another, but the years 1914 and 1915 were years of expansion,
when the fire of change spread, consuming much dead poetic timber. Alfred
Kreymbourg, who was active as an editor at the time, said the effect was much
like that of a civil war, in which the victory soon went to the rebels.

As in France, it was free verse which seemed the most striking change in
the new poetry, and over it most of the battles were fought. As late as 1917, Eliot
said "It is true that up to very recently it was impossible to get free verse printed
in any periodical except those in which Pound had influence . . . ."[2] Amy Lowell
used her influence in favor of free verse, and eventually gained support from the
critics. But it is Pound who deserves credit for being the initiator of free verse.
Even *Poetry* was at first hesitant to print it, and doubted the efficacy of the new
form. But when Rabindranath Tagore visited Chicago after receiving the Nobel
Prize, he said that free verse was the only true poetry he had found in America;

and after that Pound's word became sacred, and free verse assumed respectability.

The same arguments both for and against free verse were heard in America as had once been heard in France, but the opponents of it were not very forceful, and by 1915 there were few talented poets who were still expressing themselves in regular verse. Conrad Aiken was one exception, but the articles which he wrote on the question of free verse were directed more against the abuse of it than against the principle. And Edwin Arlington Robinson was another exception, though he never wrote a line against the new poets, and when questioned, said that he appreciated the new form, but that his talent was for regular verse.

Pound and Amy Lowell were not the sole spokesmen for the new verse, for Harriet Monroe, the editor of *Poetry* magazine, wrote several editorials, tracing the origin of free verse back to classical verse (much as Gustave Kahn had once shown the common origin of French vers libre and the classical alexandrines of Racine). She ended by citing the innovations of Vildrac and Duhamel.[3] John Gould Fletcher carried on the argument with reviewers in the larger magazines, and Arthur Davidson Ficke took exception to Eunice Tietjens, when she spoke of "the spiritual danger of writing free verse."[4] But Amy Lowell finally settled matters by adapting the methods of science.

It was she who put scientific instruments to the service of free verse, not contenting herself with earlier French experiments of this kind, but making new experiments of her own in the psychology laboratory at Columbia University. Her proof was valuable in settling the origin of American free verse, for when the new technique was said to be imitative of George Meredith, or Walt Whitman, or Stephen Crane, she loudly proclaimed that modern free verse came from the French Symbolists, and her authority prevailed over the guesses of her opponents. The influence of Amy Lowell as a poet was limited, but the success of free verse and above all its popularity owed more to her than to the greater artistry of Pound and H. D. The very popularity of free verse led to a reaction against it after 1919, and the death of Amy Lowell was a further blow to the development of free verse, and an occasion for the return to regular forms.

The success of free verse, in spite of its critics, was almost instantaneous. To many, it seemed the whole point of Imagism — just as in France, to the public at large, vers libre was the whole point of Symbolism.

> Free verse is no longer an experiment, no longer even a new move-
> ment. Nearly every modern poet uses it either exclusively or in
> addition to its counterpart, regular verse.[5]

And Robert Cutler remarked in 1917 that "the world is deluged with free verse."[6] It was apparent that the Imagist movement had come of age, and that its results could be seen. Not that free verse and Imagism were to be confused, but the two things—the theory of intensive images and exact diction, and the practice of free verse—had purged poetic language of jargon, clichés, trite rhythms, jingling cadences: "abject, slavish, tired, jogtrot, copycat poetry."[7] The advent of Imagism had eliminated a number of respectable names in important magazines, and within a few years had transformed the attitude of poets toward the practice of verse, disposed of the notion of polite verse, empty perfectionism, dictionary rhymes—of the whole idea that poetry had a role to play other than that of expressing sensations and emotions in the very rhythm of these emotions. For these services, modern poetry in English is still in debt to the Imagists.

Freedom in poetry was in the air. Aldington expressed the feeling of the time when he wrote that "the artist has to deny and disapprove principles erected by his ancestors in order to keep intact their great common principle of freedom."[8] It was because Rémy de Gourmont best represented this spirit of independence that he had so many admirers during the period, and that Pound recommended his writing as a civilizing influence to all his countrymen.

But de Gourmont, in spite of the praises accorded him by the Imagists and by such critics as Havelock Ellis and James Huneker, in spite of the studies of his work which appeared at the time, in spite of the large number of translations of his essays, had only an indirect influence on the poets of 1916 and 1917, and this solely through the Imagists. It was a little later that his direct influence, especially in the notion of a "dissociation of ideas," made itself felt among intellectual rebels. Conrad Aiken showed the resistance to de Gourmont's influence in his remark: "Today, the tendency is toward individualism at any cost. The result is a fierce pursuit of novelty, and the too-hasty condemnation of any work which at first reading does not seem to be strikingly original."[9] There was indeed a disdain of the commonplace and a cult of originality, but surely it was preferable to the sort of doldrums in which English poetry slept in 1910. The taste for eccentricity reappears in every poetic era, at precisely the moment when originality is displayed, and excesses of youthful enthusiasm. Moreover, the excesses that Aiken criticized would not seem surprising to anyone acquainted with the history of French Symbolism. It was only in England and America that Pound passed for a "mystifier," whose aim, some thought, was to astonish the public by coming out every month with a new French poet for others to imitate, on pain of death. Amy Lowell may well have given a similar impression, but if so, it was because of her personal eccentricities rather than her poetic originality, her mannerism rather than her manner.

In spite of all objections, there was a real poetic life in America from 1910 to 1920: poets no longer slept in Boston chimney-corners; and if they did not try to shock the middle class, it was because the American middle class was not worth their time; they contented themselves with railing at magazine editors and trying to convert them to the new movement.

Thanks to Pound, who was working on their behalf, and thanks to Amy Lowell, who was working on behalf of everyone in general—from poets to universities, women's clubs, and even clergymen—a certain number of new ideas, whether clear or vague, had enough impact to turn the thinking minds of the day from the poetic theories of Wordsworth, the verse of Longfellow, and the republican sentiments of Whitman. Whether the subject was free verse, images, symbols, or French poetry, people were talking of new things, and especially of new technique. Amy Lowell may have lacked the necessary critical sense, balance, and humor, which would have been of the greatest service to her contemporaries. But someone had to go into the marketplace and bargin with the public, and Amy Lowell was self-appointed to the task. Someone had to spread the new ideas, even though, in the beginning, they were not particularly exotic. But they seemed exciting to aspiring poets, who were for the most part energetic and innocent. Folly and ineptitude were as much in evidence as before, but better questions were being raised: they were no longer exclusively about religion, morality, or psychology. Instead, people were becoming accustomed to the notion that poetry was an art, and a knowledgeable art which required skill and hard work.

Amy Lowell was not the person to teach the value of careful work and of perfection of style. The articles and poems of Richard Aldington, the poems of H. D., and above all the various writings of Pound were the educating force for poetry in the United States. In 1918, Eliot wrote that there were very few serious writers who did not owe something to Pound, and that all discussion of poetry had to take his ideas into consideration. He had brought the revolutionary spirit to *Poetry*—a spirit which it lost on the day he left it. Pound was not a critic, if a critic is one who produces a systematic program of ideas, but he had the rare gift of perceiving things clearly, and of saying what needed to be said at the right moment and in the right tone. He knew how to sound an alarm, if not how to conduct a discourse. Thus, he was able to provide some excellent leadership at a critical moment in American poetic history, and he continues to this day to give vigor to American letters.

American criticism was launched with the Imagist movement, and has continued to develop from it, including even the work of Eliot. From 1914 on, the *Little Review* had taken notice of the need for a new critical spirit, and in an editorial had made it clear that the new magazine was searching to recover this forgotten art:

. . . criticism as an art has not flourished in this country. We live too
swiftly to have time to be appreciative; and criticism, after all, has only
one synonym: appreciation. Criticism that is creative—that is our high
goal.[10]

Poets at this time were working toward a poetic criticism, a practical
criticism which would help the poet himself in his search for technique. Pound
was the first master in this kind of criticism, followed by Eliot, the true master.
Conrad Aiken was also trying, but with less success, to form his taste into a critical
method; though he fell short of synthesis, he did achieve a rightness of judgment
which made his book, *Skepticisms*, one of the best to be written at this time by
an American on American poetry. However, he had little influence. Although
Aiken was not far from Eliot in his interpretation of particular poets, he did not
succeed in achieving the concentration and systematic objectivity of Eliot. Aiken
was one of the most accomplished American poets, who borrowed techniques from
many sources. He owed his style in part to English Romantics like Keats, but
followed the evolution of more modern American poets as well, Eliot in particular.
In *Turns and Movies* and *The Jig of Forslin* (both 1916), he searched for a
musical poetry that was a sort of latter-day French Symbolism. The strong
influence of Eliot may be seen in such lines as:

> It is morning. I stand by the mirror
> And tie my tie once more,
> While waves far off in a pale rose twilight
> Crash on a white sand shore.[11]

Probably it was Eliot's poems, "Prufrock" and "Portrait of a Lady," which made
Aiken aware of the symphonic possibilities in poetry, of expressing emotions by
verbal resonance and harmony, in poems divided into parts equivalent to the
movements of a symphony. He isolated himself from the Imagists and from the
main current of poetry in his time, and cultivated nebulous musical qualities in
the manner of Verlaine. His tradition was principally English, though it owed
something to Sidney Lanier, as well as to Eliot, Fletcher, and the French Symbolists.

Another critic who worked in the same direction, but remained even farther
from the goal, was Maxwell Bodenheim. He was also infected with a vague
Symbolism and an imprecise Imagism, but his simple tastes led only to imitation.
He dimly perceived that the question of style had to be considered first in poetry,
but got no further than statements like this:

> Literary style alone remains a comparatively untouched region, be-
> cause the great majority of writers, since the beginning of the Chris-
> tian era, have always been clutched by some great burning message

> which they fancied the world needed . . . or by some important moral
> that required a hundred pages for illustration.[12]

or this, which sounds like an inchoate T. S. Eliot:

> Pure poetry is the vibrant expression of everything clearly delicate
> and unattached with surface sentiment in the emotions of men toward
> themselves and nature.[13]

Or, again, in the same essay:

> True poetry is the entering of delicately imaginative plateaus, uncon-
> nected with human beliefs or fundamental human feelings.

The same stylistic preoccupations were also to be seen in Marsden Hartley's writings of this time—preoccupations which were fertile and legitimate, but were not supported by a constructive criticism in his case. "I believe I must count myself among those who love stylistic irradiation: the sun is not enough for me, but I must have the radiance around the prismatic face, the iridescence around the sphere."[14] One cannot go very far with metaphors of this kind, and for this reason, it is impossible to exaggerate the importance of T. S. Eliot, whose criticism *was* constructive.

Pound's criticism was not constructive in the same sense as Eliot's: his ideas were definitive enough to do without a system. His articles always contained precise and practical advice, which answered the immediate need of poets. From 1915 on, he indicated how the faults of American literature might be corrected, publishing prescriptions and prohibitions, and giving as models the best works of world literature: he first presented the masterpieces of the Middle Ages, then what was best in contemporary French literature: "we should develop a criticism of poetry," he said, "based on world-poetry, on the work of maximum excellence."[15]

It was with this intention that he introduced contemporary French poets to America. Beginning in 1912, he brought their names into every literary discussion in which he was engaged. He also cited authors of other countries and other periods, of course: to give his readers an idea of the "image," he cited Rimbaud, and also Catullus; to give them an idea of the intensity that a poetic style could attain, he cited Corbière, and also Villon. It was to contemporary French poets that he turned most often, because they were the most immediately available. In presenting them on a universal scale of poetic value, he was necessarily severe. He did not show the sentimental and naive indulgence of a Francophile, as Amy Lowell did; but it was because he considered the French moderns superior to the modern poets of any other country that he pointed them out as models for American poets.

Two different aspects of Pound's propaganda must be distingushed. Sometimes he armed himself with a name, such as Rémy de Gourmont, to combat American vulgarity. De Gourmont gave him the prestige of his name, and also some commonsense ideas which served him as further weapons in the attack on bad taste. Later on, Pound was to make use of Confucius in much the same way. Again, sometimes he used French poets as the best examples of modern verse techniques—or what he took to be modern verse technique. He chose Rimbaud (but not the Rimbaud of the *Illuminations* or "The Drunken Boat"), Corbière, and Laforgue as his chief examples, though it might seem that Mallarmé's poetry and Rimbaud's *Illuminations* exhibit more modern methods than the "Vénus anadyomène," which Pound preferred, and than the whole work of Corbière and Laforgue, just as it might also seem that the poetry of Apollinaire was more modern than that of Romains, who seemed to Pound the most important French poet of his generation. In any case, Pound's ideas were accepted and they fulfilled the needs of the time. From 1912 to 1920, he spoke of Corbière as the master of the most intense poetry; of Corbière and Laforgue as masters of irony and satire; of Corbière and Gautier as masters of the clear, "hard" style. He constantly and patiently directed his propaganda toward the artistic problem that most needed to be solved. Some, in their enthusiasm for the whole of contemporary French literature, criticized Pound for his arbitrary choice, and for the large number of important French poets whom he ignored or discredited. But by his constant advocacy, he caused serious minds among his American contemporaries to be influenced by certain necessary and valuable ideas about poetry.

If it was Pound who taught the principles of poetic style, it was Amy Lowell who taught the principles of free verse. She gave popular lectures, wrote articles, and recited frequently in public: she read French poetry admirably, knew how to communicate her enthusiasm to a large public, and how to use humanitarian sympathies to inspire admiration for French literature:

> It is a strange thing that while so many Americans and English repair
> every year to France, so few of them, in either country, realized what
> a serious and self-sacrificing people the French were making of themselves, before the present war brought the fact to their notice. To
> students of French literature, this was no matter for surprise.[16]

Of all the Imagists, Amy Lowell had the largest public. Her books of poems sold like novels; her study of French poets alone reached a very large number of readers, having been written for popular appeal. There was not a single idea in the book, *Six French Poets*, which had not already been expressed by a French critic; and even the presentation was that of a popular lecturer. For each of the poets she included, she tried to give a few facts about their lives and some illustrative anecdotes; then she took their works in chronological order, citing the longer poems that were included in the standard French anthology. It was she who made the names of Paul Fort and Francis Jammes familiar to American readers of the period. She remarked that the Boston Public Library did not contain a single volume by Paul Fort, explaining in her good-natured fashion that "the excellent gentlemen who buy the French books for the public libraries are a bit behind the time, and a prose which jumps at one in unexpected rhymes is a fearsome thing in a foreign language."[17] Apollinaire had observed that the New York Public Library was forced to order the entire works of Henri de Régnier when he was elected to the French Academy, because it did not have a single one of his volumes up to that time. Probably it was thanks to Amy Lowell's propaganda that the larger libraries in the United States acquired most of the important works of modern French poetry.

Pound and Amy Lowell were not the only Americans who popularized French poetry. A number of other advocates appeared on the scene, and the war itself provided a common cause to arouse the interest of American readers. The death of Verhaeren brought forth a spate of funeral orations; Paul Fort was the subject of a study of Richard Aldington, following Amy Lowell's success; and his ballads soon appeared in translation, while Rémy de Gourmont was accorded studies by James Huneker, Burton Rascoe, and Aldington, the last of whom brought out a selection of his works in 1928. Max Michelson in *Poetry*, Aldington in *The Little Review*, and Paul Rosenfeld in *The New Republic* kept their readers in touch with French literature from several points of view. Havelock Ellis wrote about Rémy de Gourmont and Henri de Régnier in *The North American Review*, and little by little the better magazines began to admit French writers as a subject of importance. The smaller magazines had begun about 1915 to publish not only articles about French poets but also their poems, and after their example, the large magazines began to publish translations of the best French poets—*Books*, for example, printed much of Verlaine, Baudelaire, and Mallarmé, while the *Literary Digest* was printing Paul Fort and Verhaeren. In the *Mercure de France* of the time, Theodore Stanton was pleased to note the interest which American poets were taking in French literature and its technique. He mentioned such widely varied evidence as *Eris, A Dramatic Allegory*, by Blanche Shoemaker Wagstaff (a philosophical poem dedicated to Bergson) and William Rose Benet's *The Falconer of God*, in which he saw "a powerful French influence" represented in such titles as "Le Baiser de Rodin," "Le Café Tortoni," "La Vivandière," etc. He also mentioned that Claudel's *Connaissance de l'Est* had been translated, as well as translations of Maeterlinck and Cammaerts, and that a study of Henri de

Régnier had appeared in *The Nation* under the title, "A French Poet of Yester-day."[18]

It seems, therefore, that in the wake of the Imagists, diverse writers helped to reestablish French literary influence in America. The English response to French literature at this time was much more limited; and if the bulk of American poetry was nourished by French technique, the same could not be said for English poetry. A separation had occurred, in which England remained much as it had been before 1914. Though the same oppportunity for development had been presented to poets in both countries, Imagism passed in England without having affected the literary tradition very strongly. American poets had received the full shock, and it had produced many interesting reactions. Perhaps it could be said that Imagism gave America an artistic tradition which the sterile and facile imitation of England had long prevented. The vitality that this short movement had, deriving as it did from a prolonged current of French influence, would seem to prove that, now as in the era of Jefferson, American intellectual life responds best to the influence of France.

All the movements which attempted to give a national character to American literature, independent of foreign influences, had failed, for the success of Masters, Sandburg,[19] and Frost were individual exceptions, not the source of new movements. The Imagist movement had found the country ready to receive it, just as French painting had already awakened sympathetic response in American artists.

Some people expressed surprise that the commonsense rules which Pound published in *Poetry* magazine in 1913 should have been the basis for a revolution in American poetry. What they did not realize was that the rules had been drawn from a study of the whole Latin tradition in European poetry, and from such diverse sources as Browning, Flaubert, and T. E. Hulme (who knew French Symbolism well). Pound established a common ground, based on good sense about poetry, and this common ground was what was most needed at the moment by American poets. By extracting the essence of Latin culture for the benefit of his contemporaries, he was able to stimulate the American intelligence, and teach it to appreciate the sort of literature from which his principles had come.

French poetry gained an ever-widening influence in America, transcending the limits Pound had envisioned. Mallarmé, Rimbaud, and Laforgue showed increasing numbers of American poets the arts of expressing dreams, complex emotions, and irony. In time, many poets had learned the new language invented by the masters of French Symbolism, and were employing it in ever-subtler and richer forms.

It was Eliot, more than Pound, who led American poetry in this new direction. But Eliot was a dangerous master to follow, for although his manner worked very well for himself, those who imitated him found themselves often imitating imitations—of Laforgue, and of the Elizabethans. To study his art, and make use of combinations other than his own, was fine, but very few found combinations as successful as that of the Symbolists and the Elizabethans; his imitators tended, therefore, to follow him too closely, rather than trying to surpass him. They also lost, many times, the stylistic qualities which Pound had taught them. But Eliot's criticism remained the soundest foundation for the modern concept of poetry. For that reason, the third part of this study will be devoted to his activity, and to the renewed activity of Pound.

PART THREE

THE SPREAD OF FRENCH INFLUENCE

The Effect of Mallarmé, Rimbaud, Laforgue, and Other French Poets on the New Poetic Diction

IN 1917, the final Imagist anthology appeared, and about 1920, *Poetry* ceased to be the dominant poetic journal in America. Of the original Imagists, only Pound and H. D. continued to have influence, and even H. D. was more admired than imitated. Amy Lowell, in spite of her propaganda, interested the public more than she interested other poets. And free verse, the focus of most of the debate, had long since triumphed as a poetic form in America.

It was at this time that *The Little Review*, with Pound and Eliot as its most prominent contributors, became the center of poetic force. The French influence on this magazine was much stronger than it had been on *Poetry*, and was of a different nature. While *Poetry* had mainly admired the free verse disciples of the great poets of the nineteenth century, Rimbaud and Mallarmé, *The Little Review* turned attention to the masters themselves. Amy Lowell had a rapid success with the secondary poets of the French movement, but Pound and Eliot had a less rapid but more lasting success in giving their contemporaries Gautier, Corbière, Laforgue, and Rimbaud as models for the new poetry.

CHAPTER 1

Pound, Eliot, and *The Little Review*

ROM 1914 TO 1918, *The Egoist* magazine in England had presented first Imagism, then Eliot, and then other important American poets, notably Marianne Moore. The American magazine, *Poetry*, directed by people with much good will but little originality, had its chief impetus from the Imagists. In 1917 Pound parted company with it and accepted Margaret Anderson's invitation to join her *Little Review*. In May of that year, Pound wrote a short announcement for the latter magazine which explained his departure from *Poetry:*

> I would say, however, in justification both of *Poetry* and myself, that *Poetry* has never been the "instrument" of my "radicalism." I respect Miss Monroe for all that she has done for the support of American poetry, but in the conduct of her magazine my voice and vote have always been the voice and vote of a minority.[1]

Harriet Monroe had held on to certain illusions about the "heart of American democracy," the "voice of the West," and the "soul of Chicago." As soon as Pound and his friends left, she gave the magazine over entirely to these ideals.

As for *The Little Review*, on the other hand, its position was much more bold:

> A contempt for the "vulgus" is the inevitable reaction of any man or woman who observes the antics of the "flies in the marketplace." There's nothing supercilious about it. It's a fact that humanity is the most stupid and degraded thing on the planet—whether through its own fault or not is beside the point where you're weighing values. You're not blaming humanity when you say that: it isn't interesting to blame; the interesting thing is to put the truth of it into a form that will endure.[2]

Thus culminated the drive toward individualism which had been nourished for at least twenty-five years by the writings of Nietzsche. *The Little Review* and several other little magazines were criticized by many readers for the scorn which they appeared to express for all of life. Letters to the edtior often inquired why the journals were not interested in the World War, and the answer of *The Little Review* was: "Perhaps it's because none of us consider this war a legitimate or an interesting subject for Art, not being the focal point of any fundamental emotion for any of the peoples engaged in it."³

The Little Review seemed particularly designed to complete the work which had been begun by *The Egoist*, a fact which Pound recognized from the moment he joined it:

> In so far as it is possible, I should like *The Little Review* to aid and abet *The Egoist* in its work. I do not think it can be too often pointed out that during the last four years *The Eogist* has published serially, in the face of no inconsiderable difficulties, the only translation of Remy de Gourmont's *Chevaux de Diomèdes;* the best translation of Le Comte de Gabalis, Mr. Joyce's masterpiece *A Portrait of the Artist as a Young Man,* and is now publishing Mr. Lewis's novel *Tarr . . .* but *The Egoist* has not stopped there; they have in a most spirited manner carried out the publication in book form of the *Portrait of the Artist,* and are in the act of publishing Mr. Eliot's poems, under the title *Mr. Prufrock and Other Observations.*⁴

Poetry had published a number of articles on French poetry, but far fewer than *The Egoist*, and had rarely included translations; it had never given Pound the free hand he desired. *The Little Review* allowed him to continue the work begun in *The Egoist*, and to publish not only articles and translations from the French, but also poems and prose in the original.

In order to establish a critical standard based on the masterpieces of world literature, Pound sought the support of the best European writers. Jules Romains was named foreign editor of *The Little Review*, (a purely honorary title, since he did not contribute a single line of copy). Several years before, with a similar intention, Pound had asked Rémy de Gourmont to lend his name to the movement, and received a letter from the French writer which he printed in *The Little Review*, with this explanation:

> At a time when most of our now vocal and prominent American bellifists were still determined that the United States should take no part in saving civilization, I desired to found a magazine which should establish some sort of communication between New York, London, and Paris. To that end I asked the assistance of Mr. Yeats, who is without question the greatest living poet of these islands; of Ford Madox Hueffer, founder of *The English Review . . .* and of Rémy de Gourmont. None of these men refused. Other complications delayed the project. The present arrangement with *The Little Review* is the ultimate result of the scheme. If de Gourmont had lived he would now be among our contributors. His last letter concerning the project is therefore of personal interest to our well-wishers. It is of far wider interest, in so much as there are few amiable and dispassionate critics

of America, and that de Gourmont's few words on the subject are not
without some enlightenment.

Cher Monsieur,

J'ai lu avec plaisir votre longue lettre, qui m'expose si clairement
la nécessité d'une revue unissant les efforts des Américians, des
Anglais, et des Français. Pour cela, je vous servirai autant qu'il sera
en mon pouvoir. Je ne crois pas que je puisse beaucoup. J'ai une
mauvaise santé et je suis extrêmement fatigué, je ne pourrai vous
donner que des choses très courtes, des indications, d'idées plutot que
des pages accomplies, mais je ferai de mon mieux. J'espère que vous
réussirez à mettre debout cette petite affaire littéraire et que vous
trouverez parmi nous des concours utiles. Évidemment si nous pouvions
amener les Américains à mieux sentir la vraie littérature française et
surtout à ne pas la confondre avec tant d'oeuvres courtantes si
médiocres, cela serait un résultat très heureux. Sont-ils capables
d'assez de liberté d'esprit pour lire sans être choqués, mes livres par
exemple, il est bien douteux et il faudrait pour cela un long travail de
préparation. Mais pourquoi ne pas l'entreprendre? En tous les pays,
il y a un noyau de bons esprit, d'esprits libres. Il faut leur donner
quelque chose qui les change de la fadeur des magazines, quelque
chose qui leur donne confiance en eux-mêmes, et leur soit un point
d'appui. Comme vous le dites, il faudra pour commencer les amener
à respecter l'individualisme français, le sens de liberté que quelques-
uns d'entre-nous possèdent à un si haut point. Ils comprennent cela
en théologie. Pourquoi ne le comprendraient-ils pas en art, en
poésie, en littérature, en philosophie? Il faut leur faire voir—s'ils ne
le voient pas déjà—que l'individualisme français peut, quand il le faut,
se plier aux plus dures disciplines.

Conquérir l'Américain n'est pas sans doute votre seul but. Le
but de *Mercure* a été de permettre à ceux qui en valent la peine
d'écrire franchement ce qu'ils pensent—seul plaisir d'un écrivain.
Cela doit aussi être le vôtre.

Votre bien dévoué
RÉMY DE GOURMONT

This interesting letter expressed completely the view of de Gourmont toward
America; his mind was always interested in both the Americas, and frequent
judgments about them appear and reappear in his essays. He died too early to
see his work become widely known in the United States, and to know that it was
the basis for establishing a "corps of free spirits" there, as elsewhere. Though his
direct influence did not go beyond a small circle of writers, the circle included
such men as Aldington, Pound, and Eliot, and through them his intellectual ideals
were transmitted to a wide circle of readers and writers. In 1919, *The Little*

Review devoted an entire issue to him, including articles by Pound, Aldington, and others.

But de Gourmont was chiefly a moral influence. Other French writers had a more precise literary influence on Americans, the chief among them being Laforgue and Rimbaud. These three French names, in fact, appeared more often in the pages of *The Little Review* than any others, and their influence was evident in many ways. In February, 1918, *The Little Review* printed a whole anthology of French poetry, interspersed with quotations and critical remarks by Ezra Pound, among them the remark that the "summit" of modern French poetry was reached with Rimbaud, Corbière, and Laforgue. The list of poems published in this issue is instructive enough to be given in its entirety:

> Jules Laforgue: "Pierrots (on a des Principes)"
> "Pierrots, III"
> "Complainte des Consolations."
> "Locutions des Pierrots"
> "Complainte des Printemps"
> "Complainte des Pianos"

> Tristan Corbière: "La Rapsodie Foraine et le Pardon de Sainte Anne," and other fragments

> Arthur Rimbaud: "Au Cabaret Vert"
> "Venus Anadyomène"
> "Les Chercheuses de Poux"
> "Roman"
> "Comédie en Trois Baisers"

> Rémy de Gourmont: "Litanies de la Rose"

> Henri de Régnier: "Odelette: Si j'ai parlé"
> "L'Accueil"

> Emile Verhaeren: "Les Pauvres"

> Francis Vielé-Griffin: "In Memoriam Stéphane Mallarmé"

> Stuart Merrill: Fragments

> Laurent Tailhade: "Hydrothérapie"
> "Quartier Latin"
> "Rues"
> "Rondel"
> "Dîner Champêtre"

Francis Jammes: "J'Aime l'Ane"
"J'Allais à Lourdes"
"La Jeune Fille"
"Il Va Neiger"
"Le Poète (fragment)"

Moréas: Some verses

Klingsor: Some verses

André Spire: "Dames Anciennes"

Vildrac: Fragment

Jules Romains: Some quotations

In October of the same year, Pound published a long article on *La Wallonie*, a Belgian review of which the editor, Albert Mockel, had sent him a number of issues. The article was studded with quotations from French poems, among them those of Mallarmé, Stuart Merrill, and other Symbolists such as Hanton, Delaroche, Saint-Paul, Bois, Rodenbach, Vielé-Griffin, and Mockel himself.

The French number of *The Little Review* was a landmark in Pound's propaganda for a new poetry, and cleared the way for a new wave of French influence in the United States. It created much discussion, some of it adverse: a critic writing in *Poetry*, for example, thought the idea absurd, and took exception even to the choice of poems. Some readers were dismayed to receive a magazine written almost entirely in French, for Amy Lowell's book on French poetry had not widened the circle of readers of French poetry in America (though it had popularized the idea), and Flint's earlier articles in English reviews had reached only a very small public. But Pound's French issue made an impression on all the aspiring young poets in the country; he presented them a living tradition of modern poetry, by means of some of its best examples. He showed them the technical prowess developed by French poets from Gautier to Rimbaud, and they began immediately to emulate it.

After this issue, there were others in which French studies or translations appeared—Pound, for example, printed some translations from Laforgue, and Malcolm Cowley published an adaptation of the "Complaints." In the July 1917 *Little Review*, there were translations of some of the *Illuminations* of Rimbaud by Helen Rootham, and more importantly, Eliot's French poems, which demonstrated in an original fashion the effect of French influence on one American poet.

Poetry was not the only kind of literature which showed a French influence in the pages of *The Little Review*. The stories of Ben Hecht, which certain readers found "decadent," were of the same line as the stories of Gautier, Huysmans, Loüys, and de Gourmont. And American criticism was clearly basing itself on French standards, led by the example of Pound and above all by Eliot, both of whom owed much to de Gourmont.

For the second time, then (*Poetry* having been the first), a magazine had succeeded in America without the aid of political or philosophical articles, a magazine devoted entirely to art, and making "no compromise with the public taste." There were other attempts, at about the same time, but none of them had the success of *The Little Review*. The main contributors had already established their reputation in Europe, and they had enough confidence in themselves, and were decisive enough in their style, so that they were bound to be listened to.

Pound and Eliot had many disciples in America by now, as the poems that were appearing in the period from 1917 to 1920 clearly showed. Imagism had borne fruit: there was a new precision of imagery, an absence of abstraction, a clarity of form, and an irony of tone which owed as much to Pound and Eliot as to Laforgue and Corbière; and finally, there was an elegance and a harmony of style which represented both a discovery of the French tradition and a recovery of an earlier English tradition of poetry.

Though no magazine which represented an interlingual poetic tradition, as Pound dreamed of, achieved complete success, the knowledge of French poetry became more and more widespread. Pound was criticized often for trying to make a bilingual magazine of *The Little Review*, but he continued to maintain that an English writer who did not know French was only half-educated, and that a French writer who did not know English was also half-educated—though he seemed more committed to the first principle than to the second. The bilingual basis for American poetry received material support, however, with the publication of Eliot's French poems in July 1917, more by Aldington in March 1919, and with the publication of French poems of André Spire and Jean de Bosschère in October, 1918—not to mention the issues dedicated to French moderns, to *La Wallonie*, and de Gourmont.

From 1917 on, one could clearly see in *The Little Review*, and in other magazines dedicated to the new literature, techniques developed by the Imagists, mixed with French elements that gave the writing a special charm. Many of the poets had never read the French Symbolists in the original, and many did not even know a word of French, yet their style was French in flavor. There is nothing mysterious about this fact: American poets were now working with forms invented by their masters—Pound and Eliot, who had discovered in the great poetry of the past and in the best poetry of recent France the forms which they needed to write the poetry of their time. The poets who followed their example would add new works to this tradition to the extent of their own talent, dedication, and education.

CHAPTER 2

After Pound, Eliot and *The Little Review*

AN EXAMINATION OF *The Little Review*, the three anthologies called *Others*, published in 1916, 1917, and 1919, and the first of Louis Untermeyer's anthologies, which appeared in 1920, would show clearly that most American poems were influenced by the practice of French poets who had written before and after the turn of the century. This influence is more notable in the first volumes than in Untermeyer's collection, for this last was representative of a longer span of time and of a taste for the most diverse tendencies in modern poetry.

Alfred Kreymbourg has explained how he happened to found his magazine-anthology, *Others*.[1] The idea of such a magazine was not new: he hoped to bring together a number of American poets who were otherwise unknown. Harriet Monroe had done the same when she founded *Poetry*, but she had remained hostile to certain talented writers—among them, Alfred Kreymbourg. If one goes back far enough in American poetry, he could cite the example of Poe, and his *Southern Literary Messenger*, and of Emerson, and *The Dial*. In Greenwich Village, he made the acquaintance of Guido Bruno, editor of *Bruno's Chapbook*, which recalled the original *Chapbook* of Chicago, and continued the series of decadent reviews of which the English *Yellow Book* was the most famous. He also became acquainted with Walter Conrad Arensberg, a devotee of the works of Baudelaire, Verlaine, and Rimbaud, and a patron, as well, of French painting. Kreymbourg was not sure what modern poetry needed, but was determined to do something: he had already edited *The Glebe*, which sought to bring out unknown poets at regular intervals, on no principle except that they be interesting. And since, about 1913, writers were seeking new models, there was a demand for translations, and Kreymbourg had succeeded in translating several German and Russian works. It was his Glebe Press which had printed the first Imagist anthology, Pound's *Des Imagistes*, in 1914.

The Decadent note was evident in the first edition of *Others* (critics called it "The Yellow Dog"); but Imagism was also an influence on its pages, as in the pages of *Poetry*. Kreymbourg did not have the prestige of Harriet Monroe, who had ventured to publish the first free verse in America, had first presented Imagism to the American public, and had introduced such diverse new poets as

Carl Sandburg and T. S. Eliot. But he helped to complete the first presentation of the new American poetry.

1. CONTINUERS OF THE DECADENT MOVEMENT

Others helped to perpetuate, not without some attendant scandal, the Decadent tradition which had begun in London in the 1890s. Bruno, in his Chapbooks, included sketches of the Beardsley type, poems of the Verlaine type, and naturalistic stories, and once got himself in trouble with the police over a novel by Kreymbourg, *Mina, The Girl of the Streets. Rogue,* another lively review which smacked of London of the 1890s, also appeared on the scene at this time. It published the works of Donald Evans, Arensberg, Carl Van Vechten, Mina Loy, Louis and Allen Norton, Wallace Stevens, Gertrude Stein—most of them writers who later achieved fame. Bruno's *Bohemia,* started in 1913, had the distinction of publishing the first poems of Hart Crane. During 1912 and 1913, the number of such magazines was as great as in the previous wave of 1895 to 1900. But few of them are remembered now, except those which in some way escaped the fin de siècle influence.

Donald Evans

Donald Evans was a direct inheritor of the Decadent movement, who preferred Baudelaire and Verlaine to all other poets. He even modeled his life on that of his heroes. He was not gifted enough to see what poetry demanded to be in his time, and he was too gifted to become an imitator of the Imagists or any other of the new styles. His first book, *Discords,* published in 1912, was written under the influence of Verlaine, as the titles clearly show: "Tristesse," "Nuptial Night," "Amants, amantes," "Tout passe, tout casse, tout lasse," "In the Boudoir," "Cette maladie qui S'appelle la Vie," "Souvenir," "Jadis et naguère," "Moonlight Violins," "Ressemblance," "Je ne vis plus: J'assiste à la vie," and "In the Gardens—Versailles."

He borrowed everything from Verlaine—his rhythmic technique, his refrains, his echoes, his tone—as can be seen in such lines as:

> 'Tis cold in my heart as the woods are cold
> 'Tis chill in my heart as the air is chill.

or:

> The tuneless drip of the twilight rain
> Keeps time with my heart beats as I stray
>
> "Night Song of Autumn"

The *Sonnets from the Patagonian*, published in 1914, brought him popular acclaim, and showed a little more originality than his first volume. But the tone was still that of the Decadents who had written twenty years before him. His images were often pleasing, but never total—a fact which separates his work, as well as that of Arensberg and Bodenheim, from the true Imagists, and from Eliot and Williams. His often gracious and elegant images do not completely render the object, and it is only by accumulation that they become suggestive:

> It loosed the tongues, and the four were free.
> As four portraits on a wall come to life they stirred
>   the silence with a babbling that gleamed.
> The drawing-room was draped in a wistaria mist,
> And the flutter of the phrases patted the cheek with an
>   alien charm.[2]

In a small pamphlet published under the name of Cornwall Hollis,[3] Evans described his intentions thus:

> Create evil, not because it is evil, but because it is good . . . One must marry a woman who loves another man, and attempt a crime, so as to taste the fear of being lost and experience the shades of remorse. One must always lie, because by lying only can one test the truth . . . One must always be a decoration on the scene; even in dying, one must be careful to make a good scene.

In 1916, such absurdities were no longer amusing; however, it was through them that Evans found his reason for writing. *Two Deaths in the Bronx* (1916) and *Ironica* (1919) added nothing to the art of poetry, though Evans' diction was clearer and more modern. It was the period for irony, which served as an effective weapon against the least taint of sentimentality. Evans was following all the currents of style: he imitated Verlaine in *Two Deaths in the Bronx*, employing the rhythms of the *Ariettes* in such lines as these:

> Dearest,
> But not the nearest . . .
> If I call
> Will you come
> To the dying?
> I am lying
> Brumal, dumb
> By the wall.
> Dearest,
> But never the nearest
> When I fall

Through the gods,
Or the odds.

There was increased force in these volumes, particularly in the second, where the cynicism is intense enough at times to give the effect of a true work of art.

However, the originality of Donald Evans was not conspicuous: he was a retarded Symbolist, who had a virtuosity of language, a talent for suggestion, but made no important contribution to the new poetry of his time.

Walter Conrad Arensberg

The poems of Walter Arensberg were few, but they were fine. He maintained a studio, in which he displayed the works of Picasso, Duchamp, Gleizes, and Brancusi—all very avant-garde, for 1914. He espoused the new theories that artists in Paris were then advocating, and translated French and Italian poems into English. He even presumed to explain the moderns by means of the ancients—Mallarmé, for example, by means of Dante.

Poems (1914) contained translations of Baudelaire, Verlaine, Mallarmé, Nerval, Laforgue, and Musset. His own poems show the same qualities as those of Evans—qualities of the fin de siècle school, such as cleverness in handling slight subjects, and elegance of style. In *Idols* (1916), Arensberg made use of free verse, and dealt with the even slighter subjects in a still more elegant style. Mallarmé's influence was to be seen in these poems—a rare thing at this time in American poetry. He borrowed imges and forms from Mallarmé's poems, as in "Voyage à L'Infini":

> The swan that is
> Reflects
> Upon the solitary water—breast to breast
> With the duplicity:
> *"The other one!"*
>
> And breast to breast it is confused.
> O visionary wedding! O stateliness of the processional
> It is accompanied by the image of itself
> Alone.
>
> All night
> The lake is a wide silence,
> Without imagination.[4]

He derived some of his effects from the divided image, as Mallarmé had done (e.g. "Autobiographic"), and from the negative image, as in "The Night of Ariadne":

The night had grown oracular
With tongues of licking that were not he,
She knew not how she knew, reluctantly.[5]

and sometimes his syntax was as involved as Mallarme's: "Stalactites to her credulous chastity" or "Heavy the darkness that she lay beneath." He also translated "L'Après-midi d'un faune," but in an uninspired fashion, even when taken with the accompanying, absurd "explanation."

Arensberg did not come near discovering a new poetic style, but only borrowed certain small refinements from Mallarmé. This disciple of the Symbolist Master had learned from him by interpreting his method in a very broad fashion. The name of Arensberg deserves to be remembered, however, along with that of Evans, for illustrating a tendency which had lasted thirty years in America, and which had produced no better poets than they.

Maxwell Bodenheim

The stylistic qualities of these latter-day Decadents attained their greatest virtuosity in the poetry of Maxwell Bodenheim, who was good at formal inventions and tricks. He surprised many people with his cleverness, and came to be regarded as one of the most promising poets of his generation. They took him for a pure artist, who needed neither rhyme nor emotion to write poetry, and for whom a dictionary, a piece of paper, and a pen were sufficient equipment. He wrote things about poetry which sounded new and modern, but which were really trivial. Eliot wrote that poetry was an escape from human emotion, thereby creating a new theory of art; Bodenheim wrote, "Words are selected and combined *only in the mind* and spoken or written emotion must be a blending of animal feeling and conscious thought,"[6] and thereby appeared to be saying something important. Eliot sought to diminish the importance of emotion, but not to deny it; Bodenheim sought to do away with it altogether, and substitute irony, sarcasm, and other critical attitudes which poets like Laforgue had employed before him.

What Bodenheim took from French and American poets was only their external techniques—what for them was a suitable instrument for their emotion became for him a pose or mannerism. His metaphors flowed forth in astonishing profusion, but answered no human aim. Carl Zigrosser wrote of him: "He has tricks and mannerisms *pour épater le bourgeois*. He is the typical Bohemian poet, living a sordid, urban life, yet at moments 'browsing among the stars.' When I see him, I can imagine the life of Verlaine, and all the other vagabond poets of the Latin Quarter."[7]

Bodenheim's whole art consisted in pouring out images as false as these:

Their lives are the centers of half-cloudy days,
With now and then a noisy evening
In which they hang the crude little japanese-lanterns
   of their thoughts.
On the ever-swaying strings of their minds . . .[8]

My mind is a naked child
Living in the little half-crimson garden of my soul.[9]

And his lines were enriched by occasional Oriental allusions, which were perhaps reminiscent of Imagism or Symbolism. Malcolm Cowley noticed echoes of Laforgue in the lines of Bodenheim. Bodenheim himself, in order to attract attention, went around saying that he was a second Rimbaud, and even appeared to believe it, up to a point. At any rate, he thought that with French Symbolism, poetry had found its true expression: "Only with the coming of the French Symbolists did poetry enter into the completion of its second large trend," he said, explaining that this "trend" was "the proclamation that poetry needed no link with the most important human themes, but only needed to paint a picture, without commentary."[10] This discovery of Bodenheim's, however, smacked more of the Parnassians than of the Symbolists.

Bodenheim was not sure of his ideas, and did not try to clarify them by examination of actual works: he simply drifted, hiding the poverty of his thought under the umbrella of a pretentious style. It was true of his criticism as of his poetry that the front was decorated but the shop was empty. It consisted of a few facile metaphors, sometimes crowded against each other, sometimes extended into paraphrases and allegories, but never the symbol as Mallarmé understood it, never the image as the Imagists understood it; instead, there was flag-waving, parades, costumes without actors, and sideshows stolen from other contemporary poets.

2. THE MAINSTREAM OF AMERICAN POETRY

We can turn our attention to the poets who emerged as the best and most interesting of that time, and who carried forward modern experiments in talented fashion, in the style of their contemporaries among the French poets. The direct or indirect influence of French poetry can be shown in the work of Marianne Moore, Wallace Stevens, Mina Loy, William Carlos Williams, Alfred Kreymbourg, and other poets who became known before 1920, as well as in that of poets whose recognition came after that date, namely Hart Crane, Malcolm Cowley, E. E. Cummings, and others.

Marianne Moore

Marianne Moore's first poems appeared in *The Egoist*, and showed all the earmarks of Imagist experiments. She was an Imagist by virtue of the clarity and novelty of her images; her art, which Pound likened to that of Laforgue, was distinguished by an extraordinary gift for picturesque imagery, and an equally remarkable gift for speculation, by means of metaphors, literary references, and aphorisms. An object released in her mind a train of images and memories, present and past, as if she were a naturalist who collected specimens of animals and vegetables, and then studied them with the aid of scientific textbooks. Laforgue's mind worked in a similar fashion, but with a different sensibility and irony. It is unlikely that Marianne Moore had read either Laforgue or Rimbaud when she published her first poems in 1915, even though some critics supposed they could see the influence of these two Symbolists in her work.[11] But in any case her poetry spoke the Symbolist language, and in an idiom not too far from those poets or even from Mallarmé.

She belonged to the Symbolist tradition, first, because of her exceptional powers of observation. With Mallarmé, these powers were used in the search for beauty of forms and sensual grace; with Rimbaud, in one of two ways—either for visual fidelity or for expressive vision; with Laforgue, for the translation of a sensibility burning to express itself. But with Marianne Moore, observation was directed toward the object, to fix it vividly and in its utmost reality. Her method had more of physics than of metaphysics about it, and it was in minute observation that she displayed her greatest strength.

Observation, however pure, is not poetry: it must be placed in context, and Marianne Moore had a weakness for using observation to point a moral or illustrate a principle, rather than to fill out a poetic idea. Since precepts and morals were passé as a basis for modern poetry, she tended to emphasize elements of style, such as irony and allusion, rather than composition. Laforgue had the same weakness, to a lesser degree, being content often with exhibiting a virtuosity of diction and a wealth of irony. Both poets were alike in their delight with the dance of words, their pleasure in ideas studded with striking and ingenious observations, and their ability to use verbalism and imagism to perfection.

The verbalism of Marianne Moore is without musical accompaniment, but it is not absurd to compare her poetry with that of Laforgue: they borrowed from different sources, but to the same advantage. Like both Pound and Laforgue, Miss Moore liked to play with learned diction:

> To popularize the mule, its neat exterior
> expressing the principle of accommodation reduced to a

minimum.

"Labors of Hercules"[12]

In these noncommittal, personal impersonal expressions of
appearance,
the eye knows what to skip.

"People's Surroundings"[13]

Why should continents of misapprehension have to be
accounted for by the
fact?

"England"[14]

It would be vain to look in French poetry for a style that gives the same
kind of pleasure as that of Marianne Moore, and this fact sets her apart from other
poets in this study. It is not because her technique is so different, or because each
aspect of her art cannot be found in some contemporary French poet; but because
she has eliminated almost all emotion from her observations, and because she does
not deal in literary clichés nor in popular songs, but in clippings from American
newspapers (from the political news to the sports pages) worked together into a
special harmony, by means of her gift for observation and her originality in the
choice of words. She made a poetry very new in appearance by using new
materials, but the techniques of diction and composition, the ironic effects, are
those used by the French Symbolists, particularly Laforgue. Finally, it was with
something like a Latin ease and solidity that she built her observations of common
objects and prosaic expressions of the day into a structure of true poetry.

Wallace Stevens

As for Wallace Stevens, he was also a poet for whom style was the primary
gift. But he used it for elegance, and it was toward the perfection of elegance that
he directed his powers of observation.

He knew French poetry. He even translated French poems; but he never
imitated them directly, though one can see many evidences of French stylistic
influence in his poetry.

He once wrote a letter to William Carlos Williams on the subject of Imagist
principles of poetry:

> My idea is that in order to carry a thing to the extreme necessity to
> convey it one has to stick to it . . . Given a fixed point of view, realistic,
> imagistic, or what you will, everything adjusts itself to that point of
> view; and the process of adjustment is a world in flux, as it should be
> for a poet. But to fidget with points of view leads always to new
> beginnings and incessant new beginnings lead to sterility.

... One has to keep looking for poetry as Renoir looked for
colors in old walls, wood-work and so on.[15]

This is a revealing commentary on his method: he was a patient observer and a
careful craftsman, taking from real objects whatever he could find of details,
colors, and forms for making his poetic garlands:

> Just as my fingers on these keys
> Make music, so the selfsame sounds
> On my spirit make a music, too.
>
> Music is feeling, then, not sound;
> And thus it is that what I feel,
> Here in this room, desiring you,
>
> Thinking of your blue-shadowed silk,
> Is music . . .
>   "Peter Quince at the Clavier"[16]

Thus, while Marianne Moore was seeking connections between real objects,
Stevens was seeking correspondences of feeling or of thought between objects and
an impalpable reality:

> The body dies; the body's beauty lives.
> So evenings die in their green going,
> A wave interminably flowing.
> So gardens die, their meek breath scenting
> The cowl of Winter, done repenting.
> So maidens die, to the auroral
> Celebration of a maiden's choral.[17]

One recognizes the familiar style of the Symbolist poets in this passage; the
enjoyment of prolonged echoes of emotion in extremely delicate form were a
source of pleasure to many of the poets of this school. But Stevens was being true
to his own feelings; he was always guided by his own tastes and instincts, and
attached less importance to learning than Pound and Eliot did. He recognized that
French poetry exerted an influence over him, though he did not seek it: "The
lightness, grace, sound, and color of French have had an undeniable and precious
influence on me," he said.[18]

This influence of the French language on English and American writers was
not a new phenomenon, since French has always been an inspiration to English
writers in developing elegance of thought and of expression. But the influence of
language does not come without influence from literature, particularly in the case
of poetry. It is a generally accepted opinion that English has strength and richness

as a language, while French has elegance and nuance. Pursuing these qualities
in style, Stevens naturally cultivated the genius of the French language, in works
where its peculiar virtues existed to the highest degree. Writing in a period when
French poetry was widely known and even unconsciously imitated by Americans,
he drew benefit from the subtleties of expression and experiments with technique
that were emanating from France. This is true not only in the passage cited, but
in the totality of his work. He not only used a French vocabulary extensively, but
even the movement of his sentences was French, involving more exclamations and
questions than are usual in English poetry. Also notable are his word-bouquets,
his multi-colored images, his impeccable dandyism, his vibrations of joy or of
"spleen," all of which are qualities never encountered before in American poetry,
but which were very evident in French Symbolist poetry:

> Who, then, in that ambrosial latitude
> Out of the light evolved the moving blooms,
>
> Who, then, evolved in the sea-blooms from the clouds
> Diffusing balm in that Pacific calm?
> *C'était mon enfant, mon bijou, mon âme.*
>
> The sea-clouds whitened far below the calm
> And moved, as blooms move, in the swimming green
> And in its watery radiance, while the hue
>
> Of heaven in an antique reflection rolled
> Round those flotillas. And sometimes the sea
> Poured brilliant iris on the glistening blue.
>
> "Sea Surface Full of Clouds"

In short, in his tradition, Wallace Stevens was French, being related to
Baudelaire by his taste for elegance and his dandyism, and to Laforgue by his
nonchalant irony and the "Pierrot" tone of his poems—though his Pierrot is
dressed formally in black and wears a silk top hat. He was a Symbolist in his art
of evocation, his search for correspondences, for words which form an image and
words which cause an echo in the mind.

Stevens's case, more than any other, raises the question of whether modern
American poetry is an exotic creation, with an artificial veneer of manners rather
than an authentic style, or whether, instead, in taking their modern technique
from the example of the French poets, American poets did not borrow elements
proper to their own nature. One American critic, Gorham Munson, answered this
question for Stevens, when he showed what made his poetry distinctly American.
And certainly it may be said that if a poet of Stevens's genius is rare, Americans

were always open to what was new, and had produced many partially successful experimenters before Stevens appeared. The number of pseudo-Parnassians, quasi-Tennysons, neo-Wordsworths, and would-be Baudelaires among American poets before the time of Stevens would serve to prove that there was nothing exotic about his success. Discipline was lacking in these half-poets, and their attempts therefore contributed nothing lasting; as soon as discipline was introduced by the Imagists, and the easy imitation of English poetry was given up for good, the qualities striven for by earlier American poets were finally realized as part of the new poetic style.

Unfortunately, subjective lyricism and facile style appeared again after the initial discipline was assimilated; but in lines like these, the strict precision of the language of Rimbaud and of the French Parnassians is to be seen embodied in the familiar pattern of English blank verse:

THE WORMS AT HEAVEN'S GATE

Out of the tomb, we bring Badroulbadour,
Within our bellies, we her chariot.
Here is an eye. And here are, one by one,
The lashes of that eye and its white lid.
Here is the cheek on which that lid declined,
And, finger after finger, here, the hand,
The genius of that cheek. Here are the lips,
The bundle of the body and the feet.
. . . .
Out of the tomb we bring Badroulbadour.

William Carlos Williams

It may have been Williams who produced the best formula for an American art. By 1918, at any rate, it could be seen that a fairly large number of poets were contributing to the new style that had developed out of Imagism, and that all were members of the same "family." American poetry had attained a state of temporary equilibrium: it was no longer a question of experimenting, but of exploring a newly discovered vein. All the poets possessed three qualities in particular: imagism, verbalism, and musicality. All were joined in seeking a luminous, yet objective vision, for which Pound had first given the formula. All agreed with Pound that "the natural object is the best symbol." Never before had America produced a group of poets who knew so well how to handle the music and dance of words.

French influence had undoubtedly helped to shape these poets. The problem of tradition was paramount, and Pound solved it for himself—and he hoped, for other Americans—by the study of significant literature in all the languages of the world. Eliot solved it somewhat differently, but the difference was not crucial, since both poets followed Rémy de Gourmont in matters of tradition. Amy Lowell, who had seen the renaissance of 1912 as an effort to "express America," began to feel the urge to do so herself rather late in life, and took up the American legend in particular, probably a relaxation after her revolutionary battles for an international poetry. It remained to be seen whether the English tradition, exemplified by Edwin Arlington Robinson and Edna St. Vincent Millay, or the native American tradition, perpetuated by Sandburg, Masters, and Frost, would provide the best solution for American poetry. Both seemed possibilities at that time, but proved to have little life left in them.

Whether or not Williams found a better solution, it is clear that his effort had much in common with that of Pound, Marianne Moore, and H. D. He applied imagination to American subjects, it is true, but it was an imagination similar to that of H. D., though applied to a different world; and this imagination was not European. One could even find in earlier American literature some precedent for their kind of visual clarity and sensual precision. Their effort at founding an American style of poetry was a serious one, and had little to do with Whitman's American ideals and prejudices. Williams, particularly, was concerned with the direct contact of man with life, human or natural.

But Williams's poetry did not grow out of the American soil like a dogwood, or some other indigenous tree. When questioned about his "influences," he replied in terms of his own family: his maternal grandmother had been a French colonial, from Martinique; his mother had studied painting in Paris, with Carolus Duran; and he himself had attended school in Switzerland when he was a boy—all of these seemed to constitute a French influence in his background. Perhaps more important was his interest in French painting, for he had a great admiration for Picasso and Juan Gris (a fact which he attributed to his Spanish ancestry), and met Marcel Duchamp on his visit to New York in 1915. However, he had not read, as he admitted "beaucoup les Français contemporains ni même les classiques, bien qu'il soit assez au courant de ce qu'ils ont fait."[19]

Williams was at that time one of a new group of poets who were carrying on what the earlier Imagists had started. For a period of years, Williams had depended on Pound for news on the important things that were going on in contemporary French poetry and criticism, especially wherever they might be useful to the formation of modern American poetry. It may seem surprising that this strongly American poet, who prided himself on being independent of European influence, turned to French models to form his characteristic style, yet the fact is that it was the contemporary French tradition which helped him the most.

This fact is clear from the first in Williams's development, and not only from the fact that he appeared in the original Imagist collection, *Des Imagistes*. Some of his early poems reflect the manner of Browning, but even then he had the capacity for strict and intense observation which all the best Imagists shared, the talent for shaping hard and clear images, and the ability to give them a latent emotional quality with great hidden force. Finally, he sought, in common with all the Imagists, to express emotion by the briefest possible means, in the sparest and most striking language, as though on a straight line from the object to the observer. He always worked for the simplest possible expression, stripped of all sentiment, beginning with his very first book, *Al Que Quiere* (1917), and continuing through *Kora in Hell* (1920) and *Sour Grapes* (1923).

About 1918, when he began working on *Kora in Hell*, he broke away from the Imagist discipline of free verse into an even freer form, not abandoning his poetic aims but allowing them still greater liberty, and so wrote his "Improvisations," as he called them, very much in the manner of the *Illuminations* of Rimbaud. As he said in the "Prologue" to this work: "It is to the inventive imagination we look for deliverance from every other misfortune as from the desolation of a flat Hellenic perfection of style."[20] To critics who objected to this experiment in the free association of ideas, he replied that his earlier poetic discipline had enabled him to make this change without losing his sincerity, and that his concern had been to break out of "the trammels of literature, beating down every attack of its *retiarii* with my *mirmillones.*"[21]

It is evident that after his first book, Williams had become concerned with making a more faithful transcription of his emotions, and began to doubt the efficacy of pure Imagism, seeking a more complete means of communicating with his audience. Having tried the strict discipline of the Imagists, it was perhaps natural that he should have turned to the unrestrained manner of Rimbaud in the effort to express himself, for as he put it: "It is seldom that anything but the most elementary communications can be exchanged one with another."[22] Hence he resolved to try the experiment of unleashing his imagination altogether, hoping to force a connection between objects most intimate and most remote:

> Of what other thing is greatness composed than a power to annihilate
> half-truths for a thousandth part of accurate understanding. Later life
> has its perfections as well as that bough-bending time of the mind's
> florescence with which I am so discursively taken.[23]

Rimbaud had declared, "Il faut se faire voyant." And Williams responded:

> In the mind there is a continual play of obscure images which coming
> between the eyes and their prey seem pictures on the screen at the
> movies. Somewhere there appears to be a maladjustment. The wish

would be to see not floating visions of unknown purport but the imaginative qualities of the actual things being perceived accompany their gross vision in a slow dance, interpreting as they go. But inasmuch as this will not always be the case one must dance nevertheless as he can.[24]

This image of the dance was as real for Williams as it had been for Rimbaud, as can be seen by comparing parallel passages from the two works:

J'ai tendu des cordes de clocher à clocher; des guirlandes de fenêtre à fenêtre; des chaines d'or d'étoile à étoile, et je danse.

. . . . . Puis un ballet de mers et de nuits connues, une chimie sans valeur, et des melodies impossibles.

"Illuminations"

—And I? must dance with the wind, make my own snowflakes, whistle a contrapuntal melody to my own fugue![25]

I could say so much were it not for the tunes changing, changing, darting so many ways.[26]

It can be seen that these two poets resemble each other in many respects. Given the different languages which separated the genius of Rimbaud from that of Williams, there is a remarkable similarity of gifts, intuitions, even spirit. "Il faut se faire voyant," declared Rimbaud, and "We must make contact," said Williams. The aims seem opposite, yet in pursuit of them the two poets were alike, uniting free impulse with visionary imagination. They possessed two apparently contradictory sensibilities, each of which could express itself in turn. The same Rimbaud who wrote "Venus Anadyomène" also wrote "La Saison en Enfer." The same Williams who wrote *Al Que Quiere* also wrote the *Improvisations*. Both were accomplished ironists: Williams, like Rimbaud, sometimes used a trite phrase or commonplace construction to arrest the reader and prepare him for an unexpected meaning. Or sometimes he would fasten his sight on the minutest details of an object, in order to discover some new aspect of it.

On joue aux cartes au fond de l'étang, miroir évocateur des reines et des mignonnes . . .

Pendant que les fonds publics s'écoulent en fêtes de fraternité, il sonne une cloche de feu rose dans les nuages . . .

How smoothly the car runs. And these rows of celery, how they bitter the air—winter's authentic foretaste . . . [27]

Up over the dark factory into the blue glare start the young poplars.
They whisper: It is Sunday! It is Sunday! But the laws of the country
have been stripped bare of leaves[28]

Further examples would show that a similar psychological process took place
in the two poets. They shared the same kind of verbal intoxication, but always
showed restraint in using it. Sometimes intensity of emotion broke through this
restraint, and a beautifully simple and calm statement would suddenly be made.
In every case, the poetry was kept in control by irony, ingenuity, and visual
clarity.

In Williams's disciplined dreams, the unfolding images responded to the logic
of association and often the associations were fortuitous. A work of art can never
really abandon itself to disorder, even when it imitates the formlessness of dreams,
nor is any association of images sufficient unto itself. Rimbaud, Mallarmé, even
Apollinaire, enchanted though they were with the realm of fantasy, never surren-
dered themselves to it, and neither did Williams. In evoking a landscape which
is equivalent to a state of mind, he attained a mastery comparable to that of the
French poets who preceded him:

Hercules is in Hacketstown doing farm labor. Look at his hands if
you'll not believe me. And what do I care if yellow and red are Spain's
riches and Spain's good blood. Here yellow and red mean simply
autumn! The odor of the poor farmer's fried supper is mixing with the
smell of the hemlocks, mist is in the valley hugging the ground and
over Parsippany—where an oldish man leans talking to a young
woman—the moon is swinging from its star.[29]

Pound wrote to Williams, before the publication of *Kora in Hell*:

I was very glad to see your wholly incoherent unAmerican poems
in the *Little Review*.
Of course Sandburg will tell you that you miss the "Big drifts,"
and Bodenheim will object to your not being sufficiently decadent.
The thing that saves your work is *opacity*, and don't you forget
it. Opacity is NOT an American quality. Fizz, swish, gabble of verbiage, these are echt Amerikanisch.[30]

Pound thus pointed out to Williams the French quality in his poetry: what
he meant by "opacity" is essentially French, deriving from Symbolist poetry.
Later on, after the publication of *Kora in Hell: Improvisations*, Pound wrote to
Williams:

But what the French real reader would say to your *Improvisations:* "Qui, ça j'ai déjà vu ça; ça c'est de Rimbaud!"[31]

And in an essay on Williams written some years after that, Pound commended this French influence, saying that "if he did some Rimbaud forty years late it was nevertheless composition, and I don't think he knew it was Rimbaud until after he finished his operation."[32]

This book, *Kora in Hell*, which contained the *Improvisations*, was probably the most important work in the early evolution of Williams's poetry, even if that fact has not been generally acknowledged. In composing the book, he clearly confronted himself with the leading artistic questions of the time, and in writing it, he gained a firmer grasp of his own gifts.

He had discovered that the basic truths of Imagism needed further development, and so he added a new shade of meaning to the principle that reality is a solid object, and that the eye is the most important organ of the consciousness. He accepted the Imagist principle that poetic expression must have the "hardness of marble." "All I do is try to understand something in its natural colours and shapes," he once wrote to Pound."[33] In the Prologue to *Kora in Hell*, he wrote:

> By the brokenness of his composition the poet makes himself master of a certain weapon which he could possess himself of in no other way. The speed of the emotions is sometimes such that thrashing about in a thin exaltation or despair many matters are touched but not held, more often broken by the contact.
>
> Thus a poem is tough by no quality it borrows from a logical recital of events nor from the events themselves but solely from that attenuated power which draws perhaps many broken things into a dance giving them thus a full being.[34]

In such passages as these, one perceives the true character of Williams's genius. He completed the work of Pound and Eliot in an entirely personal fashion, without adding any fundamentally new discoveries to what they had done. He gave a vigor and enthusiasm to the language which no other American poet had equaled. Looking at the *Improvisations*, and at certain other early poems (such as "A Goodnight," for example) one can see, besides the power of precise observation, an art of movement which approaches the dance, and which makes all other attempts of the sort appear artificial.

> This that I have struggled against is the very thing that I should have chosen—but all's right now. They said I could not put the flower back into the stem nor win roses upon dead briars and I like a fool believed them. But all's right now. Weave away, dead fingers, the darkies are dancing in Mayaguez—all but one with the sore heel and sugar cane will soon be high enough to romp through. Haia! leaping over the ditches, with your skirts flying and the devil in the wind back of you—no one else. Weave away and the bitter tongue of an old woman

is eating, eating, eating venomous words with thirty years' mould on them and all shall be eaten back to the honeymoon's end. Weave and pangs of agony and pangs of loneliness are beaten backward into the love kiss, weave and kiss recedes into kiss and kisses into looks into the heart's dark—and over again and over again and time's pushed ahead in spite of all that. The petals that fell bearing me under lifted one by one. That which kissed my flesh for priest's lace so that I could not touch it—weave and you have lifted it and I am glimpsing light chinks among the notes! Backward, and my hair is crisp with purple sap and the last crust's broken.[35]

Williams understood the working of the poetic imagination in its most robust power, as well as its most refined. Early critics of his poetry failed to recognize his grasp of the resources of the imagination, a grasp which was equal, in its way, to that of the French Symbolists and their disciples. Indeed, by a comparison with French poets such as Rimbaud, Williams's peculiar excellence can be best appreciated. Even Williams's obscurity, such as it is, is much like that of Rimbaud—and is formidable only to those who do not like to read critically.

Williams's avowed aim was to achieve a distinctly American poetry with an American tone, and one can say with confidence that no more purely American sensibility has yet appeared in poetry. He can be compared to H. D., Marianne Moore, or perhaps even Henry James, all of whom had a high degree of sensitivity to real objects, in the presence of which they felt something akin to an electric shock. Contact with the world was painful, but its absence was equally so. Between these extremes, there was the joy and pleasure of life.

There are days when leaves have knife's edges and one sees only eye-pupils, fixes every catchpenny in a shop window and every wire against the sky . . . [36]

But there's a small comfort in naked branches when the heart's not set that way.[37]

Williams gave American poets good advice when he urged them to "cultivate their emotions," but the technique he offered was not American in origin. Henry James had shown a similar inconsistency, for he once advised American artists to steep themselves "up to the neck in anything that their country and climate can give them," and then steeped himself up to the neck in Flaubert.

CHAPTER 3

Conclusions

Other POETS could be mentioned who, early in the twentieth century, helped to rescue American poetry from conventionality and artificiality, for example Alfred Kreymbourg, John Rodker, and Mina Loy (the last of whom was perhaps the first to introduce Surrealism into English poetry). On these poets, and on all those who sought to develop concentrated imagery and flexible rhythm, the French influence was strong, even if it was not always direct. In their pantheon, de Gourmont and Corbière, who had done so much to bring clarity and sharpness to French expression, took their places beside Rimbaud, the master of fused images, and Laforgue, the master of verbal wit.

These American poets did not all read French, but they could avail themselves of translations from the French which were appearing at the time, and they had the example of Eliot (and to a lesser extent, of Aldous Huxley) as a continuator of Laforgue's manner in English. It is Eliot who must be credited with developing American poetry from pure Imagism into the new and more complex Symbolist style, and with providing the link between a first generation of poets who sought sincerity of expression and freer rhythm, and a second generation who wished to convert their impressions of the outer world into inner experiences. From their time on, American poetry spoke French.

It was Imagism which had first opened new possibilities of expression in American poetry, by introducing free verse, and stripping language of clichés and circumlocutions; but in time a reaction set in against the skilled simplicity of the Imagist poem, and it was then that the combined efforts of T. S. Eliot, Marianne Moore, and William Carlos Williams were needed to end the dominance of the English tradition for good. Through their experiments, not only the rhythm and imagery but the very diction of English poetry was changed, and the language was, in Eliot's phrase, "dislocated into meaning"—in the same way as French had earlier been "dislocated" into new capabilities of expression by Baudelaire, Rimbaud, Mallarmé, and poets of a later generation such as Jean Cocteau.

Among the youngest generation of American poets, Allen Tate was one who had a firm grasp of what was happening. He wrote:

> French Decadence, from Baudelaire, prospers here with an eager
> fecundity. Baudelaire's Theory of Correspondences—that an idea out
> of one class of experience may be dressed up in the vocabulary of
> another—is at once the backbone of modern poetic diction and the
> character which distinguishes it from both the English tradition and
> free verse . . . We think of this as Decadence, but in a wider sense,
> if it may be repeated here, it is Elizabethan. It is not direct continuity
> from the immediate past of English poetry. It is development out of
> the whole of it under French direction; and it is no more startling than
> the progress from Wyatt to John Donne.[1]

There is no question that American poetry had reached new maturity
through the influence of French Symbolism. The date when this event occurred
may be set with some certainty: it was about 1915, when it could be said with
assurance that a new American poetry had been created and was flourishing. No
more needs to be added to prove the case, but some further examples of the poetry
written after this year may serve to confirm the lasting effect of French influence
on American poetry.

After the first shock of Imagist contact with French poetry had been felt,
it is not surprising that subsequent shocks were somewhat less startling, though
no less effective. Fewer articles were written on French poetry, and fewer translations appeared, than during the Imagist period, but this was because there was
not as much need for them. It is significant that one of the most promising
American poets of the Twenties, Hart Crane, came very near matching Rimbaud
in his use of imagery, but hardly knew enough French to read him in the original.
It is probably a fact that during the period immediately following World War I,
there were more poets in America who were actively experimenting with French
Symbolist techniques than there were in France. By then, American poetry had
found its bearings in French Symbolism and was proceeding along a clearly
marked path of development of its own. Surrealism, the French poetic movement
which followed Symbolism, had some effect on American poetry, but did not
change its direction or its force in any considerable way. The more active younger
poets, such as E. E. Cummings, Hart Crane, Allen Tate, and Malcolm Cowley,
became skilled at adapting French techniques to suit their own purposes. Cummings's work showed a richness of diction and imagery that ranged all the way
from the purely descriptive to the profoundly evocative. He could make use of
elegance, irony, caricature, or lyricism, according to his mood, and excelled at
creating striking images in words:

> In the street of the sky, night walks, scattering poems.

or,

> The sea through her blind miles of crumbling silence.

or,

> Thy fingers make early flowers of all things.

And in these early verses of Cummings, the echo of French Symbolism may be clearly heard:

> when learned darkness from our searched world
> wrestled the rare unwisdom of the eyes,
>
> if thy two hands flowers of silence curled
> upon a thought, to rapture should surprise
>
> my soul slowly which on thy beauty dreamest. . .

In these lines, the influence of de Gourmont mingles with that of Rimbaud, and it is clear that Cummings had learned very early from the French how to concentrate a multitude of images around a single emotion. He was undoubtedly affected by the *Calligrammes* of Apollinaire, and successfully adapted many of Apollinaire's techniques into English, though at times he was too much influenced by the French poet's tricks and superficial novelties of style.

Malcolm Cowley enjoyed a brief career as a poet during the Twenties, and showed a marked influence of French poetry on his style. He was well acquainted with French from his college days, and had imitated Laforgue and Tailhade even as an undergraduate. He made several interesting translations of Laforgue's poetry, and was strongly affected by the reading of Rimbaud—particularly "Le Bateau Ivre," which he both translated and imitated. His imitation was called "Leander," and appeared in the *Dial* magazine in September, 1927, with an epigraph from Rimbaud which gave the clue to its source: *Un noyé pensif parfois descend.* The effect of the imitation was to be felt in the rhythm of the poem, as well as in its phrases, imagery, diction:

> —Leander, I will show you all my treasures
> cavern of pearl, Leander, constellations
> of incandescent fish. Leviathan
> my servant shall attend you, and my sharks
> surround you. . . .
>
> Regal and tired O corpse that mapped the countries
> of Ocean, saw pelagic meadows where

the sea-cow grazes, traveller who skirts
the unicellular gardens of the foam

Southward you drift where archipelagoes
of stars deflect the current, and waters boil
with lava, through indefinite Marquesas
spinning in the typhoon. . . .

Some of these phrases are taken directly from Rimbaud, such as "archipelagoes of stars" and "indefinite Marquesas," and others are only slightly altered from "The Drunken Boat," for example "constellations of incandescent fish," and "unicellular gardens of the foam." In other poems written at this time, Cowley showed a similar influence, as for instance in "The Fishes and Starlings," which appeared in the *Dial* in May, 1923:

And rather as a feather drops he fell
he floated down past layer after layer
of vegetation, larch, beech, poplar and farther
descending faster and faster he sees the palm
the cactus, orchids, banyans heavy with creepers
and creeping snakes over the dead lagoon.

One can also see in his verses some influence from the Surrealists, particularly from Philippe Soupault, in addition to that of Rimbaud.

But most important of all in that period was the style of Hart Crane, which was so remarkable an example of visionary eloquence, powerfully expressive of the author's stream of consciousness and will. Crane had studied all the translations of Rimbaud which he could get his hands on, particularly those which appeared in *The Dial* in July and August, 1920, consisting of selections from *A Season in Hell* and the *Illuminations*. He had previously written poems in the Imagist manner which were published in *Bohemia* and the *Pagan Anthology*. In addition, the early influence of Symbolism was to be seen in the short poem, "In Shadow," which was printed in *The Little Review* in 1917. It was clear that Crane was learning the difficult art of transforming his feelings into images, and of surrounding the images with reflections and echoes of thought. And he could elevate occasions into poems, as he showed impressively in "My Grandmother's Love Letters," "Pastorale," and "Praise for An Urn," poems which were published in *The Dial* in 1920, 1921, and 1922.

The most prominent French influences to be seen in Crane's work were those of Laforgue and Rimbaud in the moments of vision and "illumination." One could almost believe that Crane's method, like that of Rimbaud's, consisted in letting his imagination flow through a free process of association, obeying a "logic of metaphor," as Crane himself once explained: "The logic of metaphor is so organically entrenched in pure sensibility that it can't be thoroughly traced or explained outside of historical science like philology and anthropology." Crane did not push the "rational disordering of the senses" to the extreme point, as Rimbaud did; his images were kept under the control of his will; but there is no question that he saw in Rimbaud's *A Season in Hell* and *Illuminations* the models which best suited his own talent, and a method for developing his image-making powers to the fullest. Such a characteristic Crane poem as "Repose of Rivers," which appared in *The Dial* in September, 1926, is full of echoes of Rimbaud:–

> Flags, weeds. And remembrance of steep alcoves
> Where cypresses shared the noon's
> Tyranny; they drew me into hades almost.
> And mammoth turtles climbing sulphur dreams
> Yielded, while sun-silt rippled them
> Asunder . . .
>
> How much I would have bartered! the black gorge
> And all the singular nestings in the hills
> Where beavers learn stitch and tooth.
> The pond I entered once and quickly fled—
> I remember now its singing willow rim.

The influence of Rimbaud is even more evident, in these lines from his first long poem, "For the Marriage of Faustus and Helen" (1923):

> O, I have known metallic paradises
> Where cuckoos clucked to finches
> Above the deft catastrophes of drums,
> While titters hailed the groans of death
> Beneath gyrating awnings I have seen
> The incunabula of the divine grotesque.
> This music has a reassuring way.

Finally, as evidence of Crane's debt to Rimbaud, one must cite the beautiful set of poems called "Voyages," in which the poet seems to have combined the compelling rhythm and tumultuous images of Rimbaud's "Drunken Boat" with certain "metaphysical" qualities derived from reading Eliot:

> Take this Sea, whose diapason knells
> On scrolls of silver snowy sentences,
> The sceptred terror of whose sessions rends
> As her demeanors motion well or ill,
> All but the pieties of lovers' hands.

And onward, as bells off San Salvador
Salute the crocus lustres of the stars,
In these poinsettia meadows of her tides,—
Adagios of islands, O my Prodigal,
Complete the dark confessions her veins spell.

Mark how her turning shoulders wind the hours,
And hasten while her penniless rich palms
Pass superscription of bent foam and wave,—
Hasten, while they are true,—sleep, death, desire,
Close round one instant in one floating flower.

From Eliot, perhaps, came the device of posing two images against each other, alternating from one to the other in a mutually illuminating fashion. But certainly the style, construction, rhythm, movement of these verses are distinctly French.

In sum, it was as if a new language had been created by poets, first in French and then in English, a language freed of the logic of reason and obeying the logic of life, freed of the laws of the syllogism and responding to the laws of musical harmony. This language was not the discursive language of traditional poetry (for even when that poetry became artificial and conventional, it was still discursive): it did not move with a conversational tone and rhythm, but with a new gravity, capable of expressing in clear visions the varying moods of the human soul. This language has its own discipline; it has its own harmony; above all, it has its own mystery, which the best poets of the American Renaissance evolved as the French poets had before them.

Hart Crane was certainly among these poets, and the best of his poetry possessed all the qualities of the new style; he had profited from the example of Eliot and from that of the best French Symbolists, and in this practice the poetic phrase had become almost a solid object, the image a brilliant splash of color, the form a free and harmonious fluency, the whole poem a durable creation which seemed to have weight and substance as well as an invisible reality.

The Symbolist epoch, in spite of the number of minor poets who have been raised to a sudden and undeserved fame, has been a distinguished epoch in European poetry, during which many major talents engaged in the search for an exact language for human feelings. It has been in every way comparable in greatness to the age which preceded it in all European languages: the Romantic age. Such Symbolists as Mallarmé and Rimbaud led the way toward discovering in the French language a means of condensing, synthesizing, and recording, in free rhythms and images, the experiences of an interior world and a whole interior life, more directly and realistically than had ever been possible before. In the English language, it was the Imagists, led by Pound and following the example of the French Symbolists, who stripped poetry of sentiment and ornament, and renewed the poetic potentialities of the language.

CONCLUSION

Beyond French Symbolist Influence

MAJOR AMERICAN POEMS AFTER 1920

by William Pratt

LATE IN HIS career, T. S. Eliot reflected on the poetry that had been written in the first half of the twentieth century and concluded:

> I think it is just to say that the pioneers of twentieth century poetry were more conspicuously the Americans than the English, both in number and quality . . . . In the nineteenth century, Poe and Whitman stand out as solitary international figures; in the last forty years, for the first time, there has been assembled a *body* of American poetry which has made its total impression in England and in Europe.[1]

Eliot's judgment had no taint of patriotism; he had long ago given up his American citizenship, and was speaking from a European perspective. As the "more radical experimenters" who had brought world attention to American poetry, he named Ezra Pound, W. C. Williams, Wallace Stevens, Marianne Moore, e. e. cummings, Hart Crane, John Crowe Ransom, and Allen Tate, but he made no mention of himself. He was, however, being faithful to the principle he had maintained at the beginning of his career, which held that "really new" works alter "the whole existing order" of world literature to which they belong. ("Tradition and the Individual Talent.") Implied in his view that modern American poetry has had an impact on an international scale, is the assumption that American poets have been as influential in creating new works and fashioning a new poetic style as were the French poets who first influenced them: in other words, that they had progressed from being influenced to being an influence.

The history of modern American poetry starts with the period from 1910 to 1920, which was the focus of Taupin's study, when Imagism was the paramount poetic movement, for it was during that creative decade that the new style emerged. The early poems of Pound, Eliot, Stevens, H. D., Williams, Moore, appearing in the pages of little magazines like *Poetry, The Egoist, The Little Review, The Dial*, were the harbingers of a new poetic tradition that seemed unprecedented to many readers, although they were, as Taupin has shown so convincingly, the offspring of an earlier modern poetry. Not that Imagist poems were the only kind being published; they were simply the freshest and most original, most identifiably modern. "The aims of the imagist movement in poetry provided the archetype of a modern creative procedure,"[2] and in time the sort of short, visually arresting, free verse lyric which it produced became the characteristic modern poem, regardless of which poet wrote it—much as the sonnet became the characteristic form for poets in the early Elizabethan period. And just as the Elizabethan sonnet had sprung from a foreign tradition, the Italian sonnet of the thirteenth century, the period of Dante and Petrarch and the *dolce stil nuovo,* so the Imagist poem had its inception in the French poetry of the nineteenth century. The value of Taupin's study is that it shows how a new poetic tradition can grow out of an older tradition, in another time and language, by what almost seems a process of organic cultural growth, changing the tradition as it proceeds to adapt from it, and giving credence to Eliot's notion that in the transmission of literary influence "the past should be altered by the present as much as the present is directed by the past."[3]

If Imagist poems were the dominant form during the period of initial experiment that Taupin studied, Ezra Pound was unquestionably the dominant poet. As Randall Jarrell, one of the ablest of a later generation of American poets and critics, put it:

> Athens was called the education of Hellas; from 1912 till 1922 Ezra
> Pound could have been called the education of poetry . . . . His advice
> to poets could be summed up in a sentence: Write like speech—and
> *read French poets!*[4]

It was therefore logical that Taupin should have concentrated most of his study on Pound, as the central figure in modern American poetry, because there would hardly have been a common movement among poets without him. He was the theorist and practitioner with the most definite program, and the most ebullient enthusiasm, for a genuinely modern style, and he was personal liaison between American poets as diverse, and antipathetic, as Frost and Eliot, Williams and Sandburg, H. D. and Marianne Moore. It was Eliot who said of the initial period:

> Pound did not create the poets: but he created a situation in which,
> for the first time, there was a "modern movement in poetry" in which
> English and American poets collaborated, knew each other's works,
> and influenced each other.[5]

Certainly Taupin was right to focus attention on Pound and Imagism for the period when modern American poetry began, but any true account of the period after 1920 would have to focus on longer poems than the Imagist, and on Eliot as the poet whose poetic practice and critical theories assumed the dominant place.

Eliot always gave Pound credit for starting the modern movement, and in his well-known dedication to *The Waste Land*, called Pound *il miglior fabbro*, "the better craftsman" who had helped him prune and shape the poem that became the centerpiece of that movement, the most influential of all twentieth-century poems. Eliot's debt to Pound was as great as any major poet ever owed to another, and he never allowed himself to forget it, nor to forget the equally crucial part certain French Symbolist poets played in the making of his style. Since Eliot was the dominant influence on American poetry after *The Waste Land* appeared, anyone who wants to understand the main developments of modern poetry after 1920 must give the closest attention to Eliot's work as a poet and critic. Taupin had begun this effort himself, recognizing Eliot's leadership in what he called the second stage of Imagism, towards greater complexity and a more unified structure of images in poetry, increased irony and a more impersonal expression of emotion, and a more controlled use of literary allusion. Taupin saw that Eliot was building on the Imagism of Pound by successfully combining the styles of French Symbolist and English Metaphysical poetry, proving, as he put it, "that John Donne and Jules Laforgue were compatible poets," and reintroducing subtleties in English poetic style that had been lost for three centuries. This blending of an earlier English with a later French poetic style was Eliot's first method for making new poetry from old, renewing the tradition in a bold and revolutionary manner.

What was not clear at the time Taupin wrote was that Eliot was leading the way toward longer poems in the Imagist style, and that the second stage would feature the long poem as much as the first stage had favored the short poem. *The Waste Land* was Eliot's opening venture into what might be called the Super-Imagist poem, made up of cumulative images of drought and sterility that implied (but never stated) that modern civilization was undergoing a living death, suffering spiritual exhaustion from the loss of religious belief with its hope of immortality. He followed it with a shorter companion poem, "The Hollow Men," and then, at the end of the decade, he produced another long poem, *Ash Wednesday*, which was his first explicitly religious poem, an extended penitential prayer in six sections, drawing its major theme from St. Paul: "Redeem the time." In the following decade, between 1935 and 1942, Eliot wrote four separate long poems that were eventually united into his largest work, *Four Quartets*, a series of meditations on time and place and human destiny, reaching through exalted moments of Incarnation towards "the still point in a turning world," a sense of mystical union with God. These three long poems of Eliot are not only impressive in themselves, as unified and complete works of high poetic intensity, but they seem to form a connected sequence which together makes a trilogy of spiritual progress, rising from the despair of lost belief in *The Waste Land*, through the confessional repentance of *Ash Wednesday*, to the visionary moments of inner peace and grace in *Four Quartets*. Together Eliot's three major poems constitute what must be regarded as the greatest poetic achievement of the twentieth century, a work comparable in visionary power, profundity of thought, and emotional intensity with the greatest epic in the whole Western tradition, Dante's *Divine Comedy*. Indeed, the parallels are so suggestive as to be striking, for if *The Waste Land* can be seen as Eliot's *Inferno*, *Ash Wednesday* easily becomes his *Purgatorio*, and the *Four Quartets* are his *Paradiso*.

To draw such a comparison is to go beyond the influence of French Symbolism in Eliot's poetry, for there is no poem or sequence of poems by a French poet (not even Rimbuad's *Season in Hell* and *Illuminations*, which would be the nearest parallel) that could afford an adequate model of such magnitude. Having effectively combined French Symbolist and English Metaphysical styles in his early poetry, as Taupin credited him with doing, Eliot made a further synthesis in his later poems of the Imagist style with the allegorical style of Dante. That he had such a fusion in mind, of the modern with the medieval, is certainly discernible in his critical essays, as it is also discernible that he was led in this direction by the earlier French influence, particularly that of Baudelaire, the Symbolist poet he most admired.

From the outset of his career, Eliot had maintained that a poet is most himself when he is most traditional, that "not only the best, but the most individual parts of his work may be those in which the dead poets, his ancestors, assert their immortality most vigorously," as he wrote in "Tradition and the Individual Talent." As a critic, he was ever alert to his own influences, constantly citing his indebtedness to poets as different as Laforgue and Gautier, Pound and Donne, Baudelaire and Dante. As he progressed both poetically and critically, he tended to value certain influences above others, and to see the limitations as well as the strengths of the poets from whom he had learned. Thus, he paid Laforgue the high compliment of being the poet "to whom I owe more than to any one poet in any language," because "he was the first to teach me how to speak, to teach me the poetic possibilities of my own idiom of speech," but he went on to say more critically that "the poet who can do this for a young writer, is unlikely to be one of the great masters." It was after learning all he could from Laforgue that he set himself the task of assimilating a larger influence, that of Baudelaire:

> I think that from Baudelaire I learned first, a precedent for the
> poetical possibilities, never developed by any poet writing in my own
> language, of the more sordid aspects of the modern metropolis, of the
> possibility of fusion between the sordidly realistic and the phantasma-

goric, the possibility of the juxtaposition of the matter-of-fact and the fantastic. From him, as from Laforgue, I learned that the sort of material that I had, the sort of experience that an adolescent had had, in an industrial city in America could be the material for poetry; and that the source of new poetry might be found in what had been regarded hitherto as the impossible, the sterile, the intractably unpoetic. That, in fact, the business of the poet was to make poetry out of the unexplored resources of the unpoetical; that the poet, in fact, was committed by his profession to turn the unpoetical into poetry.[6]

For Eliot, then, Baudelaire was a more profound and mature poet than Laforgue, and moving from the influence of one French poet to another meant to develop in the direction of poetic mastery, widening his subject matter and broadening his viewpoint. Eliot believed that Baudelaire had been the first poet to deal directly with the modern city, using "the imagery of common life" and elevating it "to the *first intensity*—presenting it as it is, and yet making it represent something much more than itself." In this achievement, Eliot said:

> Baudelaire is indeed the greatest exemplar in *modern* poetry in any language, for his verse and language is the nearest thing to a complete renovation that we have experienced.[7]

It was in this same essay, written about the middle of his career, with *The Waste Land* behind him, and *Ash Wednesday* and *Four Quartets* ahead of him, that Eliot expressed his admiration for Baudelaire, yet compared him unfavorably with Dante, signifying that he was then moving from a profound to a profounder poetic influence, and turning from a concern with expressing the spiritless sterility of modern existence to a concern for expressing the inner spiritual longing of modern human beings for what Dante described as "E'n la sua voluntate é nostra pace" (*Paradiso*, III) and Eliot translated as "Our peace in His will" (*Ash Wednesday*, VI). At this moment of change in his style and point of view, it was natural for Eliot to seek in Dante what had been lacking for him in Baudelaire. Although, as he wrote, "It is true that many people who enjoy Dante enjoy Baudelaire," he saw Baudelaire as at best but a "fragmentary Dante," who had a great capacity for perceiving evil in himself and others and suffering guilt about it, but could only "study his suffering," lacking the capacity to transcend it. "And in this limitation he is wholly unlike Dante," Eliot said; "Baudelaire's inferno is very different in quality and significance from that of Dante." Not that he saw Baudelaire as a Satanist, who relished evil—a frequently held view; rather, he viewed him as a "rudimentary or embryonic" Christian, who had a powerful conviction of evil, but only a "vague romantic conception of Good," and who therefore could vividly express the possiblity of damnation, but could only dimly conceive of the possibility of salvation. "What is significant about Baudelaire," Eliot thought, "is his theological innocence. He is discovering Christianity for himself." And Eliot felt that Baudelaire's preoccupation with *ennui,* or boredom, as the cardinal sin of modern man, was "a true form of *acedia,* arising from the unsuccessful struggle towards the spiritual life."

Much of what Eliot said of Baudelaire applied to his own early poetry, from "The Love Song of J. Alfred Prufrock" through "The Hollow Men": there, one finds, as he finds in *Les Fleurs du mal,* the acute suffering of a sensitive human consciousness amid the sordid and disgusting scenes of city life, the sense of shame and horror at the triviality and wastefulness of an existence too much determined by sensual appetites. The characteristic tone of Eliot's early poetry is *revulsion,* seldom relieved by any positive emotions except those expressed ironically. But in the later poetry of Eliot, from the Ariel poems and *Ash Wednesday* through the *Four Quartets,* the mood changes to expectation and to hope, while the imagery changes from the sordid and disgusting to the peaceful and refreshing:

> And beyond the hawthorn blossom and a pasture scene
> The broadbacked figure drest in blue and green
> Enchanted the maytime with an antique flute.
> Blown hair is sweet, brown hair over the mouth blown,
> Lilac and brown hair
>
> *Ash Wednesday,* III

Eliot's later style owes more to Dante than to any other poetic influence, and if it is true, as he said in his long essay on Dante in 1929, that the Italian poet's work "belongs to the world of what I call the *high dream,* and the modern world seems capable only of the *low dream,*"[8] it is nevertheless the case that in Eliot's later poetry the aspiration towards a mystical vision of the soul's union with God is as convincingly expressed as in any poetry since Dante's time. Perhaps Eliot would have viewed himself as necessarily limited, like Baudelaire, to the "low dream," because the "high dream" is possible only in a time of unity of faith, but certainly Eliot had progressed far beyond the "theological innocence" of Baudelaire to a conscious expression of religious hope, even if the hope is no more than that:

> The only wisdom we can hope to acquire
> Is the wisdom of humility: humility is endless.
>
> "East Coker," II, *Four Quartets*

There is much of the wisdom of humility in Eliot's later poems, but there is more; there are moments of vision and exaltation pointing towards a condition of spiritual blessedness, the ultimate hope of the Christian believer, in Eliot's time as in Dante's. It is the view of many critics that "Little Gidding," the last of the *Four Quartets*, is Eliot's supreme poetic achievement, and there the influence of Dante is most consciously at work:

> Twenty years after writing *The Waste Land*, I wrote, in *Little Gidding*, a passage which is intended to be the nearest equivalent to a canto of the Inferno or the Purgatorio, in style as well as content, that I could achieve. The intention, of course, was the same as with the allusions to Dante in *The Waste Land:* to present to the mind of the reader a parallel, by means of contrast, between the Inferno and the Purgatorio, which Dante visited and a hallucinated scene after an air raid. But the method is different: here I was debarred from quoting or adapting at length—I borrowed and adapted freely only a few phrases—because I was *imitating*.[9]

In the memorable visionary passage to which he refers, Eliot was not only expressing his belief in the reality of a life beyond death, in which the dead can speak to the living as believably as they did in Dante's great poem, but he is acknowledging his debt to other poets who guided him in shaping his own original but constantly changing poetic style. Though he is imitating Dante's allegorical method, the spirit that he meets in the world beyond the living is not identified with Dante; rather, it is described as a composite shade:

> I caught the sudden look of some dead master
> Whom I had known, forgotten, half recalled
> Both one and many; in the brown baked features
> The eyes of a familiar compound ghost
> Both intimate and unidentifiable.
> "Little Gidding," II, *Four Quartets*

Much speculation has revolved around the identity of this "dead master," with suggestions ranging from Shakespeare to Henry James, from T. E. Hulme to James Joyce, but the only clues Eliot gives within the passage are lines paraphrased from Mallarmé:

> Since our concern was speech, and speech impelled us
> To purify the dialect of the tribe.

which clearly echo:

> Donner un sens plus pur aux mots de la tribu

> ("To give a purer sense to the words of the tribe")
> "Le Tombeau d'Edgar Poe"

and a general allusion to various passages in Dante, especially those in the Purgatorio:

> From wrong to wrong the exasperated spirit
> Proceeds, unless restored by that refining fire
> Where you must move in measure, like a dancer."

The middle line here recalls the line in the Purgatorio which ends Dante's meeting with the spirit of the Provençal troubadour, Arnaut Daniel (*il miglior fabbro*):

> Poi s'ascose nel foco chegli affina
> (Then he hid himself in the fire that purifies)

Knowing that this same line is quoted in Italian at the end of *The Waste Land*, we can be sure that the echo is intentional, and that Dante is as much inside the "familiar compound ghost" as is Mallarmé. It seems quite likely that Eliot intended this figure to represent all the poets who had influenced him, and whom in various ways he had reincarnated somewhere in his poetry. Yet the probability remains that Dante was the chief of them all, for Eliot once paid Dante the supreme compliment, saying that "there is no poet in any tongue—not even in Latin or Greek—who stands so firmly as a model for all poets," and praising the last Canto of the *Paradiso* as "to my thinking the highest point that poetry has ever reached or ever can reach."[10]

If we take "Little Gidding" as the nearest to Dante's Paradiso in Eliot's poetry, we can say that though he continued in his later poetry to derive a beneficial influence from the French Symbolists, as indicated by his deft adaptation from Mallarmé, he had moved from their modern realm of private and subjective symbolism, through the deepening influence of Dante, into the more traditional realm of Christian allegory, until, at the end of the *Four Quartets*, he has approached very near to the final mystical vision of Dante's Paradise:

> And all shall be well and
> All manner of thing shall be well
> When the tongues of flame are in-folded
> Into the crowned knot of fire
> And the fire and the rose are one.

Clearly, Eliot's fire is Dante's purgatorial flame, and his rose is Dante's image of paradise as a multifoliate rose with God at the center. Though such allusions require as much knowledge on the reader's part as do those in any of Eliot's early poems, their significance does not depend wholly on private poetic intuitions, but upon a continuity of religious belief and doctrine; that is to say, they are not only poetic images but traditional symbols of Christian faith.

In so far as Eliot's later poetry is the most influential American poetry after the time of Taupin's study, then, it may be said to show a transcendence of French Symbolist influence, for if Eliot had learned from Laforgue and Baudelaire how to find an adequate language to symbolize modern experience, he learned from Dante how to give a more universal meaning to the symbols he employed, and in so doing, he found a way of unifying a set of longer poems, by drawing into them parallels, echoes, and even direct imitation, from Dante's allegory. Eliot's revolutionary kind of traditionalism produced a fusion of widely differing styles, ranging from the nineteenth century French Symbolist to the seventeenth century English Metaphysical to the thirteenth century Italian allegorical, but in the end, what matters is that the fusion resulted in great poetry. In his *Notes Towards the Definition of Culture* (1949), Eliot defended such eclecticism as he practiced by saying, "I think the reason why English is such a good language for poetry is that it is a composite from so many European sources," and he went on to say that the beneficial influence of French Symbolism was such that in the modern period, the work of poets as different as Yeats, Rilke, and himself "would hardly be conceivable" without it. The same may be said for other major poets in the twentieth century, that they started with the primary influence of French Symbolism but went considerably beyond it in developing their later and longer poems. Eliot's transcendence of French influence through the influence of Dante has parallels in the longer poems of such contemporary American poets as Pound in the *Cantos*, Hart Crane in *The Bridge*, William Carlos Williams in *Paterson*, and Wallace Stevens in *Esthétique du mal*, and to look at these poems with Eliot's example in mind is a way of tracing the course of American poetry in the period after 1920, where Taupin's study effectively ended.

If Eliot tended to overshadow Pound in the period following *The Waste Land*, it was not because his poetic efforts were more ambitious: certainly, Pound's *Cantos* form the longest and most complex poetic work written in the twentieth century in any language. But their very length and complexity have been their weakness, for the 117 *Cantos* are even longer than the *Divine Comedy*, and they lack the thematic unity and poetic symmetry so notable in Dante's poem, which make it possible for the reader to grasp the whole while struggling to understand the parts. Pound was too ambitious ever to complete his epic: the final *Cantos* are admittedly "Drafts and Fragments," not finished poems, and there is no clear indication that if they had been finished, the epic itself would be complete. Eliot's three longer poems are, in contrast, complete in themselves, and they form a continuity that makes the whole greater than the parts, and more intelligible as well, especially when seen in parallel with Dante's poem. Pound's *Cantos* are more comprehensible in the part than in the whole, in spite of numerous attempts to see some kind of unity in them, and they remain a bewilderingly rich diversity for most readers. They are probably best approached as an autobiographical poem, somewhat like Whitman's *Song of Myself*, but with far more prosodic variety and intellectual range. Whitman spoke with one voice, while Pound spoke through many voices and in many languages, and Whitman's American "kosmos" seems provincial in comparison with Pound's history-encompassing vision. So far as the *Cantos* have a central subject, it is the mind of Pound moving through time and space, and its sustaining interest is the richness of that mind, the brilliance of his poetic imagery, the ever-fresh lyricism of his ear, the immense imaginative scope of his intelligence, which ranges through all human history to discover and record those moments of metamorphosis, when men see through the visible to the invisible reality, and mortal experience partakes of immortality.

> Then a partridge-shaped cloud over dust storm.
> The hells move in cycles,
> No man can see his own end.
> The Gods have not returned. "They have never left us."
> They have not returned.
> Cloud's processional and the air moves with their living.
>
> Canto CXIII

For the persistent and patient reader, Pound's *Cantos* do form an epic, but it is an Imagist epic, in which fragmentary lyrics coalesce into a panorama of the poet's mind: erudite, whimsical, tragic at some moments, comic at others, often brilliant, sometimes, alas, tedious, obsessed with the usury, or greed, that reduces art to a mere commodity, but stubbornly insistent that art alone enables man to transcend the mortal plane, to see downward into Hell, where

> The light has gone down into the cave,
> Splendour on splendour!
>
> Canto XLVII

and upward into Paradise:

> The fourth; the dimension of stillness.
> And the power over wild beasts.
>
> Canto XLIX

In short, in Pound's *Cantos*, through the recurrent images of darkness and light, one is able to experience in the transformations of the poet's language something like the simultaneity of all human consciousness, connecting the remotest ages—the classical Chinese and Greek—with the present age of America and Europe,

as if there were a single intelligence perceiving it all and expressing it in momentary flashes of vision and ecstasy:

> To have gathered from the air a live tradition
> or from a fine old eye the unconquered flame
> This is not vanity.
>
> Canto LXXXI

No, it was certainly not vanity that led Pound to move from the simple, brief
Imagist poems that he derived early in his career from French vers libre and
Japanese haiku, to the complex, extended Imagist poems, or Ideograms, of his
interminable and irrepressible epic, which derived from a greater variety of
influences than any poet has ever dared to incorporate in a single work. There
is tragic nobility in the last fragments of the *Cantos*, which do bring it to an end,
with the sense of coming death to a man who has never in his life ceased singing:

> That I lost my center
>   fighting the world.
> The dreams clash
>   and are shattered—
> and that I tried to make a paradiso
>   terrestre.
>
> Notes for Canto CXVII

The *Cantos* are a lifelong poem that could end only with death, fifty years
of "trying to make a paradiso terrestre" which ends in failure, but a magnificent
failure, a noble poetic ruin. Hart Crane's *The Bridge*, on the other hand, was
written in a single decade, and was deliberately constructed to be a positive poetic
symbol of the modern world. Crane conceived of it as the "answer" to Eliot's
Waste Land, which he had found enormously impressive as a poem, but completely negative in its implications for modern civilization. Against Eliot's metaphor of
the modern city as a desert of lost souls, Crane set out to create a metaphor of
the modern city as a bridge connecting people, a marvel of human technology
that could serve as "the symbol of consciousness spanning time and space," as
he put it in a letter during the composition of the poem. He had prepared himself
for this major work by reading voraciously in the modern poets he most admired,
especially Pound and Eliot, and then learning enough French to acquaint himself
with the Symbolist poets to whom, as he knew, they were indebted. He regarded
Rimbaud as the greatest of all modern poets, but as his friend Allen Tate wrote
at the time of Crane's suicide in 1932:

> The career of Hart Crane will be written by future critics as a chapter
> in the neo-symbolist movement . . . . Like most poets of his age in
> America, Crane discovered Rimbaud through Eliot and the Imagists:
> it is certain that long before he had done any of his best work he had
> come to believe himself the spiritual heir of the French poet. He had
> an instinctive mastery of the fused metaphor of symbolism, but it is
> not likely that he ever knew more of the symbolist poets than he had
> got out of Pound's *Pavannes and Divisions*.[11]

Crane began writing poems in the Imagist style, then building them into larger wholes, "For the Marriage of Faustus and Helen," and "Voyages," and during the decade from 1920 to 1930, he labored to produce his epic, *The Bridge*, consisting of fifteen sections, many of which were published as separate poems in little magazines (including Eliot's *Criterion*), and finally as a complete poem in 1930. Its strength—and even the severest critics have agreed that it contains many powerful poetic passages—is in its simplicity of conception, with the central symbol, the Brooklyn Bridge, described in the initial section, or Proem, and left to carry implicitly the weight of meaning through the rest of the poem. But the bridge barely supports the other fourteen sections, each of which is separately titled, some with American historical or legendary names, "Van Winkle," "Powhatan's Daughter," "Cape Hatteras," and some with foreign names, "Ave Maria," "Cutty Sark," "Atlantis." All the sections have something to do with the American landscape, whether natural or industrialized, and it was Crane's intention to produce a "mystic consummation" of images converging into the Bridge as "myth of America," a poetic embodiment of its conversion from wilderness into civilization through the triumph of technology. But Crane's Machine Age epic did not cohere in quite the way he intended; in spite of its initial symbol, it remains less a bridge than a set of disjunct pontoons, a work more impressive for what it seeks to say than for what it actually says. The problem Crane encountered was that his symbol was inadequate for his purpose; in attempting to make a utilitarian engineering product, however large in scale, into a profound religious and artistic symbol, Crane found himself faced with a conflict between the real and the ideal. When only half way through the poem, he began to realize that he had set himself an impossible task, as he confessed in a letter to one of his chief intellectual patrons, the American social philosopher, Waldo Frank:

> Emotionally I should like to write *The Bridge;* intellectually judged
> the whole theme and project seems more and more absurd . . . . The
> very idea of a bridge, of course, is a form peculiarly dependent on such
> spiritual convictions. It is an act of faith besides being a communica-
> tion. The symbols of reality necessary to articulate the span—may

not exist where you expected them, however . . . . The bridge as a
symbol today has no significance beyond an economical approach to
shorter hours, quicker lunches, behaviorism, and toothpicks.[12]

Crane doggedly continued writing until he had finished the poem, despite his
misgivings, but the very unevenness of the work betrays the loss of inspiration
which he had suffered in the course of his poetic labors. If *The Bridge* does have
its exalted moments, it sinks at other times into depths of bathos from which no
serious interpretation can rescue it, and the total impression it makes is of
ambition wrecked, not so much by failure of poetic talent as by failure of belief.
Crane had simply not been able to sustain the symbolic import of the bridge, try
as he might:

> O harp and altar, of the fury fused,
> (How could mere toil align thy choiring strings!)
> Terrific threshold of the prophet's pledge,
> Prayer of pariah, and the lover's cry

The lover's cry is that of the poet himself, who wishes with all his heart to make
an artifact of stone and steel into an altar of worship. Objective reality was at odds
with symbolic purpose, and though, as Allen Tate affirmed, "some of the best
poetry of our generation is in *The Bridge*," as a whole the work stands as a
monument to unfulfilled optimism about the modern world, like an architectural
folly constructed partly of rhetoric and partly of poetry, an ironic lesson in the
truthfulness of poetic language. "Far from 'refuting' Eliot," as Allen Tate said,
"his whole career is a vindication of Eliot's major premise—that the integrity of
the individual consciousness has broken down."

Soon after publishing *The Bridge*, Crane dramatically ended his life—as
much from despair over the failure of his major work, as for any other reason—
but not before he had written one of his finest poems, "The Broken Tower," a
truer and more tragic symbol for Crane than *The Bridge*, and a moving confession
of his final doubts about his poetic achievement:

> And so it was I entered the broken world
> To trace the visionary company of love, its voice
> An instant in the wind (I know not whither hurled)
> But not for long to hold each desperate choice.
>
> My word I poured. But was it cognate, scored
> Of that tribunal monarch of the air
> Whose thigh embronzes earth, strikes crystal Word
> In wounds pledged once to hope—cleft to despair?

The question Crane asked remains for us to ponder; still, with all its flaws, *The Bridge* stands as a major poetic symbol of modern civilization, but more ironic than Crane meant it to be: the truth lies somewhere between the ideal and the real, between the soaring, mythical bridge of Crane's imagination and the actual Brooklyn Bridge that carries men and machines back and forth every day in the giant metropolis. Crane had hoped to find an objective and universal symbol for the city that would affirm man's social and material progress, and America as the promise of a New World, but the transcendent message he wanted the bridge to convey was at odds with its utilitarian character. Crane's poem is proof that a too deliberate and willful symbolism turns against itself, however great the poetic talent may be that goes into trying to make it valid.

William Carlos Williams's *Paterson* is the perfect complement to *The Bridge*, because Williams took as his subject the same teeming city, the vast New York urban sprawl, but treated it in a style and tone which are, though modern, the opposite of Crane's. Williams does not idealize the city; he personifies it: his Paterson is a projection of his consciousness of the environment in which he grew up, an ugly industrial suburb of New York City that was once a verdant natural landscape with an impressive waterfall. Williams's presentation of the city is a set of contrasting images of past and present, some by poetic projection, some by historical record, a kind of kaleidoscope of selected pieces of observation and fact that makes up a mosaic of the American urban personality. In contrast to Crane's fused metaphors and pulsating rhythms, Williams offers a deliberately prosaic style, conversational and forthright:

> —Say it, no ideas but in things—
> nothing but the blank faces of the houses
> and cylindrical trees
> bent, forked by preconception and accident—
> split, furrowed, creased, mottled, stained—
> secret—into the body of the light!
>
> *Paterson*, Book One

The central symbol of Williams's long poem is not a thing but a person, "Dr. Paterson," a poet-doctor like Williams himself, who lives, observes, and sensitively records the things he sees, in all their common ugliness and their occasional, unexpected beauty. This figure is appealing for his modesty and his frankness; he is an ordinary human being with an extraordinary appetite for experience of all kinds, and a knack for sifting out of it the significant images, the telling anecdotes, and expressing them in the idiom of American colloquial speech—city-speech, not a rural dialect, but highly informal, at times even illiterate, yet usually with a faint but detectable rhythm. Williams had been one of the first Imagists, and he remained one of the truest to the original principles, favoring direct treatment and a simple free-verse cadence as if such a style were natural to him, and fashioning it into a collection of sharp images that mirror the abrupt contrasts of vulgarity and delicacy that were to Williams the essence of urban life:

> Beautiful Thing!
> And the guys from Paterson
>   beat up
> the guys from Newark and told
> them to stay the hell out
> of their territory and then
> socked you one
>   across the nose
>   Beautiful Thing
> for good luck and emphasis
>   cracking it
> till I must believe that all
> desired women have had each
>   in the end
>   a busted nose
> and live afterward marked up
>   Beautiful Thing
>
> *Paterson*, Book Three

The poem was composed in five long sections, or books, which are intentionally fragmentary, shapeless as modern experience itself, yet unified by the dual personality of the poet and his city. The whole poem is in a much lower key than *The Bridge*, never rising to the dithyrambic heights of Crane's poem at its best, yet never sinking into the ironic disillusionment that punctuates Crane's rhapsodic passages, remaining characteristically detached, unsentimental, wrily good-humored. Dr Paterson is not an idealist, but a generous realist, and his city is neither the sterile Waste Land of Eliot nor the towering Bridge of Crane. If there are not as many quotable lines in Williams's poem as in Eliot's or Crane's, he has nevertheless created his own epic of the modern city, dominated by a believable personality with a familiar human voice, a common man with uncommonly keen perceptions to whom nothing human is alien or unredeemable. *Paterson* is Williams's longest poem, reflective of his strongly masculine sensibility; for his tenderer side, one must go on to read *Asphodel, That Greeny Flower*, a later masterpiece which is an extended love poem addressed to his wife, Flora, whose name was a flower, for in it he symbolized their marriage with sustained lyric force; the poem is a rare and convincing expression of conjugal love enduring

through a lifetime, "a life filled, / if you will, / with flowers," and conquering
even the fear of approaching death:

> I have learned much in my life
> from books
> and out of them
> about love.
> Death
> is not the end of it.
> There is a hierarchy
> which can be attained,
> I think,
> in its service.
>
> *Aspodel*, Book One

Love asserted itself impressively at the end of Williams's career, though it
was generally true that "Williams, by nature, is more of a realist than is commonly
true in the case of a poet," as Wallace Stevens observed, and "the anti-poetic
was his spirit's cure." Poetry was the cure of Wallace Stevens's spirit, and the
imagination was his antidote against the anti-poetic. A native of Reading, Pennsyl-
vania, which he called "the acme of dullness," and a lawyer and insurance
executive by profession, Stevens led a life as outwardly prosaic as Williams, but
poetry was his refuge: "Seek those purposes that are purely the purposes of the
pure poet," he told himself, and he followed his advice so well that he became
in time the pre-eminent American Symbolist poet, a transatlantic counterpart of
Mallarmé or Valéry, a philosopher-poet who wrote his poetic theories in poetic
forms. Stevens was one of the successful experimenters with Imagism, but he had
a natural affinity for the abstract as well as the concrete, and was at ease as much
in the long, meditative poem as in the short, vivid lyric. Any list of Stevens's major
poems would be bound to start with "Sunday Morning," which was published in
its first version in *Poetry* magazine in 1915, the year when Eliot's "Love Song
of J. Alfred Prufrock" appeared in its pages, and would probably culminate with
"Notes Towards a Supreme Fiction," published some thirty years later. Along the
way, the list would have to include "The Comedian as the Letter C," "Idea of
Order in Key West," and "The Man with the Blue Guitar," as well as other long
poems suited to the taste of individual readers. Each of these major poems
represents Stevens at his best, expressing in varying poetic moods his expanding
theory of what a poem should be. Any reader of Stevens who is also a reader of
French Symbolist poetry will think of appropriate parallels for these poems on
poetics: Baudelaire's "Correspondances," Verlaine's "Art poétique," Mallarmé's *Un Coup de dés*, or Valéry's "Le Cimitière marin." Thoroughly versed

in French poetry as Pound or Eliot, Stevens—who never visited France—even contended that "French and English constitute a single language," a belief which is borne out by many French titles and phrases in his poetry, early and late. Difficult as it is to single out one major long poem from such an extensive repertoire, there is a later poem which owes as much as any to the French Symbolists, yet is definitely Stevens's own work and a somewhat neglected master-piece, *Esthétique du mal*. This poem can serve admirably as the culminating American long poem of the post-Imagist period, which takes its point of departure directly from French Symbolism—the title is of course a pun on Baudelaire's *Les Fleurs du mal*—and goes on to make capital of this influence, constructing an original set of variations on a major modern theme, the relation of poetry as an ideal good to the reality of evil in human life.

Esthétique du mal, like most of Stevens's long poems, is a monologue in the form of fifteen sections, or blank verse paragraphs, each about 25 lines long. It is a form admirably suited to Stevens's purpose of philosophical speculation, rather like a verse essay centering on a major theme, loose enough to allow for digressions yet formal enough to give the sense of orderly thought, and always rich in the verbal music which made even the most abstract of Stevens's poems a pleasure to the ear. If Williams maintained that there could be "No ideas but in things," Stevens proved himself ready to entertain almost any idea that was poetically interesting. His first important poem was "Sunday Morning," which takes the idea of religious worship and performs eight different variations on it, ranging from the traditional and sacramental—"The holy hush of ancient sacri-fice"—to the primitive and natural—"Supple and turbulent, a ring of men / Shall chant in orgy on a summer morn / Their boisterous devotion to the sun"— without finally settling on any one of them as most satisfactory, but finding in each a symbolic action with poetic possibilities. Similarly, in "The Idea of Order at Key West," he takes the relation of art to nature as his subject, and using the figure of a woman singing by the seashore, he muses on the way in which human expression alters the order of nature, giving significant form to the changing movements of the material world, and effecting a unity of subject and object— "when she sang, the sea, / Whatever self it had, became the self / That was her song, for she was the maker." In *The Man with the Blue Guitar*, the idea becomes the play between imagination and reality, and in *Notes Towards a Supreme Fiction*, it is the projection of myth through poetry. Though it is never easy to paraphrase one of Stevens's long poems—as R. P. Blackmur once observed, "Stevens' ambiguity is that of a substance so dense with being, that it resists paraphase"[13]—each poem, however lengthy, usually revolves around a single theme, often stated or implied in the title. There is no question that

Esthétique du mal refers to Baudelaire, not only in its title, but within the poem, where a musician named "B." is connected with a book called "Livre de toutes sortes de fleurs d'après nature"—oblique references, as are typical of Stevens's elusive technique, but still the dark perfumes of *Les Fleurs du mal* can be sniffed in the shadowy background.

The immediate occasion of this poem was different, as we learn from Stevens's *Letters*, where it appears that he was inspired to write the work because of something he had read in the *Kenyon Review*. The time was 1944, during the Second World War, and John Crowe Ransom had happened to quote a correspondent's question about the possible relation between poetry and pain. Stevens responded with a letter to Ransom in which he said that "it might be interesting to try to do an esthétique du mal."[14] Within a month, Stevens had completed the poem and sent it to Ransom, who published it in the Autumn, 1944, issue of his journal. Thus we may suppose that along with the scent of the flowers of evil in the background, there is also the noise of war. If so, Stevens made only passing reference to it in the poem, where he does mention "soldiers" and "paratroopers" but never speaks of any battles. As usual with Stevens, the poem creates its own imaginative context, using pain as a source of poetry without naming any specific agent of the pain.

Baudelaire had prefaced *Les Fleurs du mal* with an explanation of the meaning of his title:

> Certain illustrious poets have long since divided among themselves the more flowery provinces of the realm of poetry. I have found it amusing, and the more pleasant because the task was more difficult, to extract *beauty* from *Evil*.[15]

Stevens's *Esthétique du mal* is similarly ironic in the import of its title, but with the difference that his poem will be about the principle of deriving beauty from evil rather than a presentation of poems so derived. Baudelaire's source of evil is clearly human, a city of alienated men and women who are tormented as if they were living in hell, but for Stevens the source is not so clear; he simply begins by asserting that "Pain is human," and going on to contrast human with inanimate nature in this respect:

> Except for us, Vesuvius might consume
> In solid fire the utmost earth and know
> No pain
>
> *Esthétique du mal*, I

Stevens here uses as one possible source of pain the fiery destruction of Pompeii many centuries ago—a vivid enough example of human suffering, but remote enough to be more abstract, a subject of speculation as much as a cause of emotion, rather than the more immediate pain of a world war. He then reflects that man cannot be spared from pain, not even by "A too, too human god, self-pity's kin" (as direct a reference to Christ as Stevens ever allowed himself to make), for suffering is an inevitable part of every life and must be endured:

> The genius of misfortune
> Is not a sentimentalist. He is
> That evil, that evil in the self
>
> (IV)

There is, of course, the bond of human sympathy which in some measure helps to relieve the pain:

> Within the actual, the warm, the near,
> So great a unity, that it is bliss,
> Ties us to those we love.
>
> (V)

In this unity of affection binding man to man, there is consolation for a soldier's death, when "the shadows of his fellows ring him round," and our mourning is a way of sharing the pain of death together, an unspoken acknowledgement that "his wound is good because life was." Thus one kind of good, that of human fellowship, does come from one kind of evil, the pain of death, and Stevens's problem of the aesthetics of evil has a partial resolution.

He is seeking a total resolution, however, and is led in Section VIII of the poem to confront a larger aspect of the problem: how are men to see evil as somehow working to their good, when they no longer believe in any transcendent cause of good or evil?

> The death of Satan was a tragedy
> For the imagination.

Satan was a personification of evil in the universe, and as such an active agent of malevolence who could be blamed for the misfortunes and suffering of men; now, we have only impersonal physical forces causing pain. In Stevens's assumption that Satan is dead to the imagination, there may well be a conscious echo of something else Baudelaire said in his preface to *Les Fleurs du mal:*

> It is more difficult for people nowadays to believe in the Devil than
> to love him. Everyone smells him and no one believes in him. Sublime
> subtlety of the Devil.[16]

What modern man has instead of the figure of Satan is "the mortal no" of pain and death, an ever-present reality against which, "in the imagination's new beginning," the poet must speak:

> the yes of the realist spoken because he must
> Say yes, spoken because under every no
> Lay a passion for yes that had never been broken.
>
> (VIII)

It is the poet's affirmation of good, then, the "yes of the realist," that must take the place of God, as the "mortal no" has taken the place of Satan, and in the remaining sections of *Esthétique du mal,* Stevens deals with what the poet can do in a time when transcendent personifications of good and evil are no longer believed in. Accepting that "Life is a bitter aspic," the poet's task is to make an aesthetics of evil, opposing the pain of mortal suffering with the healing power of poetic expression:

> Natives of poverty, children of malheur,
> The gaiety of language is our seigneur.
>
> (XI)

Our *seigneur,* our modern savior, is thus the poet, who creates through the beauty of his language a "third world" beyond good and evil, where knowledge intuitively draws good from evil:

> It accepts whatever is as true,
> Including pain, which, otherwise, is false.
> In the third world, then, there is no pain.
>
> (XII)

Stevens thus has arrived at an overarching view that every man's suffering is "a fragmentary tragedy / Within the universal whole," and that good and evil are comparative and complementary forces, neither of which can exist without the other. He has rejected any possible political solution to human pain — "Revolution / Is the affair of logical lunatics," he says — and accepted instead an aesthetic solution, where poetry makes art out of the tragedy of existence. The poet's belief is that "The greatest poverty is not to live / In a physical world," and, discarding the earlier myths by which men have been able to reconcile themselves with pain, he becomes an "adventurer in humanity" who conceives of "a race / Completely physical in a physical world." In this way, the poet changes evil into good, pain into pleasure, by a metaphysical transformation, a kind of modern alchemy of emotions:

And out of what one sees and hears and out
Of what one feels, who could have thought to make
So many selves, so many sensuous worlds,
As if the air, the mid-day air, was swarming
With the metaphysical changes that occur,
Merely in living as and where we live.

(XV)

The significance of Stevens's poem as a whole is that it generalizes ethics into aesthetics and aesthetics into metaphysics. The poem is at once an expression of the problem of evil in the world, the oldest of human problems, and a resolution of it by art. Whereas Baudelaire dealt with evil as a concrete reality in human experience, an intense feeling of the seductiveness of sin, Stevens deals with evil as a generative idea which is sensuous only in the words that express it, and which the poem can assimilate and sublimate, distilling honey out of venom, making poetry out of pain. Stevens was one who believed that "Poetry is a means of redemption," and in this poem he made it into a means of transmuting evil into good, transforming Baudelaire's *fleurs du mal* into an *esthétique du mal*, a grand poem which has as its principal idea the conversion of physical pain into aesthetic pleasure and thus into metaphysical good. This firmly held belief in the transcendent power of poetry, apart from any supporting religious doctrine, makes Stevens the purest Symbolist among American poets, and *Esthétique du mal* is his vanquishing of the powers of darkness by the light of the poetic imagination. Certainly it is one of his major poems, and one of the major modern poems in any language, though its ability to convince readers of the possibility of overcoming evil with good through the power of poetry must depend on their willingness to share his belief that "It is possible to etablish aesthetics in the individual mind as immeasurably a greater thing than religion."[17]

Looking back over the fifty years since Taupin completed his study, we see evidence that the later, longer modern American poems are impressive for continuing to draw on French Symbolist influences while at the same time passing considerably beyond them, exceeding the limits of the brief Imagist model with which they began and building it into works of epic scope. There are no equivalents in French poetry for the *Four Quartets*, the *Cantos*, *The Bridge*, *Paterson*, or *Esthétique du mal*, yet it is highly unlikely that any of them would have been written without the original French example. The achievement of American poets in the twentieth century has been truly international, providing new forms and styles of poetic expression, new ways of symbolizing human experience, American in flavor, yet like the French poets, broadly interpretive of modern Western civilization, both in its ugliness and its beauty, its moments of despair and of exaltation. Even Eliot said that his poetry remained "purely American," yet it was as cosmopolitan as any poetry that has ever been written. Perhaps being international came naturally to Americans because of their origins in so many national and racial strains, and it did not matter whether they became expatriates like Eliot and Pound, or stayed at home and absorbed foreign influences from their reading, like Crane and Williams and Stevens. The French Symbolists were the first poets to discover how to make poetry out of the limitations of modern city life, the experience of the lonely individual in the vast metropolis created by an industrial civilization, but the American poets greatly extended the inclusiveness of that experience, its historical range and philosophical as well as religious profundity, and added immensely to the variety of forms and styles in which it could be embodied. As Taupin so ably put it, true influence does not occur when writers imitate earlier models, but only when they surpass them. It seems probable that the singular greatness of modern American poets will be seen in their ability to be influenced by so many other poets, yet to remain identifiably themselves, incorporating in their poems the widest possible diversity of human experience in uniquely individual creations.

Notes

Introduction

1. "A Few Don'ts by an Imagist," *Poetry* (March, 1913).
2. *Gaudier-Brzeska* (first published in 1916; reprinted by New Directions, New York, in 1960), p. 85.
3. Eliot, *Selected Essays* (New York: Harcourt, Brace, 1950), p. 9.
4. *Ibid.*, p. 248.
5. *Ibid.*, p. 377.
6. For a discussion of the general principle of *synaesthesis*, see *The Foundations of Aesthetics* by I. A. Richards and C. K. Ogden (New York: Lear Publishers, 1925) Chap. XIV.
7. *The Mirror of Art: Critical Studies by Baudelaire* (New York: Doubleday Anchor Books, 1956), p., x.
8. Jacques Maritain, *The Situation of Poetry* (New York: Philosophical Library, 1955), p. 42.
9. T. E. Hulme, *Speculations*, ed. Herbert Read (first published in London, 1924; reprinted in New York by Harcourt, Brace, 1961), pp. 3–71.
10. *Ibid.*, pp. 143–69.
11. "Credo," *Poetry and Drama* (London, 1912).
12. "Lecture on Modern Poetry," in *Further Speculations*, ed. Sam Hynes (Minneapolis: U. of Minnesota Press, 1955), p. 74.
13. *Ibid.*, p. 72.
14. "Romanticism and Classicism," *Speculations*, p. 135.

Part One / Chapter 1

1. Ezra Pound, "Patria Mia," *The New Age* (26 September 1912).
2. H. L. Mencken, "Puritanism as a Literary Force," *A Book of Prefaces* (New York: Aflred A. Knopf, 1917).
3. Excerpt from a letter published in *Mercure de France* (15 October 1927).
4. "The contributors make the magazine and the magazine makes the contributors. This is the reason why America no longer produces anything that can be called art . . . with the exception of political articles." Ezra Pound, "Patria Mia," *The New Age*, (3 October 1912). See also Baptist von Helmholst, "Those American Publications," *The Egoist* (15 October 1914).
5. Anonymous, "A Bitter Complaint of the Ungentle Reader," *The Chap-Book: Semi-Monthly*, I, 1 (15 May 1894), p. 10.
6. Sidney Lanier, *The Science of English Verse* (New York: Charles Scribner's Sons, 1891).

Part One / Chapter 2

1. Preface to *Complete Poetical Works of Joaquin Miller* (San Francisco: Whitaker and Ray, 1897), p. v.
2. *Ibid.*, xii.
3. *Ibid.*, xiii.

Part One / Chapter 3

1. A very lively portrait of this period has been traced by Thomas Beer in *The Mauve Decade* (New York: Alfred A. Knopf, 1926).
2. *Les Gammes* was issued by Vanier the same year that Merrill was in New York.
3. Edgar Fawcett, for example, and also Edgar Saltus.
4. "Gerard de Nerval," *The New York Times*, 22 April 1888; "Lohengrin in Paris," *New York Evening Post*, 7 May 1887; "The Legend of Siegfried," *New York Evening Post*, 19 November 1887; "The Dusk of the Gods,"*New York Evening Post*, 2 February 1888.
5. Stuart Merrill, "Oscar Wilde," *La Plume* (15 March 1893).
6. London: Macmillan and Co., 1878.
7. See especially *French Dramatists of the Nineteenth Century; Gateways to Literature, and Other Essays; Books and Playbooks; Essays on Literature and the Drama; Aspects of Fiction and Other Ventures in Criticism.*
8. Not yet known for his paintings.
9. Paul Bourget, *Outremer*, p. 96.
10. Mark Twain, "What Paul Bourget Thinks of Us,"*North American Reveiw* (January, 1895).
11. London: Swan, Sonnenschein and Lowrey, 1888.
12. London: Nutt, 1891.
13. Anonymous, "A Trio of French Tourists: Gautier, Mery, de Nerval," *Blackwood's* (March, 1853); Andrew Lang, "Gerard de Nerval," *Fraser's Magazine* (May, 1873); Garnet Smith, "Gerard de Nerval," *Gentleman's Magazine* (March, 1889.)
14. Stuart Merrill, "Gerard de Nerval," *The New York Times*, 22 April 1888.
15. London: Macmillan, 1878.
16. Cited by James. G. Huneker, "The Baudelaire Legend," *Egoists*, p. 80.
17. "Charles Baudelaire," *Southern Magazine* (January, 1873).
18. "Charles Baudelaire," *Nation* (27 April, 1876).
19. Anonymous, "A Poet of the Lower French Empire," *Fraser's Magazine* (December, 1869); George Saintsbury, "Charles Baudelaire," *Fortnightly Review* (1 October 1875), reproduced in the *Nation* (April 27, 1876).
20. Such at least is the opinion of Ezra Pound, Cf. *Little Review* (August, 1918).
21. H. MacCulloch, "The Poetry of Charles Baudelaire," *Harvard Monthly*, (February, 1890).
22. "The Poet Verlaine," *Fortnightly Review* (1 March 1891); review of *Bonheur* by Paul Verlaine, *Academy* (18 April 1891).
23. *Impressions and Opinions*, p. 19.
24. Gosse, "Stéphane Mallarmé," *Academy* (January 7, 1893); F. Carrell, "Mallarmé," *Fortnightly Review* (2 March 1895).

25. Harry Thurston Peck, "Stéphane Mallarmé," *The Bookman* (November, 1898).

26. Virginia Crawford, "Emile Verhaeren, The Belgian Poet," *Fortnightly Review* (1 November 1896).

27. "A Year of Continental Literature," *Atheneum* (July, 1891).

28. "A Pessimist Playwright," *Fortnightly Review* (1 September 1891).

29. *The Blind* and *The Intruder*, translated from the French of M. Maeterlinck by Mary Vielé (Washington, D. C., Morrisson: 1891).

30. John Heard, in *The Forum*.

31. New York: Harper Bros., 1890.

32. See René Taupin, *L'Interpretation americaine de la poèsie française contemporaine*, p. 5.

33. Theodore Child, "Literary Paris," *Harper's Monthly* (August, 1892). pp. 327–40.

34. Esmé Stuart, "Charles Baudelaire and Edgar Poe," *Nineteenth Century Review* (July, 1893), reprinted in *The Living Age* (September, 1893).

35. *The Critic* (16 December 1893).

36. *Nation* (14 December 1893).

37. "The Decadent Movement in Literature," *Harper's Monthly* (November, 1893).

38. London: W. Heinemann, 1899.

39. Aline Gorren, "The French Symbolists," *Scribner's* (January-June, 1893).

40. Cf. "Impressions of Mr. Maeterlinck," *Poet-Lore*, VII, 8 (1895).

41. *The Bookman: An Illustrated Literary Journal* (New York: February, 1895).

42. "This new edition will contain supplementary articles of immediate importance to American readers. *The Bookman* will give each month a biography of some new author. From time to time it will also give portraits." (Preface to first edition of *The Bookman*.)

43. *Degeneration*, translated from the second edition of the German work (New York: D. Appleton & Co., 1895).

44. G. Robert, "Richard Wagner et Max Nordau," *Ermitage* (August, 1894); Leon Bazalgette, "Note sur Max Nordau," *Ermitage* (August, 1894); Charles Tenib, "Defense de P. V." *La Plume* (15 September 1894).

45. *The Forum* (June, 1909). See, along with the articles of Huneker, *Regeneration: A Reply to Max Nordau*, with an introduction by N. M. Butler (New York: G. P. Putnam's Sons, 1896). See also J. C. Leclercq, *The Legend of French Decadence in the United States* (U. of California, 1922).

46. *Chap-Book*, No. 1, 1 May 1894. On the flyleaf of the first number, this announcement appeared in mock-Old English: "The Chap Book; a miscellany of curious and interesting Songs, Ballades, Histories etc; adorned with a variety of pictures, and very delightful to read; newly composed by many celebrated writers to which are annexed a large collection of Notices of Books. Chicago, Printed for Stone and Kimball of the Caxton Building where Shopkeepers, Hawkers, and others are supplied."

47. *Chap-Book* (1 July 1894).

48.
> Mon âge mur qui ne grommelle.
> En somme qu'encore tres peu . . .
> *Chap-Book*, (15 September 1894).

49. "The Green Tree Library, a series of books representing what may broadly be called the new movement in literature. The intention is to publish uniformly the best of the so-called decadent writings of various countries done into English." *Chap-Book* (15 September 1894).

50. *Chap-Book*, (15 May 1896).

51. See in particular W. Sharp's "The Birth of a Soul," in the *Chap-Book* (September 15, 1894), and Josephine Preston Peabody's "The Woman of Three Sorrows," in the *Chap-Book* (1 September 1895).

52. *Ermitage* (1895), p. 307. See also *Magazine International* (May, 1895).

53. "Their flowers are flowers of evil and their trees bear sodom apples." *Chap-Book* (1 September 1896).

54. *Chap-Book* (1 December 1894).

55. Lansing, Mich. (April, 1896).

56. New York (February, 1896).

57. *A Humorous and Artistic Periodical*, (May, 1895).

58. *The Criterion*, New York (16 October 1897).

59. Portland, Me. (January, 1895).

60. "Avis au Lecteur,"*The Lark* (1 September 1895).

61. For instance, the famous jingle by Burgess:

> I never saw a purple cow,
> I never hope to see one,
> But I can tell you anyhow,
> I'd rather see than be one.

62. Edited by Burgess, Oliver Herford, and Carolyn Wells (New York, 1 April 1898).

63. *The New Bohemian*, (1895).

64. *M'lle New York* (November, 1895).

65. *Ibid.* (January, 1896).

66. New York, Summer, 1904. The death of the editor ended the magazine. In its single issue, however, it printed Mallarmé's "L'Eventail de M'lle Mallarmé," Stuart Merrill's "Chambre d'Amour," and Gustave Kahn's "Votre Domaine est Terre de Petit Fee."

67. "Notes," *The Nation*, LXVI (17 February 1898), p. 131.

68. See the article by J. G. Cooke in *The Bookman* of April, 1900.

69. French architectural style was much in evidence there, as at the Pan American Exposition of 1900. French painting was being more and more appreciated: from 1900 to 1910, the Metropolitan Museum bought canvases of Degas, Sisley, and Monet. A very important showing of French Impressionists at Buffalo, followed by two others at Pittsburgh and Cincinnati, in 1908, did much to turn public attention toward the new conception of art.

70. Boston: Richard G. Badger, 1900.

71. *French Portraits*, p. 167.

72. *Ibid.*, p. 183.

73. *Ibid.*, p. 115.

74. "Just as Poe created modern French prose, Whitman re-created modern French verse." *Ibid.*, p. 103.

75. He wrote for the New York *Sun*, the New York *Recorder*, the *Morning Adviser*, *The New York Times*, the *World*, and the Philadelphia *Press*.

76. "The Evolution of an Egoist: Maurice Barrès," *Atlantic Monthly* (August, 1897).

77. "A Pessimist's Progress: J. K. Huysmans," *North American Review*, (September 1907).

78. "The Baudelaire Legend," *Scribner's* (February, 1909).

79. Reprinted in *Iconoclasts* (New York: Charles Scribner's Sons, 1905), p. 350.

80. See "Notes," *The Nation* (March, 1897), where *Livre de Masques* is referred to as an unappreciated work.

81. "Rémy de Gourmont," New York *Sun* (14 June 1900).

82. "There are a hundred books called *Impressionist*, and only two called *Promenades*, Stendahl's and de Gourmont's. Hence my *Promenades of an Impressionist."* Huneker to W. C. Brownwell, 29 January 1910.

83. New York: Charles Scribner's Sons, 1909, reprinted AMS, 1975.

Part One / Chapter 4

1. "À Stéphane Mallarmé," *To the End of the Trail,* (New York: Duffield & Co., 1908), p. 45.

2. "The Faun. V." *Along the Trail* (Boston: Small, Maynard & Co., 1898), pp. 87–88.

3. *To the End of the Trail,* p. 148.

4. "Spring. V." *Along the Trail,* p. 56.

5. "The Laurel. An Ode to Molly Day Lanier." *To the End of the Trail,* p. 8.

6. *Launcelot and Guinevere, A Poem in Dramas: Dedication; The Quest of Merlin: The Marriage of Guinevere.* (New York: John Lowell Co., 1891).

7. Boston: Small, Maynard & Co., 1898.

8. Maeterlinck, *Preface to Theatre,* Vol. I.

9. Letter of Mallarmé to Hovey, Nov. 19, 1898, published by Barbara Matulka in "Letters of Mallarmé and Materlinck to Richard Hovey," *Romanic Review,* XVIII (Autumn, 1927), p. 233.

10. Letter from Maeterlinck to Hovey, 12 September 1898. loc. cit., p. 236.

11. *The Plays of Maurice Maeterlinck: Princess Maleine, The Intruder, The Blind, The Seven Princesses, Alladines and Palomides, Pelleas and Melisande, Home, The Death of Tintagiles,* translated by Richard Hovey (Chicago: Stone & Kimball, 1894–1896).

12. *Ibid.,* Introduction: "Modern Symbolism and Maurice Maeterlinck," p. 7.

13. *Ibid.,* p. 8.

14. "Richard Hovey, Poet, in Town," *The Boston Record* (1 September 1898).

15. Boston, New York: Lamson Wolffe & Co., 1895.

16. Boston: Copeland & Day, 1894. See also *More Songs from Vagabondia* (Boston: Copeland & Day, 1896); and *Last Songs from Vagabondia* (Boston: Small, Maynard, & Co., 1901).

17. Boston, New York: Lamson, Wolffe & Co., 1898.

18. "Presence," *New York Nocturnes,* p. 21.

19. "A Street Vigil," *New York Nocturnes,* p. 30.

20. L. C. Page & Co., 1903.

21. "On the Upper Deck," *The Book of the Rose,* p. 5.

22. "The Fear of Love," *The Book of the Rose,* p. 23.

23. See *First Poems and Fragments* (Boston: Copeland & Day, 1895).

24. See *The Wayfarers* (Boston: Copeland & Day, 1898), and *Fortune and Men's Eyes* (Boston: Small, Maynard & Co., 1900).

25. "We have been in Paris now seven weeks and I have learned this dainty Sodom tolerably well, I flatter myself." Letter to Robert M. Lovett, Paris. Nov. 22, 1892. *Some Letters of William*

Vaughan Moody, ed. Daniel G. Mason (Boston and New York: Houghton, Mifflin Co., 1913), p. 6.

26. Moody to Daniel G. Mason, Chicago, 18 December 1899, in *Some Letters of William Vaughan Moody*, p. 119.

27. Moody to Mrs. C. H. Toy, 17 February 1909, *Some Letters*, p. 169.

28. Moody to Percy MacKaye, 15 August 1904, *Some Letters*, p. 148.

29. Moody to Josephine Preston Peabody, 5 January 1902, *Some Letters*, p. 143.

30. *The Fire Bringer*, Act I, p. 54.

31. Translator's note: This assumption of Taupin's is undoubtedly based on an article about Moody by C. M. Lewis, which appeared in the *Yale Review* in July, 1913, suggesting the French poem as a "probable source." The parallels are certainly striking, but the conjecture is without confirmation in Moody's published writings; in fact, in *Letters to Harriet* (Boston, New York: Houghton Mifflin Co., 1935), p. 172, he refers to *The Death of Eve* as "a new piece," and says distinctly that "The idea of it came on me out of a clear sky the other day, and almost lifted me out of my skin."

Part One / Chapter 5

1. Buffalo: C. W. Moulton, 1894.

2. Buffalo: C. W. Moulton, 1891.

3. Philadelphia: J. B. Lippincott, 1873.

4. "Lines to a Corpse," *Honey and Gall*, p. 186.

5. "Negra Venus," *Honey and Gall*, pp. 141–2.

6. "Souvenirs," *Honey and Gall*, pp. 128–29.

7. "Vicenza," *Honey and Gall*, p. 116.

8. Gautier, "La Basilique," *Poésies Complètes* (Paris: Bibliothèque Charpentier, 1905).

9. "Tours," *Honey and Gall*, p. 133.

10. "Turquerie," *Honey and Gall*, p. 98.

11. "A . . . ", *Honey and Gall*, p. 8l

12. "In Summer," *The Poems of Trumbull Stickney* (Boston, New York; Houghton Mufflin & Co., 1905), p.22.

13. "Charles Baudelaire," *Nineveh and Other Poems* (New York: Moffatt, Yard & Co., 1907), p. 130.

14. "The Haunted House," *Nineveh and Other Poems*, pp. 149–50.

15. *The Candle and the Flame*, (New York: Moffatt, Yard & Co., 1912), p. 15.

Part One / Chapter 6

1. *Modern American Poetry* (New York: Harcourt, Brace, and Co., Inc., 1919).

2. "Modern American Poetry," *Poetry Review* (October, 1912), p. 469.

3. *Literary Friends and Acquaintances* (1900).

4. Preface to *Tendencies in American Poetry* (New York: Macmillan Co., 1917).

5. Here is the list:

1908	G. Sterling:	*A Wine of Wizardry*

1909	R. Burton:	*From the Book of Life*
	L. I. Guiney:	*Happy Ending*
	T. A. Daly:	*Carmina*
	J. Oppenheim:	*Doctor Rash*
		Monday Morning and Other Poems

1910	E. A. Robinson:	*The Town Down the River*
	A. H. Branch:	*Rose of the Wind*
	H. Kemp:	*Judas*
	H. Traubel:	*Optimos*

1911	G. Sterling:	*The House of Orchids*
	B. L. Taylor:	*A Line o' Love or Two*

6. "Aftermath," *A Dome of Many-Coloured Glass* (Boston: Houghton Mifflin & Co., 1912,) p. 104.

7. "Aedh Wishes for the Cloths of Heaven," *The Wind Among the Reeds*, 1899.

8. *Chariot d'Or*, p. 97.

9. *The New Republic*, Poetry Number (November, 1916).

10. Edited by F. Earle (New York: Mitchell Kennerley, 1912).

11. *Boston Evening Transcript*, 14 October 1912.

12. Ezra Pound described the state of mind in this way: "1912 was a bad year, we all ran about like puppies with ten tin cans tied to our tails. The tin cans of Swinburnian rhyming, of Browningsians, of Kiplingsians, a resonant pendant, magniloquent, Miltonic, sonorous." *Egoist*.

13. See "Poetry Banquet," *Poetry*, IV (April, 1914), pp. 25–28.

Part Two / Chapter 1

1. *Speculations: Essays on Humanism and the Philosophy of Art* (London: Kegan Paul, Trench, Trubner & Co., 1924).

2. "Notes on Language and Style," published by Herbert Read in the *Criterion* (July, 1925).

3. *Ibid.*

4. *Ibid.*

5. *Problème du Style*, p. 69.

6. "Notes on Language and Style," *Ibid.*

7. *Ibid.*

8. *Ibid.*

9. *Ibid.*

10. *Ibid.*

11. *Des Imagistes* (London: Poetry Book Shop; New York: Albert and Charles Boni, 1914).

12. Rémy de Gourmont in *La France*, 5 May 1915; reprinted in *Mercure de France*, June, 1915; then in the preface to *Some Imagist Poets*, 1916, by Aldington in *Bruno's Chapbooks*, 1915, and by others in various places.

13. Pound, *Blast*, July, 1914.

14. Richard Aldington, "The Art of Poetry," *Dial* LXIX (August, 1920), p. 168.

15. *Problème du style*, p. 41.

16. "A Consideration of Modern Poetry," *North American Review* (January, 1917).

17. *L'Attitude du Lyrisme Contemporain*, p. 112.

Part Two / Chapter 2

1. "Contemporary French Poetry," *Poetry Review* (August, 1912).

2. "The Approach to Paris," *The New Age* (4 September-16 October 1913).

3. Ezra Pound, "Paris," *Poetry* III (October, 1913), p. 27.

4. "The Approach to Paris," *New Age* (2 October 1913), p. 662.

5. *Ibid.*, p. 663-64.

6. "The Approach to Paris, VI," *The New Age* (9 October 1913), p. 696.

7. *Egoist*, I (16 March 1914), p. 101.

8. *Six French Poets: Studies in Contemporary Literature* (New York: Macmillan Co., 1915).

9. *La Poésie d'Andre Fontainas*, (Paris: Editions du Monde Nouveau, 1919).

10. "The Case of French Poetry," *The Little Review*, I (February, 1915) pp. 18-19.

11. See "Albert Mockel et la *Walhonie*," *The Little Review* (October, 1918).

12. "Approach to Paris," *The New Age* (11 September 1913).

Part Two / Chapter 3

1. Georges Bonneau, *Albert Samain, poète symboliste* (Paris, 1925), p. 15.

2. "A Restrospect," *Pavannes and Divisions* (New York: Alfred A. Knopf, 1918) p. 96.

3. Harold Monro, "Imagists Discussed," *The Egoist* II (1 May 1915), p. 18.

4. *Symbolistes et decadents*, p. 92.

5. Albert Thibaudet, *La Poèsie de Stéphane Mallarmé* (Paris: Librairie Gallimard, 1926), p. 85.

6. *Ibid.*, pp. 87-88.

7. *Ibid.*, p. 86.

8. May Sinclair, Introduction to *The Closed Door* by Jean de Bosschère, trans. F. S. Flint (New York: John Lane, 1917).

9. O. W. Firkins, "The New Movement in Poetry," *The Nation*, CI (14 October 1915), p. 459.

10. "Hérodiate," *Poésies*, p. 58.

11. "The Pool," *Some Imagist Poets* (1915), p. 21.

12. Thibaudet, *La Poésie de Stéphane Mallarmé*, pp. 124-24.

13. Lora Marsden, "The Gentle Act of Appreciation," *The Egoist* II (2 August 1915), p. 102.

14. "Oread," *Some Imagist Poets* (1915), p. 28.

15. "The Faun Sees Snow for the First Time," *Some Imagist Poets* (1915), p. 16.

16. "Le Vierge, le vivace et le bel aujourd'hui," *Poésie*, p. 124.

17. May Sinclair, "On Imagism," *The Egoist* II (1 June 1915), p. 88.

18. *Pavannes and Divisions*.

19. See "Considerations of Modern Poetry," *North American Review* (January, 1917). Amy

Lowell, on the other hand, made suggestion one of the innovations of the new school, but she and Fletcher were latter-day Symbolists.

20. See Louis de Saint-Jacques, "La Protestation Mallarmophile de M. Gide et les Divagations de Mallarmé," *La Plume* (15 March 1897).

21. "Paul Claudel," *Poetry*, VI (July, 1915), p. 204.

22. "Au Vieux Jardin," *Poetry* (November, 1912), and *Des Imagistes*, p. 11.

23. See "A Retrospect," *Pavannes and Divisions*, p. 97.

24. It was Aldington who best showed this dreamlike atmosphere in H. D.'s poetry. See "A Young American Poet," *The Little Reveiw* (March, 1915).

25. Ford, *Thus to Revisit*, pp. 137–38.

26. *Ibid.*, p. 140.

27. "A Pact," *Lustra*, p. 23.

28. "Ortus," *Lustra*, p. 10.

29. *Some Imagist Poets* (1916), p. vi. *Livre des masques*, Preface. p. 13.

30. *The Phoenix, A Magazine of Individuality*, South Norwalk, Conn., 1914–1916.

31. Ford, *Thus to Revisit*, p. 132.

32. Richard Aldington, "Modern Poetry and the Imagists," *Egoist* I (1 June 1914), p. 202.

33. Preface to *Some Imagist Poets* (1915), p. vi.

34. Ford, *op. cit.*, p. 160, and *Le Probleme du style*, p. 43.

35. See above, Part II, Chapter One, footnote 12.

36. Aldington, *Bruno's Chapbooks*, 1915, special series, No. 15.

37. J. K. Huysmans, Preface to *Rimes de joie* by Théophile Hamon, cited by Aldington in *Bruno's Chapbooks*, Special Series, No. 5.

38. *Problème du style*, p. 32. Cf. Richard Aldington, in *The Dial* (August, 1920): "Style is thinking, perceiving, and expressing oneself precisely and individually."

39. There was perfect accord between Rémy de Gourmont, the Symbolists, and the Imagists on this subject. The notion had been explored in particular by Jules de Gaultier (*Mercure de France*, 1 March 1924): poetry was to be thought of as a sort of return to a poetic language, which was no more than "the prolongation and exteriorization in a resonant medium of the nervous vibration identified with the very reality of physical feeling." Poetry was also to be "a tentative biology aimed at reconstituting, by new means appropriate to the circumstances of a new language, the ancient power."

40. Pound, "A Retrospect," *Pavannes and Divisions*, p. 97.

41. "Presentation: Notes on the Art of Writing," *The Chapbook*, II (London: Poetry Bookshop, March, 1920), p. 17.

42. Margaret Anderson "The Piano and Imagism," *The Little Review*, II (August, 1915), p. 9.

43. F. S. Flint, "H. D.," *The Chapbook*, II (London: Poetry Bookshop, March, 1920), p. 24.

44. "Studies in Contemporary Criticism," *The Egoist* (October, 1918).

45. *Le Problème du style*, p. 32.

46. "A Retrospect," *Pavannes and Divisions*, p. 103.

47. *Some Imagist Poets* (1915), Preface, p. vii.

48. Pound, "A Retrospect," *Pavannes and Divisions*, p. 95.

49. *Lustra*, p. 55.

50. Barre, *Le Symbolisme*.

51. Richard Aldington, "A Young American Poet," *The Little Review*, II (March, 1915). p. 22.

52. F. S. Flint, *In the Net of the Stars* (London: Elkin Mathews, 1909), p. 14.

53. See the issues of *Occident* for 1909.

54. *Du Rhythme en français* (Paris: Welter, 1912).

55. F. S. Flint, "Presentation: Notes on the Art of Writing," *The Chapbook*, II (London: Poetry Bookshop, March, 1920), p. 19.

56. Amy Lowell, "The Rhythm of Free Verse," *The Dial* (17 January 1918).

57. "Poetry as a Spoken Art," *The Dial* (25 January 1917), p. 49.

58. "The Rhythm of Free Verse," *The Dial* (17 January 1918).

59. The influence of certain modern theories on the Imagist movement, such as accelerated Impressionism, or Futurism, and such as one school which reacted against Symbolism by searching for the soul of the group rather than of the individual sensibility (which they thought the Symbolists had overemphasized), and by seeking direct nonmusical expression—the school which called itself "Unanimiste"—this influence was real, but vague, indecisive, and paradoxical. These schools influenced the Imagists in some respects, for the Imagists loved the classical beauty of Greece, and they cultivated individualism; but in other respects, the Imagists reacted in their own way to the new ideas, especially in their desire to prune the dead branches from English poetry, sentimentality, abuse of adjectives, and use of abstractions. They did take from the French, however, the idea of grouping themselves into a "school."

60. F. S. Flint, "Henri Ghéon and the 'Vers Libre,' " *Poetry Review* (August, 1912), pp. 363–64.

61. F. S. Flint, "Georges Duhamel," *Poetry Review* (August, 1912), p. 387.

62. Aldington "Free Verse in England," *The Egoist* (15 September, 1924); Pound, *Poetry* (March, 1913), and *Pavannes and Divisions*; H. Monroe, "Rhythms of English Verse," *Poetry* (13 November 1913); A. Lowell, Preface to *Some Imagist Poets* (1915).

63. Preface to *Some Imagist Poets* (1916), p. lx.

64. Vildrac and Duhamel, *Notes sur la technique poétique*.

65. *Ibid.* This same idea was expressed by Amy Lowell in her article, "The Rhythms of Free Verse," *The Dial* (17 January 1918), when she said that the vers libre poem as a whole keeps to a single recurring psychological beat.

66. De Gourmont, *L'Aesthetique de la Langue Française*.

67. Aldington, *The Egoist* (15 September 1914).

68. Preface to *Some Imagist Poets* (1916), pp. x–xii.

69. F. S. Flint, "Presentation: Notes on the Art of Writing," *Chapbook* (London: Poetry Bookshop, March, 1920).

70. *The Egoist* (15 September 1914).

71. *Ibid.*

72. Richard Aldington, "The Art of Poetry," *The Dial* (August, 1920).

73. "Three Imagist Poets," *The Little Review* (June, 1916).

Part Two / Chapter 4

1. F. S. Flint, Preface to *Otherworld: Cadences* (London: Poetry Bookshop, 1920), p. v.

2. *The Love Poems of Emile Verhaeren* (1916), and *The Closed Door* by Jean de Bosschère (1917).

3. Aldington, *Collected Poems*, p. 3.

4. Aldington, *Rémy de Gourmont: A Modern Man of Letters* (Seattle: U. of Washington Bookstore, 1928), and *Rémy du Gourmont: Selections from All His works*, chosen and translated by Richard Aldington (New York: Covici-Friede, 1929).

5. Aldington, *Rémy de Gourmont: A Modern Man of Letters*, p. 27.

6. Pound, "The Approach to Paris," *The New Age* XIII (11 September 1913), p. 577.

7. *Personae: The Collected Poems of Ezra Pound* (first published 1926, republished by New Directions, New York), pp. 13, 6–7, 14–15.

8. See Jean de Bosschère, "Ezra Pound," *The Egoist* (January-March, 1917).

9. Ezra Pound, *The Spirit of Romance*, (first published by Dent, London, 1910, and republished by New Directions, New York), p. 126.

10. Personal letter of Ezra Pound. [This letter (in French) is to be found entire in *Letters of Ezra Pound* (1907–41), ed. D. D. Paige (New York: Harcourt, Brace, 1950), pp. 216–18.]

11. F. S. Flint, "History of Imagism," *The Egoist* (1 May 1915).

12. Pound, "The Approach to Paris, II," *The New Age* (11 September 1913), p. 577.

13. "The Approach to Paris, V.", *The New Age* (2 October 1913), p. 663–64.

14. "A Retrospect," *Pavannes and Divisions*, p. 98.

15. *Ibid.*

16. *Ripostes of Ezra Pound, Whereto Are Appended the Complete Poetical Works of T. E. Hulme* (Boston: Small, Maynard, & Co., 1913).

17. "N. Y.," *Personae*, p. 62.

18. "A Girl," *Personae*, p. 62.

19. *Ibid.*

20. "Apparuit," *Personae*, p. 68.

21. "The Approach to Paris," *New Age* (11 September 1913), p. 579.

22. Between "Apparuit," in which Pound had experimented with stanzaic structure, aided by his reading of de Gourmont, and "The Return," one of his most successful poems, in which he had profited by reading de Régnier, a period of six months had elapsed. The latter poem was written in only a quarter of an hour!

23. Pound, "Vortex," *Blast*, No. 1 (20 June 1914), p. 154.

24. "Salutation the Third," *Personae*, p. 145.

25. *Personae*, p. 161.

26. *Ibid.*, p. 163.

27. *Personae*, p. 179.

28. *Personae*, p. 181.

29. *Ibid.*, p. 182.

30. "How to Read," *New York Herald Tribune Books* (January, 1929).

31. *Ibid.*

32. *Ibid.*

33. See "A Study in French Poets," *The Little Review*, IV (February, 1918), pp. 6-7. (The entire passage is worth quoting verbatim: "After Gautier, France produced as nearly as I can understand, three chief and admirable poets: Tristan Corbière, perhaps the most poignant poet since Villon, Rimbaud, a vivid and indubitable genius, and Laforgue—a slighter, but in some ways a finer artist than either of the others. I don't mean that he writes better than Rimbaud, and Eliot has pointed out the wrongness of Symons's phrase: 'Laforgue the eternal adult; Rimbaud the eternal child.' Rimbaud's effects seem often to come as the beauty of certain silver

crystals produced by chemical means; Laforgue always knows what he is at; Rimbaud, the 'genius' in the narrowest and deepest sense of the term, the 'most modern' seems, almost without knowing it, to hit on the various ways in which the best writers were to follow him, slowly. Laforgue is the 'last word'; out of infinite knowledge of all the ways of saying a thing, he finds the right way. Rimbaud, when right, is so because he simply can't be bothered to do it anyhow else.")

34. Pound's poem, "To a Friend Writing on Cabaret Dancers," quoted above, contains Gautier's phrase in French.

35. "A Study in French Poets," *loc. cit.*, p. 23.

36. "How to Read," *loc. cit.*

37. The entire text of this letter is to be found in *The Letters of Ezra Pound* (1907–41), p. 217.

38. "A Study of French Poets," *loc. cit.*

39. "Irony, Laforgue, and Some Satire," *Poetry*, XI (November, 1917).

40. *Ibid.*

41. Pound, *Instigations*, p. 253.

42. For example, he reproduced "Oh, le Tétrarque sur la terasse, cariatide des dynasties" with "The tetrarch appeared on a terrace, removing his ceremonial gloves," but he did not understand the popular expression "procédé instantané" and translated it as "a speedy procedure." Also, he shortened "Quant aux lointains du ciel, ils étaient loin" to "The heights of heaven were distant."

43. *Mauberley* (1920), III, *Personae*, p. 202.

44. *Ibid.*, p. 199.

45. *Ibid.*, p. 187.

46. *Ibid.*, p. 196.

47. *Ibid.*, p. 200.

48. *Ibid.*, p. 196.

49. "Paris," *Poetry* (October, 1913).

50. *Personae*, p. 198.

51. Émaux et camées.

52. *Personae*, p. 180.

53. *Ibid.*, p. 192.

54. *Ibid.*, p. 194.

55. *Ibid.*, p. 195.

56. One can see some truth in Louis Untermeyer's judgment, in his early book, *The New Era in American Poetry* (New York: Henry Holt & Co., 1919, p. 211) that Pound "does the stock French thing . . . which seems new only because Anglo-Saxons generally know so little of French literature."

57. Harriet Monroe, Editorial, *Poetry*, I (October, 1912).

58. "Night," *Collected Poems of H. D.*, p. 47.

59. "Pygmalion," *Ibid.*, p. 71.

60. "Adonis," *Ibid.*, p. 69.

61. "Pygmalion," *Ibid.*, p. 72.

62. "Eurydice,"*Ibid.*, p. 76

63. "Lethe," *Ibid.*, p. 280.

64. *Ibid.*, pp. 44–45.
65. "Adonis," *Ibid.*, p. 68.
66. "Phaedra," *Ibid.*, p. 199.
67. "Lethe," *Ibid.*, p. 280.

Part Two / Chapter 5

1. *Six French Poets* (Boston, New York: Houghton Mifflin, 1915), p. 274.
2. *Ibid.*, p. 236.
3. *Ibid.*, p. 257.
4. Preface to *Sword Blades and Poppy Seed* (New York: Macmillan Co., 1916), p. ix.
5. "Walt Whitman and the New Poetry," *Yale Review* (April, 1927), p. 509.
6. Preface to *Men, Women and Ghosts*, pp. vii–viii.
7. *East Wind* (Boston, New York: Houghton Mifflin, 1924); *What's O'Clock* (Boston, New York: Houghton Mifflin, 1925); and *Ballads for Sale* (Boston, New York: Houghton Mifflin, 1927).
8. "A Consideration of Modern Poetry," *The North American Review* (January, 1917), p. 105.
9. *Ibid.*, p. 104.
10. "Absence," *Sword Blades and Poppy Seed*, p. 85.
11. *Ibid.*, pp. vii–ix.
12. Heredia, *L'Orient et les tropiques.*
13. "The Pike," *Sword Blades and Poppy Seed*, p. 234.
14. *Ibid.*, p. 54.
15. "La Vigile des Grèves," *Poèmes anciens et romanesques.*
16. *Sword Blades and Poppy Seed*, p. 160.
17. *Men, Women and Ghosts*, p. 351.
18. *Sword Blades and Poppy Seed*, p. 31.
19. *Ibid.*, p. 57.
20. Title poem to *Les Medailles d'Argile.*
21. *Sword Blades and Poppy Seed*, p. 34.
22. André Barre, *Le Symbolisme*, p. 372.
23. "Pantomime in One Act," *What's O'Clock*, p. 208.
24. "Le Pavillon," *La Cité des Eaux.*
25. *Men, Women and Ghosts*, p. 150.
26. *Six French Poets*, p. 51.
27. *Sword Blades and Poppy Seed*, p. 242.
28. *Ibid.*, p. 91.
29. "The Middleton Place. Charleston, S. C.," *What's O'Clock*, p. 90.
30. *Men, Women and Ghosts*, p. 136.
31. *Sword Blades and Poppy Seed*, p. 38.
32. *Six French Poets*, p. 250
33. In an unpublished letter, dated 21 January 1915, Rémy de Gourmont wrote to her: "Mademoiselle, j'ai retrouvé les 3 manuscrits dont j'avais parlé à M. Aldington en lui disant mon intention de vous les envoyer en souvenir de votre délicate bonté pour moi. Vous les recevrez

bientôt. Veuillez les accepter en excusant leur peu de valeur, qui serait très grande si elle égalait ma reconnaissance ... Cette guerre m'a touché bien directement; ma santé trés atteinté, mes revenus brusquement disparus. Bref j'ai fait naufrage, et je n'oublierai jamais que vous êtes venue noblement à mon secours, vous qui ne me connaissiez que par mes écrits."

34. "The Bronze Horses," *Can Grande's Castle*, p. 170.

35. "The 'Prince of Poets,' " *Literary Digest* (17 August 1912), p. 261.

36. Preface to *Sword Blades and Poppy Seed*, pp. xi–xii.

37. Preface to *Roman de Louis XI*, by Paul Fort.

38. "A Consideration of Modern Poetry," *The North American Review*, pp. 103–117.

39. "Vers Libre and Metrical Prose," *Poetry* (March, 1914).

40. *Six French Poets*, p. 316.

41. "In a Castle," *Sword Blades and Poppy Seed*, p. 172.

42. *Six French Poets*, p. 449.

43. "The Basket," *Sword Blades and Poppy Seed*, p. 167.

44. "Richard Coeur de Lion," *Chansons pour me consoler d'être heureux*.

45. "Miss Lowell's Discovery, Polyphonic Prose," *Poetry* (April, 1915).

46. See M. C. Cestre, "L'Oeuvre poétique d'Amy Lowell," *Revue Anglo-Américaine* (1925), for a discussion of this poem.

47. Preface to *Can Grande's Castle*, pp. xi–xiii.

48. "The Bronze Horses," *Can Grande's Castle*, p. 176.

49. *Can Grande's Castle*, pp. 157–158.

50. Paul Fort, "Louis XI," translated by Amy Lowell in *Six French Poets*, pp. 448–449.

51. Paris, Honoré Champion, 1927. See also articles by W. L. Schwartz in *La Revue de littérature comparée* and in *Modern Language Notes*.

52. *Six French Poets*, pp. 287–88.

53. *Ibid.*, p. 304.

54. "The Sadness of Summer," *The Book of Nature*.

55. "Song of a Night," *The Dominant City*.

56. "Pleasure's Awakening," *The Dominant City*.

57. "Les Nombres," *Les Flambeaux noirs*, p. 141.

58. "The Poet's Autumn," *Fire and Wine*.

59. "The Vowels," *Fire and Wine*.

60. "The Three Transformations of Poetry," *Fire and Wine*.

61. It is worth noting that in this same early collection he also imitated Rémy de Gourmont, in the poem "Hands," which begins:

> There is a great mystery, my love,
> In the movements of your hands.

echoing the beginning of de Gourmont's poem:

> Simone, il y a un grand mystère
> Dans la forêt de tes cheveux.

62. Personal letter to the author.

63. *Irradiations*, XIX p. 31.

64. *Irradiations*, X, p. 12.
65. See his book *Skepticisms*, p. 105.
66. "Three Imagist Poets," *The Little Review* (May, 1916).
67. *Irradiations* (Boston: Houghton Mifflin, 1915), I, p. 3.
68. "Steamers," *Irradiations*, p. 56.
69. Verhaeren, "Londres," *Les Soirs*, p. 35.
70. *Irradiations*, XXVI, p. 28.
71. "The Gale," *Irradiations*, p. 44.
72. *Irradiations*, XXVI, p. 28.
73. "Le Fléau," *Les Campagnes hallucinées*, p. 70.
74. "La Dame en noir," *Les Flambeaux noirs*, p. 124.
75. *Irradiations*, VII. p. 9.
76. "The Groundswell," *Irradiations*, p. 53.
77. "Les Cordiers," *Les Villages illusoires*, p. 277.
78. *Irradiations*, V, p. 7.
79. *Irradiations*, IV, p. 6.
80. *Goblins and Pagodas*, p. 11.
81. "Bedroom," *Goblins and Pagodas*.
82. "Green Symphony," *Goblins and Pagodas*, p. 44.
83. *Ibid.*, pp. 43–45.
84. "Solitude in the City (Symphony in Black and Gold)," *Goblins and Padogas*, p. 34
85. *Ibid.*, pp. 36–37.
86. "The Endless Lament," *Japanese Prints*, p. 57.
87. "The Empty Days," *The Tree of Life*, p. 72.
88. *Breakers and Granite*, p. 114.
89. "New York," *Breakers and Granite*, p. 5.
90. "The Windmills," *Breakers and Granite*, p. 107.
91. *Ibid.*, p. 108.
92. "In the City of Night," *Breakers and Granite*, p. 140.

Part Two / Chapter 6

1. T. S. Eliot, *The Sacred Wood* (London: Methuen Co., 1920), p. 12.
2. Ezra Pound, "Drunken Helots and Mr. Eliot," *The Egoist* (June, 1917).
3. *Problème du style*.
4. "Tradition and the Individual Talent," *The Sacred Wood*, p. 58.
5. "The Perfect Critic," *The Sacred Wood*, pp. 14–15.
6. "Henry James: In Memory," *The Little Review*.
7. "A French Poet on Tradition, authorized translation by Richard Aldington," *Poetry*, (July, 1914). De Gourmont had sent this article to Aldington, with this note: "Disposez de l'article selon que vous le jugerez" (Unpublished letter).
8. "Tradition and the Individual Talent," *The Sacred Wood*, p. 51.

9. "Hamlet and His Problems," *The Sacred Wood*, p. 100.

10. Pound, *The Spirit of Romance*, p. 14.

11. See *The Spirit of Romance*, p. 116: "In Tuscany the cult is a cult of the harmonies of the mind. If one is in sympathy with this form of objective imagination and this quality of vision, there is no poetry which has such enduring, such, if I may say so, indestructible charm. The best poetry of this time appeals by its truth, by its subtlety, and by its refined exactness."

12. *Homage to John Dryden* (London: Hogarth Press, 1927).

13. *Ibid.*, p. 23.

14. *Ibid.*, pp. 31–32.

15. *Ibid.*, p. 30.

16. T. S. Eliot, *Collected Poems, 1909–1935* (New York: Harcourt, Brace & Co. 1936), p. 48.

17. Bosschere, *The Closed Door*, p. 36.

18. *Alcools.*

19. "Les Veufs de rose," *Créances*, p. 209.

20. "Contemporanea," *The Egoist* V (June–July, 1918), p. 84.

21. Ramon Gomez de la Serna, preface to Apollinaire's *Il y a.*

22. "Sur Guillaume Apollinaire," *Mercure de France* (15 November 1923).

23. "Poet and Saint," *The Dial* (May, 1927).

24. "Gerontion," *Collected Poems*, p. 45.

25. Sometimes the influence is found more as parody than as imitation. For example, Baudelaire wrote:

> Voici venir le soir . . .
>
> Aux uns portent la paix aux autres le souci,

whereas Eliot wrote:

> When evening quickens faintly in the street,
>
> Wakening the appetite of life in some,
>
> And to others bringing the Boston Evening Transcript.

26. T. S. Eliot, "Note sur Mallarmé et Poe," *Nouvelle revue française* (November, 1926).

27. Richard Aldington, "T. S. Eliot," *Literary Studies and Reviews* (London: George Allen & Unwin, Ltd., 1924), pp. 183–184.

Part Two / Chapter 7

1. Anne Knish and Emmanuel Morgan, *Spectra* (New York: M. Kennerly, 1916). See also W. Bynner, "The Spectric Poets," *New Republic* (18 November 1916).

2. *Ezra Pound: His Metric and Poetry* (New York: Knopf, 1917), p. 10. See also Richard Aldington in *The Little Review* (March, 1915): "For in 1911, when H. D. began to write the poems I am considering, vers libre was practically unheard of outside of France."

3. See her editorials, "The Rhythm of English Verse," *Poetry* (November-December, 1913).

4. *The Little Review* (November, 1914).

5. Edward Storer, "Form in Free Verse," *New Republic*, VI (11 March 1916), p. 154

6. "And the Flood was Forty Days upon the Earth," *Nation* (February, 1917).

7. Ezra Pound, "Status Rerum," *Poetry* (April, 1916).

8. "Free Verse in England," *The Egoist*, I (15 September 1914), p. 351.

9. "The Impersonal Path," *Poetry Journal* (December, 1916).

10. "Announcement," *The Little Review* (March, 1914), pp. 1–2.

11. Conrad Aiken, "Morning Song from 'Senlin,' " *Turns and Movies*.

12. Maxwell Bodenheim, "Style and American Literature," *The Little Review* IV (October, 1917), p. 23.

13. Bodenheim, "What is Poetry?" *New Republic*, XIII (December 22, 1917), p. 212.

14. *The Little Review* (Octboer, 1917).

15. "The Renaissance, III," *Poetry* (February, 1915).

16. Preface to *Six French Poets*, p. v.,

17. *Six French Poets*, p. 273.

18. A fuller list is to be found in Taupin, *L'Interpretation americaine de la poesie française*, which shows how fully French culture had penetrated America by the 1920s.

19. Incidentally, French poetry exerted an influence on Carl Sandburg not of the same kind, but nevertheless pronounced. Sandburg had read French contemporary poetry, and particularly admired Paul Fort and Verhaeren, as he makes clear in his short preface to the translation of Fort's *Ballades françaises* by John Strong Newberry, in 1922. Sandburg's form is often like that of Fort, and he even used certain techniques of verse and rhythm to greater effect than the French poet, making Fort's verses appear anemic in comparison.

Part Three / Chapter 1

1. "Editorial," *The Little Review* IV (May, 1917), p. 3.

2. Editor's note by Margaret Anderson, *The Little Review* IV (July, 1917), p. 29.

3. *The Little Review* (August, 1917), p. 25.

4. *Ibid.*, p. 5.

Part Three / Chapter 2

1. See Kreymbourg, *Troubadour: An Autobiography* (New York: Boni & Liveright, 1925).

2. "Four Portraits on a Wall," *Others* (1919).

3. Cornwall Hollis, *The Art of Donald Evans* (Philadelphia: N. L. Brown, 1919). Evans himself was the author of this book.

4. Walter C. Arensberg, *Idols* (Boston, New York: Houghton Mifflin & Co., 1916), pp. 12–13.

5. *Ibid.*, p. 25.

6. Introduction to *Introducing Irony*.

7. Zigrosser, *Modern School* (February, 1919).

8. "Sunday in a Certain City Suburb," *Others* (1916).

9. "After Writing Poetry," *Others* (1916).

10. *New Republic* (13 October 1917), p. 211.

11. For example, Ezra Pound, in *Pavannes and Divisions*. But Miss Moore herself wrote, in a personal letter to the author: "I know that the influence of Rimbaud and Laforgue has been found in my poetry, although I had read neither of them at the time I wrote it."

12. *Observations*, p. 63.

13. *Ibid.*, p. 68.

14. *Ibid.*, p. 58.

15. Quoted by William Carlos Williams in *Kora in Hell: Improvisations* (Boston: Four Seas Co., 1920), pp. 17–18.

16. *Others* (1919).

17. *Ibid.*,

18. Personal letter to the author. See also Gorham Munson's comments in *Destinations*, p. 81: "He will say 'harmonium' instead of 'small organ,' 'lacustrine' instead of 'lakeside,' 'sequin' instead of 'spangle'; he speaks of hibiscus, panache, fabliau, poor buffo . . . .

19. Personal letter of Williams to the author.

20. William Carlos Williams, *Kora in Hell*, p. 16.

21. *Ibid.*, p. 18.

22. *Ibid.*, p. 19.

23. *Ibid.*, p. 24.

24. *Ibid.*, p. 70.

25. *Ibid.*, p. 36.

26. *Ibid.*, p. 35.

27. *Ibid.*, p. 39.

28. *Ibid.*, p. 55.

29. *Ibid.*, p. 50.

30. Quoted by Williams in the Prologue to *Kora in Hell*, p. 14. [Reprinted in *The Letters of Ezra Pound: 1907–41*. p. 124]

31. *Letters of Ezra Pound*, p. 160.

32. "Dr. Williams' Position," *Dial* (1928). Reprinted in *The Literary Essays of Ezra Pound*, ed. T. S. Eliot (New York: New Directions, 1954), p. 393.

33. Quoted by Pound in his article in *The Dial*.

34. Prologue to *Kora in Hell*, p. 19.

35. *Ibid.*, p. 66.

36. *Ibid.*, p. 70.

37. *Ibid.*, p. 35.

Part Three / Chapter 3

1. "One Escape from the Dilemma," *The Fugitive* (Nashville, Tenn. April, 1924), pp. 35–36.

Conclusion

1. "American Literature and the American Language" (1953), in *To Criticize the Critic* (New York: Farrar, Straus & Giroux, 1965), p. 59.

2. Stephen Spender, *The Struggle of the Modern* (Berkeley: University of California Press, 1963), p. 110.

3. "Tradition and the Individual Talent," *Selected Essays* (New York: Harcourt, Brace & Co., 1950), p. 5.,

4. "Fifty Years of American Poetry," *Prairie Schooner* XXXVII (Spring, 1963), p. 1.

5. "Ezra Pound" (1946) in Peter Russell, ed., *Ezra Pound: A Collection of Essays* (New York & London: Peter Nevill, Ltd., 1950), p. 29.

6. "What Dante Means to Me," (1950), *To Criticize the Critic*, p. 126.

7. "Baudelaire," (1930), *Selected Essays*, p. 377.

8. *Selected Essays*, p. 223.

9. "What Dante Means to Me," in *To Criticize the Critic*, p. 128.

10. "Dante," *Selected Essays*, pp. 229, 212.

11. "Hart Crane," in *Allen Tate: Essays of Four Decades* (Chicago: Swallow Press, 1968), p. 310.

12. *The Letters of Hart Crane, 1916–1932*, ed. Brom Weber (New York: Hermitage House, 1952), p. 261.

13. "Examples of Wallace Stevens," in *Form and Value in Modern Poetry* (New York: Doubleday Anchor, 1957), p. 184.

14. *Letters of Wallace Stevens*, ed. Holly Stevens (New York: Alfred Knopf, 1966), p. 468.

15. *Baudelaire: Flowers of Evil*, ed. Jackson Matthews (New York: New Directions, 1955), p. xviii.

16. *Ibid.*, p. xvii.

17. "Adagia," *Opus Posthumous*, ed. Samuel French Morse (New York: Alfred Knopf, 1957), p. 166.

Index of Names